Elements
of
Hypermedia Design

Techniques for Navigation & Visualization in Cyberspace

Peter Gloor

Springer Science+Business Media, LLC

Library of Congress Cataloging In-Publications Data

Gloor, Peter A. (Petr Andreas), 1961-
  Elements of hypermedia design : techniques for navigation and
visualization in cyberspace / Peter Gloor.
  Includes bibliographical references and index.
  ISBN 978-0-8176-3911-2
  1. Interactive multimedia   I. Title.
QA76.76I59G56   1997
025.04--dc20   96-39026
                                                            CIP

Printed on acid-free paper
© 1997 Springer Science+Business Media New York
Originally published by Birkhäuser Boston in 1997

ISBN 978-0-8176-3911-2   ISBN 978-1-4612-4144-7 (eBook)
DOI 10.1007/978-1-4612-4144-7

9 8 7 6 5 4 3 2 1

This book is dedicated to Irene, my wife, and my children, Sarah and David, who had to share me too long with my computer while this manuscript was being written.

Table
of
Contents

Preface

The hypermedia authoring process has been vividly described in a special issue of the *Economist* as a combination of writing a book, a play, a film, and a radio or television show: A hypermedia document combines all these elements and adds some of its own. The author's first job is to structure and explain all of the information. The author then must distill the information into brief, descriptive nodes. Each node has to contain a list of the ingredients, and instructions on how the ingredients are mixed together to the greatest advantage. The structure of the material provided is translated into an architectural metaphor of some kind; much of the designer's work is the creation of this imaginary space. Then, the designers must chart the details of what to animate, what to film, who to interview, and how to arrange the information in the space to be built [Eco95a].

This book presents guidelines, tools, and techniques for prospective authors such that they can design better hypermedia documents and applications. It surveys the different techniques used to organize, search, and structure information in a large information system. It then describes the algorithms used to locate, reorganize, and link data to enable navigation and retrieval. It looks in detail at the creation and presentation of certain types of visual information, namely algorithm animations. It introduces new mechanisms for editing audio and video data streams. Finally, it presents several examples of using these techniques in a large-scale project (conference proceedings) and describes the problems associated with bringing such projects to completion. It also suggests ways in which the process of creating electronic conference proceedings can be improved and partially automated.

Three different design elements have to be considered when designing a hypermedia product: *structure, presentation,* and *contents* (Figure 1) elements.

1. *Structure:* It gives in-depth coverage to how to structure information for optimal navigation and access and presents a broad overview of the state of the art in this field as well as a new classification of tools and mechanisms for information structuring. Part II introduces the Cyber-Toolbox, a set of tools developed by the author and his group for optimal navigation and information structuring.

Figure P.1

Hypernedia
design elements
and correspond-
ing book parts.

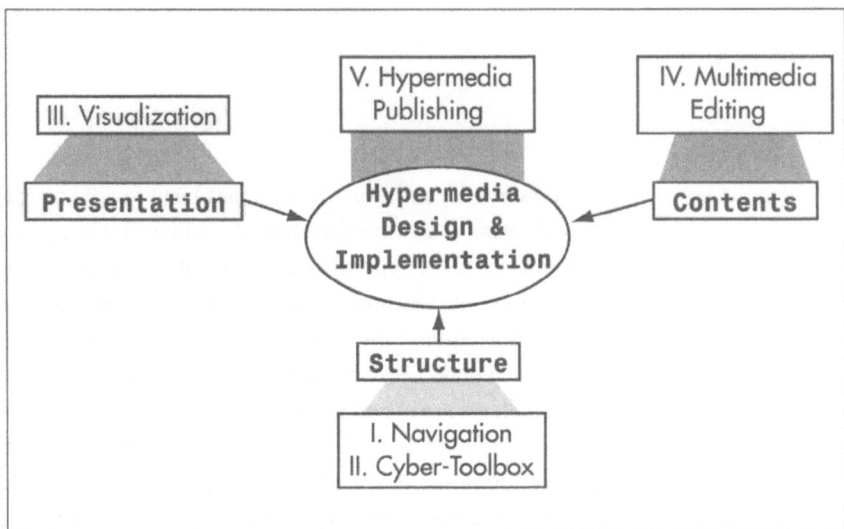

2. *Presentation:* It describes how to present and visualize complex concepts by introducing the reader to algorithm animation.

3. *Contents:* It also outlines a novel approach for authoring and editing of multimedia contents.

In the final part, the book illustrates how these three design elements can be put together to produce user-friendly hypermedia documents.

After a careful introduction to information retrieval, user modeling, and the World Wide Web, Part I introduces the seven concepts for *navigation in cyberspace*—linking, searching, sequentialization, hierarchy, similarity, mapping, and agents—and gives a broad overview of the state of the art by discussing a palette of existing systems, tools, and techniques to implement these concepts.

Part II presents a toolbox of *cybertools* for authoring and editing hypermedia documents. Navigation Diamond, Viewfinder, Hiermap, Cybermap, and Cybertrees have been developed by the author and his group to address various aspects of the navigation-in-cyberspace problem.

Part III introduces *algorithm animation*, an aspect of visualization that has been around for some decades but has been used only sporadically outside the computer science domain. Using algorithm animation to its best offers an author a unique way to explain complex concepts that are very hard to convey by other means. After a short survey, Part III focuses on experiences collected when implementing Animated Algorithms, a large scale project that combined a hypertext version of the textbook *Introduction to Algorithms* [Cor90] with animations of the most important algorithms. Later, a blueprint for algorithm animation and a concept called "algorithm animation by scripting" are presented.

Most digital multimedia editing tools have been based on visual, easy-to-use direct-manipulation interfaces. Part IV describes a complementary *language-based multimedia editing* system called *VideoScheme* that combines a common direct-manipulation interface with a programming language enhanced to manipulate digital audio and video streams. The resulting system can automate routine audio and video editing tasks, as well as perform jobs based on sophisticated media recognition algorithms.

Part V discusses elements of hypermedia design that are key to hypermedia publishing. An example application that covers many facets of the hypermedia creation and authoring process is the production of a series of *multimedia conference proceedings*. The DAGS (Dartmouth Institute on Advanced Graduate Studies) multimedia proceedings were produced first on CD-ROM. The latest proceedings have been published on the Web.

This book makes original contributions in five areas:

1. The seven design concepts for navigation in cyberspace (Part I) propose a novel framework for categorization and classification of tools and mechanisms for navigation in cyberspace and information structuring.

2. The Cyber-Toolbox (Part II) provides a unique collection of tools and mechanisms for the visual exploration and the structuring of large information spaces.

3. The Animated Algorithms system (Part III) proposes a universal hypermedia learning environment for algorithms of high educational value, as well as a novel approach for algorithm animation based on scripting.

4. The VideoScheme system (Part IV) offers a combination of direct-manipulation and programming language-based editing that implements a highly flexible test bed for automation as well as exploration of new algorithms in the field of multimedia authoring.

5. A series of sophisticated hypermedia applications (Part V) combine different media types to achieve a tightly integrated hypermedia learning environment.

This sign denotes chapters and sections that contain "further reading" — material that, while of significance, is not necessary for the overall understanding of the book. These sections are intended for students and practitioners alike who are looking for background information on a certain topic. The sign also marks sections describing systems that are primarily of historical interest.

Acknowledgments

The work described in this book grew out of my stay at the Laboratory for Computer Science at MIT as a postdoctoral associate from 1990 to 1993. I am deeply indebted to David Tennenhouse for all the support he gave me during this time as a member of his group. I am also grateful to Glorianna Davenport at the MIT Media Lab, as well as to Chris Lindblad and the other members of the TNS group at MIT, for the many stimulating discussions.

Many of the projects described in this book have come out of a long and fruitful cooperation with Fillia Makedon from the Department of Computer Science at Dartmouth College. I truly enjoy the cooperation with a very creative and inspiring colleague.

Frank Yeean Chan, Ralph Santos, and Ethan Mirsky were instrumental in various phases of the Cybermap project, implementing much of the system on the Macintosh and on the Connection Machine as part of their UROP (Undergraduate Research OPportunity) responsibilities at MIT. Chris Langmead implemented the Java version of Cybermap at Dartmouth College. The timbral Cybermap is based on Chris's own research. Apple Computer provided financial assistance to the project in the form of an equipment grant. Bill Bleier implemented the first version of the Path Tool for the Web.

The algorithm animations are the work of Frank Chan, Brian Dunkel, Scott Dynes, Mark Haseltine, Donald Johnson, Norman Koon, Clif Kussmaul, Irene Lee, Jim Matthews, Takis Metaxas, Corby Page, Angel Velez, and Yihao Zhang. Without their tireless work, the system would have been impossible. Angel Velez did a terrific job as animation editor-in-chief by polishing the rough edges in the animations and eliminating zillions of bugs. Frank Chen programmed the map XCMD, patiently changing its functionality upon our numerous modification suggestions. Brian Dunkel did a great job as a last-minute hypertext troubleshooter. Scott Dynes not only assumed overall responsibility as hypertext editor but also was essentially involved in the design of the Gloor/Dynes hypertext engine. William Ang, Tom Cormen, Terry Ehling, Fillia Makedon, Ron Rivest, David Tennenhouse, and Albert Vezza provided essential support for different aspects of the project. I am deeply indebted to Charles Leiserson, whose initial support and long-term assistance made the whole project possible.

Jim Matthews did a tremendous job independently implementing VideoScheme. He was also instrumental in the DAGS '92 CD-ROM project. Matthew Cheyney did most of the programming for the DAGS '92 CD-ROM, while Takis Metaxas assumed responsibility as hypertext editor. Oliver Van Ligten was responsible for the DAGS '95 talks on the Web, and Charles Owen and Jamie Ford provided indispensable support. Both of these projects were done within the auspices of the DEVLAB at Dartmouth, whose director, Fillia Makedon, and co-director Sam Rebelsky were essential for the success of these projects.

I am grateful to Professor Kurt Bauknecht of the Department of Computer Science at the University of Zurich for his continuing support in various phases of this project.

The final version of this book was compiled during a term as visiting scholar at the Department of Computer Science at Dartmouth College. I am grateful to the chair, Scot Drysdale, and Fillia Makedon for providing me with the excellent infrastructure to complete such a project in a timely fashion. Finally, I express my gratitude to Donald Johnson, the deceased first chair of the Dartmouth Computer Science Department, who not only provided essential support but also actively participated in various projects. I also gratefully acknowledge the support of my employer, Coopers & Lybrand, which allowed me to use its infrastructure for the final preparation of the manuscript.

The quality of this book owes greatly to the positive criticisms of the reviewers of the draft of this manuscript:

- Marc Brown, DEC Systems Research Center, Palo Alto
- George Cybenko, Dartmouth College
- James Ford, Dartmouth College
- Fillia Makedon, Dartmouth College
- Hermann Maurer, Technical University of Graz, Austria
- Viera Proulx, Northeastern University, Boston
- David Tennenhouse, MIT

Finally, I thank Wayne Yuhasz, the editor at Birkhäuser Publishers, for his continuing support and the excellent collaboration during the editing and production phase of this book, as well as Jennifer Matheny for preparing the HTML version of this book.

p a r t **I**

Structuring Information

> "*Information anxiety afflicts modern society. In most cases—for example, when surfing on the World Wide Web— we suffer from data overload and become confused, disoriented, and inefficient.*"
>
> **—Ramesh Jain.**
>
> *[Jai 95]*

The vast amount of information accessible on CD-ROM, and exponentially more on the Web, demands careful structuring and provision of access mechanisms. Chapter 1 starts with an introduction into basic information retrieval techniques to lay the groundwork for understanding the tools and techniques for information filtering and exploration presented later in this book. Chapter 2 discusses general user modeling techniques and its application to information retrieval. It is not the goal of this book to give a general introduction into information retrieval and user modeling. Rather, the focus of chapters 1 and 2 is on discussing the concepts employed for the tools described in the Seven Design Concepts for Navigation in Cyberspace and the Cyber-Toolbox introduced in Part II. For a general introduction to information retrieval the reader is referred to [Sal88], [Sal89a], and [Bel87]. [Chi89] gives an overview of user modeling techniques. Chapter 3 introduces the World Wide Web and its basic navigation mechanisms. Chapter 4 discusses emerging systems for Web programming that have been used for our own Web navigation tools presented later in the book.

Chapters 5 to 12 introduce the Seven Design Concepts for Navigation in Cyberspace. Hypermedia authors, who follow these concepts, will produce better–navigable and thus more easily usable hyperdocuments. At the same time, we use the seven concepts as a classification mechanism to present a wealth of tools and techniques for navigation in cyberspace. These methods can then be adapted by authors to fit their own needs.

CHAPTER 1

A Brief Introduction

to

Information Retrieval

Gerard Salton [Sal83] defines an information retrieval system as a system used to store items of information that need to be processed, searched, retrieved, and disseminated to various user populations. Theoretically, there is no constraint on the type and structure of the information items to be stored and retrieved with the information retrieval (IR) system. In practice however, large–scale IR systems are mostly processing textual information. If the information is particularly well structured, database management systems are used to store and access that information. If this is the case, the data are normally structured in the form of networks (for network databases), hierarchies (for hierarchical databases), tables (for relational databases), or objects (for object–oriented databases). Contrary to databases, classical IR systems are concerned with storing and retrieving unstructured or narrative information. To be searchable, information has to be stored in machine–readable format. This means that until recently, information retrieval systems were limited to searching textual information.

The advent of large, multimedia digital libraries has focused attention on retrieving documents consisting of multiple media types, including the traditional focus on textual sources and the increasing emphasis on media with spatial and temporal properties (e.g., sound, maps, graphics, images, video). Exciting research in language processing, speech processing, image and video processing, and spatial and temporal reasoning addresses these problems [Smo94][Yos94][Kem95][Kaz96]. Content-based retrieval uses features of multimedia objects in their native form for indexing, storage, and retrieval. Identifying features that make a difference is a nontrivial research challenge since different sets of features, from the same multimedia object, may be needed by different applications.

The IR terminology is still based on fundamental techniques introduced in the 1980s for text-based IR. Additionally, searching on the Web is currently mostly text based. We will therefore limit our discussion of IR here to a very brief introduction to text-based IR, while referring the readers to [Smo94][Yos94][Kem95][Kaz96] and the Special Interest Group on Information Retrieval (SIGIR) [Sig95] and RIAO [Ria94] proceedings for an in-depth treatment of multimedia information retrieval.

1.1 Classification of Retrieval Techniques

This section briefly reviews a classification of text retrieval techniques that has been proposed by Nicholas Belkin and Bruce Croft [Bel87]. At the highest level, Belkin and Croft distinguish between exact and partial match techniques. Exact match techniques are currently at use in most conventional IR systems. Queries are usually formulated using Boolean expressions. The search pattern within the query has to match exactly the text representation inside the document to be retrieved.

Within the partial match retrieval techniques are many different variants. *Individual* techniques search single document nodes without considering the document collection as a whole. For the *feature-based* techniques, documents are represented by sets of features or index terms. The index can be defined manually or computed automatically. The most prominent representative of this category is the *vector space* model, based on a *formal* model of document retrieval and indexing. In the vector space model, each document is represented by an index vector containing a set of weighted terms. For each query, documents are ranked in decreasing order of similarity to the query. The *probabilistic* approach is similar to the vector space model: the basic goal is to

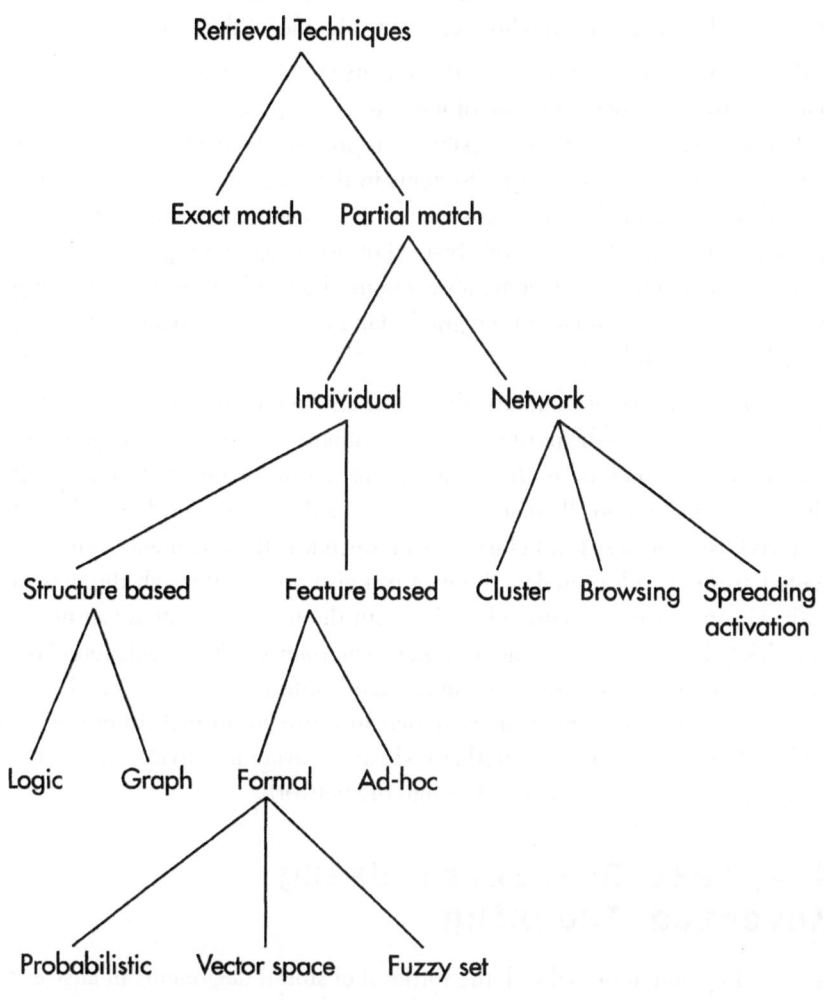

Figure I.1

Classification of retrieval techniques

retrieve documents in order of their probability of relevance to the query. The probabilistic retrieval model was developed by Steve Robertson and Karen Sparck Jones in the 1970s. In the probabilistic model (as contrasted with a Boolean retrieval system), a query typed by a user to retrieve information is taken as an unstructured list of words or phrases. These terms are then matched to the documents in the database. Some authors also have suggested a *fuzzy set* approach for feature–based formal IR systems. Contrary to formal feature–based IR systems, there have also been a number of ad hoc similarity measures proposed. Most of the feature-based approaches have the problem that small differences in weights can lead to significant differences in results.

For *structure–based* techniques, documents are represented in a more complicated structure than just a set of index terms as used for the feature–based techniques. It is theoretically possible to represent the contents of the document collections in formal *logic*. Systems in this category could, for example, use rules to describe how relevant fragments of a document are related to the query (see the RUBRIC system). Instead of using logic to represent the contents of a document, the document's contents also can be described as a *graph* where the edges and nodes of the graph stand for ideas and relationships contained in the document.

With *network–based* methods, the set of all documents and their relationships are used to find the most relevant documents with respect to a query. The most prominent method is *clustering*, where the most similar documents are clustered together and all documents are grouped into a cluster hierarchy until a ranked list of lowest-level clusters is produced. If the documents are represented as a network of nodes, the user can also *browse* through the network with system assistance. Through dialog with the user, the system can use the network to build a model of the user. Based on relevant documents found during the browsing session, a model of the user's information needs can be constructed. *Spreading activation* is similar to browsing in that, from the start node, other nodes connected to that node are activated. Activated nodes then propagate or spread themselves through the network.

1.2 Text Retrieval Using Inverted Indexing

As noted by Salton in [Sal89a], the retrieval of stored documents in answer to an information request is based on determining the similarity between the query and the stored documents (Figure I.2). The stored documents are represented by a set of *index terms*, sometimes called *term vectors*. Terms can be unweighted, or each term has an associated weight, called *importance weight*, to reflect its relative importance. To speed up access to the documents, an inverted index for each term in the index set can be created that lists all the addresses of the documents containing that particular term.

The addition of importance weights is done for document and query terms to distinguish between terms that are more important for retrieval purposes and

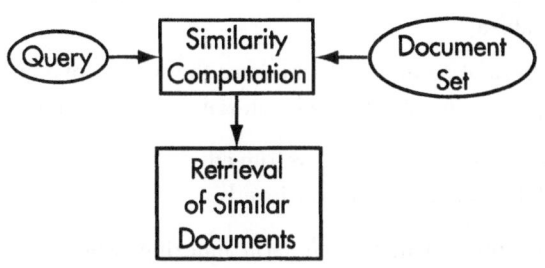

Figure I.2

Concept of text retrieval

terms that are less important. This addition of weights can be done manually or automatically. A particular document would then be represented, for example, as $D_i = (T_{1i}, 0.2; T_{2i}, 0.6; T_{3i}, 0.1)$ meaning that term 2 of document i (T_{2i}) has an importance weight of 0.6 while term 3 has a weight of 0.1. A possible weight assignment strategy is described in the next section.

An obvious way to get more broadly applicable terms is to use truncation. For example, the expression *philosoph** represents the whole list of philosopher, philosophic, philosophical, philosophically, philosophize, philosophizer, philosophizing, philosophy, and so forth. Various term truncation methods can be used, including suffix and prefix truncation. For a more in–depth treatment of this subject see [Sal89a:240ff.]. Most commercial IR systems are using truncation to improve precision; our own Cybermap system is using it also.

1.3 Automatic Indexing

The careful selection of index terms is of utmost importance for successful retrieval. Indexing can be done manually, by choosing appropriate index terms for each document by hand, or automatically. The goal is to find identifiers that describe the contents of a document as closely as possible. If manual indexing is done by a human expert using a limited vocabulary, a considerable degree of indexing uniformity can be achieved, and high–quality is sometimes obtained [Sal89a:276]. Unfortunately, manual indexing is an extremely tedious, time–consuming, and error–prone process. It is thus highly desirable to use automatic indexing. Because of the complexity of indexing, any automatic indexing operation will necessarily perform imperfectly. Nevertheless, retrieval results obtained by using advanced automatic indexing techniques are generally superior to queries executed in systems based on manually constructed indexes, due to the uniformity of the automatically generated index [Sal89a].

The most important parameter to measure the success of a query is the precision (*P*): the proportion of retrieved material that is relevant [Sal89a:278]:

$$P = \frac{\text{Number of relevant items retrieved}}{\text{Total number of items retrieved}}$$

Indexing can be divided into *single-term* indexing, where each index entry consists of a single term, and indexing with *terms in context*, where each index entry is composed of a group of terms. Obviously the latter is much more complex to handle than using single-term indexing vocabularies. In the rest of this introduction we will limit the discussion to single-term indexing.

term frequency

To find appropriate weights for a term, the *term frequency*—the number of occurrences of a term in the document—is commonly used. Unfortunately, it is not sufficient to count only the number of occurrences of a term in the document. Using only term frequency would entail, for example, grouping the documents having the highest occurrences of the word *apple*. Rather, the precision requirement also demands terms with a high discrimination value. In fact, the precision function is better served with terms that occur rarely in individual document collections. The best discrimination can be reached by terms that occur frequently in one document but rarely in the whole document collection. A useful term weight for a term T_k in document D_i is, for example,

collection frequency

defined as the term frequency multiplied by the inverse *collection frequency*—the number of occurrences of the term in the whole document collection [Jon72]. The two factors for computing weights are therefore:

- *Collection frequency*. Terms that occur in only a few documents are likely to be more useful than ones occurring in many.

- *Term frequency*. The more frequently a term appears in a document, the more important it is likely to be for that document.

The weight of term *k* in node *i* is thus computed as:

$$wi_k = termFrequency_{ik} \times \log\left(\frac{numofDocuments}{CollectionFrequency_k}\right)$$

This means that the more a term occurs in one document, and the less frequent it is in the whole document collection, the better is its discrimination value. Additionally, the document length could also be taken into consideration, since a term that occurs the same number of times in a short document as in a long one is likely to be more important to the short document than it is to the long one.

A strategy for automatic indexing is given in [Sal89a]:

1. After having identified the individual words in a document collection, use a *stop word list* to eliminate the words that produce only noise, but are of no discrimination value (*and, but, or, the*, etc.).

2. Use truncation to get only the word stems (use only *philosoph** instead of *philosopher, philosophic, philosophical, philosophically*, etc.).

3. For each remaining word stem T_k (= term) in each document, compute its term weight w_{ik} using the formula:

$$w_{ik} = termFrequency_{ik} \times \log\left(\frac{numOfDocuments}{CollectionFrequency_k}\right).$$

4. Represent each document by the vector containing the set of terms together with the corresponding weights $D_i = (T_1,w_{i1}; T_2,w_{i2}; T_3,w_{i3};...)$

In [Sal91], Salton describes experiments that use content structure for the improvement of text retrieval. One problem with this technique is that a word can have different meanings depending on its context, and thus retrieval based on simple pattern matching works only in very limited cases. One solution is to include the node length into the computation of the similarities to account for the length factor.

1.4 The Vector Space Model

Contrary to the basic Boolean query model, the vector space model allows one to find the documents that are the most similar to the query without the need for a 100 percent match. In the vector space model, queries and documents are represented as term vectors of the form $D_i = (d_{i1}, d_{i2}, ...,d_{it})$ and $Q = (q_1, q_2, ...,q_t)$, where D_i is a document vector composed of terms d_{i1} to d_{it}, and Q is a query vector composed of terms q_1 to q_t. A document collection is then represented as a term-document matrix A, where a_{ij} is the weight q_{ij} of term j in document i:

$$
A = \begin{array}{c} \\ D_1 \\ D_2 \\ \\ \\ D_n \end{array}
\overset{\displaystyle T_1 \ \ T_2 \ ..T_t}{
\begin{bmatrix}
a_{11} & a_{12} & ..\,a_{1t} \\
a_{21} & a_{22} & a_{2t} \\
\cdot & & \\
\cdot & & \cdot \\
a_{n1} & a_{n2} & a_n
\end{bmatrix}}
$$

The similarity $sim(D_i, Q)$ between a query vector Q and a document term vector D_i can then be computed as:

$$
sim(D_i Q) = \sum_{1 \le l \le t} d_{li} q_l
$$

This method of computing similarity coefficients between queries and documents is particularly advantageous because it allows one to sort all documents in decreasing order of similarity to a particular query. This also permits one to adapt the size of the retrieved document set to the user's needs. (On the other hand, the similarity measure is reduced to a vector, which makes it hard to discriminate various types of similarity.)

1.5 Document Clustering

centroid

The vector space model has the main disadvantage that the information pertaining to a particular document is distributed among many different inverted-term lists. Furthermore, documents containing similar information are not stored in physical proximity. If browsing is to be allowed, however, documents containing similar information should be stored close together. Therefore, what is needed is the capability to cluster related documents that are physically distributed together. Normally, hierarchies of clusters are constructed, where the leaves are the actual documents. Virtual nodes on the higher levels are used to group the related documents. The virtual nodes on the higher levels are represented by *centroids*, or average term vectors (Figure I.3). Our Cybermap system is using this mechanism to build hierarchical overview maps of document collections.

The centroid may actually be the term vector of one of the documents in the cluster it represents, but generally it is computed using some statistical method to be in the center of the cluster. One obvious way is to compute some average of each vector element for all documents in the cluster.

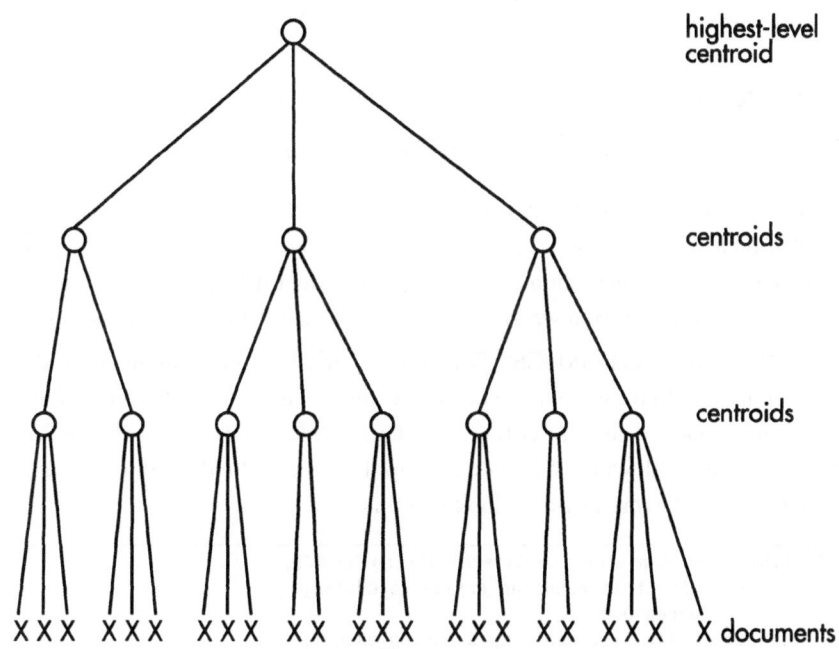

highest-level
centroid

centroids

centroids

X X X   X X X   X X X   X X   X X X   X X X   X X   X X X   X documents

Simple clustering is normally done using some variant of the following method [Sal89a:329]:

1. Compute all document similarity coefficients $sim(D_i, Q)$.

   ($\dfrac{n \times (n-1)}{2}$ coefficients for n documents).

2. Put each of the n documents into its own cluster.

3. Create a new cluster by combining the two most similar clusters C_i and C_j, delete the rows and columns for i and j in the similarity matrix, recompute the centroid for the newly created cluster, and update the similarity matrix.

4. Repeat step 3 if the number of clusters left is greater than 1.

Once the cluster hierarchy has been created, it is relatively efficient to process a query by searching the cluster tree doing either a top–down or a bottom–up search. The problem is that the clustering process itself is rather CPU intensive.

1.6 Rule-based Expert Systems for Information Retrieval

Contrary to feature-based systems, structure-based IR systems demand structured knowledge about the document collection to be searched. The basic concepts described in this section are very similar to the CYC system presented in Chapter 10. In this section we illustrate this approach with a classical example.

The RUBRIC system [McC83][Ton85] does rule-based reasoning about the knowledge base to be searched. This means that each document needs to have some rules attached that describe its contents. Rules in RUBRIC also define the probability with which a certain rule applies to a particular subject area. A sample rule for terrorism would look like this:

```
if (the story contains the literal string "bomb"),
     then (if it is about an explosive_device)
       to degree 0.6;
     but if also (it mentions a boxing_match),
     then (reduce the strength of the conclusion)
       to degree 0.3;
```

To find a story about violent acts of terrorism, RUBRIC tries to build an internal representation of how a story about this subject could look like. There are four elements that should be included in such a prototype: an actual violent event, a terrorist actor, the effect of the event having occurred, and the reason for the event (Figure I.4). Each edge in the tree has an attached relevance value, such that the intermediate topics and key word expressions contribute according to their relevance value to the actual concept at the root of the tree. Unlabeled edges have an implicit relevance value of 1.

Obviously, systems like RUBRIC allow one to build a close model of the real world and thus offer high–precision queries. The big drawback of these systems is the need for a rule-based description of the documents to be searched. In the prototypical system described here, the rule base has been constructed manually. Until it is possible to compute accurate, rule-based descriptions of documents automatically, the practical use of such systems will be very restricted. In practice, although the concepts of rule-based IR look very interesting, there are currently no large-scale commercial systems based on this approach. This might change when the huge rule base of the CYC system described later

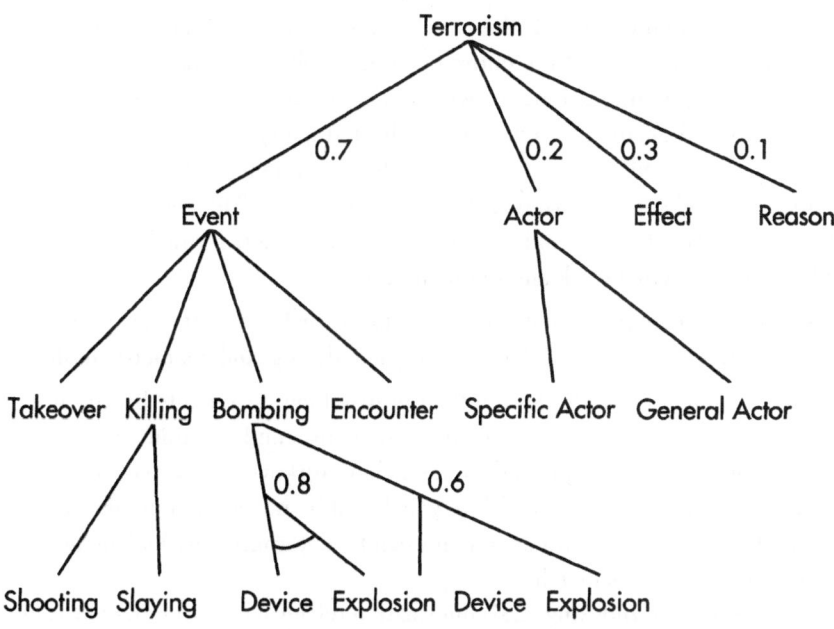

Figure I.4

Rule-evaluation tree for terrorist query

in this book is more widely available. In the meantime, most commercial IR systems are based on combinations of the vector space model and probabilistic approaches [Cro95].

1.7 Hypermedia and Information Retrieval

Apparently the idea of combining IR and hypertext is as old as the hypertext idea itself. Making available all knowledge known to humanity in the Memex[1] as envisioned by Vannevar Bush demands extremely powerful information location capabilities. Since then, many efforts have been made to combine the two techniques, resulting in powerful systems combining the best of both worlds [Kah88]. One obvious combination of hypertext and IR is the *action link*, where the link consists of an IR query. If users follow the link, they implicitly execute the query and get a graphical representation of the result set.

---

1 The Memex is a hypothetical hypertext engine that was described by Vannevar Bush in his seminal paper, "As We May Think". It was to be realized based on microfiches and mechanical links [Bus45].

For the hypermedia system Intermedia [Yan88], a query sheet builder has been implemented that assists the user by graphically visualizing an idea map. It gives the user a view of the entire document collection, shows the location of the most important documents (with respect to the query), and gives access to the retrieved documents. Once a complicated query sheet has been assembled, it can be saved and later applied to other document collections while still maintaining links to the original document collection. The result of a query sheet can be saved as a set of links to the actual documents, which can then be linked into the actual work environment of the user.

Among the many promising approaches for textual and nontextual searching methods are n-gram analysis, latent semantic indexing, and geometric hashing.

n-gram analysis

N-gram analysis[Dam95] is a method of matching documents based on the statistical similarity of occurrences of n-grams (n-length combinations of letters) in the text. For example, a document about turkeys will have occurrences of the trigrams *tur*, *urk*, *rke*, and *key*, which will be uncommon in other documents. The similarity of two documents can be determined by looking at how many of their n-grams match.

latent semantic indexing

http://www.cs.utk.edu/~lsi/

Latent Semantic Indexing (LSI) information retrieval uses the singular value decomposition (SVD) to reduce the dimensions of the term-document space. LSI explicitly represents terms and documents in a rich, high-dimensional space, allowing the underlying ("latent") semantic relationships between terms and documents to be exploited during searching. LSI assumes that the variability of word choice partially obscures the semantic structure of the document. By reducing the dimensionality of the term-document space, the underlying semantic relationships between documents are revealed, and much of the noise (differences in word usage, terms that do not help distinguish documents, etc.) is eliminated. LSI statistically analyzes the patterns of word usage across the entire document collection, placing documents with similar word usage patterns near each other in the term–document space, and allowing semantically related documents to be near each other even though they may not share terms [Let96].

Geometric Hashing

Geometric hashing is a technique to generate candidate matches between a model database and a set of measurement features. It was first employed by Lamdan et al. [Lam88]. Geometric hashing performs recognition with a set of points. Each of these points may have an attribute list to accommodate features that carry more information than just a position, such as a line. The algorithm works in two stages. In the first stage, which can be performed off-line with just the model database, a hash table is generated from the set of object models. In the second stage, the actual recognition, this hash table is used to perform recognition on a set of measurement features.

While Intermedia, although somewhat dated, is still a classic in the field of hypermedia IR, Chapter 4 introduces actual search systems for the Web such as WAIS and SWISH that are based on the IR concepts described in this chapter. Later in the book we present our own system for the exploration of large information spaces, Cybermap. Cybermap uses the IR techniques described in this chapter, in particular, extensions of the vector space model and document clustering to give an overview and provide a means of navigation to browse and explore large hypermedia documents.

User

Modeling

This chapter briefly introduces user modeling, with an emphasis on its application to information retrieval. An accurate model of the user can considerably improve the success of an IR system session, as IR systems often lack the capability of adapting their behavior to different categories of users. Naive users, users with a specific background in the search domain, newcomers, and experienced users are all treated the same. The goals that should be reached by applying user modeling techniques to IR are threefold:

1. Linguistic gaps between the user and the system should be closed.

2. Users should be supported at the conceptual level in the analysis of their information needs, the formulation of an appropriate search strategy, and the evaluation of the results.

3. A user needs a customized preview of the information space in order to decide on meaningful queries. Cybermap applies user modeling techniques described in this chapter to provide such an overview.

2.1 Classifications and Taxonomy

Generally, user models are grouped into two categories: empirical quantitative models and analytical cognitive models [Bra87]. *Empirical quantitative models* are based on an abstract formalization of general classes of users. These models contain only surface knowledge about the user, and no internal reasoning takes place. The knowledge about the user is usually taken into consideration explicitly only during the design of the system and is then hardwired into the system. Most conventional help systems follow this approach.

Analytical cognitive models, on the other hand, try to simulate the cognitive user processes that are taking place during permanent interaction with the system. These models incorporate an explicit representation of the user knowledge. The integration of a knowledge base that stores user modeling information allows for the consideration of specific traits of various users. In this chapter we will discuss only analytical cognitive user models.

Rich [Ric83] introduces a taxonomy that classifies (analytical cognitive) user models along three dimensions. In the first dimension, Rich distinguishes between *canonical* and *individual* user models. In a canonical model, there is one single, typical user; an individual user model has to be able to tailor its behavior to a heterogeneous variety of users. In the second dimension, Rich separates *explicit* from *implicit* user models. An explicit model is built manually by the user; an implicit model is built by the system through monitoring user behavior and acquiring unobtrusively other user information. Rich's third dimension categorizes *long-term* and *short-term* modeling; the short-term modeling systems focus on building up a user model during a single session, and the former models concentrate on information that changes more slowly over a whole series of sessions.

The capabilities of today's user modeling systems are still very limited [Jon89]. There are many interesting academic systems, but they are applied to limited problem domains; they contain many simplifying assumptions, and their underlying knowledge bases have been hand-coded for the specific problem domain.

 ## 2.2 User Modeling in UC, the UNIX Consultant

To give a better impression of what user modeling is for, this section discusses a concrete application of user modeling in an expert system. The UNIX Consultant (UC) is a natural language help system for the UNIX operating system environment. UC was developed at the University of California at Berkeley [Chi89]. "Users can ask UC how to do things in UNIX, get definitions

of UNIX terminology, and get help debugging problems in using commands"
[Chi89:74].

The user modeling component of UC has been named KNOME
(KNOwledge Model of Expertise). The example in Figure I.5 illustrates how
KNOME can infer the user's level of expertise from a conversation with the
user and how this knowledge then is used advantageously to assist the user.
Obviously, user 2 is a more experienced UNIX user than user 1, because user
2 knows about the inode concept. Therefore the answer to the first question is
much shorter than for user 1. Also question 2, the same for both users, gets
answered on a more technical level for user 2.

To accomplish a task like the one outlined, a user modeling system must first
determine what the user knows and then represent this information internally.
To determine the knowledge level of the user, the system could quiz the user
exhaustively, an extremely time–consuming process. It would be much better
if the system were able to predict the user's knowledge level based on the
user's behavior while using the system, which is exactly what KNOME is trying to do. KNOME represents what UC believes users know about UNIX.

In KNOME users are grouped into four categories according to their level
of expertise in using UNIX: *novice, beginner, intermediate,* and *expert*. These
categories are called *stereotypes*. Individual users are represented as members
of one of the stereotypes and inherit the generic properties of their stereotype.
Specific information about one user can then override the generic information
of the stereotype. To present the UNIX help information, KNOME categorizes

---

User 1	User 2	Figure I.5
Hi.	Hi.	UC session with
How can I help you?	How can I help you?	user 1 (left) and
# How can I delete a file?	*# How can I find out the inode of a file?*	user 2 (right)
Use rm.	Use ls -i.	(from [Chi89])
For example, to delete the file		
named foo, type 'rm foo'.		
# What does ruptime do?	*# What does ruptime do?*	
ruptime is used to list the uptime of	ruptime is like uptime, except ruptime is	
all machines on the network, list the	for all machines on the network.	
number of all users on them, and list		
their load average.		

all the commands, command formats, terminology, and other relevant information into four stereotype categories: *simple, mundane, complex,* and *esoteric.* Command stereotypes and user stereotypes are then matched using deduction tables (Figure I.6).

Figure I.6 shows an example of a deduction table for facts that are (not) known to the user. Using rule-based reasoning, KNOME does a likelihood rating of the user. When the likelihood rating of a stereotype reaches TRUE, it is selected as the user's category.

The reasoning in Figure I.7 is not yet conclusive; the user is somewhat unlikely to be intermediate, and the system would now proceed to find out that the user is somewhat likely to be an expert.

User modeling in KNOME is relatively simple (only four user categories or stereotypes); nevertheless, it allows a huge improvement in adaptability to the needs of a user. On the other hand, it is a very labor-intensive and mostly manual process to adjust the knowledge base to the different user categories. This means that user modeling can be done in expert and intelligent tutoring system environments, where it is tolerable that the knowledge base has to be laboriously hand crafted. However, it will be very difficult to adapt similar user modeling procedures and techniques to IR systems for very large, heterogeneous data collections. Obviously, IR user models have to be simplified further.

2.3 User Modeling in Information Retrieval

In IR the user model is used to provide assistance to the user in the query formulation process. The goal is to express the informational need in a way that

User	**Difficulty level of fact**			
Stereotype	*simple*	*mundane*	*complex*	*esoteric*
Novice	somewhat unlikely	false	false	false
Beginner	somewhat likely	somewhat unlikely	false	—
Intermediate	likely	somewhat likely	somewhat unlikely	—
Expert	likely	likely	somewhat likely	—

Figure I.6

Deduction table whether user knows some fact (from [Chi89])

Hi.

How can I help you?

 # How can I find out the inode of a file?

KNOME:	Asserting *USER* knows INODE1
KNOME:	Since INODE1 is an INODE, asserting *USER* knows INODE
KNOME:	INODE has difficulty COMPLEX, so deducing:
KNOME:	ruling out *USER* = NOVICE
KNOME:	ruling out *USER* = BEGINNER
KNOME:	*USER* is SOMEWHAT-UNLIKELY to be INTERMEDIATE

=> likelihood(*USER* = INTERMEDIATE) = SOMEWHAT-UNLIKELY

etc.

Figure I.7

Reasoning with intermediate user (from [Chi89:96])

---

provides the system with enough information to retrieve all documents relevant to the user. Unfortunately, the result of a search can only be as good as the description of the items that are sought. Users frequently have a hard time specifying what exactly they are looking for. It is the task of the user modeling component of the IR system to complement the users' interests automatically based on their previous search behavior.

The user model as maintained by the IR system thus augments the search specification issued by the users. The expanded search specification then reflects the users' needs and interests more closely. Figure I.8 illustrates the central position that user modeling can assume in information retrieval systems.

An IR system enhanced with user modeling techniques normally starts by getting the user's preferences — for example, a statement of the user's interests, a self–description, or an SQL-based query. This input is subsequently analyzed, using the user model, and the user model is updated accordingly. Then the formal query is constructed and processed, based on the user's preferences. Afterward, in close interaction with the user model, the output is prepared for presentation to the user (e.g., results of the query sorted based on user's interests) and the user model is refreshed. Finally, the user can evaluate the query and restart the whole cycle if needed.

Figure I.8

User models in
information
retrieval (from
[Kok91])

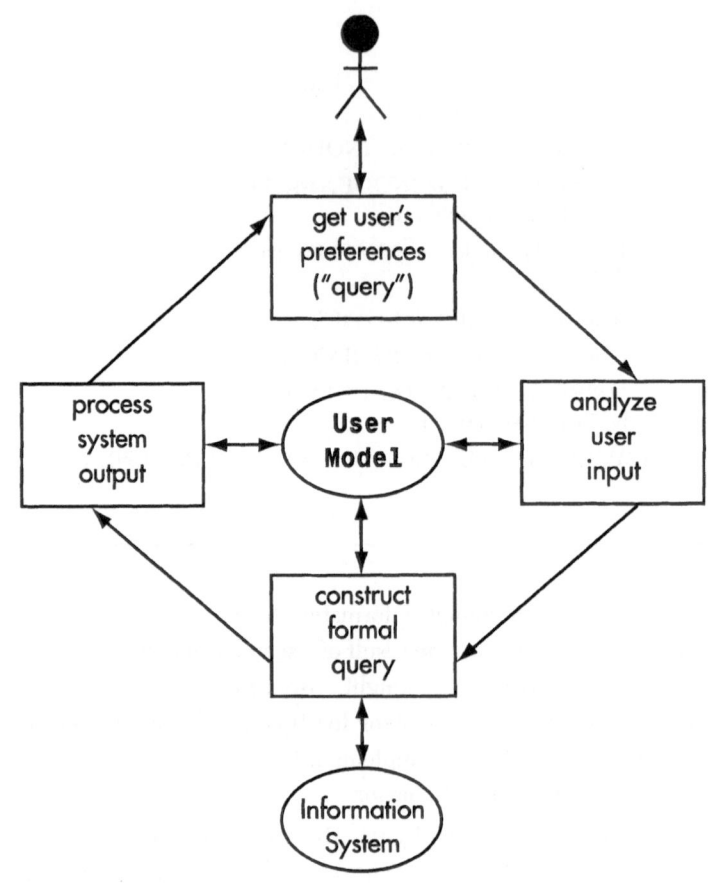

Users must be able to communicate their wishes to the system in the form of
interests, and the system needs a way to return to the users its predictions of
what the reflected interests in the system are.

2.4 User Modeling in I³R

This section describes I³R (Intelligent Interface for Information Retrieval),
which incorporates user modeling to increase the effectiveness of an intelligent
information retrieval system [Bra87:308]. (The I³R system has been developed
at the University of Massachusetts at Amherst by Rebecca Thompson and

Bruce Croft.) I^{3}R exhibits all the fundamental IR and user modeling concepts discussed so far and can be considered a blueprint for the application of user modeling techniques in IR. The I^{3}R user model incorporates both *long-term knowledge* for a general characterization of the user, such as the user's domain knowledge, summary of previous interactions and requests, and *short-term knowledge* concerning specific user needs submitted in the current session. The model of the user built during the initial session is refined during subsequent interactions with the system in order to improve the accuracy of the user's characteristics.

Croft and Thompson propose a domain-independent search heuristic: If the current document is interesting:

- What else has been written by its authors?
- Are any of its references interesting?
- Are any of the documents that reference it interesting?
- Are any of the documents in the same journal issue or conference proceedings interesting?
- Are there any other documents that are very similar to it in the database?

If the current term is interesting:

- Does it have synonyms, narrower terms, or something else of relevance?
- What documents is it used in?

This heuristic can be applied manually by an experienced searcher, depending, of course, on the features of the IR system available. Better still, the system should apply this or similar heuristics automatically.

The I^{3}R system is based on the blackboard model. It is composed of a number of autonomous components (here called "experts") that are controlled by a scheduler and operate independently from each other. All the experts have access to a declarative knowledge base that consists of two parts: the user records, and the concept–document knowledge. The *user records* store the user model in framelike structures called *stereotypes*. For each session, the user records contain the expression of the information needs ("the queries"), the stereotypes that were applied, the request model that was constructed, and the documents that were judged relevant.

The *concept–document* knowledge base contains meta–information about the documents that can be accessed through the I^{3}R system on three levels:

1. *Concept level.* Contains a semantic network of the core concepts that the document collection is about.

2. *Document level.* Contains general knowledge about the documents that are accessible through I^{3}R. This knowledge is extracted from the document title, key words, and abstract.

3. *Journal issue level.* Based on the observation that from time to time, many journals have whole issues devoted to special topics. It is therefore a reasonable assumption that documents in the same journal issue have related topics.

Besides the scheduler (in I^{3}R called "controller expert"), the system contains three other experts: the user model builder, the request model builder, and the domain knowledge expert. The *user model builder* collects information about the user relating to a particular session. This information is stored in stereotypes based on questions answered by the user and stereotypes of the same user from previous session. The values stored in a stereotype are summarized in Figure I.9.

As Figure I.9 illustrates, the stereotypes used in I^{3}R are rather simplistic; there are just two user categories. The user model builder collecting information about the user assumes an expert to find 20 relevant documents during an exhaustive search within two searches, while a novice user is expected to find 15 relevant documents during four searches.

Figure I.9	**Domain Knowledge Expertise**	**Novice**	**Expert**
Values stored in a stereotype	Number of relevant documents expected (exhaustive search)	15	20
	Maximum number of searches expected (exhaustive search)	4	2
	Number of relevant documents expected (selective search)	5	5
	Maximum number of searches expected (selective search)	2	1
	System Experience		
	Number of nodes to be shown in Browse Map Neighborhood	4	7
	Number of documents judged relevant while browsing triggering a new search	3 automatic	5 confirmed

The I^{3}R *request model builder* constructs a detailed representation of the user's information needs ("query"). It records evaluations and frequency information of terms, evaluations of documents, and term dependencies that have been identified by the user. I^{3}R further contains a *domain knowledge expert* component that is responsible for suggesting additional concepts to the users that may be relevant for their information needs. The knowledge base of the domain knowledge expert can be extended interactively by experienced users and can record their domain knowledge as typed connections between concepts.

Compared to UC/KNOME, I^{3}R has a very simple user model that distinguishes only between novice and expert users. Similar to KNOME, I^{3}R combines the user model with a domain knowledge base (the concept–document knowledge base). The IR system I^{3}R thus uses the same user modeling concepts and techniques as the UC expert system. But the domain knowledge base has to be constructed mostly manually, which means that as long as we lack a reliable way to automate this process, it will be almost impossible to apply these concepts to very large data collections, except on a very rudimentary level. Nevertheless, I^{3}R shows a reasonable way to integrate user modeling into IR systems for moderately large data collections and illustrates the problems that need to be solved if we want to apply user modeling for really large–scale information systems.

CHAPTER 3

World Wide Web:

an

Introduction

*Thus my theory is that the Web arose from the chaotic behavior of
a delicately balanced packet ecosystem. Somewhere in Argentina,
perhaps, a butterfly flapped its wings. A gentle breeze was felt in
Brazil. Storm clouds gathered in New York City, and a hurricane
blew in Europe. The Web was born. An instantiation of chaos theory: Deus ex machina.*

—**Robert W. Lucky, 1995**
[Luc95]

The World Wide Web system [Ber92] originated around 1989 at CERN
(Organisation Européenne pour La Recherche Nucléaire) in Geneva as a
practical initiative to bring a global information universe into existence
using available technology. Contrary to most examples presented later in
this book, the primary goal of WWW was never to extend hypermedia
research but to apply existing technologies and standards to get a working,
world wide hypertext web.

3.1 WWW Overview

*Pick up your pen, mouse or favorite pointing device and press it
on a reference in this document—perhaps to the author's name,
organization, or some related work. Suppose you are directly presented with the background material—other papers, the author's
coordinates, the organization's address and its entire telephone
directory. Suppose each of these documents has the same property
of being linked to other original documents all over the world. You
would have at your fingertips all you need to know about electronic publishing, high-energy physics or for that matter Asian
culture. As you are reading this book on paper, you can only
dream, but read on.*

—**Tim Berners-Lee et al., 1992**

[Ber92]

http://www.w3
.org

When Tim Berners-Lee wrote the above sentences in 1992, the scenario he
described was still mostly visionary. Since then, the Internet has experienced
a phenomenal growth, mostly due to the enormous popularity of the Web, such
that the dream Tim Berners-Lee described, has come true.

WWW is the most successful experiment so far that realizes Vannevar Bush's
vision of creating the information universe by linking together all knowledge
known to humanity. It implements a bottom-up approach by defining an architecture and lightweight protocol that runs on a variety of platforms. There have
been other visionaries, most prominently Theodore Nelson, who has been
working on his Xanadu system for the last 25 years. Contrary to Xanadu
[Nel90], which is incompatible with all existing systems, WWW offers gateways to link existing systems like Gopher [McC92], NetNews, and WAIS
[Kah89] into the World Wide Web (Figure I.10).

The WWW architecture copes with a wide range of hardware platforms,
operating systems, network protocols, information systems, and graphical
user interfaces using the client-server model. The client's task is to resolve
a document address into the actual document using its repertoire of network
protocols and then to display the retrieved document. WWW clients currently understand HTTP (hypertext transfer protocol), FTP (file transfer
protocol) and NNTP (network news transfer protocol). The server provides
the basic data in a format that has to be negotiated with the client. WWW
thus covers:

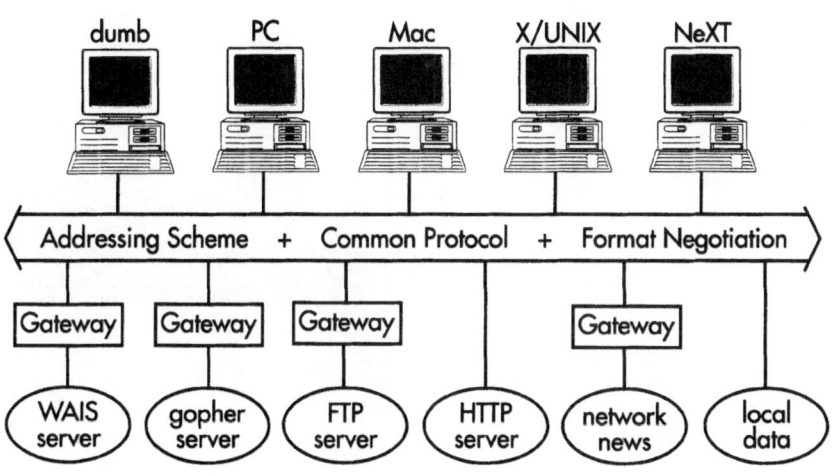

WWW
architectural
overview

- A common naming scheme for documents (URL—uniform resource locators): http://www.w3.org/pub/WWW/Addressing/Addressing.html

  URL specification

- Common network access protocols (HTTP): http://www.w3.org/pub/WWW/Protocols/

  HTTP specification

- Common data formats for hypertext (HTML—hypertext markup language): http://www.w3.org/pub/WWW/MarkUp/

  HTML specification

Almost any existing information system can be represented using the WWW data model. WWW offers an architecture that stretches seamlessly from small, personal notes to large information networks on other continents. Documents on the Web do not have to exist as actual documents. They can be created on the fly by the server as an answer to a query and can, for example, represent views of a database or snapshots of changing data.

Figure I.11 illustrates different representations of an original WWW document which is specified in HTML, a language based on SGML[Gol90].[1]

---

1 SGML (Standardized Generalized Markup Language) is a text formatting language standardized by the International Standardization Organization (ISO/IEC 8879-1986). It allows documents to be described independent of any platform in terms of their logical structure. SGML provides a metasyntax for expressing agreed-on syntaxes for individual documents. Each such syntax, called a *document type definition* (DTD), consists of a set of tags for coding a particular type of document, together with the allowable contents and attribute sets. Starting with HTML 2.0, HTML is specified as a SGML DTD.

Figure I.11

WWW hypertext
encoding and
display

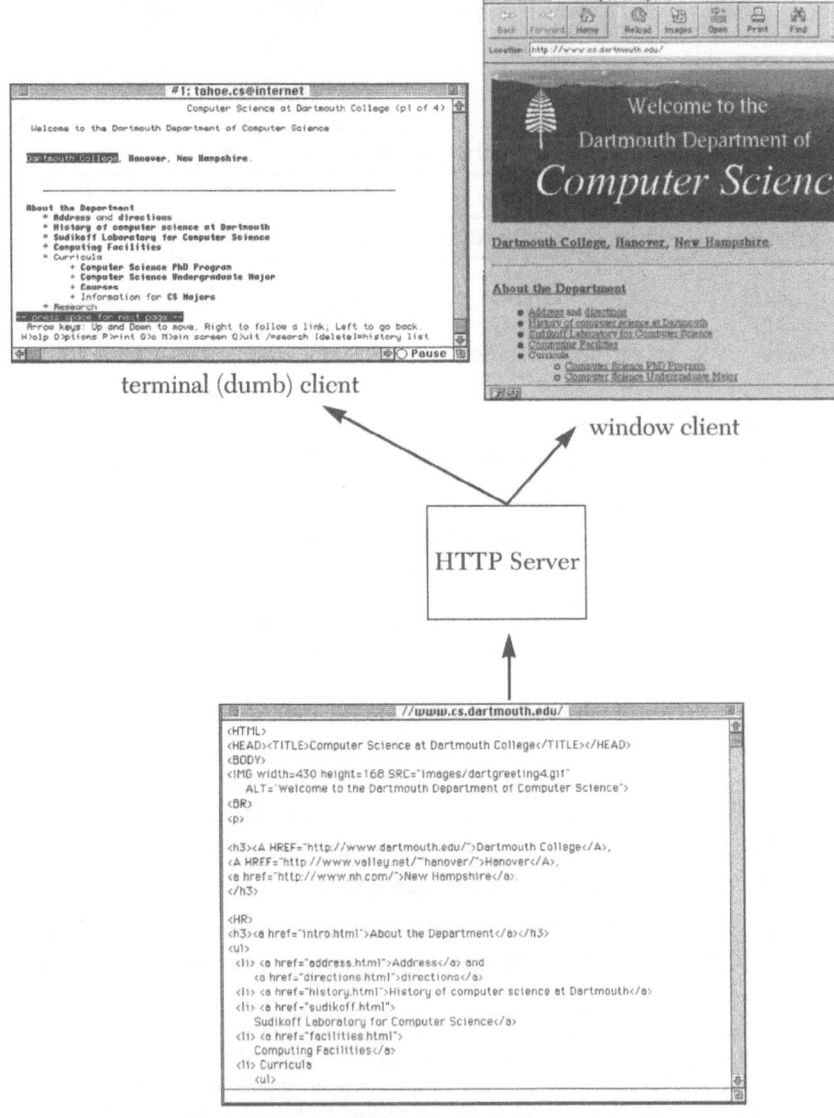

terminal (dumb) client

window client

HTTP Server

HTML source on server

The document contains, in addition to the text body, embedded links that are mapped into the different user interfaces to the Web, the so-called Web browsers, depending on the capabilities of the actual system. These links may point to any other document integrated into the Web, anywhere on the world.

3.2 Basic WWW Navigation Mechanisms

The basic Web navigation mechanisms were developed for the first Web browsers at CERN and are, even for state-of-the-art browsers like Netscape (which was about to release version 3.0 at the time this book went to press), still the same. The basic idea is to follow a trail (*trailblazing*) through the multidimensional cyberspace by clicking on hyperlinks on the Web page currently loaded on the browser. Each user declares a preferred point of reference, the user's *home page*, from where she or he starts and can always return to if she or he gets lost in cyberspace. Figure I.12 shows the basic Netscape browsing interface with the Return button to go back to the user's home page, as well as the Back and Forward buttons to advance or go backward on the trail that the user has established by following hyperlinks.

Besides the option of selecting links and going sequentially backward, and forward again, Web browsers also offer a history of places that have recently been visited. Netscape's history menu (Figure I.13) lists the titles of pages that have been visited in the current session and allows the user to jump directly to any of these by selecting the entry in the menu. In Figure I.13 the user went to the Computer Science at Dartmouth College page, and jumped from there to the Dartmouth College home page. Using the Back and Previous menu commands or arrow-buttons, the user can browse sequentially through the pages that have been visited before in the same session.

A final core feature of Web browsers is the ability to mark special Web pages for later direct access by setting bookmarks. Netscape's Bookmark window (Figure I.14) allows users not only to store bookmarks but to create a hierarchical menu system organizing them for easier access. It also allows them to change defaults for appearance, their home page, and how nontextual media are handled.

Netscape's basic
navigation
mechanisms

Back-   Forward-   Home-Button-

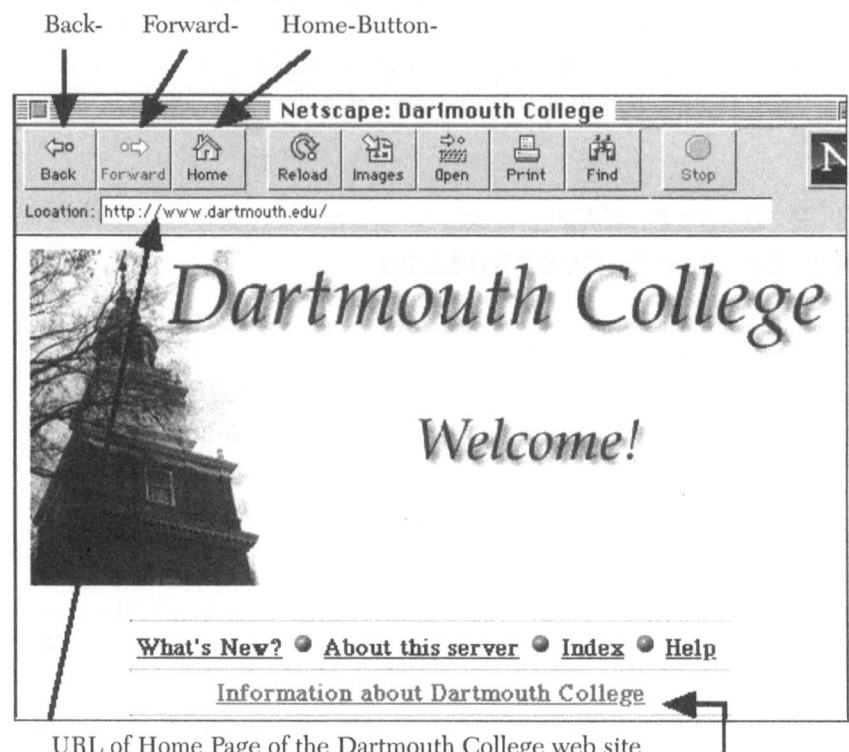

URL of Home Page of the Dartmouth College web site

Link to "information about Dartmouth College"

3.3 Hyper-G

http://www.iic
m.tugraz.ac.at

Hyper-G is a technically superior information server developed at the
Technical University of Graz [Mau96]. The Hyper-G team calls its system
the first 'second generation', publicly available, networked hypermedia
information system running over the Internet [Hyper-G Readme]. Hyper-G
integrates hyperlinking, hierarchical structuring, sophisticated search, and
access control facilities into a single system and is interoperable with other
network information tools like Gopher and WWW [And95]. It has its own
SGML-based text format: Hyper-G Text Format (HTF). When accessed by a
Web client, older versions of Hyper-G servers converted text documents on
the fly into HTML documents. The newest version of Hyper-G directly sup-

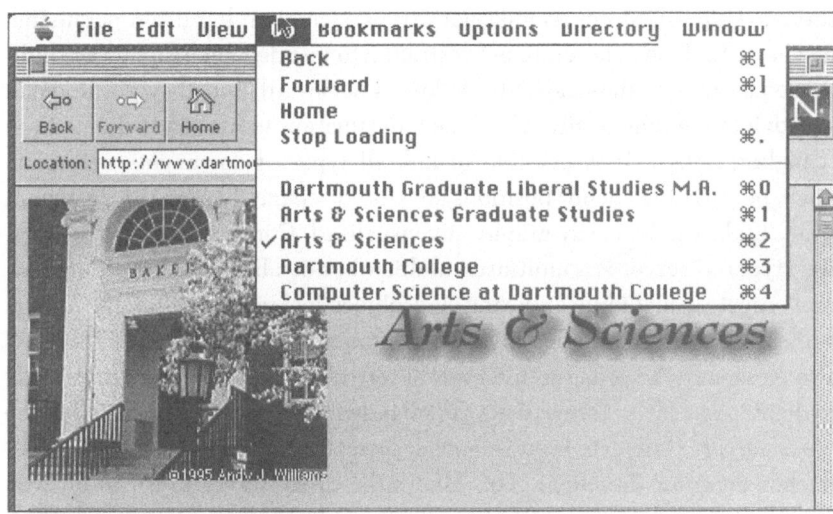

Figure I.13

Netscape's history mechanism

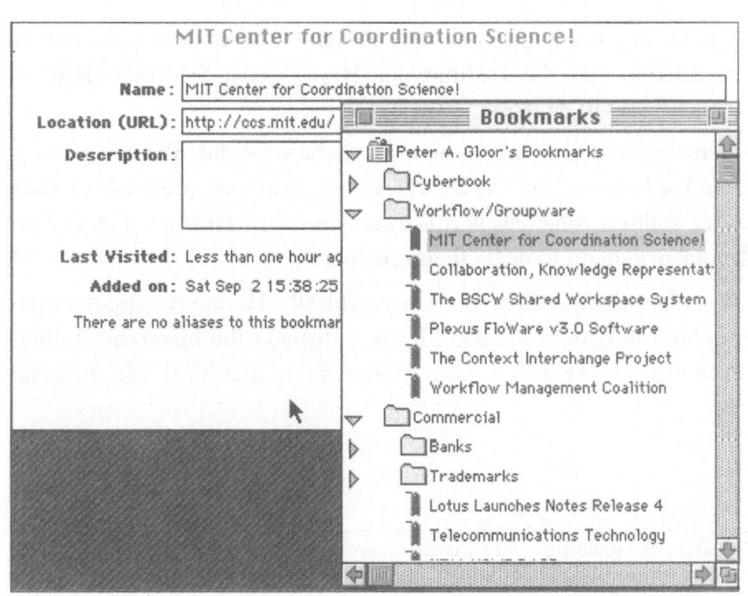

Figure I.14

Netscape's Bookmarks window

ports HTML 3.0. Like Intermedia (see Chapter 11), but unlike WWW servers, Hyper-G stores its links not within documents but in a separate link database. Links are therefore not restricted to text documents; they are bidirectional and can thus easily be followed backward, and they are updated and deleted automatically when their destination moves or is deleted (no "dangling links"). It is possible to link all types of documents with each other, because the anchor positions are stored separately from the document itself. Links can be easily graphically visualized. Contrarily to Web servers, the Hyper-G server is a multiuser, multiauthor database that allows concurrent updates, including indexing and object locking by different authors while the system continues to serve information to other users[2]. Hyper-G also pioneered the proxy architecture where clients are supposed to connect to their "nearest" (in terms of network bandwidth) server, which is called the *proxy server*. If objects from remote servers are required, the proxy server fetches them for the client. This allows the proxy server to cache or even store permanent replicas of frequently requested information. In addition, the proxy architecture is based on a connection-oriented, stateful protocol between client and server, resulting in increased performance. The proxy architecture has also been adopted by most Web servers.

Hyper-G is being developed jointly by the Institute for Information Processing and Computer Supported New Media (IICM) of Graz University of Technology, Austria, and the Institute for HyperMedia Systems (IHM) of JOANNEUM RESEARCH, Graz, Austria.

Hyper-G includes a line mode browser, a browser for Windows called Amadeus, and a browser for UNIX/X11 called Harmony. Because of their much broader abilities Amadeus and Harmony are now positioned as authoring and data management tools by their creators.

ftp://ftp.iicm
.tugraz.ac.at/
pub/Hyper-
G/Harmony

Hyper-G's information is structured hierarchically. Harmony supports hierarchical browsing in that its Session Manager displays the hierarchical information structure of Hyper-G data similar to a graphical file browser (Figure I.15).

---

2 Hyper-G tackles many problems of authoring in cyberspace that are not addressed in this book, such as linking multimedia data (e.g., MPEG movies), or issues arising in large-scale data management such as managing metainformation (e.g. author, opening date, expiration date key words, and access restrictions).

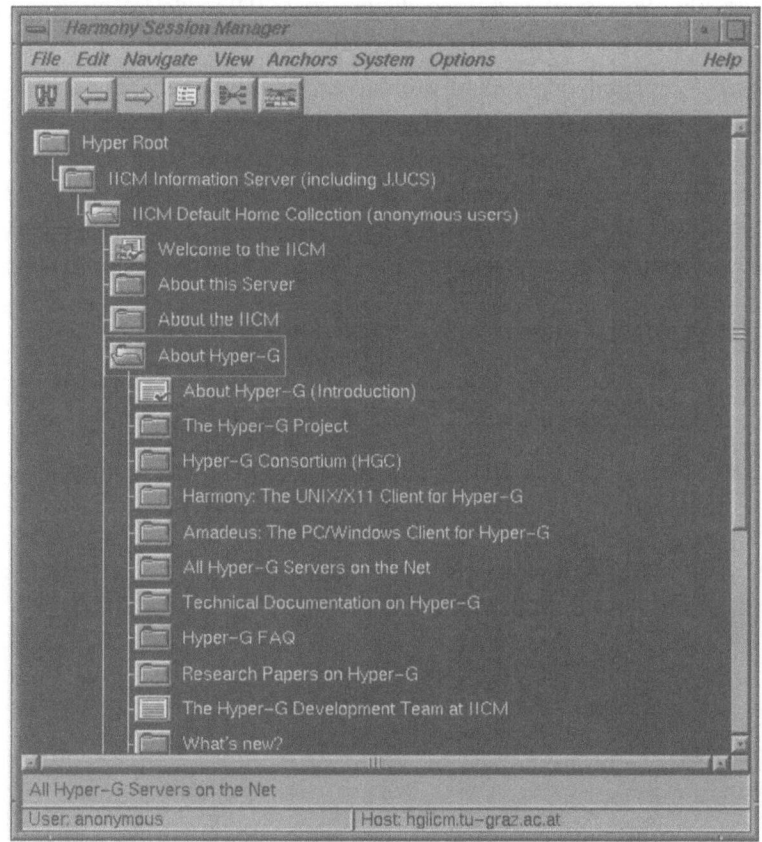

Figure I.15

Hyper-G
Harmony
Session Manager

Because the Hyper-G server is built on top of a powerful object-oriented database engine, every Hyper-G object (documents, links, collections) can be globally searched for. Harmony provides sophisticated search capabilities. It supports both attribute (key word, title, author, creation time, etc.) and content (fulltext) searches. Search results are presented as a ranked list. The scope of searches is user definable, ranging from individual collections to all collections on all Hyper-G servers worldwide. Selecting a document or collection in the local map, in the search result list, or following a hyperlink causes the location of the corresponding object to be displayed automatically in the collection browser, providing a powerful aid to orientation.

Harmony supports hyperlinks between arbitrary document types, including text, image, film, PostScript, and three–dimensional (3D) models. Source and destination anchors can be defined interactively.

Harmony's Local Map (Figure I.16) presents a dynamically generated graphical overview of the link relationships of a chosen document; incoming and outgoing hyperlinks are represented. The depth of the "look back" and "look ahead" can be dynamically adjusted by the user. Normally the user selects depth 1 to get the immediate surroundings of the current node. Selecting an object toward the edge of the map and generating a new display offers another means of associative browsing.

The Information Landscape (Figures I.17 and I.18) is a 3D graphical overview map of the collection structure. Users can fly over the information landscape looking for salient features, select interesting documents, and so on.

Figure I.16

Hyper-G
Harmony local
map with center
"About
Hyper-G"

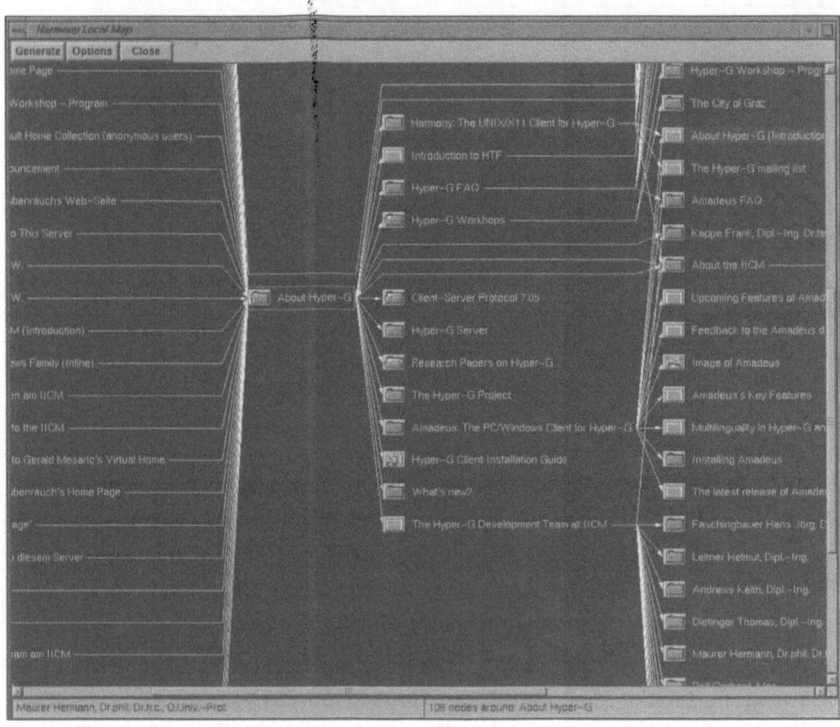

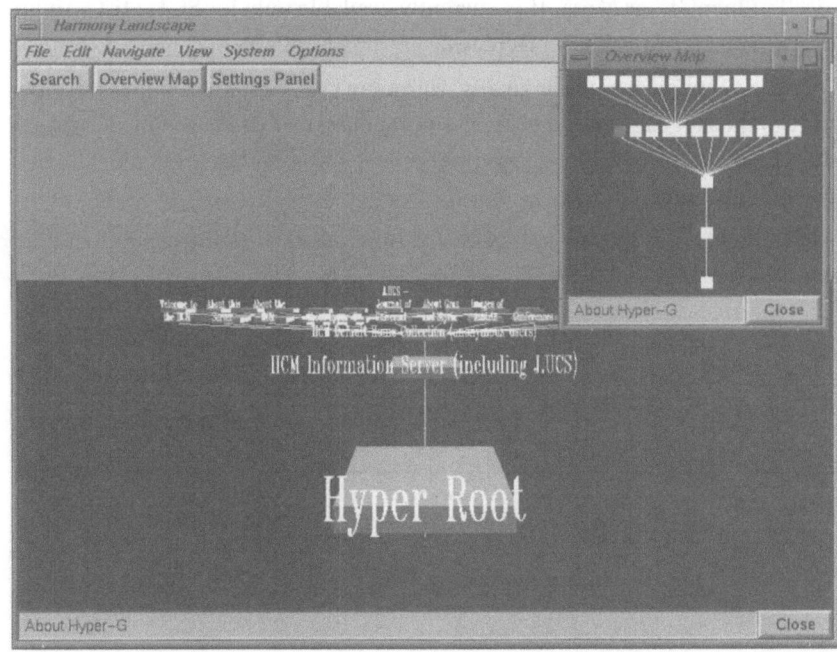

Figure I.17

Hyper-G
Harmony
Information
Landscape

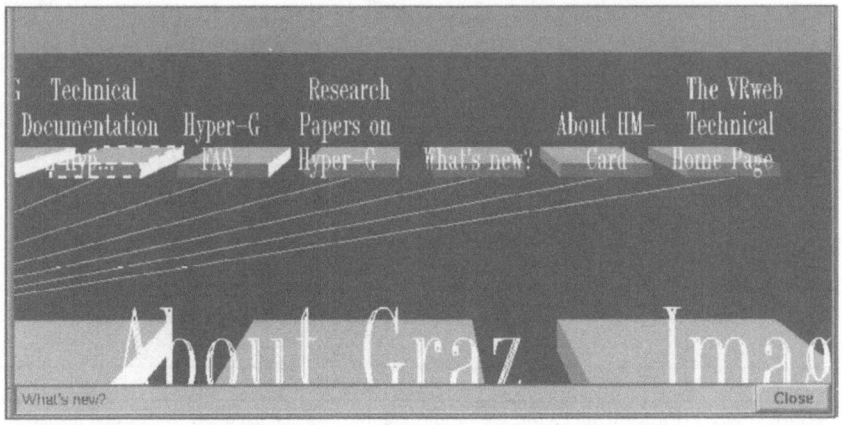

Figure I.18

Hyper-G
Harmony
Information
Landscape,
zoomed in
virtual reality

This feature requires platform support for a 3D graphics package such as IrisGL, OpenGL, or Mesa. It is currently available only for SGI, DEC Alpha, Solaris, Linux, and HP/UX machines.

Hyper-G supports multilinguality. Harmony's user interface adjusts dynamically to the language of first choice, documents available in multiple languages are selected in order of language preference, and searches are optionally language dependent.

Documents in Harmony are displayed by separate viewer processes in their own windows:

* *Text.* A generic SGML parser is used to display Hyper-G (HTF) and WWW (HTML) texts. Inline images in GIF, JPEG, XPM, XBM, and TIFF formats are supported (Figure I.19).[3]

Figure I.19

Hyper-G
Harmony Text
Viewer

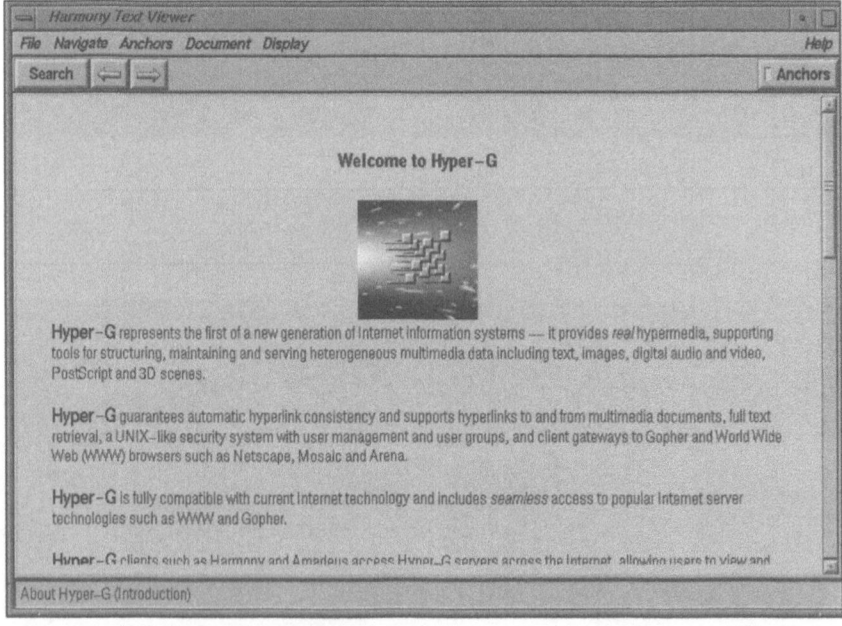

---

3 GIF, JPEG, TIFF, XPM, and XBM are various graphic formats that allow storing and displaying images independent of a particular platform.

- *Images.* GIF, JPEG, and TIFF images are supported and may be zoomed, panned, and so forth.

- *Movies.* MPEG-1 video streams are supported. Options include live display while loading, double size display, alternative dithering methods, and gamma correction. After loading, selective portions of the film may be replayed, for example, or the frame rate altered.

- *Audio.* The Audio Player supports both the Network Audio System (NAS) and local audio commands provided by the client system.[4]

- *PostScript.* PostScript files can be displayed page by page, zoomed, printed, and so forth.

- *3D scenes.* 3D model descriptions are displayed and can be manipulated or traversed in three dimensions. Hyperlinks are attached to objects in the model. This feature requires platform support for a 3D graphics package such as IrisGL, OpenGL, or Mesa and is currently available only for UNIX clients on SGI, DEC Alpha Solaris, Linux, and HPUX machines. The Hyper-G team also developed one of the first VRML viewers.

- *PDF* and *SGML.* PDF tools as well as a SGML parser are scheduled to appear in the fall 1996.

All built-in Harmony viewers support both activation and interactive definition of incoming and outgoing hyperlinks. Harmony can also be configured to use external programs to display any document types (but without linking capabilities).

Clearly Hyper-G offers superior functionality compared to WWW and its browsers such as Netscape. It is undergoing the transition from a research system to a commercial product, there is a growing number of Hyper-G servers (around 200 in spring 1996) in daily practical use all over the world. The creators of Hyper-G have founded a company, HyperWave, that markets a commercial version of Hyper-G under the name HyperWave.

---

4 The Network Audio System was developed by NCD for playing, recording, and manipulating audio data over a network. Like the X Window System, it uses the client–server model to separate applications from the specific drivers that control audio input and output devices.

CHAPTER 4

Programming

the

Web

This chapter surveys existing tools and techniques for programming on the
Web. The goal is not to teach how to program on the Web, but to show the
capabilities and limitations of existing tools and give readers an understanding
of the subject and point them to further reading. The tools discussed here have
been evaluated as a basis for our own Web-enabled navigation tools described
later in the book.

4.1 CGI (Common Gateway Interface)

http://hoohoo.
ncsa.uiuc.edu/
cgi/overview
.html

The Common Gateway Interface, or CGI, is an interface for running external programs, or gateways, under an HTTP information server. What is
referred to as gateway are really programs which handle information
requests and return the appropriate document or generate documents on
the fly.

Gateway programs, or *scripts*, are executable programs that can be run by
themselves. Users normally start a CGI program on the Web server by send-
ing a request to the server. The server processes this request by executing the
CGI program, while the browser on the client site waits until the program

43

has been completed and the output has been sent back to the client (top of Figure I.20). A sample application might be to connect a database such as a search engine to the World Wide Web to allow people from all over the world to query it. The search engine provider then needs to create a CGI program that the Web server will execute to transmit information to the search engine, and receive the results back and display them on the client.

Gateways conforming to the CGI specification can be written in any language that produces an executable file: C and FORTRAN programs, PERL scripts, Bourne and C shell scripts, AppleScript, Visual Basic, Tcl, and others.

Figure I.20

Program execution over the Web: CGI program versus Java applet

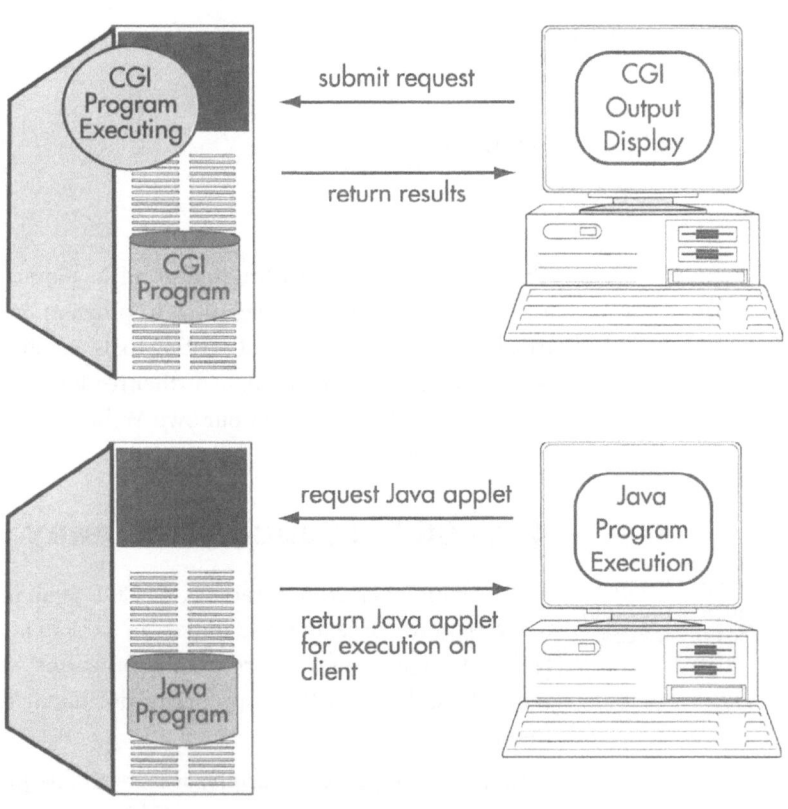

4.2 Java

CGI programs are executed entirely on the server. After completion of the CGI program, the server sends back the output to the browser that posted the request. Contrarily, Java applets are loaded from the server over the network and executed directly by the client browser (bottom of Figure I.20). This approach offers obvious advantages, because each task can be executed in its optimal environment. In particular, server and network load can be reduced by moving computation to the client. Also, an applet can be executed on any client platform where a Java-enabled browser is available. Unfortunately, transmission of executable code over the network introduces potential risks and security leaks. The Java developers have gone to great lengths to close those gaps.

`http://www`
`.javasoft.com`
`http://java`
`.sun.com`

Sun not only recommends Java for extending Web browsers by applets, but also positions it as the next–generation application development language. Consequently, the Java development environment allows programmers to build stand-alone Java applications.

The Java API provides a platform-independent run time environment for Java applets and applications, the Abstract Window Toolkit (AWT). The API contains classes for the GUI, networking, and input/output (I/O), plus a collection of utilities. The programmer accesses the API through a Java class library.

`http://www`
`.javasoft.com/`
`JDK-1.0/api/`
`packages.html`

4.3 JavaScript

In addition to Java, Netscape and Sun also developed JavaScript, formerly called LiveScript, a cross-platform object scripting language for the creation and customization of applications on enterprise networks and the Internet. The initial version of JavaScript was released as part of the Netscape Navigator 2.0 browser.

`http://home`
`.netscape.com/`
`comprod/`
`products/`
`navigator/`
`version_2.0/`
`script/`
`script_info/`
`index.html`

JavaScript is an easier-to-use object scripting language designed for creating live on-line applications that link together objects and resources on both clients and servers. Java programs and JavaScript scripts are designed to run on both clients and servers. JavaScript scripts can be used to modify the properties and behavior of Java objects. JavaScript is analogous to Visual Basic in that people with little or no programming experience can use it to construct simple applications quickly. (See Table I.1.)

Table I.1	**Java**	**JavaScript**
Comparison between Java and JavaScript	Compiled on server before execution on client	Interpreted by client, not compiled
	Object-oriented; programs consist of object classes, with inheritance, etc.	Object based; no classes or inheritance; built-in, extensible objects
	Applets distinct from HTML (accessed from HTML pages)	Integrated with/embedded in HTML
	Must declare variables' data types (strong typing)	Do not declare variables' data types (loose typing)
	Static binding; object references must exist at compile time	Dynamic binding; object references checked at run time
	Secure: cannot write to hard disk	Secure: cannot write to hard disk

With JavaScript, an HTML page might contain an intelligent form that performs loan payment or currency exchange calculations right on the client in response to user input. A multimedia weather forecast applet written in Java can be scripted by JavaScript to display appropriate images and sounds based on weather readings in a region. A server-side JavaScript script might pull data out of a relational database and format it in HTML on the fly.

JavaScript has been proposed by Netscape and Sun to the W3 Consortium (W3C) and the Internet Engineering Task Force (IETF) as an open Internet scripting language standard.

4.4 Tcl

http://www
.sunlabs.com/
research/tcl/
index.html

Java and Tcl [Ous90] are both being promoted by Sun as Web programming languages. Nevertheless, both occupy quite different niches. Tcl is a high-level scripting language allowing programmers to create small and medium-sized applications quickly and to glue together existing components. It has a simple syntax and almost no structure, which makes it good for scripting. However, Tcl as an interpreted language is not well suited for very large tasks involving iterative calculations. Java, on the other hand, is a system programming language like C or C++. Much more structured than Tcl, it requires a higher initial learning effort, as it is more complex to build applications with, but this structure also makes it easier to build large, complex applications. Java is compiled, which results in greater efficiency and supports multithreading; Tcl does not.

Sun envisions a symbiosis between Tcl and Java in which Java is used to build new primitives, which are then glued together into various applications by Tcl/Tk [Ous94].

Safe-Tcl has been developed by Nathaniel Borenstein and Marshall T. Rose based on John Ousterhout's Tcl language. The Safe-Tcl extension to Tcl/Tk disables Tcl functions that might cause damage to the downloading environment in a hostile or poorly written script.

http://www
.qualcomm.com/
ProdTech/quest/
times/ETFall94/
SafeTcl.html

Agent-Tcl adds remote programming capabilities to Tcl similar to the features of Telescript, described next. It is being developed by Robert Gray in the Agents group at Dartmouth College. The agents migrate from machine to machine using the Jump command. Execution resumes on the destination machine at the statement immediately after the jump. Modifications to the Tcl core allow the capture of the complete internal state of an executing script.

http://www.cs
.dartmouth.edu/
~agent/

4.5 General Magic Telescript

Telescript is an object-oriented programming language designed to support a remote programming model. It has been developed by General Magic, a Silicon Valley startup, as a basis to develop remote agents that execute tasks autonomously on behalf of the user.

http://www
.genmagic.com

http://www.sel.
sony.com/SEL/
Magic/

Telescript is an interpreted language. The interpreter and run time environment is called a Telescript engine and is implemented as one or more processes under the native operating system (currently some flavor of UNIX). A host can support the simultaneous execution of multiple Telescript engines, while a Telescript engine allows the simultaneous execution of multiple lightweight processes. Each process represents a distinct thread of execution. Telescript applications consist of communicating processes taking advantage of each other's resources via interprocess communication.

Telescript differs from other environments in its model for interprocess communication, a new model it introduced called *remote programming*. To support remote programming, Telescript divides all processes into *agents* and *places*, and it introduces an instruction called go, which is built into the language and provides the basis for interprocess communication. A place is a process that can contain other processes. When an agent needs the services defined at a given place, it must go to that place and then call operations there. Typically an application's Telescript component is set up around a single major place, which

**remote
programming
paradigm**

contains other places and agents whose operations implement the functionality of the application. Agents interact with each other by going from one place to the other and sometimes meeting with agents in different places.

Telescript engines permit agents to travel between places residing on different engines. For each go, a destination place is specified, and the Telescript engines and their supporting infrastructure take responsibility for the transport of the agent to the new place. When an off-engine go is executed, the agent's execution is momentarily suspended, and the agent is encoded for transport. A route to the requested place is determined, and the agent is sent over the network to its destination place. The agent is unpacked in the new place, all of its context is restored, and it resumes execution with access to the operations defined there.

The Seven Design Concepts *for* Navigation in Cyberspace

We commonly mistake data for information. Information starts with data, but data is not information—it is a source of information.

—Ramesh Jain, 1995
[Jai95]

The general problem addressed in this and the following eight chapters is how hypermedia documents should be structured and what navigation mechanisms should be provided such that readers can orient themselves in large information spaces. These large information spaces can consist of free-text articles, structured databases, hypertext documents, or knowledge bases. The orientation and information exploration problem can easily be experienced by anybody browsing on the Web: How often in a browsing session did the reader inadvertently stumble on an interesting site, only to search desperately for the same site in the next session? Also called the problem of *being lost in hyperspace*, this question has met high attention in the hypertext community, and many different solutions have been proposed.

We have identified seven concepts that need to be considered when designing the structure of a hypermedia document. The following seven chapters discuss these concepts and their application for the design of usable hypermedia documents in detail. By illustrating the basic principles by a large collection of practical examples, we are simultaneously using the seven design concepts to classify existing tools for navigation and information structuring into seven categories.

Frisse suggests a classification [Fri90] of navigation tools for hypertext documents distinguishing between signposts, shallow guides,[1] and deep guides. *Signposts* are the menus and buttons that indicate the existence of a link and allow the user to follow this link. They may be represented by electronic bookmarks. *Shallow guides* are overview maps and index lists that indicate the structure of the hypertext document. *Deep guides* extend the notion of shallow guides by incorporating knowledge not only about the structure of the hypertext network but also about the semantic contents of the hypertext document.

Frisse's taxonomy needs refinement. We are suggesting a more elaborate classification of navigation tools into seven categories (Figure I.21). At the same time, these seven categories serve as design principles for designing usable hypermedia documents. The seven design concepts cover a broad range of navigation tools and techniques ranging from appropriate structuring of information to the application of artificial intelligence techniques.[2]

The *linking* structure is the most distinguishing feature of a hypertext document. Links allow direct access to a designated location within the information space through markers that are embedded into the documents. We distinguish between straightforward *static links* and context–specific, automatically generated *dynamic links*.

Providing *searching* capabilities is an obvious means for locating information. In hypertext documents, this is mostly done using full-text search, although there are also systems that provide additional databases for searching. In this book we limit the discussion to full-text search tools mostly for the Web.

---

1 Instead of the expression *navigation tool*, Frisse uses the term *guide* in the general sense of a sign or mark that serves to direct. We will be using the term *guide* later in the more restricted meaning of a guide as a person or agent who shows the way by leading, directing, or advising.

2 The categorization into seven design concepts treats the information exploration problem on a practical, application-oriented level. The underlying theoretical information retrieval and user modeling techniques have been discussed in the preceding chapters.

		Description	Example	Figure I.21
	Linking	Global linking structure of document	Hyperlink	The seven design concepts for navigation in cyberspace
	Searching	Mechanisms for full-text search	Full-text search	
	Sequentialization	Mechanism for sequentially visiting selected locations within hyperdocument	Path	
	Hierarchy	Hierarchical table of contents	Table of Contents	
	Similarity	Connection between not-yet-linked but semantically related nodes	Index	
	Mapping	Graphical visualization of contents of hyperdocument	Overview map	
	Agents	Mechanism to execute complex tasks on behalf of the user	Shopping agent	

For novice or first-time users it can be very helpful to reduce the complexity of the n-dimensional hypertext document to one dimension by offering them a *sequential* path or guided tour through the hyperdocument.

A *hierarchical* document structure is very well understood by humans. Almost all printed books are organized hierarchically. Prospective authors are well advised to employ a hierarchical document structure for a new hyperdocument, but there are also tools, like Superbook, that compute a hierarchical map from existing documents. The hierarchical information structure is then made obvious to the users and put at their disposal as their principal navigation aid.

Similarity links connect nodes that have similar contents but might not yet be linked. An index is a very simple means to discover similarities between different nodes, because pages that have common index entries might exhibit some sort of similarity. More complex tools in this category are based on the assumption that the system has knowledge about not only the document structure but also the contents of the information contained in the document. There are two approaches to this problem. IR-based systems (see section 1.4) compute similarities based on statistical approaches, and knowledge-based systems try to use a deeper understanding of the semantic contents of a document. Obviously, this latter requirement is very hard to accomplish and needs some sort of expert system. It is not surprising that the systems of this category have not moved beyond the state of early prototypes.

Mapping is a technology to structure, visualize, and manage webs of information. Similar to real maps, graphical maps show readers where they are and where they can go from here, and it gives them an overview of their local and global context. They are thus one of the most flexible, versatile, and user–friendly means for navigation in cyberspace. Mapping is orthogonal to the previous concepts in that maps can be used to visualize links, search results, sequential paths, hierarchies, and similarities.

The concept of *guides* and *agents* is popular for navigation and many other areas. The agent metaphor is well understood by humans, because agents simulate human assistants. The systems in this category incorporate artificial intelligence–based techniques derived from the metaphor of agents' assisting human readers in their complex orientation tasks. The agents are implemented in different ways, ranging from simple, hardwired guides to rule-based agents that are able to react more flexibly to different needs of different users. Agents can use any of the other six concepts to assists users in their navigation task.

Most of the tools and techniques described in the following chapters have been developed explicitly for hypermedia documents. With the advent of the

Web, the distinction between hypertext and sequential documents has been blurring, as many existing, sequential documents have been converted to hypertext. It is one of the goals of this book to have authors not only change the format from, say, Microsoft Word to HTML, when converting a document from text to hypertext, but to redesign the document for presentation in another, much richer, environment.

Linking

There have been many attempts to classify links [Con87a] [Fri90] [Myk95]. Designers of hypermedia documents need to decide about the main linking structure of their documents, as well as about what additional linking facilities to supply to the user. To limit cognitive overload, it can be helpful to provide only a subset of different link types. We propose a link classification that closely fits the first four concepts for navigation in cyberspace (Figure I.22):

- *Page links—sequentialization*. Page links rebuild the original ordering sequence of the nodes and thus reflect the primary sequential reading order as intended by the hypermedia author. They connect a particular page with its predecessor and successor and thus recreate a locally sequential context for the node.

- *Hierarchical links*. Hierarchical links reflect the logical ordering of the original sections of the document. Because most documents are inherently hierarchically structured, hierarchical links are the most powerful means for achieving easily navigable and user–friendly hyperdocuments.

- *Similarity links*. Similarity links connect nodes that have similar contents but are not yet connected by page or hierarchical links. They are

Figure I.22

The four types of
links

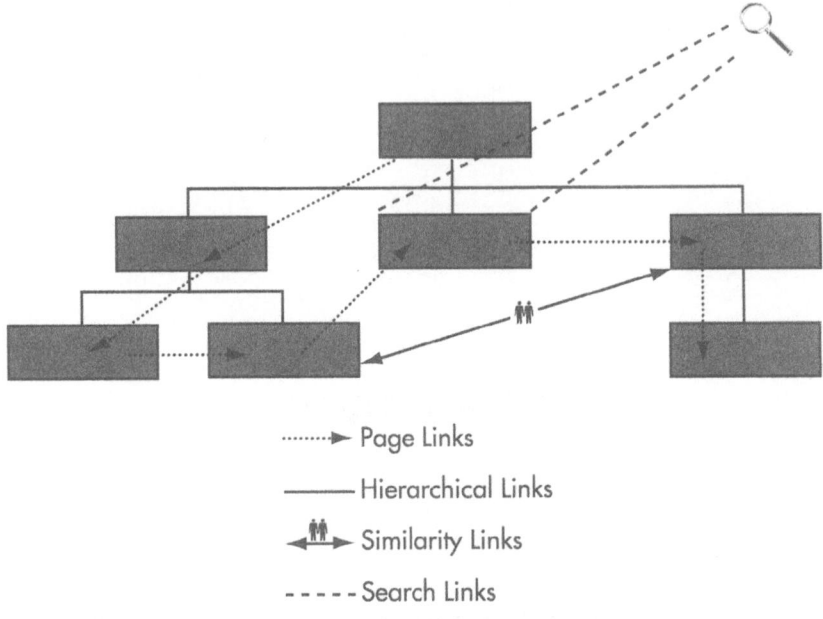

........► Page Links

———— Hierarchical Links

◄—👫► Similarity Links

- - - - - Search Links

frequently computed automatically based on similar terms in different
nodes and are generated by means of a statistical evaluation of the node
collection. Similar nodes can be ranked using the vector space model or
with knowledge-based approaches.

- *Search links*. Search links are generated automatically in answer to a query
  made by the retrieval system.

In addition to these first four categories of links that reflect the document
structure and thus also offer a primary means for structuring information, we
can identify another link category that embodies cross references between
nodes:

- *Reference links*. Reference links are embedded in the original text and
  refer to other nodes or text passages within the original text, for example,
  "see section 7", or [Knuth73]. Reference links are therefore a special case
  of similarity links.

This book describes many complex tools and techniques for navigation and
information location in hypertext documents. In the best of all cyberworlds,

there would be the ideal solution: If at any time the *one* link that the reader really wanted could be made available, then there would be no need for sophisticated navigation tools like an index, overview maps, fish–eye views, and cone trees, described in later chapters. To satisfy this requirement, the hypertext system would have to figure out the current needs of the users based on their user model, browsing history, and current context and then offer them the most meaningful link to the next node to be read. Unfortunately, the state of the art in automatic hypertext link generation will not be that advanced for a long time. Nevertheless, there are some promising approaches based on the concept of dynamic linking.

6.1 Static Versus Dynamic Linking

In correspondence with other literature [Fou90] [Hal91], we define static and dynamic links as follows:

- *Static links.* The common link type in most commercially available hypertext systems. Static links are defined by a hypertext author and are available afterward to the reader (<A HREF....>-links in HTML). The connections and link end points are hardwired into the document by the author. There is no easy way to accommodate different user groups and to adjust the links in a modified hyperdocument.

- *Dynamic links.* Implemented only in a few experimental hypertext systems [Irl90][Fou90][Ega91]. Dynamically linked documents do not have any fixed link end points (also called anchors). Instead the links are computed at run time according to the needs of the user.

Halasz [Hal91] calls this discussion the "literalists versus the virtualists". For literalists (believers in static links), structures and links are created and represented explicitly. Navigation is by following explicit structural connections. Examples of literalist systems are most of the existing hypermedia systems— for example, Intermedia [Utt89], NoteCards [Hal86], and KMS [Aks88]. Examples of virtualist systems include MICROCOSM [Fou90], SuperBook [Rem87], and Cybermap (described later in this book).

Dynamic links offer two distinct advantages compared to static links:

1. They propose a more flexible way of navigating in the hyperdocument because they are generated on the fly according to the varying needs of the readers.

2. Dynamically linked documents are easy to modify because newly added or deleted nodes are (un)linked automatically to and from the existing nodes. Anyone who has tried to add or remove nodes from a complex hypertext document written by somebody else knows how difficult it is to avoid dangling links within the existing body of the hyperdocument.

Similarity links, where links are computed automatically based on similarity between nodes, are a special case of dynamic links. (Similarity is discussed in Chapter 10.)

It is difficult to provide a fixed a priori linking structure for huge hyperdocuments [Fur89]. This is true in particular if the links should be able to satisfy the needs of various user groups with different capabilities and requirements. Dynamic linking addresses this problem by trying to figure out the needs of the reader dynamically and to present only the links that are appropriate in a particular situation.

6.2 MICROCOSM: A System Based on Dynamic Linking

http://cosm
.ecs.soton.ac
.uk/

Wendy Hall et al. [Fou90][Car94][Lew96] have implemented MICRO-COSM, a system based on dynamic linking. MICROCOSM is a complete hypermedia authoring system. One of its main goals is to be open to future expansion. Its authors describe it as a "loosely coupled system with a low level of interdependency" where links are separated from data objects. This idea has lead to the concept of *generic links*. Generic links allow the author to associate a document with any occurrence of a partial text string in any document. Generic links are therefore applicable not only to just one document, but may be used within a whole class of documents. This means that a new plain document brought into the system may immediately contain links. For example, if "amoeba" is a link to a video about amoebas, a new document containing "amoeba" automatically inherits this link. Another important concept of MICROCOSM is that there is no distinction between hypertext reader and hypertext author; readers are free to add a link at any place they wish.

Figure I.23 displays a MICROCOSM application. The MICROCOSM system is available for academic and nonacademic users on the PC/Windows platform.

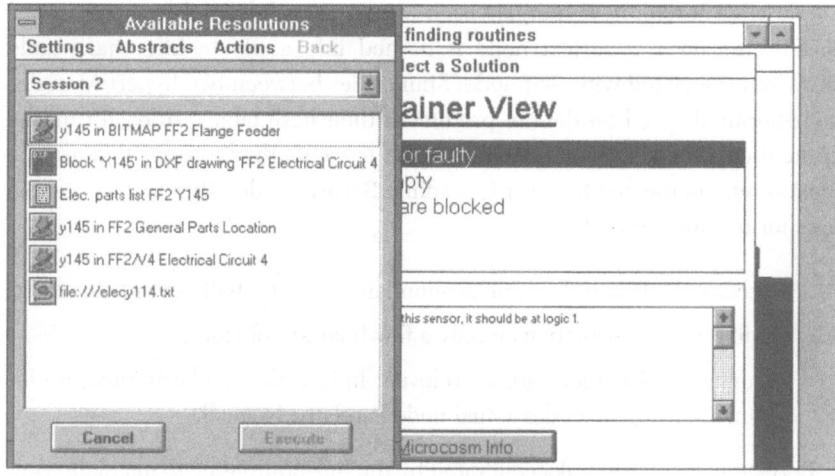

Figure I.23

Following
generic links in
MICROCOSM
http://cosm.ecs.
soton.ac.uk/pub/
ScreenCam/
FALTFIND.EXE

As MICROCOSM illustrates, the concept of the generic link allows a user to
add new plain–text documents (without links) that automatically inherit any
generic links that might point into the newly added documents. MICRO-
COSM [Fou90] does not address the problem of automatic link generation but
allows the reuse of existing, manually created links. The link apprentice,
described in the next section, tries to compute links between related documents automatically, based on simple string comparisons.

6.3 Automatic Link Generation: The Link Apprentice

Mark Bernstein [Ber90] describes a link apprentice for the automatic generation of links that delivers surprisingly effective results using a shallow link
detection technique. The link apprentice does not do any semantic analysis of
the underlying text but uses a simple pattern matching and string comparison
algorithm. Obviously a system working in this way can never expect to generate all links automatically, because if two passages of text express the same idea
differently (using different phrases and words), the link apprentice has no way
of figuring out the link. If, on the other hand, unrelated concepts are expressed
in similar words, the link apprentice computes an erroneous link.

Bernstein integrated his link apprentice into the hypertext system Hypergate [Ber90]. In Hypergate each word and each left substring of a word that occurs on a hypertext node is hashed into a Bloom filter hash table [Knu73b] associated with that node. Similarities between two hypertext nodes are computed based on the dot product of their hash tables. In each run, the apprentice scans the whole document and presents the 20 pages that are the most similar to the one the user is reading. Bernstein identifies three potential uses for his link apprentice:

1. Selecting the best links from an abundance of potentially interesting links.
2. Finding more destinations if only a few links are obvious.
3. Recognizing that there are no relevant links if the similarity measure for all links starting from the actual node is relatively small.

Bernstein compared links generated by the link apprentice to manually generated links and found that most of the time automatically generated links are at least as good as the manually generated ones. In about 10 percent of the cases, the link apprentice produced meaningless links. This means that all automatically generated links have to be verified manually, but that the link apprentice offers a valuable tool assisting the hypertext author in finding the best links. It is also well suited for automatically generating first approximations of guided tours (see Chapter 8). But to get a truly versatile automatic linking facility, there is no way around both comparing strings and analyzing the contents of a document. The VISAR system presented in Chapter 10 is representative of this kind of system.

6.4 Breadcrumbs and Bookmarks

Breadcrumb navigation aids, suggested by Mark Bernstein [Ber88], provide a visual indicator that a particular node has already been visited. The concept is inspired by the fairy tale of Hansel and Gretel, where Hansel marked their way in the dark forest by throwing breadcrumbs on the ground every few inches. Eventually breadcrumbs accumulate to a point where they are marking most of the nodes; at this point their utility is minimal. Bernstein suggests that breadcrumbs disappear after a certain time: Crumbs represent pages we have read recently, and imaginary birds remove breadcrumbs the reader leaves unvisited for more than thirty pages [Ber88:43].

The breadcrumb feature has been implemented in WWW browsers such as Netscape by coloring links to pages that have already been visited. The user can specify an expiration time to the coloring; after the time has expired, the links are reset to their original color.

Bookmarks are similar to breadcrumbs in that they mark places that the user has visited. Unlike breadcrumbs, they are permanently stored for later access. The bookmark feature, adapted from the printed book, has proved invaluable for keeping track of places useful to the reader (see Figure I.14 for Netscape's implementation of bookmarks).

Searching

One way to add new links dynamically is in response to a search query. Obviously this works only if search engines are built into the hypermedia environment. Most hypermedia authoring environments, such as HyperCard and ToolBook, have their own search mechanisms of vastly different capabilities built in. Open hypermedia systems such as the World Wide Web, on the other hand, offer information providers and authors great flexibility in implementing their own search subsystems.

This chapter introduces tools for searching in large information spaces. Although these tools can be used for searching in any large information collection, they have all been adapted to or even specifically developed for the largest information space of all, the Web. Contrary to the simple browsing mechanisms discussed in Chapter 3, the tools described here allow users to do Boolean, vector space, or probabilistic searches.

7.1 WAIS

http://www
.wais.com

WAIS (Wide Area Information Server) has been developed by Thinking Machines Corporation [Kah91] [Obr93] to use the potential of massively parallel supercomputers for information access, exploration, and filtering in very large information bases. WAIS has acquired a life of its own as one of the most popular search–and–retrieval mechanisms for WWW applications. It is available in a public domain version, and an extended version is being marketed commercially by its original inventors through WAIS Corporation, recently acquired by America Online (AOL).

relevance feedback

WAIS allows full-text search in free-text databases (called *content navigation* by its creators [Kah89]). Users enter their query in plain English and specify which databases to search. WAIS then returns a list of documents that match the key words of the query. In the example in Figure I.24 users searched for background about Kenya selecting the databases "Atlas" and "TMC Encyclopedia" out of the listing of possible sources. With *relevance feedback*, users can refine their search by using parts of documents retrieved earlier as their new search query.

Successful queries (like the one in the Figure I.24) can be saved. They then serve as action links to a collection of documents. The query in the figure defines not only what the query text is ("Please give me background on Kenya Africa") but also what data collections to search ("Atlas", "TMC Encyclopedia") and on what servers to search those. It could also contain some documents as part of the query search using relevance feedback if any of the previously

---

Figure I.24

WAIS query about Kenya

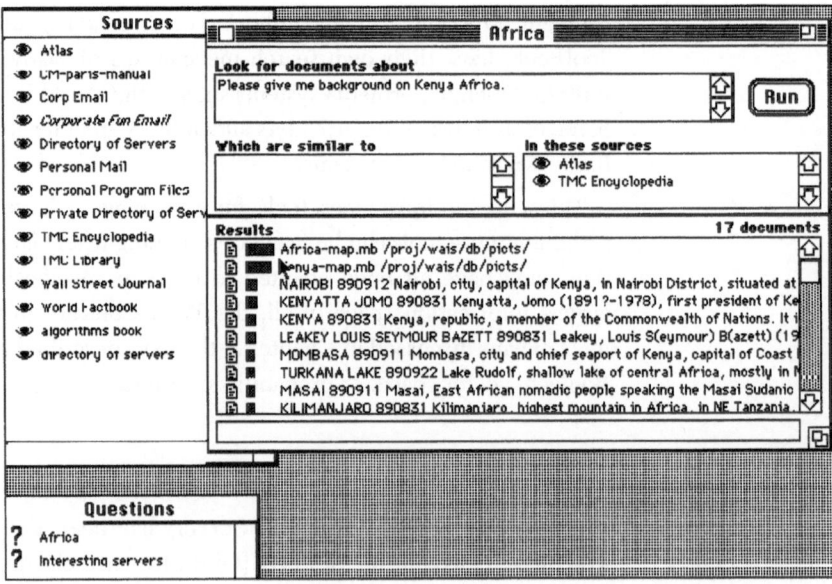

---

retrieved documents had been dragged into the "which are similar to" window. The query in the Figure has already been saved under the label "Africa" and shows up in the window "Questions" in the lower left corner of the Figure.

WAIS is based on a full-text IR architecture whose servers and clients communicate through an extension of the Z39.50 protocol standard from the U.S. National Information Standards Organization. Its architecture is depicted in Figure I.25. WAIS clients translate user queries into the Z39.50 protocol. The location and content description of the server databases can be received from the Directory of Servers database, which is located at a well-known address. Selected server databases are then queried directly from the client. Database servers maintain complete inverted indexes for all stored documents. For a query, the key words of the query are matched against the index, and a sorted list of all documents that contain some key words of the original query is returned. The clients display a numerical score for each retrieved document title that gets the larger for a particular document the more query key words are matched within the document. WAIS introduces the concept of a WAIS

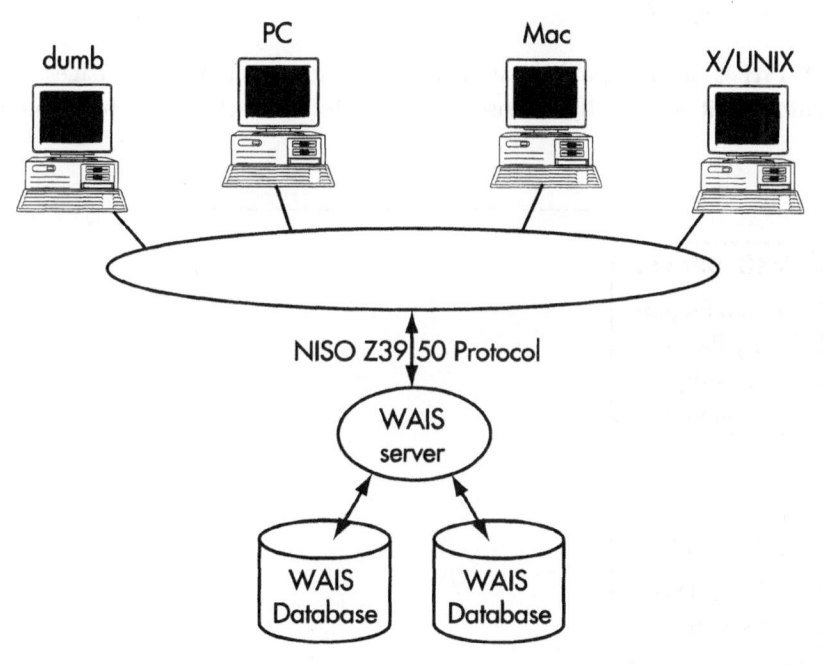

Figure I.25

WAIS
Architecture

network publisher, an information provider that supplies both a WAIS database and a WAIS server (Figure I.26).

WAIS is an excellent IR system for huge databases, but it omits some navigation functionality. The original WAIS GUI (graphical user interface), shown in Figure I.24, does not represent retrieved information graphically, and it does not give an overview of the contents of the databases, which can be used as search sources. We have addressed these shortcoming in our own Cybermap system (see Chapter 18).

http://www.eit
.com/sofware/
wwwwais/
wwwwais.html

To connect a WAIS server to the Web, a CGI gateway is needed [Pfe95]. (See Chapter 4 for a brief introduction to CGI.) There are various programs available that provide this functionality such as WWWWAIS (Figure I.27).

WWWWAIS allows the user to submit a search request via HTTP server to the WAIS server, which searches the WAIS index and then returns the result to the browser in the form of an ad-hoc generated HTML page. As can be seen from Figure I.27, advanced functionality such as relevance feedback is not normally offered on WAIS Web interfaces.

7.2 SWISH

http://www.eit.
com/goodies/
software/swish/
swish.html

SWISH is another publicly available indexing systems for Web pages. We introduce it here briefly because our own indexing mechanism is based on it.

Figure I.26

WAIS network
publisher

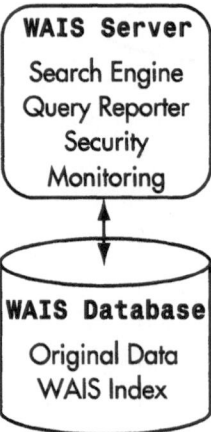

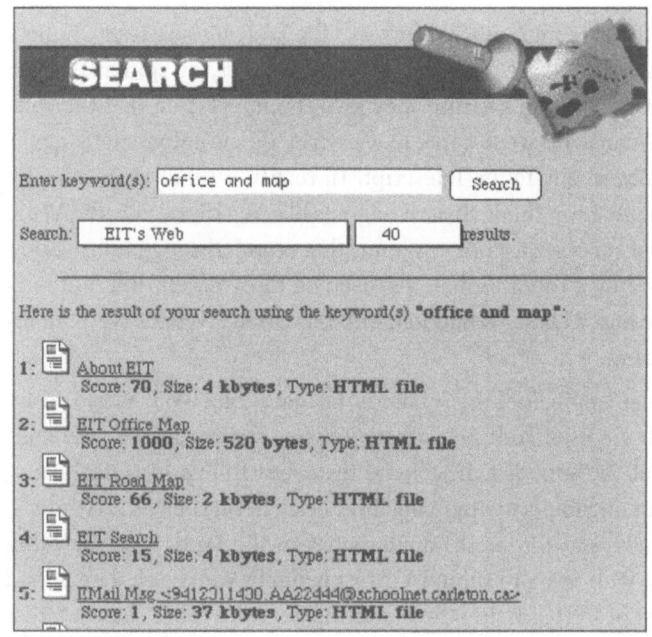

Figure I.27

WWWWAIS
search interface
for the Web

SWISH (Simple Web Indexing System for Humans) allows users to index directories of files and search the generated indexes.

SWISH has been developed explicitly for Web use, which means that it knows about the popular HTML tags and can either ignore data in tags or give higher relevance to information in header and title tags. Titles are extracted from HTML files and appear in the search results. SWISH also allows searches for words that exist in HTML titles, comments, and emphasized tags. The SWISH index consists of only one file that is about 1 to 5 percent of the size of the original HTML data.

The obvious disadvantage of the simplicity of SWISH is that it does not support advanced functions such as stemming (searching for different versions of a word) or the use of synonyms. The creator company of SWISH, Enterprise Integration Technologies Corporation (EIT) has not placed it in the public domain, but distributes it free of royalties for personal, academic, research, and internal commercial use.

7.3 Robots

http://info
.webcrawler.com/
mak/projects/
robots/robots
.html

http://altavista
.digital.com/

http://www.lycos
.com/

http://inktomi
.berkeley.edu/
query.html

Indexing robots

**Risks Using
Robots**

http://www
.w3.org/pub/
WWW/Robot/

**Keeping Robots
Out**

Web robots are software programs that traverse the Web automatically. Robots are sometimes also called Web wanderers, Web crawlers, or spiders, names that are somewhat misleading because they give the impression that the software itself would move between sites like a virus or an autonomous agent implemented in, say, Agent-Tcl or Telescript. In reality, a robot visits sites by requesting documents from them. Search engines like WAIS, Lycos, Alta Vista, and Inktomi are not robots; they are programs that search through information collections gathered by a robot. Robots are used on the Web for different purposes, such as indexing, HTML validation, link validation, "What's New" monitoring, and mirroring.

The most popular application of robots is for gathering Web pages to be indexed for search engines. Indexing robots employ various search strategies to decide what Web sites to visit. In general they start from a historical list of URLs, especially of documents with many links elsewhere, such as server lists, "What's New" pages, and the most popular sites on the Web. Most indexing services also allow Web users to submit URLs manually, which are then added to the historical list of URLs. Using those starting points, a robot selects URLs to visit and index, and to parse and use as a source for new URLs. If an indexing robot knows about a document, it may decide to parse it and insert it into its database. How this is done depends on the robot. Some robots index the HTML titles, or the first few paragraphs; others parse the entire HTML text and index all words, with weighting depending on HTML constructs.

Robots should be used on the Web only by experienced Web programmers because of the risks involved when robots are let loose without considering the consequences. If a robot is implemented improperly, it can overload networks and servers. There are guidelines available for properly implementing robots. And even if a robot is implemented properly, it can nevertheless be used improperly, resulting in network and server overload. If a robot visits one site too fast in sequence, it can slow down the server, even causing server crashes.

A potential problem with indexing robots is that centralized search databases built by Web-wide indexing robots do not scale easily to millions of documents on millions of sites.

Most robots provide valuable services to the Web community. However, a standard has been established for keeping robots away from certain pages or even blocking them totally from visiting a server. To block a robot from visiting a server, the following two lines need to be placed into the server:

```
User-agent: *
Disallow: /
```

It is also possible to specify selectively in the /robots.txt file if certain robots should be prohibited from visiting particular files. Of course, this procedure works only if the robot itself obeys this protocol.

7.4 Harvest

Harvest is an integrated set of tools to gather, extract, organize, search, cache, and replicate relevant information across the Internet. It is being developed at the University of Colorado at Boulder. Harvest software, in the public domain, consists of a robot for gathering information, indexing parts to build a searchable index, and a search engine to search the index and return the results to the Internet user. Harvest consists of the following subsystems:

`http://harvest`
`.cs.colorado`
`.edu/`

- *Gatherer.* The Harvest Gatherer is a robot that collects information optimized for indexing. It scans objects periodically, maintaining a cache of indexing information, and allowing a provider's indexing information to be retrieved in a single stream (rather than requiring separate requests for each object).

- *Broker.* The Broker provides an indexed query interface to gathered information. Brokers retrieve information from one or more Gatherers or other Brokers, and they incrementally update their indexes. The Broker records unique identifiers and expiration dates for each indexed object, garbage collects old information, and invokes the Index/Search Subsystem when it receives an update or a query. Harvest provides a distinguished Broker called the Harvest Server Registry (HSR), which registers information about each Harvest Gatherer, Broker, Cache, and Replicator in the Internet.

- *Index/Search Subsystem.* Harvest defines a general Broker-Indexer interface that can accommodate a variety of search engines. The principal requirements are that the back end supports Boolean combinations of attribute-based queries and incremental updates. One can therefore use different back ends inside a Broker. Harvest currently supports commercial and free WAIS and has its own search engines, called Glimpse and Nebula.

- *Replicator.* Harvest provides a weakly consistent, replicated wide-area file system called *mirror-d*, on top of which Brokers are replicated. Mirror-d itself is layered on top of a hierarchical group communication subsystem.

- *Object Cache*. To speed up network access, Harvest includes its own hier-archical Object Cache. The Cache sends "query" datagrams to each neighbor and parent, plus an ICMP echo to the object's home site. It chooses the fastest responding server from which to retrieve the data.

Harvest offers a complete public domain solution for building a Web-wide searchable information base. Its only disadvantage is its complexity, compared with simpler, albeit much more limited, systems such as SWISH.

Sequentialization

The high dimensionality of an interlinked hypertext document allows many ways of browsing a hyperdocument. A novice user soon gets overwhelmed by the number of possible ways to read through the document. Guided tours or paths offer a simple mechanism for quickly providing an overview of a hypermedia document. These tools hide the complexity of hypertext by constraining the user to a sequential path. Guided tours are not to be confused with guides described in Chapter 12. The idea of guided tours can be traced back to Vannevar Bush and the origins of hypertext.[1] Bush calls a guided tour a *trail* and describes it as a sequence of "links through the Memex". In this chapter we outline four implementations of his concept. Later we introduce our own means of sequentialization, the path editor.

---

1 Vannevar Bush is generally considered to be the inventor of the hypertext idea. He first presented his thoughts in the classical article "As We May Think" [Bus45], which introduced the hypertext concept with the example of the hypothetical Memex system.

8.1 Guided Tours and Travel Holidays

Hammond and Allison present a system based on the *travel holiday metaphor*
[Ham88] for educational applications. They identify two types of control in
learning support environments: control over the sequencing of material and
control over the sequencing of learning activities (e.g., reading, taking tests, or
solving problems). To minimize the amount of training needed to use their system, they have built it around a travel holiday metaphor. For inexperienced
readers, guided tours offer a means of traveling safely in unknown territory.
Subtours (excursions) can be embedded into the main guided tour. The system
offers other navigational cues, such as an index, a map, a quiz, and hints for further reading. Readers use these tools while they travel in the document in
so–called got-it-alone mode.

When evaluating the use of their system, Hammond and Allison found that
readers preferred the tour over all other mechanisms for studying unfamiliar
material, but that with increasing familiarity, readers shifted to user-controlled
navigation tools such as the index and map. Simple guided tours thus seem to
be a useful aid for novice or first–time users but are too limiting for experienced readers and need to be complemented by navigation tools that allow the
reader to browse more freely.

8.2 Guided Tours and Tabletops in NoteCards

NoteCards, one of the preeminent research hypertext systems, was developed
from 1985 to 1988 at XEROX PARC [Hal86]. NoteCards pioneered concepts
such as typed links (Figure I.28) and graphical overview maps of hypertext documents (Figure I.29).

To allow sequentialization and easier access to complex hypertext documents, Trigg suggests extending NoteCards by offering the author *guided tours*
and *tabletops* [Tri88]. Tabletops are a mechanism for defining the layout of a set
of NoteCards cards on the screen. A tabletop contains a set of cards, their
screen positions, scrolled locations, size, and overlapping arrangements.
Figure I.30 shows an example tabletop, specifying an arrangement of
NoteCards cards on the screen. A "tabletops" card contains links to other tabletops and thus defines a sequence of screen snapshots.

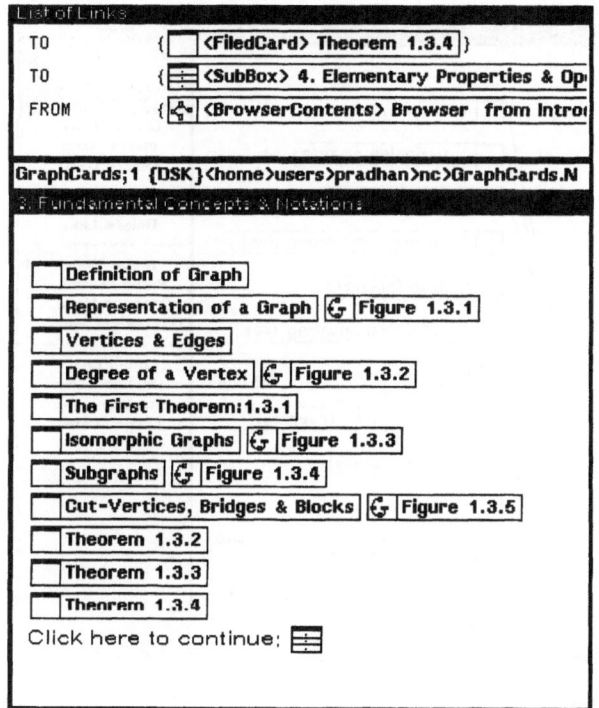

Figure I.28

Visual representation of different links from and to a NoteCards node http://vertex.cs .bsu.edu/ colloquim/ link.gif

The guided tour facility, based on the tabletops concept, offers a graphic interface to link a network of tabletops. To create a new guided tour, authors normally create an empty guided tour card and then add new tabletops by placing the appropriate icon on the guided tour card using an attached menu (Figure I.31).

To operate a guided tour, the reader uses the five buttons attached to the guided tour card. The purpose of a guided tour is to give somebody not already familiar with the NoteCards document an overview of the material contained in it.

Marshall and Irish used Trigg's guided tours and tabletops to make their hypertext documents more intelligible to readers [Mar89]. They employ a three–step process. First, they enforce a consistent screen layout by using a set of predefined tabletops. Second, they mark the tabletops with large, bold

Figure I.29

Graphical
overview map of
the linking struc-
ture of a
NoteCards
hyperdocument
http://vertex.cs.b
su.edu/
colloquim/
browser.gif

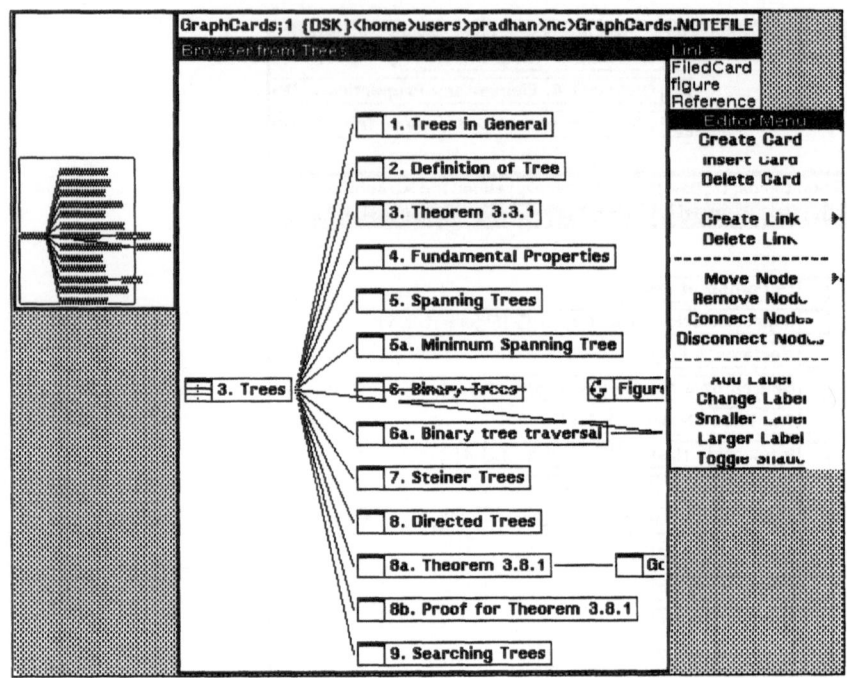

arrows to guide the reading direction of the user. Third, they link the tabletops
to build the guided tour.

Guided tours and tabletops offer a simple way to give readers a quick
overview of a hyperdocument. They have to be built manually by the document author and demand detailed knowledge about the original document.
They are static in that they are based on static links.

8.3 Scripted Paths

Polle Zellweger generalizes the notion of guided tours in her description of
scripted paths [Zel89]. She sees her path mechanism as a fundamental solution
to the two classical hypertext problems of *user disorientation* and the additional
cognitive overhead needed to create and choose among links. Obviously paths

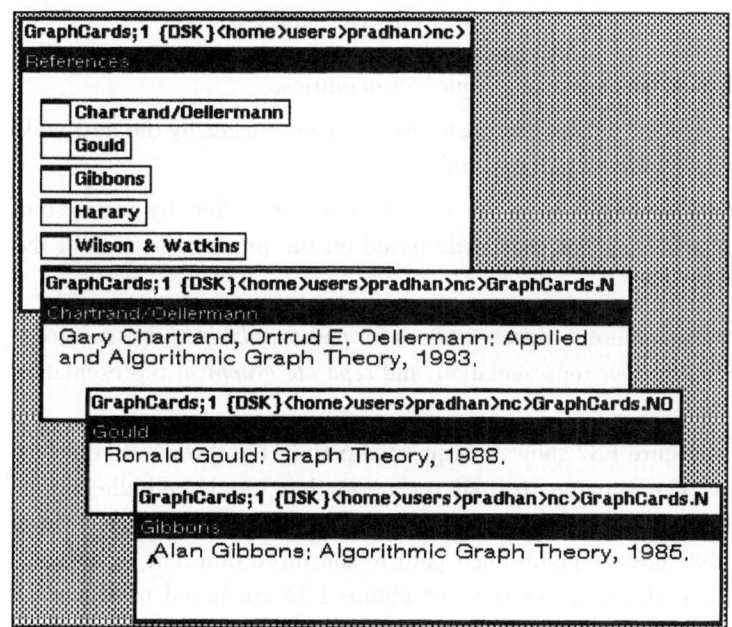

Figure I.30

Example of
NoteCards
tabletop
http://vertex
.cs. bsu.edu/
colloquim/ref.gif

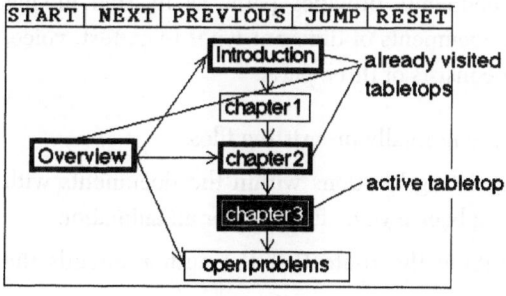

Figure I.31

A mock-up of a
NoteCards
guided tour card

should not replace browsing as main hypertext navigation mechanism but rather should augment it. Zellweger distinguishes these paths:

- *Sequential paths* or ordered sequences of entries.
- *Branching paths*, where the reader has to choose manually the next node among a selection of different links.
- *Conditional paths*, where the branching is controlled by the system (e.g., by selecting the next node based on the previous actions of the reader).

Zellweger lists different representations for paths; *embedded link* representation, *separate textual* representation, and *separate graphical* representation (Figure I.32).

The top of Figure I.32 shows a sequential path in the three different representations. The separate textual representation (in the middle) corresponds to a description of the path in a programming language. The bottom of Figure I.32 shows a conditional path in the three different representations. All six path representations of Figure I.32 are based on the same underlying hypertext structure consisting of the four linked nodes A, B, C, and D (Figure I.33).

A path as defined by Zellweger has to offer some sort of playback control. This means that the user needs an easy way to follow a path — either a single stepping control, allowing the user to step from one node of the path to the other, or automatic playback control. Users may even get full browsing control, allowing them to visit the nodes of a path in arbitrary order.

Zellweger implemented her ideas in a hypermedia system called *Scripted Documents*[Zel89]. Scripted Documents provides paths as its sole linking mechanism. The idea is to link documents of different types (e.g., text, voice, music, video) by paths. A script consists of three parts:

1. A set of documents, which are normally preexisting files.
2. A set of script entries, associating locations within the documents with actions—for example, playing back a voice fragment or an animation.
3. A path specification, describing the route that the author intends the reader to take.

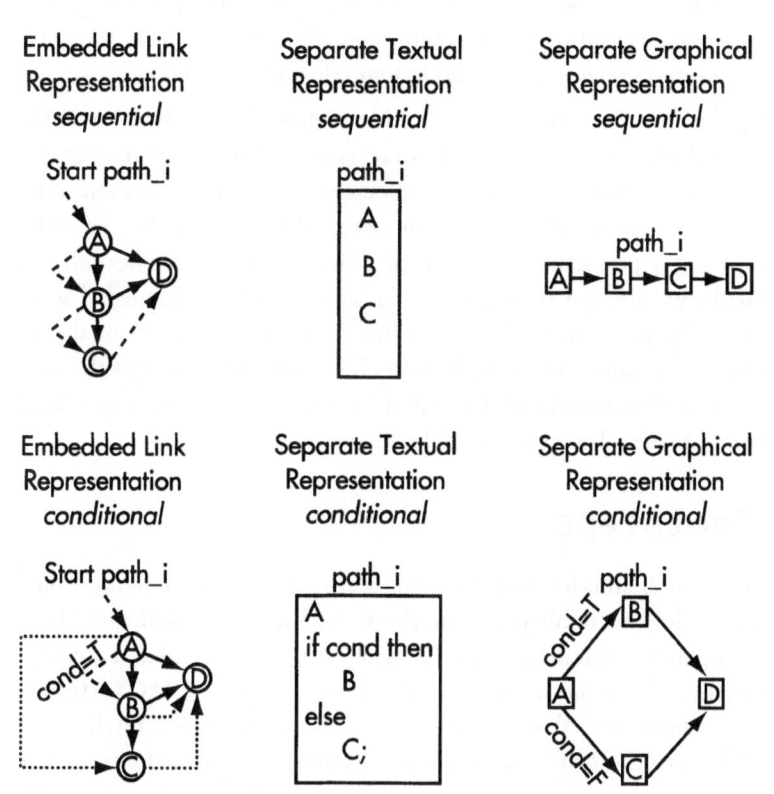

Embedded Link
Representation
sequential

Start path_i

Separate Textual
Representation
sequential

path_i

A
B
C

Separate Graphical
Representation
sequential

path_i

A → B → C → D

Embedded Link
Representation
conditional

Start path_i

Separate Textual
Representation
conditional

path_i

A
if cond then
B
else
C;

Separate Graphical
Representation
conditional

path_i

cond=T
cond=F
A B C D

Figure I.32

Alternative path
representations

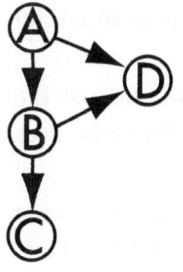

Figure I.33

Basic hypertext
structure of
Figure I.32

Scripted paths in Scripted Documents offer the types of playback control (single stepping, automatic playback, browsing) already described. They also allow the reader to preview a path and to jump directly to an entry.

Scripted Documents implements a flexible system that vastly extends the ideas of guided tours. By allowing paths to be specified in a programming language, it becomes straightforward to implement conditional paths and integrate any type of document into the path. Scripted Documents is a powerful tool for building hypermedia documents of all sorts, but with the flexibility of scripted paths we also get the capability to build complicated, tangled webs where the reader gets hopelessly lost. Authors need to use the scripted path mechanism with caution and to build hyperdocuments that prevent the user from becoming disoriented and frustrated by too much cognitive overhead needed to create and choose among links.

8.4 Footsteps

`http://`
`gorgon.eng`
`.cam.ac.uk/`
`footsteps/`
`footsteps.html`

Footsteps is much simpler than Scripted Paths, but is implemented on a much more widely available platform, the Web. Nicol, Smeaton, and Slater have developed a guided tour mechanism for the Web called Footsteps [Nic95] within the general framework of project INTERACT [Int95]. Footsteps is implemented as a single perl CGI script, which fetches and displays URLs in the order in which they should appear in the tour. The script then adds navigation buttons to the original Web page to navigate within the guided tour (Figure I.34). The tour itself is described in the tour file.

Figure I.35 shows a sample tour index, generated on the fly by the Footsteps script. It allows jumping directly to any URL within the guided tour. Figure I.35 also illustrates what happens if a tour references an invalid URL ("404 Not Found").

Footsteps offers an easy way to build sequential tours, or paths, through the Web. Web pages can obviously be reused for different tours. The script does not require any modification to either client or server.

Because of its implementation, a CGI-based tour mechanism is somewhat clumsy and slow. Initially CGI offered the only way to add user-defined features to the Web. With the advent of Java, the Web designer has much greater flexibility. (In Chapter 16 we describe our own path mechanism for the Web, which we have implemented in Java.)

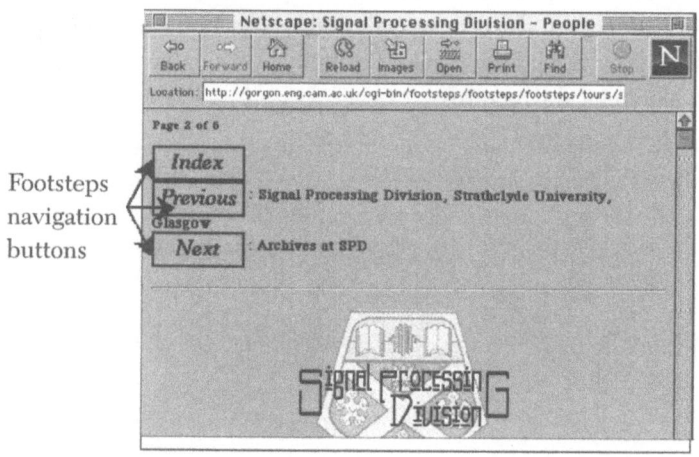

Footsteps
navigation
buttons

Figure I.34

Sample guided
tour
implemented
with Footsteps

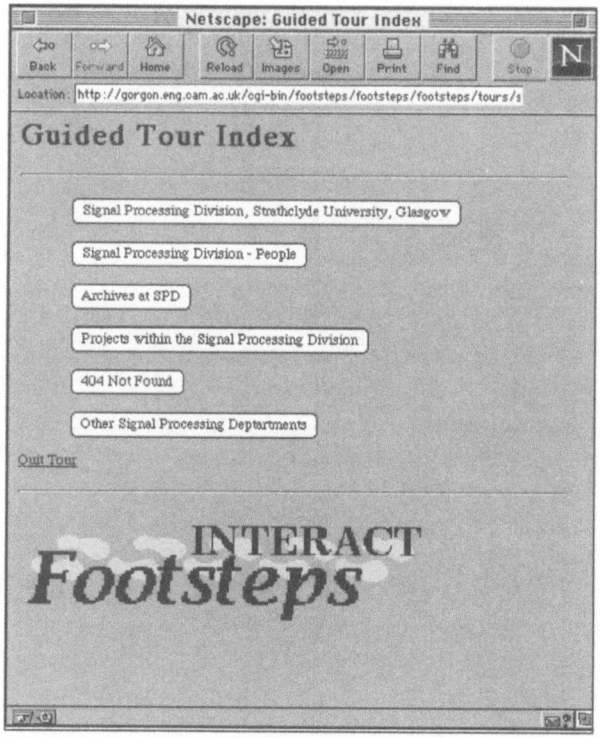

Figure I.35

Tour index
implemented
with Footsteps

While guided tours and paths assist the reader by reducing the complexity of locating information, they also take away flexibility. The tools and techniques presented in the next chapter offer greater flexibility by extending the sequential tour into a hierarchical structure.

CHAPTER 9

Hierarchy

A meaningfully structured document can substantially assist in exploring and locating information. Hierarchical structuring, as employed frequently in technical documentation and manuals, is one of the most popular means of organizing large documents. There are two ways of imposing a hierarchical document structure:

1. Ideally, a document is molded into a hierarchical structure during its creation and authoring phase. The IGD system described in section 9.3 is a typical representative of such a system.

2. It is much harder to impose a hierarchical structure on an existing document collection. Our own Cybermap system, described in Part II, computes a hierarchical structure for any information space.

9.1 Electronic Table of Contents

The table of contents is a straightforward navigation aid that covers a reader's basic needs. Its big advantage lies in its familiarity to the user because it corresponds to similar means for the printed book. Compared to printed books, an electronic table of contents offers improved access by allowing the user to jump to a chapter part directly by clicking on an entry. Electronic counterparts are also easily constructed automatically from book manuscripts based on the chapter structure. Systems like SuperBook, described at the end of this chapter, build electronic books automatically based on an enhanced notion of table of contents. Empirical results show that such systems compare favorably to more conventional computer–based information presentation systems like IR systems or data bases [Ega91]. An index and a table of contents are particularly well suited for exploring a topic that is already familiar to the reader [Ham88].

9.2 IGD: Hierarchical Display of Hypertext Structure

Steven Feiner [Fei88] describes a hypertext system that is based on a strict tree structure for the organization of the nodes. His system, IGD (Interactive Graphical Documents), supports the creation and the display of arbitrary key worded graph structures embedded in a tree hierarchy. Like most of the other systems available, IGD does not support the conversion of existing documents into a tree structure. Rather, an aspiring author is expected to write new tree-structured documents using IGD. IGD supports the creation of tree hierarchies, but the text has to be put into the hypertext nodes manually.

To make out the best tree representation for IGD, Feiner [Fei88] investigated the respective advantages and disadvantages of different ways to display tree structures, as identified by Knuth [Knu73a]. Knuth describes three standard graphical notations for displaying trees: graph trees, indentation, and nested set notation. Figure I.36 contains the popular *graph tree* notation. Feiner thinks that this representation gets too tangled and messed up as soon as the number of nodes and hierarchy levels becomes too large.

Figure I.37 displays the same graph in the *indentation view*. This view eliminates the need for explicit tree arcs and provides a clearer distinction between the hierarchical and the arbitrary graph structure. However, the indentation view suggests a sequential ordering of the children of each node.

The *nested set* notation expresses the tree structure through spatial containment by nesting each node within its parent node (Figure I.38). Steven Feiner considers this representation superior to the two other approaches for the purpose of editing the tree structure. He claims that this method offers the best visually distinct technique for showing hierarchy and graph structure. Also the

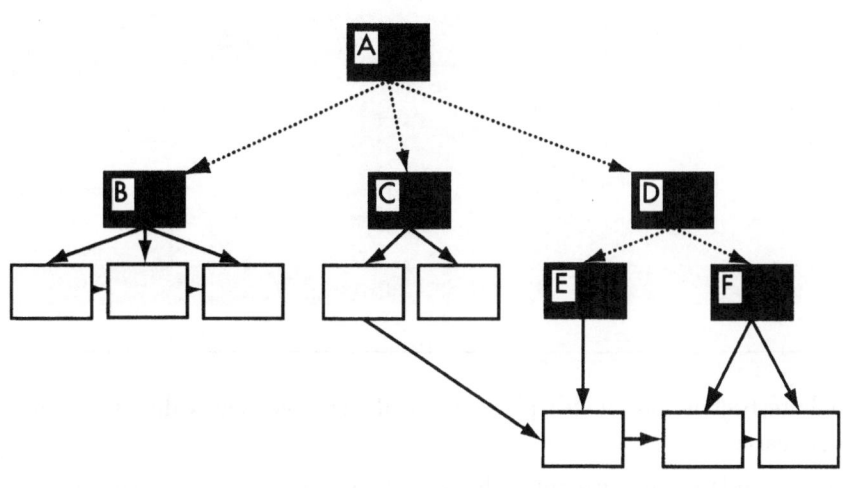

Figure I.36

Graph tree notation

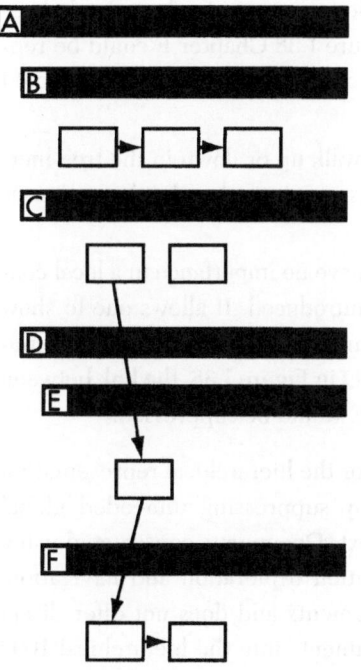

Figure I.37

Indentation graph notation

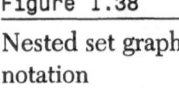

Figure I.38

Nested set graph notation

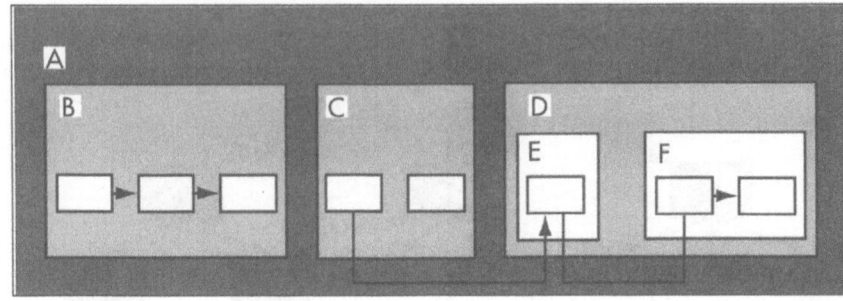

only restriction for a node's placement is the arrangement within its parent's boundaries.

IGD therefore uses a variant of the nested set graph notation. To improve the representation of information by information hiding, IGD employs three techniques:

1. *Subtree detail suppression.* It is possible to represent selected subchapters only by their bounding box. In Figure I.38 Chapter F could be represented only by the box, without showing the two nodes contained within.

2. *Subtree display selection.* The user can walk up or down in the tree hierarchy and fill each subchapter with as much enclosed information as desired.

3. *Link inheritance.* To suppress links that have no importance in a local context, the concept of link inheritance is introduced. It allows one to show only links connecting nodes with the same ancestor. For example, assuming that the user is focusing on Chapter D in Figure I.38, the link between the left node in C and the one node in E would be suppressed.

IGD offers some interesting techniques for the hierarchical representation and structuring of complex information by suppressing unneeded global information and focusing on the local context. Documents constructed using IGD offer excellent assistance for information exploration and navigation. But IGD is limited to authoring new documents and does not offer direct support for the integration of existing documents into the hierarchical IGD structure.

9.3 Tree-Maps: Visualization of Hierarchical Information Structure

Tree-Maps represent a novel way for the space-efficient representation of hierarchical information [Joh91]. Johnson and Shneiderman's work has been motivated by the problem of visualizing large directory structures on hard disk drives. Tree-Maps therefore are especially well suited for the representation of very large tree hierarchies. A Tree-Map drawing encompasses the following properties [Joh91]:

- If $node_1$ is an ancestor of $node_2$, then the bounding box of $node_1$ completely encloses, or is equal to, the bounding box of $node_2$.

- The bounding boxes of two nodes intersect only if one node is the ancestor of the other.

- Nodes occupy a display area strictly proportional to their weight.

- The weight of a node is greater than or equal to the sum of the weights of its children.

This means that each node has an associated weight that defines the area that the node occupies in the Tree-Map. Figure I.39 displays a tree in the conventional graph tree representation and as a Tree-Map. As Figure I.39 illustrates,

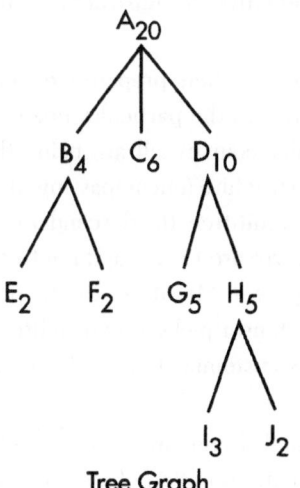

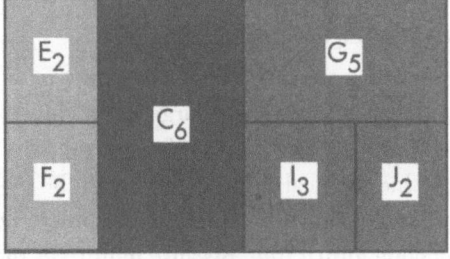

Tree Map

Tree Graph

Figure I.39

Graph tree and Tree-Map of the same graph

only nodes that are leaves are shown directly. They indicate common ancestry by using similar patterns or colors. A slice and dice algorithm, which rotates the orientation of the elements by 90 degrees on each hierarchy level, produces an appealing layout of the elements.

Tree-Maps are especially useful for giving a quick overview if the hierarchy is very large and contains thousands of nodes. In particular, they allow the easy transmission of an additional dimension to the user by varying the node size depending on the weight. By using meaningful color coding, even a third dimension can be added to the Tree-Map display.

Tree-Maps offer an unorthodox approach to the information exploration problem for hierarchically structured data. By compressing the whole structure on a computer screen, the user gets direct navigational cues, and the problem of being lost in cyberspace is therefore being tackled from another side. The addition of zooming features to a one-level Tree-Map allows the user to go into arbitrary levels of detail. Tree-Maps thus offer an additional fourth way of representing hierarchical structure, extending Knuth's listing of methods for displaying trees.

9.4 Multitrees

Recently George Furnas and Jeff Zacks introduced a new structure for representing partly hierarchical information [Fur94], the *multitree*. Multitrees are directed acyclic graphs (DAGs) that have large, identifiable substructures that are trees (Figure I.40).

Obviously, reuse of hierarchy is not new. When teachers prepare a course, they usually rearrange a large hierarchical syllabus to the particular needs of the course. If multiple professors prepare similar courses, all are using the same hierarchical subtrees, although the overall structure (encompassing multiple professors) is not a tree. More precisely, in a multitree, the descendants of any node form a tree. Because multitrees themselves are DAGs, and not trees, a node in the structure can have more than one parent. Multitrees can be perceived as unions of trees that share subtrees. Each user picks a set of subtrees of a large hierarchical resource and then places a customized hierarchy above those pieces for his or her own purposes.

As Furnas and Zacks note, genealogies, although frequently called "family trees," are in fact multitrees. Multitrees offer a natural notion of context (dis-

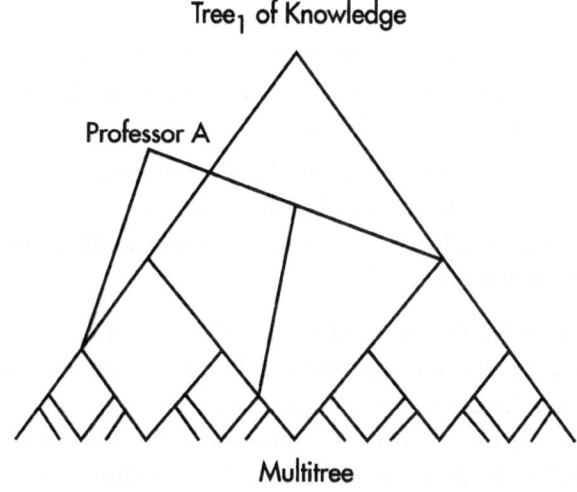

Tree₁ of Knowledge

Professor A

Multitree

Figure I.40

Sample Multitree
http://www.sils
.umich.edu/
~furnas/
HomePage.html

playing ancestors) and content (displaying descendants), and are therefore very well suited for reusing hierarchical structure.

9.5 Zooming into Hierarchically Structured Information

Once a document has been structured hierarchically, readers frequently need additional methods for navigating in the hierarchy. Girill and Luk suggest a different way of browsing that they have implemented in their system DOCU-MENT [Gir92]. Their technique is based on zooming in and out of hierarchically structured documents. DOCUMENT is mainly used to store and retrieve technical information like on-line manuals that exhibit a hierarchical document structure. Girill and Luk motivate their work by identifying four weak aspects of browsing in tree-structured documents:

1. *Order dependency.* To reach a leaf node, readers need to know the whole path, from the root of the tree to the particular leaf.

2. *Unbalanced concept discrimination.* The most discriminating concepts on the path toward a desired leaf node are near the leaves, not the root. This means that readers starting a path at the root have to deal with the most

undiscriminating nodes first to find a very specific node at the end of the path.

3. *Incomplete context.* To get complete navigation information, the siblings of a node are often essential. Unfortunately, the siblings are not included in the hierarchical path from the root to the leaf node.

4. *Semantic factoring.* Unfortunately, hierarchical paths are frequently not sufficient to offer enough information to find the wanted leaf node. This problem has to be addressed by offering other navigation facilities, like full-text search or key word index.

Girill and Luk claim that the first three of these problems can be solved by offering the functionality of zooming in and out. Order dependency can be addressed by browsing the document in hypertext fashion and zooming into the hierarchy as soon as the context seems promising. The discrimination problem is also easily solved because a zoomed-in view of the context of a node allows simple discrimination among other, similar nodes. The local and global context of a node is clarified by zooming in to and out from a particular node.

Zooming offers a simple solution for some navigation problems. Obviously the concept is not limited to hierarchically structured information but works with any graph. The zooming concept can be considered a special case of fish–eye views, which offer a general framework to display large amounts of information from a fish eye's perspective. (Fish–eye views are described in Chapter 11.)

9.6 SuperBook: Automatically Structured Documents

SuperBook, developed at Bell Labs [Rem87], preprocesses on-line text and automatically generates a dynamic table of contents, text pages, and a history of search words. Contrary to most hypertext systems, which are best suited for authoring new information, SuperBook is well qualified to postprocess existing documents by adding navigation and information exploration mechanisms. The original goal of SuperBook was simply to improve the usability of on-line text.

SuperBook takes as input formatted text (e.g., in troff, Scribe, or Interleaf format), and produces three navigation tools:

1. A dynamic *table of contents* is generated based on the formatting macros of the text processing system. This does not mean that a new document structure is being computed automatically based on the document's contents; rather the original hierarchical document structure is being replicated electronically. This electronic table of contents allows a user to jump to any subchapter by mouse click.

2. A *full-text index* is built automatically, allowing the user to search for any word, word stem, or Boolean combination thereof. The table of contents is synchronized with the key word search in the sense that it automatically displays the proportional number of matches in each subchapter and thus provides an additional method for the user to locate quickly areas of interest.

3. Because the ideas and concepts the user is searching for are rarely expressed in the same words by user and book author, an *aliasing feature* is provided, allowing the user to add index synonyms. The idea

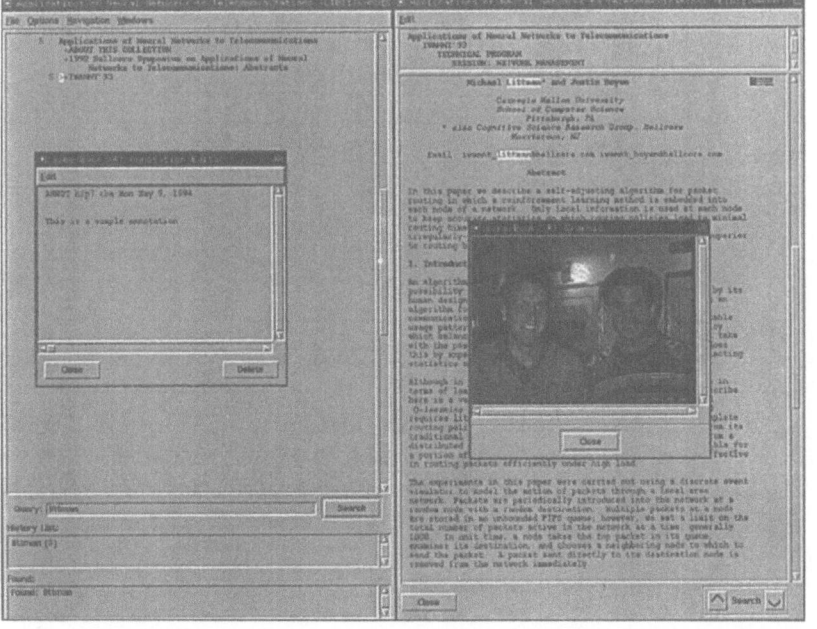

Figure I.41

SuperBook Proceedings of the 1993 International Workshop on Applications of Neural Networks. (See Part V for a brief description of these proceedings.) http:// superbook .bellcore.com/SB /IWANNT/ iwannt93.eprocs .html

is, of course, to collect a repertoire of synonyms built up by a community of users.

SuperBook (Figure I.41) has been implemented in a two-level architecture, isolating the text processing package–specific part into the lower layer. By providing an additional module for a new text processor, SuperBook can thus be adapted to process documents formatted in any text–processing package. In a comparative experiment for the Chemistry Online Retrieval Experiment (CORE) [Ega91] researchers found the SuperBook implementation superior not only to the paper version but also to more conventional electronic document retrieval systems.

SuperBook is not a true hypertext system because it does not offer explicit links between hardwired link anchors. Rather, it provides excellent navigation facilities and allows linking by query formulation, a process similar to dynamic linking.

Similarity

> *What they [users] need is infoscopes that base search operations on similarity rather than matching. Similarity is domain dependent and subjective.*

—**Ramesh Jain**
  [Jai95]

The tools and methods described in this chapter permit one to browse, edit, and retrieve information based on similarities of parts of the document. One of the main problems of this approach is that a measure of similarity needs to be defined. Similarity is also called proximity, alikeness, affinity, or association in the literature [Jai88]. Described mathematically, a similarity between two objects i and j, denoted sim(i,j), must satisfy the following three properties:

similarity properties

1. $sim\ (i,i) \geq \max_{j} sim(i,j) \quad \forall\ i$
2. $sim\ (i,j) = sim\ (j,i), \quad \forall\ i,j$
3. $sim\ (i,j) \geq 0, \quad \forall\ i,j$

91

10.1 Electronic Index: Similarity by Common Key Words

The advantage of the index lies in its familiarity to the user. Compared to books, an electronic index offers improved access by allowing the user to jump to an index reference directly by clicking on the entry in the index. Electronic counterparts are also easily constructed automatically based on a list of key words. An index is one of the simplest means to construct similarity links automatically because it can be generally assumed that if an index entry points to different pages, these pages must be somewhat related. In fact, an extension of this simple idea is normally used to compute similarities and similarity links automatically, based on an automatically generated index, and a computation of similarities based on the IR vector space model (see Chapter 1). The linking apprentice discussed in Chapter 6 uses the same idea to compute links between related nodes automatically. All of the tools presented subsequently in this section use already structured information, that is stored as semantic networks [Bra79] or as rules.

10.2 Semnet: A Test Bed for Three-Dimensional Knowledge Base Representation

SemNet is an experimental environment for exploring a variety of navigation mechanisms for structured knowledge bases [Fai88]. Its goal is to present large knowledge bases to users in ways that can easily be understood. The knowledge bases are represented as 3D directed graphs. Figure I.42 shows an optimized representation of a knowledge base consisting of Prolog rules.

The 3D graphs on the screen can be manipulated with a mouse in real time. Fairchild et al. used a two-layered architecture with the graphical representation part running on an Silicon Graphics IRIS workstation and the knowledge base running on another computer. To position the elements of the knowledge base (i.e., the nodes of the graph) as understandably as possible, Fairchild et al. experimented with a variety of different methods:

- *Random positioning.* This simple method resulted, not surprisingly, in the cognitively worst representation. Although this method may work for small knowledge bases, it results in a meaningless tangle for larger bases.

Figure I.42

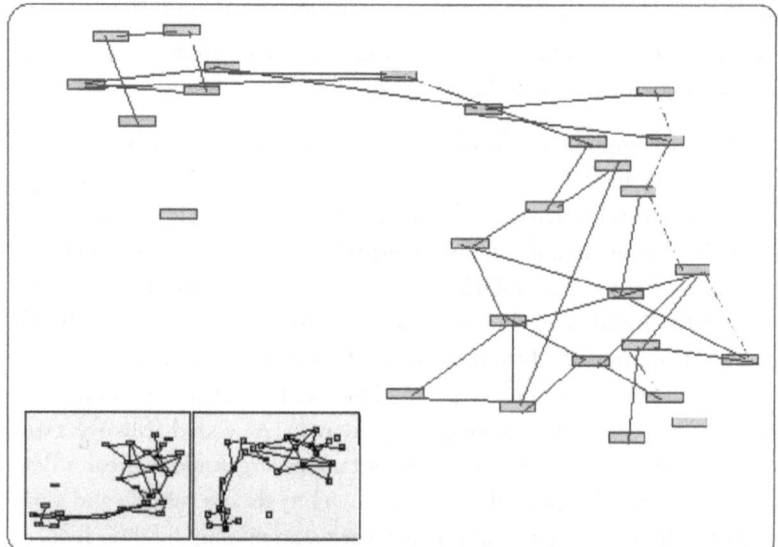

Mock up of
SemNet
representation of
a Prolog
knowledge base

- *Mapping functions.* Frequently the elements in the knowledge base have properties that allow one to map the elements into the 3D space. In a knowledge base about animals, the animals could, for example, be mapped using the three dimensions of size, predacity, and domesticity.

- *Connectivity between elements.* In a knowledge base, there are many relationships among elements. Applying some measure for the proximity or similarity of elements results in effective representations of the whole knowledge base. Among the methods Fairchild et al. used were *multidimensional scaling,* where the distance between elements is monotonically related to the number of interconnections between elements; and *clustering-based heuristics,* where the position of an element is based on the weighted mean (called *centroid;* see Chapter 1) of the positions of all related knowledge elements. One of the most effective positioning methods was based on *simulated annealing* [Kir83], where a new position for an element is computed by adding a random vector to the position of the element. The element is moved to the new position if it is closer to the centroid but not too close to other elements. This method resulted in graph layouts that by the users were subjectively judged to be the best. Figure I.42 shows a graph layout based on simulated annealing.

- *Personalized positioning.* Sometimes users wish to position nodes manually by dragging and grouping them with the mouse.

To reduce the cognitive overhead of navigating in large knowledge bases, not only do the nodes have to be placed and grouped meaningfully, but they also have to be filtered such that only the nodes of interest are actually displayed. The main technique employed for information reduction was generalized fish–eye views. As the main DOI(degree of interest)-function, Fairchild et al. used the spatial location of the elements—the tree distance among the elements. Objects more distant from the user's focus were represented by object clusters. Object clusters and user-specified elements, such as nodes high in an ISA-subtree, got higher API (a priori importance). A second fish–eye representation was achieved by showing important nodes larger and in greater detail by, for example, showing not only the node icon but also its subtitle and a brief textual description. Less important nodes were marked only by their icon.

To assist in orientation, users could place landmarks on the view to identify clusters of interesting nodes easily. But the most important navigation aid was the immediate animated 3D navigation feedback. In particular, Fairchild et al. found that the users favored absolute movement over relative movement. This means that they preferred to move to their desired viewpoint by using three two-dimensional maps showing the x-y, y-z, and x-z planes instead of using a "helicopter flight option" that allowed them to fly directly over the knowledge base.

In a newer application of the ideas first described in the SemNet project, Fairchild, Meredith and Wexelblatt extended their ideas to a *tourist artificial reality* [Fai89]. In this project, the authors tried to organize all information and documentation related to a large software project. They applied the ideas prototyped in SemNet, where the entities are represented in graphs and filtered using fish–eye views. The novel idea in their new system is the tourist artificial reality: All workstations are linked to offer a shared workspace. There is also a speaker phone link between the workstations. This means that two persons at two different workstations can walk through text or source code and discuss the same piece of information. In the tourist artificial reality, one of the two participants is the tour guide, who gets full control over all aspects of the tour and the interface on the workstation of the tourist. The tourist can record the tour and replay it later to take the same trip at a more leisurely pace.

The techniques of Fairchild et al. demand intimate knowledge of the internal structure of the knowledge base. They get this knowledge either by using well-structured information (like a collection of Prolog rules) or by manually preprocessing the information. In addition they extend their ideas to the integration of guided tours and guides. Contrary to the guides and agents described in Chapter 12, Fairchild et al.'s guides are human beings who have the necessary domain knowledge.

10.3 The CYC Browser

The most distinguishing feature of the system presented in the this section is its underlying knowledge base, CYC, which tries to model the commonsense knowledge of the average American. The CYC project [Len90] is a large-scale project that started at MCC (Microelectronics and Computer Technology Corporation in Austin, Texas, a joint research consortium sponsored by the U.S. industry), extending over a period of ten years. Its goal is to build a very large knowledge base containing a broad range of commonsense knowledge. The CYC knowledge base consists of a network of units or frames, where each unit corresponds to a physical object or an abstract concept. CYC currently encompasses a few hundred thousand rules and is projected to have several million when it is completed. The CYC browser [Tra89] uses a visual representation for navigating knowledge structures, based on a virtual museum metaphor. The browser, named MUE (Museum Unit Editor), operates in an ideal environment in the sense that the knowledge structures to be modeled are already fully machine understandable. In contrast to MUE, the knowledge bases of all other navigation systems have to be brought either manually or automatically into a format that can be understood by the computer.

The following CYC unit (adapted from [Tra89]) represents the class of all people, specifying that #%People has specializations (#%specs) such as #%workers and #%FemalePeople, generalizations (#%genls) such as Mammals, and so forth:

```
#%People:
#%english: ("The class of all human beings")
#%specs: (#%Workers  #%FemalePeople  #%MalePeople  #%USCitizens ...)
#%genls: (#%Mammals #%IntelligentEntities)
#%allElements: (#%MikeTravers #%DougLenat ...)
#%canHaveSlots: (#%citizenship #%languagesSpoken...)
 ...
```

Figure I.43 shows the MUE version of the #%people unit of the above material.

Each CYC unit in Figure I.43 is represented in MUE as a box, and units within units are represented as nested boxes. Color is used to indicate the type and the nesting depth of a relationship. The goal of MUE is not only to display statistical relationships and units as exemplified in Figure I.43, but to allow navigation through the knowledge structure. To do so, MUE walks through the graph constructed by the CYC units. The actual unit is always put at the root of the graph to be displayed. This means that for a walk through the graph, the graph is constantly rerooted to put the actual node at the root (Figure I.44).

Figure I.43
CYC #%people
unit displayed
in MUE

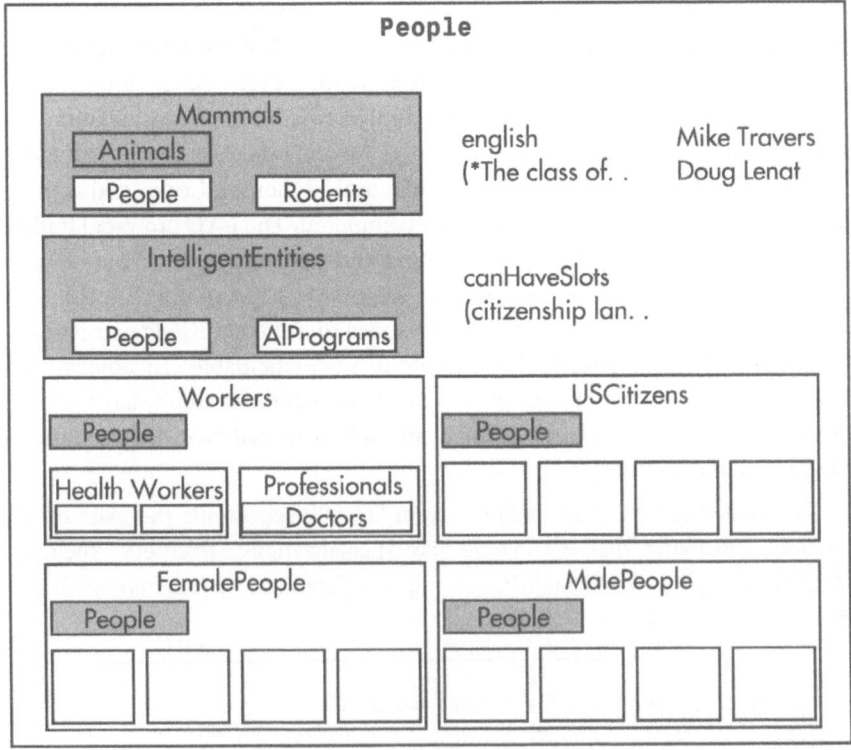

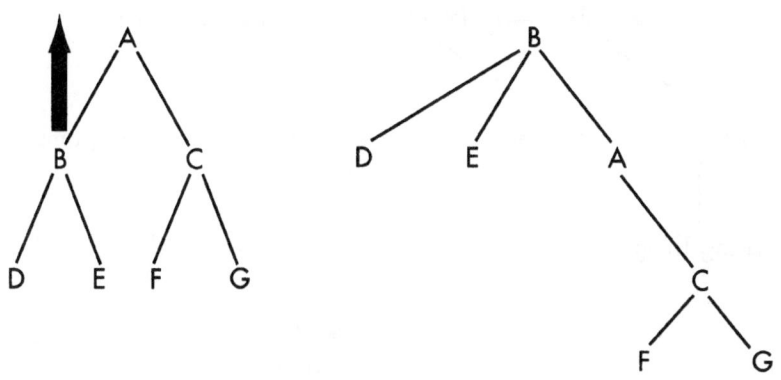

Figure I.44

Rerooting of a tree

To construct a hierarchy, directions within the graph are inverted by invert-
ing the relationships between units. Consider the #%people unit from
Figure I.43. Figure I.45 contains the original graph structure extracted
directly from the knowledge base. Figures I.46 and I.47 explain how the hierarchy is constructed.

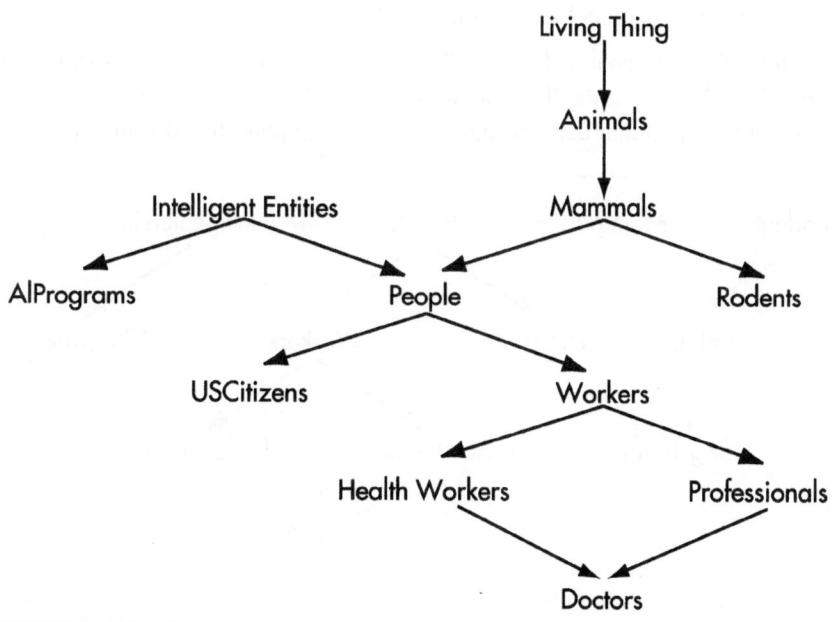

Figure I.45

Class structure
containing the
#%people unit

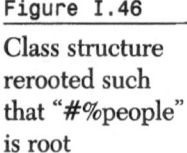

Figure I.46

Class structure rerooted such that "#%people" is root

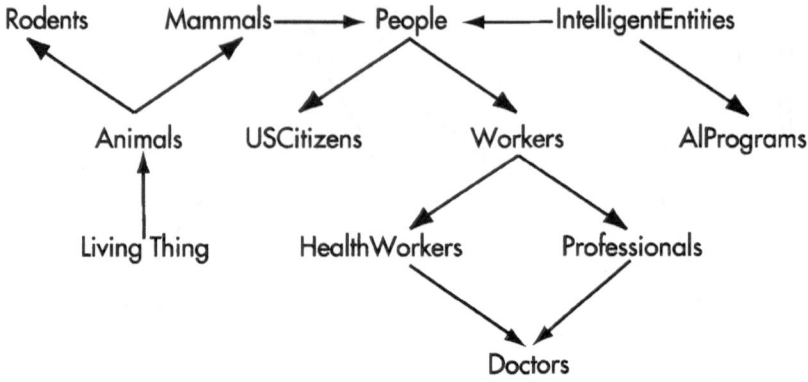

MUE offers an elegant graphical way of navigating in a very large knowledge base. But contrary to most real-world examples, the CYC knowledge base has a very strict syntax and thus makes it easy for MUE to reshape the display graph based on the CYC units. This means that the ideas of MUE are hard to apply to unstructured knowledge bases. The long-term goal, of course, is to use CYC for structuring unstructured information. When CYC will encompass the full commonsense knowledge, it may be possible to use it jointly with an extended MUE to model unstructured knowledge bases.

While the main goal of MUE is the visualization, browsing, and editing of the CYC rules and units, the system introduced in the next section uses CYC as a tool to implement content-based navigation in plain-text documents.

Figure I.47

Rerooted class structure with inverted directions to get hierarchy

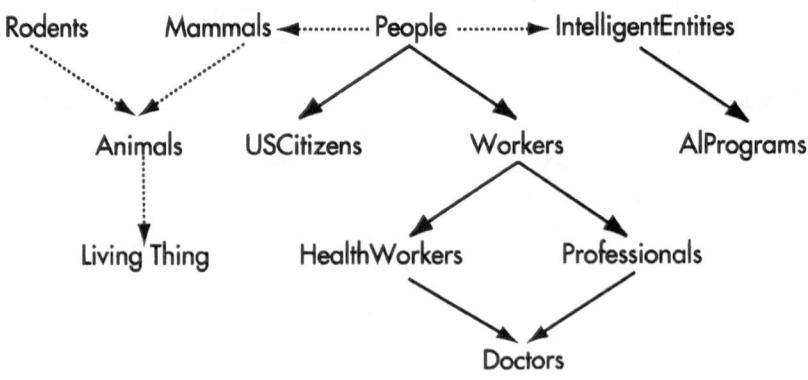

10.4 VISAR: Navigation by Inference

A reliable automatic link generation system needs some kind of semantic knowledge about the data it intends to link. The VISAR system described by Clitherow et al. [Cli89] employs a sophisticated approach using CYC. VISAR has been created to serve as an intelligent assistant to researchers in performing an initial survey in a field of interest new to them. It takes a user request and returns a set of citations that seem to be related to the user's interest. VISAR differs in two aspects from existing document retrieval systems performing similar tasks:

1. It allows the user to specify *relationships between concepts* as search input rather than key words.

2. Instead of returning a list of retrieved titles, VISAR returns a conceptual reduction of the relationship between the concepts found that are related to the query. Such a *per*sonalized *in*formation *rep*resentation of the relationship between concepts is called a *perinrep*.

Perinreps are small extracts of a larger semantic network [Bra79]. In VISAR's case, the semantic network consists of the CYC frames and rules extended by a citations knowledge base. A perinrep is displayed on the screen as a graph structure of linked nodes, where each node represents a concept. Steps 2 and 4 in Figure I.48 display generic perinreps.

The perinrep idea allows the user to get an overview of the retrieved information instead of being flooded with a list of all retrieved entries. VISAR works by transforming a textual user request into a request perinrep, based on a default perinrep. It then performs an inference process in the CYC knowledge base to find the matching conceptual relationships. Finally the matching relationships are reduced to manageable quantities and returned to the user (Figure I.48).

Figure I.48

Functional
representation of
VISAR with
perinreps

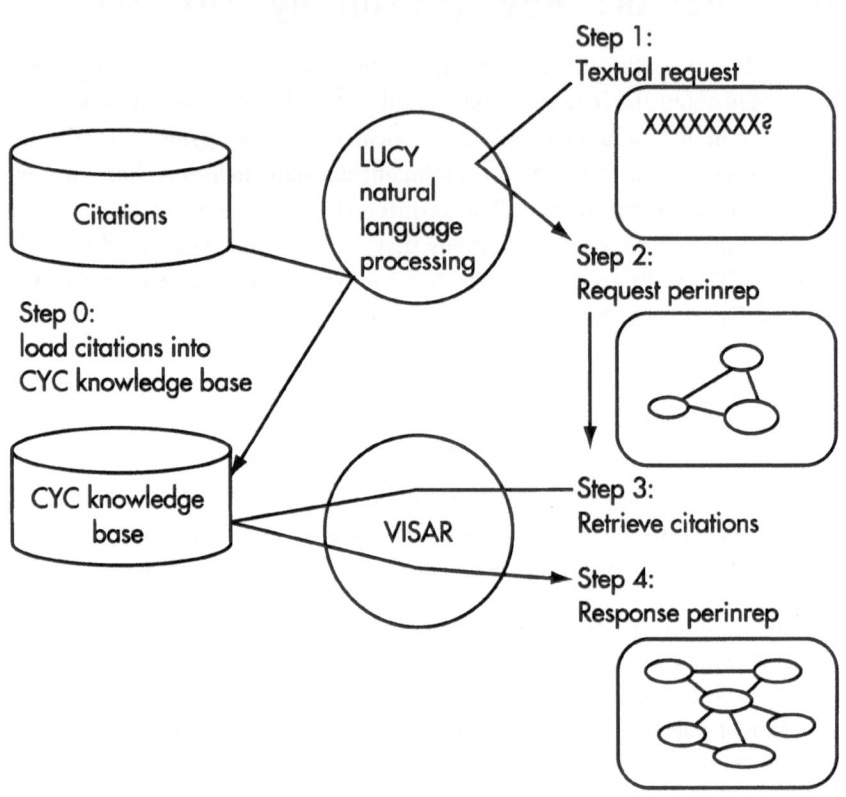

Mapping

A good map tells a multitude of little white lies; it suppresses truth to help the user see what needs to be seen.

—Mark Monmonier
[Mon91]

Geographical maps are a well-known means for orientation in the real world. Their purpose is at least threefold:

1. They show readers where they are.
2. They show readers where they can go from here.
3. They give readers an overview over their environment.

Overview maps of hyperdocuments serve exactly the same purpose. They try to impart the document structure in graphical form to the user. Figure I.49 shows a straightforward application of this idea. The overview map of the travel information system Business Class uses the map metaphor to lead readers to information about the country they are interested in.[1]

In Figure I.49 users click their way on a map of Europe to find travel information about Austria. For general use (non-geographical applications), it is much harder to find a suitable graphical representation for the overview map. Usually concepts, topics, or subjects are graphically linked by relations to give

Figure I.49

Overview map of the travel information system Business Class

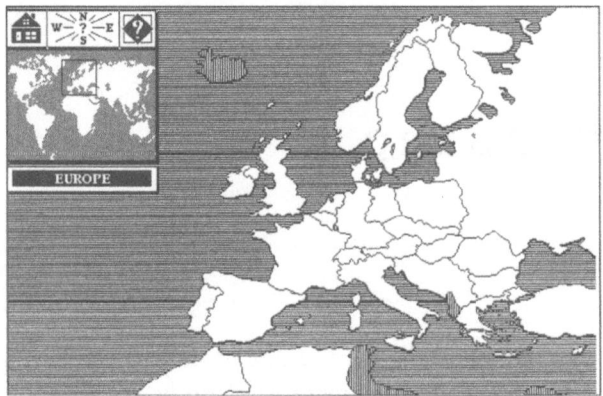

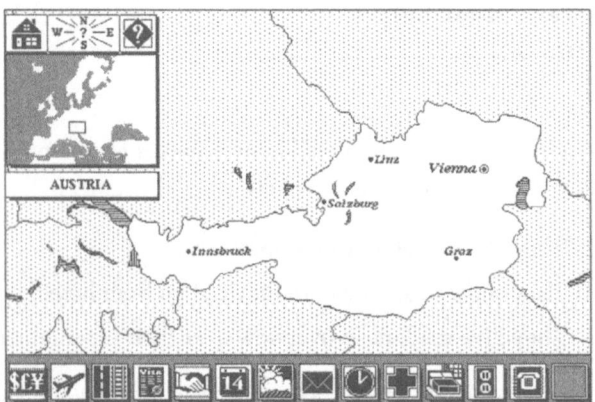

---

1 The HyperCard travel information system Business Class was developed by Danny Goodman, author of a best-selling HyperCard book, and sold through Activision, Mountain View, CA.

readers an idea of the contents of the document. Figure I.50 shows the overview map of the HyperCard version 1.x help system. Labeled icons denote the main parts of the help system with arrows describing the relationships; a ✻ marks the current location of the user in the document.

Mapping is orthogonal to the previously discussed concepts in that maps can be used to visualize links, search results, sequential paths, hierarchies, and similarities.

Overview maps of smaller documents are most easily drawn manually, but for larger documents, this becomes a tedious task. Computer support for the creation of overview maps is thus highly desirable.

11.1 Intermedia Web View

Intermedia is one of the most frequently cited research hypermedia systems [Yan88]. It was developed between 1985 and 1990 at the Institute for Research and Scholarship (IRIS) at Brown University and was used as a test bed for novel programming, hypertext, and multimedia concepts. Using object-oriented programming techniques, Intermedia offers a seamless integrated hypermedia information environment, including integrated text editor, drawing editor, pixmap painting editor, time line editor, animation editor, scripting environment, and hypermedia mail system [Yan88][Jac91]. Among

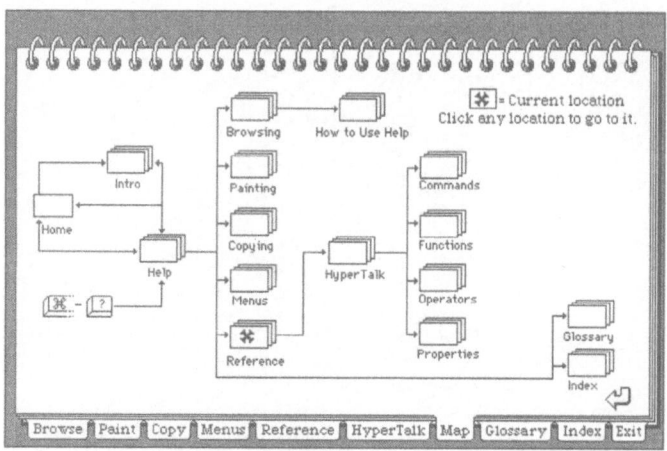

Figure I.50

HyperCard Help overview map

other issues, the Intermedia team addressed the problem of users becoming disoriented and lost in hyperspace. One of their main remedies was the automatic generation of an overview map of a hypermedia document. They implemented different versions of automatically generated overview maps, where the maps always reflected the actual linking structure. This means that their maps were based on hardwired, static links made by a designated person. In the first version, all nodes and links of a hyperdocument were represented on the screen (Figure I.51).

Figure I.51 illustrates the problem of displaying all links and nodes of a document in a single view. Obviously this overview map becomes a meaningless tangle as soon as the number of nodes or links exceeds just a few. To overcome this problem, Utting and Yankelovich describe a refined overview map based on the *Web View* [Utt89]. They distinguish between local and global maps. The type of map displayed in Figure I.51 is called a *global map*, because it shows all nodes and links in a document. A simpler global map is shown in Figure I.52.

Figure I.51

Spiderweb view
of Intermedia
document
[Con87b:Fig. 10]

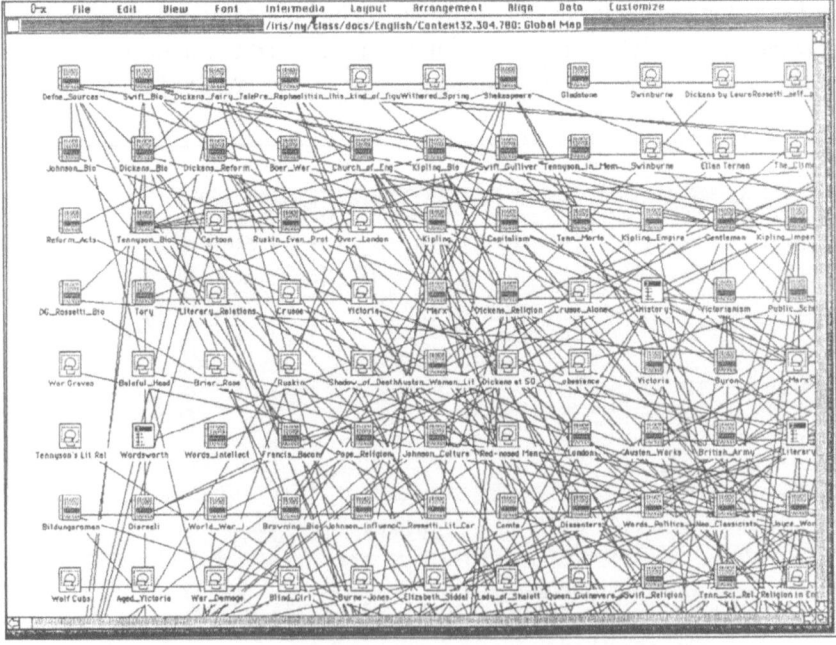

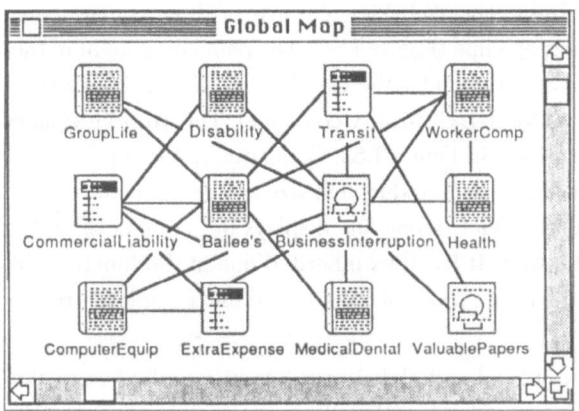

Figure I.52

Global map
[Utt89:Fig. 2]

By showing only the local context of the actual node, the global map can be disentangled. But at the same time, the global context information is lost (Figure I.53). This type of map is called a *local map*.

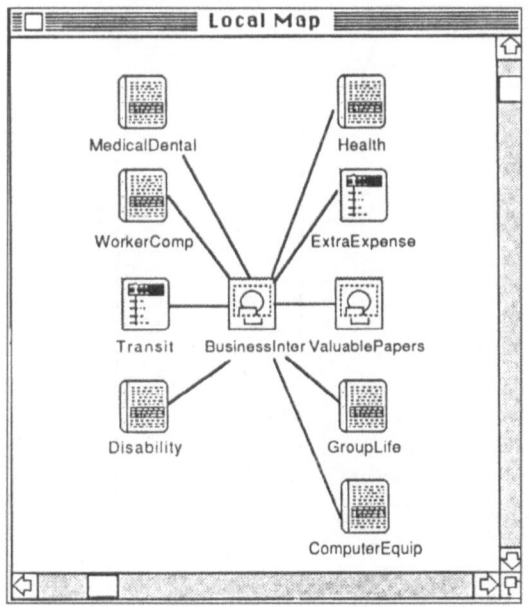

Figure I.53

Local map
[Utt89:Fig. 3]

The Intermedia Web View combines a record of the user's path with a map of the currently available links. The Web View consists of three components: the path, the map, and the scope line (Figure I.54). The *path* component of the Web View contains a catalog of the nodes the user has last visited. It is a simple sequential list similar to the UNIX history command. The Web View *map* is similar to the local map shown in Figure I.53. Compared to the original layout in Figure I.53, the icons have been reduced in size and are laid out in rows in alphabetical order. The Web View *scope line* displays the number of nodes and number of links in the web. It has thus inherited one of the functions of the global map by giving the user a sense of the size and link complexity of the actual web.

By integrating concepts of local and global map into one unified view, the Intermedia Web View achieves a high functionality on limited space. The main drawback of the Web View is that it is based on static links and thus reflects the local context of a node based on the hardwired links connected to that node. There is no way for the inherent document structure to be reflected in the Web View. The Web View also offers no easy way of scaling for very large webs. The

Figure I.54

Intermedia Web
View
[Utt89:Fig. 12]

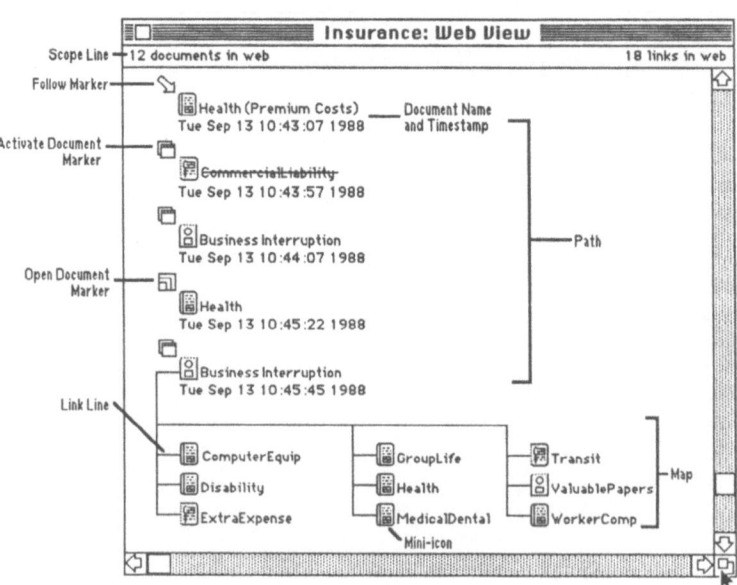

only place where the size of the web is reflected is in the scope line, which tells the user the number of nodes and links in the web.

Nevertheless, the Intermedia Web View is an excellent example of a well-thought-out overview map. It integrates all the basic concepts and offers a convenient method of orientation and information retrieval in complex hypermedia documents.

The Intermedia Web View displays a static picture of a hyperdocument. The fish–eye view concept described in the next section presents a personalized view of an information structure by permitting a user to define a focus of interest.

11.2 Fish–Eye Views

Human beings often recognize their own neighborhood in great detail, while they perceive only landmarks in greater distance. This fish–eye perspective can be observed in many real-world examples. A person living in Boston knows the street names of the local neighborhood, the names of the towns in the greater Boston area, and some major towns in Massachusetts. But the farther away and the less important the towns are, the less likely it is that the person knows them. The person very likely knows about Los Angeles and San Francisco, although they are on the other side of the continent, because they are rather large and important. A city like San Antonio, Texas, on the other hand, although it is also rather large, is much less likely to be known to the Bostonian, because it seldom appears in the Boston headlines. Generalizing our geography fish–eye example, we see that there are two things that define the perception of an object: *distance from the viewer* and *a priori importance* to the viewer. This concept was first formalized by George Furnas in a frequently cited paper [Fur86]. In this section we present Furnas' approach and then introduce a graph-based extension by Sarkar and Brown [Sar92] in the next section.

Furnas defines a *degree of interest* function (DOI function) that assigns to each point in the structure a number telling how important this point is for the viewer. The viewer is supposed to be located on one designated point y in the structure. This means, that a fish–eye view is always in relation to one particular point y in the structure, which we call *focus*. In Furnas's simple model, the DOI function is composed of the distance of each other point x from the focus y and the a priori importance that each point in the structure has. This means that for each point x in the structure its DOI function is computed using the following formula:

$\mathrm{DOI}(x)$ = a priori importance of x — distance between x and focus y.

Figure I.55 illustrates the computation of the DOI function for a small, hierarchical structure. The figure can be thought of as a management hierarchy in a company. The director of the company, located at the root of the tree, gets an a priori importance of 0; for each step down in the hierarchy level, the a priori value is reduced by 1. The number of edges between y and another node x is taken as distance.

If Figure I.55 depicts a management hierarchy in a company, y stands for a simple employee. If the employee is new to the company, he or she eventually knows only a zero–order fish–eye view of management—his or her own direct boss and the director of the whole company (Figure I.56). After some more working days, the new employee eventually proceeds to a first–order fish–eye view knowledge about the personnel: he or she now also knows colleagues in the same department and all the department heads.

Speaking more formally, we have defined a threshold k and only displayed the nodes x in the tree for which $\mathrm{DOI}(x) \geq k$. By displaying only the most

Figure I.55

Computation of DOI values for small hierarchy

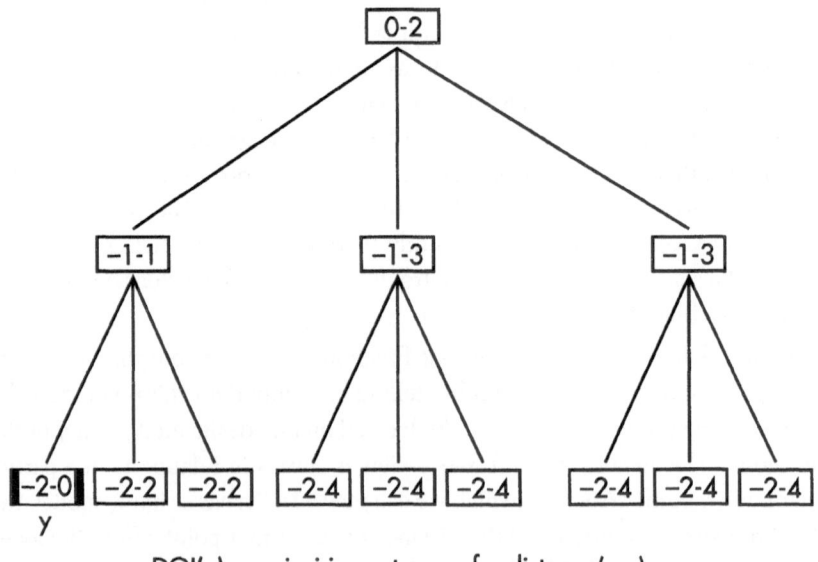

DOI(x)=a priori importance of x-distance(y,x)

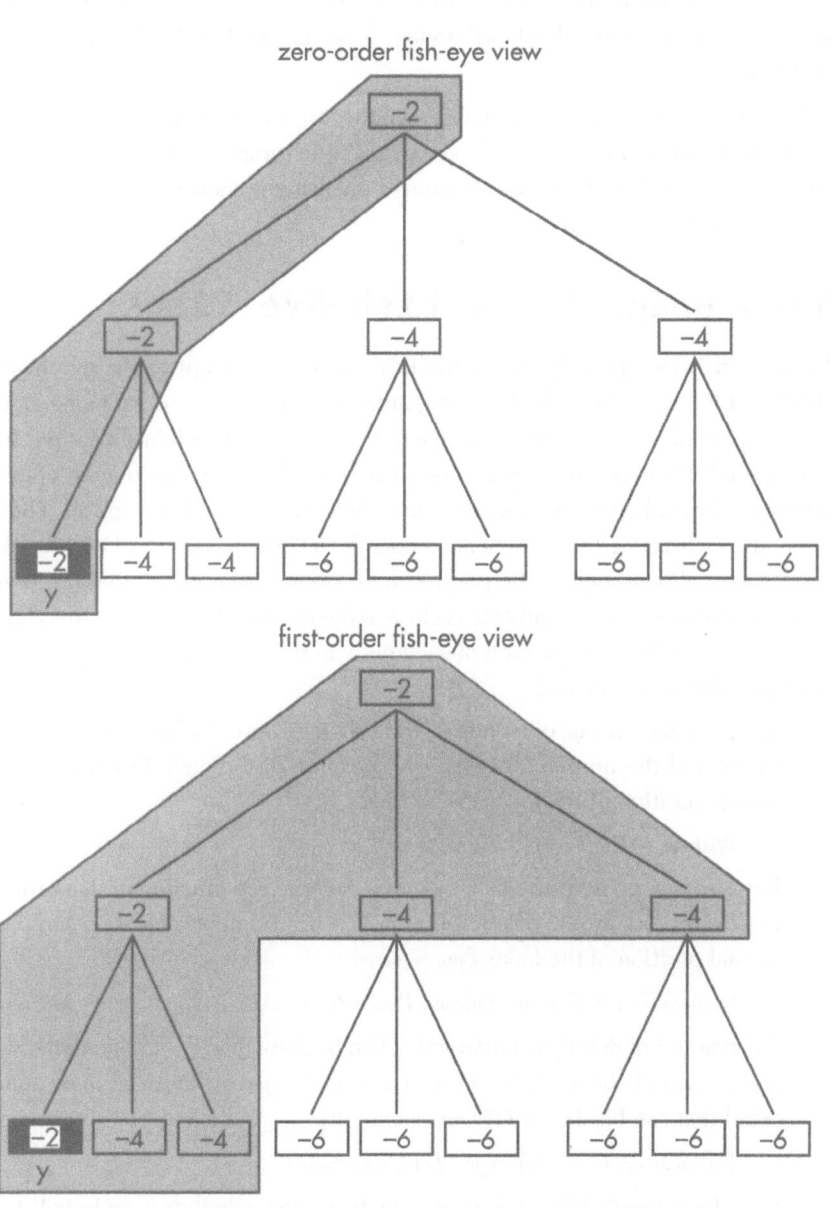

zero-order fish-eye view

first-order fish-eye view

Figure I.56

Zero-and
first-order
fish-eye views

interesting nodes, we get a zero–order fish–eye view; adding the second most interesting nodes to the displayed nodes results in a first–order fish–eye view, and so on.

Furnas describes in his seminal paper the use of fish–eye views for text-based applications like viewing large source code program fragments [Fur86]. The next section describes the extension of the fish–eye view idea to 2D graphical representations.

11.3 Graph-based Fish–Eye Views

Sarkar and Brown [Sar92] extend the fish–eye view concept to the graphical display of information in the form of graphs. In Furnas's original scheme, one node in a graph would be either shown or not shown at its original location. In Sarkar and Brown's approach, nodes can be differently sized and edges stretched depending on the importance of the node in the whole graph. They generalize Furnas's DOI function for a node by introducing a *Visual Worth VW* for a node x. Each node in the graph can be shifted from its original position and changed in size to magnify areas close to the focus and demagnify areas farther away. To define the position of each node in the fish–eye view, the following formalism is introduced:

1. The position *Pfisheye* of a node in the fish–eye view can be expressed as a function of the normal (non-fish eye) position of the node *Pnorm* and the normal position of the focus *Pnorm focus*:

   $Pfisheye = F1 \ (Pnorm, \ Pnorm \ focus)$.

2. The size of a node in the fish–eye view *Sfisheye* is a function of its normal size *Snorm* and normal position *Pnorm*, its a priori importance *API*, and the normal position of the focus *Pnorm focus*:

   $Sfisheye = F2 \ (Snorm, \ Pnorm, \ Pnorm \ focus, \ API)$.

3. The amount of detail *DTLfisheye* that can be displayed for a node depends on the size of the node in the fish–eye view *Sfisheye* and the maximum detail that can be shown *DTLmaximum*:

   $DTLfisheye = F3 \ (Sfisheye, \ DTLmaximum)$.

4. The visual worth *VW* of a node, which decides whether a node will be shown, depends on the distance between the node and the focus in normal coordinates *Dnorm* and on the a priori importance *API* of the node:

   $VW = F4 \ (Dnorm, \ API)$.

To generate useful views, the functions *F1*, *F2*, *F3*, and *F4* have to be chosen appropriately. Sarkar and Brown present a prototype implementation where they use the following function *F1* for the mapping of the Cartesian coordinates of a point *P(x,y)*:

$$Pfisheye(x) = \frac{(d+1)\dfrac{Dnorm(x,xfocus)}{Dmax}}{d\dfrac{Dnorm(x,xfocus)}{Dmax}+1} = \frac{\dfrac{(d+1)}{Dmax}}{d+\dfrac{Dmax}{Dnorm(x,xfocus)}}$$

$$Pfisheye(y) = \frac{\dfrac{(d+1)}{Dmax}}{d+\dfrac{Dmax}{Dnorm(y,yfocus)}}$$

The *x* and *y* coordinates are treated completely independently in the above mapping. *Dmax* is the distance of the boundary of the window from the focus. The constant *d* is called the *distortion factor*. If *d* = 0, then the normal and the fish–eye coordinates are the same. The larger the distortion factor *d* is, the more the nodes are shifted away from the focus and compressed near the boundaries of the graph.

Figure I.57 shows an undistorted symmetric graph. The graph at the top of Figure I.58 displays a fish–eye view of the same graph using the cartesian transformation function *F1* described above. In addition, a size transformation function F_2 has also been applied.

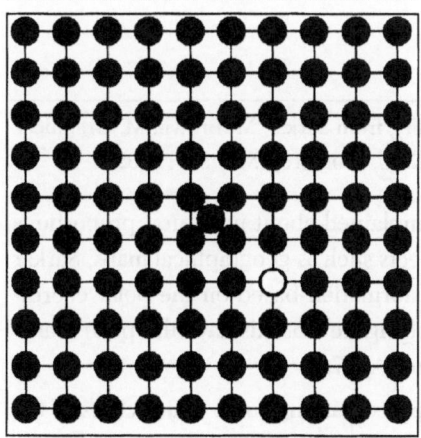

Figure I.57

An undistorted
graph
[Sar92:Fig. 3]

© 1992 Association for Computing Machinery, from Sarkar, M. Brown, M. Graphical Fish Eye Views of Graphs. *CHI '92 Proceedings*, Monterey, May 3–7, 1992.

Figure I.58

A graphical
fish–eye view
using cartesian
transformation
(top) and polar
transformation
(bottom) (d = 4)
[Sar92:Figs. 4,5]

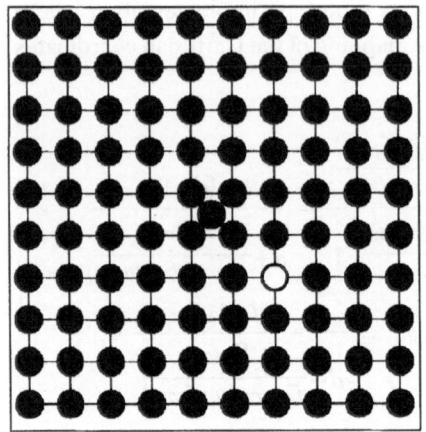

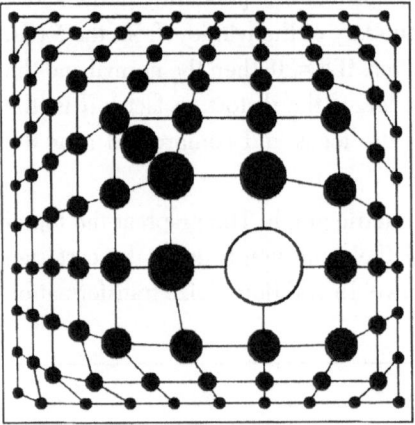

© 1992 Association for Computing Machinery, from Sarkar, M. Brown, M. Graphical
Fish Eye Views of Graphs. *CHI '92 Proceedings*, Monterey, May 3–7, 1992.

Because early users of the system complained about unnatural proportions
of the transformed graph for familiar objects such as geographical maps, Sarkar
and Brown implemented a second transformation based on the polar coordi-
nate system. The graph at the bottom of Figure I.58 displays the polar transformation of the symmetric graph of Figure I.57.

Figure I.59 shows an undistorted graph containing some major cities of the
United States at their geographical locations. Figure I.60 demonstrates the
same graph in a fish–eye view with St. Louis as its focus.

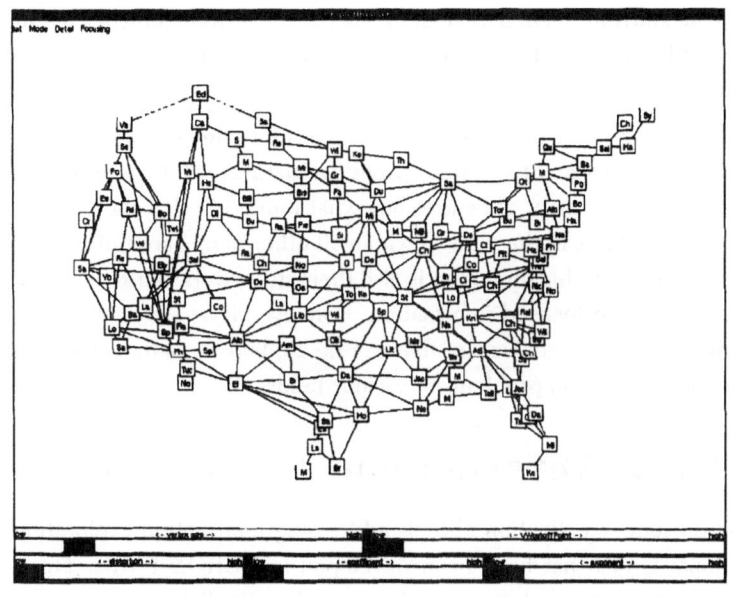

Figure I.59

The initial layout
of a graph
showing some
U.S. cities
[Sar92:Fig. 1]

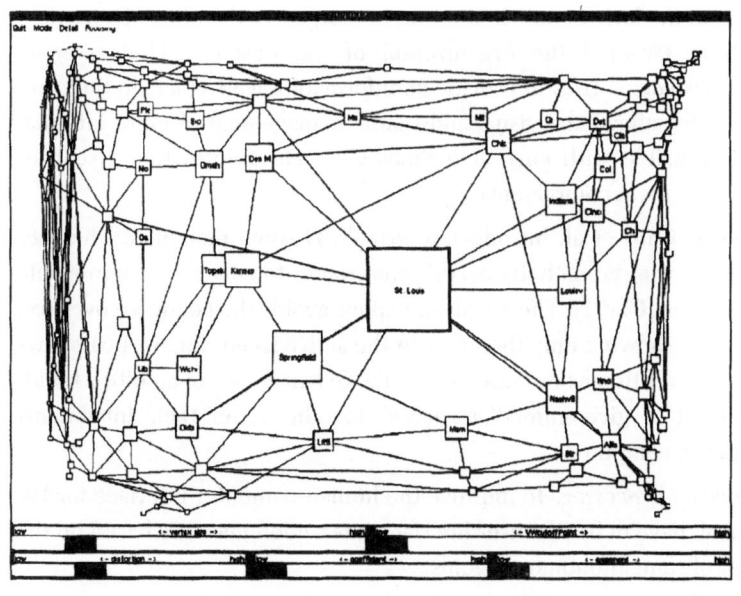

Figure I.60

A fish–eye view
of the graph
[Sar92:Fig. 2]

While Furnas can be credited with introducing the general idea of fish–eye views, the main contribution of Sarkar and Brown is the introduction of a mathematically sound formalism that can be used to generate arbitrary graph-based fish–eye views.

Obviously fish–eye views offer an excellent means for quickly getting a personalized overview of large information spaces. In that respect, they refine the concept of the overview map. They are somewhat limited in that they need a focus of interest—a point in the view to whom all other points are put in relation. On the other hand, this limitation is also their strength because users are very often interested in focused information. Fish–eye views are a promising navigation tool offering a mechanism that can be applied to many navigation and information exploration problems in various fields.

11.4 XEROX Information Visualizer

This section presents a collection of tools addressing information exploration and navigational issues that have been developed at XEROX PARC. These navigation tools are somewhat narrower in scope than the fish–eye view concept in that each of the tools described here addresses one specific problem.

The work of Card, Mackinlay, and Robertson [Car91] [Mac91] [Rob91] is embedded into the larger context of trying to reorganize the office. In particular, they have targeted the organization of the desktop. Their system, Information Visualizer, tries to provide an information workspace on the computer screen that allows the visual and spatial management of more information than is possible with current technologies. The information visualizer consists of three main components:

1. *3D/Rooms*. Card et al. introduce a virtual 3D room metaphor. The user switches on the screen between different rooms to enlarge the immediate storage space [Car91]. The rooms metaphor avoids the cognitive overload problem by showing only the items in the active room. Figure I.61 shows an obvious 3D/Rooms example where the 3D structure of an office building is used to give immediate access to offices and their inhabitants through the computer.

2. *Cognitive co-processor*. To improve the human-computer interface for IR, Card et al. have defined a user interface interaction manager based on the concept of semiautonomous agents.

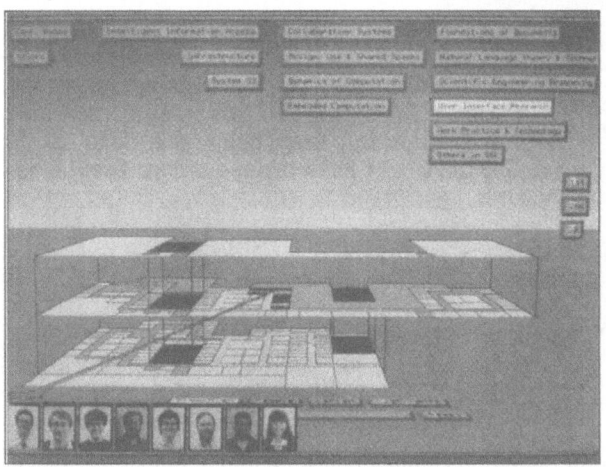

Figure I.61

Information visu-
alizer: 3D/Rooms
example
[Car91:Plate 2]

3. *Information visualizations.* To visualize the information contained in
3D/Rooms, Card et al. have developed different information representation techniques. Figure I.61 shows the office building metaphor as an
interface to people.

In the next two paragraphs two other 3D information representation techniques, *cone trees* and the *perspective wall*, are introduced.

Cone trees try to represent hierarchically structured information in a 3D   **cone trees**
space [Rob91]. The user controls the 3D environment with a conventional 2D
device, normally the mouse. Nodes in a cone tree are laid out either horizon-
tally or vertically. Figure I.62 shows a simple vertically oriented cone tree. The
user can grab any of the nodes in the tree with the mouse and rotate the whole
tree to bring the selected node to the foreground. The rotation of the tree is
animated to give the user feedback of what is happening.

Lighting cues like lighter coloring and shadows of the cones on the room floor
improve the 3D perception. To hide parts of a complex hierarchical substructure,
Robertson et al. use *gardening* operations. The user can prune or grow a substructure by manipulating a node with either a direct mouse gesture or a menu
command. Cone trees have been used by Robertson et al. to visualize file directory structures, organization structures, and a company's operating plan. During
user testing, they found that the most important component of the cone tree user
interface was the animation capability. Animating tree modifications allows users

Figure I.62

Vertically
oriented
cone tree
[Rob91:Plate 2]

© 1991 Association for Computing Machinery

to understand the current operation simultaneously. Without animation, it takes
them a long time to reassimilate the structural relationships. Robertson et al. also
found that the 3D representation permitted to represent an order of magnitude
more nodes on the screen than with a comparable optimized 2D representation.

**perspective
wall**

While cone trees are used to visualize hierarchical information, the perspective wall represents linearly structured information [Mac91]. The perspective
wall employs a simplified fish–eye view strategy by representing the linear
information in a 3D space and enlarging the current focus in the foreground
and bending more distant data to the back (Figure I.63).

Figure I.63

Perspective wall
[Mac91:Plate 2]

© 1991 Association for Computing Machinery

This intuitive 3D metaphor for distorting 2D views allows the user a smooth transition between views. As with cone trees, the user can select an element in the perspective wall, which is then moved to the center panel of the wall. This animation permits the user, similarly to cone trees, to reassimilate quickly to the modified view. The user is also able to change the level of detail by stretching the panel edges or the bent back sides of the panel.

The information representation techniques for the information visualizer exhibit some unique features not present in any other existing system. Unfortunately, today's hardware is barely powerful enough to provide the real–time, high–resolution 3D graphics needed for the information visualizer, as its interface runs on Silicon Graphics IRIS 3D graphics workstations. Nevertheless, the concepts and ideas may be guiding information management interfaces of the future, as ideas from XEROX PARC have already influenced the ways of computing frequently in the past.

11.5 Mapping the Web

The multidimensional structure of the Web is ideally suited for visualization by mapping. There have been different approaches suggested at recent Web conferences, and there is now even a commercial company that sells tools for "Web cartography."

Luis Neves and José Oliveira describe a system that analyzes Internet links [Nev95] by treating them as abstract objects.[2] Their system clusters HTML files based on contents by analyzing their title, headings, and general contents. Further analysis of different types of HTML links, such as:

- Hyperlink references—<A HREF = "URL> .. </A>.

- Image references—<IMG SRC = "URL">...</IMG>

- Embedded references—<EMBED SRC = "URL>

allows users to create local maps automatically for any HTML page displaying the page in its local context, as depicted in Figure I.64.

This local map can be used to browse in the Web. Also, the database of URLs built up by the SOUR tool can be queried directly (e.g., to find out all the pages that contain links to a certain page).

Classifying Internet Objects with SOUR

http://www.w3
.org/pub/
Conferences/
WWW4/Papers/
portugal

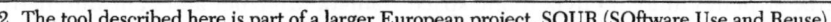

2 The tool described here is part of a larger European project, SOUR (SOftware Use and Reuse).

Figure I.64

Web browsing
using SOUR's
Result Manager
http://www.w3
.org/pub/
Conferences/
WWW4/Papers/
portugal

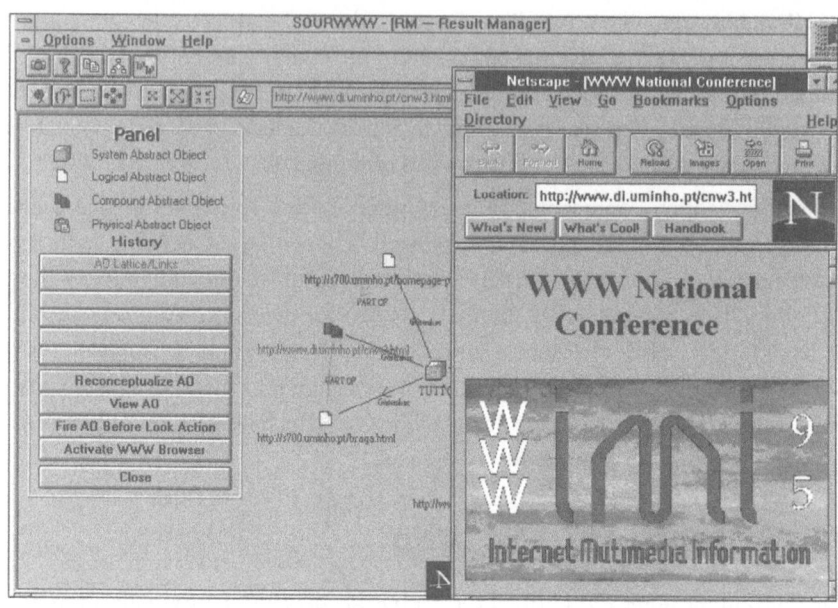

**maps of
hyperspace**

http://agora
.leeds.ac.uk/
spacenet/
ghedini.html

The SOUR system is part of a software engineering project; the "maps of hyperspace" system tackles the problem from a different side using AI concepts but comes to similar results. Ghedhini Ralha and Anthony Cohn suggest an AI-based approach to building maps of hyperspace [Ghe95]. They are trying to build spatial cognitive maps of the hyperspace influenced by the human cognitive mapping process.

Figures I.65 and I.66 display a small subset of a sample hyperspace in Venn and node graph notation, respectively. They have been drawn manually based on automatic clustering of the contents of the HTML files.

Ghedini Rahlha and Cohn's system is based on the same similarity measure as described in the previous chapter. The goal is not only to display actual links but to combine information about the linking structure with a semantic analysis of the contents of the HTML pages.

**3D hyperbolic
space**

http://www.geom.
umn.edu/docs/
research/webviz/

The next system extends the XEROX PARC Information Visualizer Cone Tree structure into 3D hyperbolic space. Tamara Munzner and Paul Burchard suggest the use of 3D hyperbolic space for the visualization of the Web structure. They use a 3D graphical representation available in their own format, as

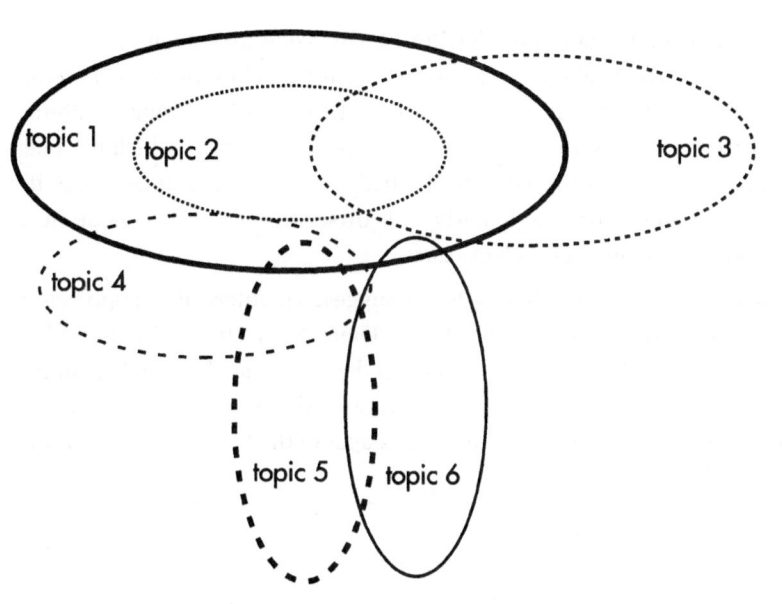

Figure I.65
Venn diagram of
sample
hyperspace
http://agora.leeds
.ac.uk/spacenet/
ghedini.html

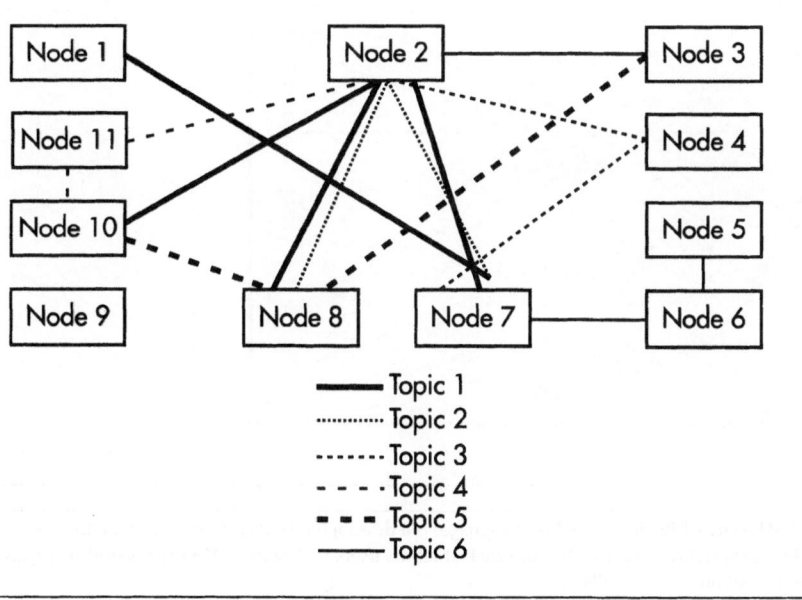

Figure I.66
Node graph of
sample
hyperspace
http://agora
.leeds.ac.uk/
spacenet/
ghedini.html

well as in the VRML format, to allow for interactive browsing in hyperbolic space.[3]

Their layout is a variant of the XEROX PARC cone tree. Contrary to original cone trees, hyperbolic cone trees are much less cluttered and therefore offer the big picture and interesting details at the same time. Using an interactive 3D browser, the user can navigate in the hyperbolic tree, which has been drawn in Figure I.67 in the interior of a ball. By selecting a single node, the user can then jump from the hyperbolic browser to the selected node in an ordinary Web browser such as Netscape.

**Navigational
View Builder**

http://www.cc
.gatech.edu/
gvu/people/
Phd/sougata/
Nvb.html

Sougata Mukherjea and James Foley suggest an interactive approach to building visual structures of the Web. Their Navigational View Builder [Muk95] uses a combination of structural and contents analysis for computing different types of visualizations. As a motivation, Mukherjea and Foley display an unfiltered, very small subset of the Web pages of the Graphics, Visualization

Figure I.67

Screen shot of a
interactive flight
in 3D hyperbolic
web space
http://www
.geom.umn.edu/
docs/research/
webviz/node2
.html#motion

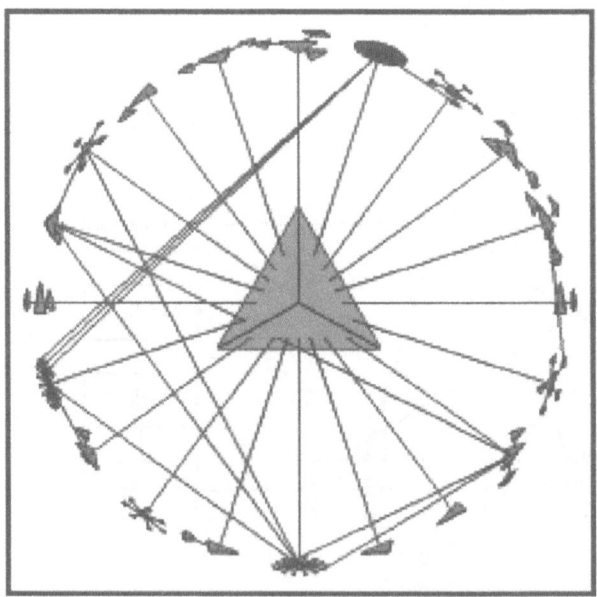

---

3 VRML (Virtual Reality Modeling Language) is a developing standard for describing interactive 3D scenes delivered across the Internet. It allows users to describe 3D virtual worlds textually for execution over the WWW.

and Usability Center at the Georgia Institute of Technology (Figure I.68). Its complexity renders this visualization almost useless.

The advantage of such a spiderweb representation is that it can be computed automatically. Mukherjea and Foley apply all sorts of filtering mechanisms to this representation. They allow filtering for file type, such as the web in Figure I.69, that displays only HTML nodes that are connected to images (gif files) and movies (mpg files).

Navigational View Builder also allows clustering by contents, such as by author or topic, and by link structure, such as distance from current, or number of children. To reduce screen clutter further, filtering criteria can be applied recursively to form clusters of similar nodes.

The system incorporates the concepts of the XEROX Information Visualizer such as cone trees (Figure I.70) and perspective walls, as well as Tree-Maps (see Chapter 9).

These research systems illustrate interesting concepts, but they are not available to non-academic users. NetCarta is a commercial system for visualizing the web structure. It calls itself the leader in the World Wide Web cartography software market. (Microsoft offers a Web administrator tool, FrontPage, which has a similar function.) NetCarta CyberPilot Pro and

NetCarta

http://www
.netcarta.com

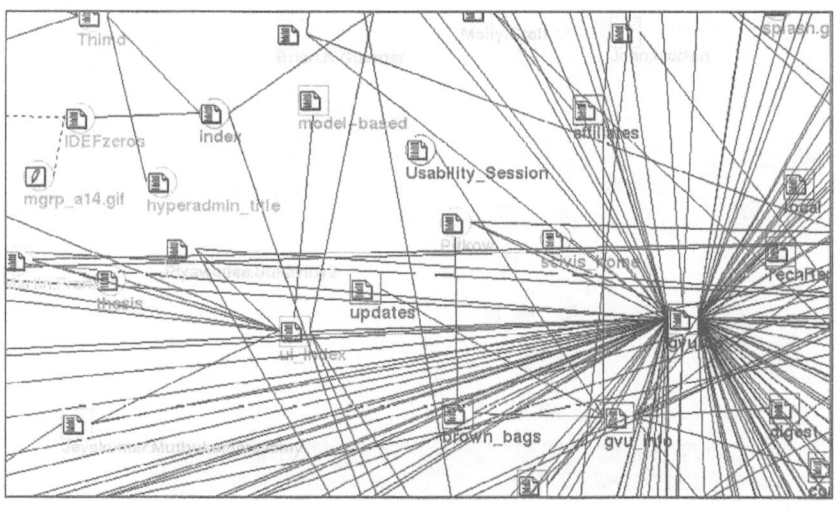

Figure I.68

Small subset of the web displaying all links ("spiderweb view") http://www.cc .gatech.edu/gvu/ people/Phd/ sougata/bind.gif

Reproduced with permission of Sougata Mukherjea, GVU Center, Georgia Institute of Technology. Copyright 1996.

Figure I.69

Example of
structure-based
filtering
http://www.cc
.gatech.edu/gvu/
people/Phd/
sougata/filter.gif

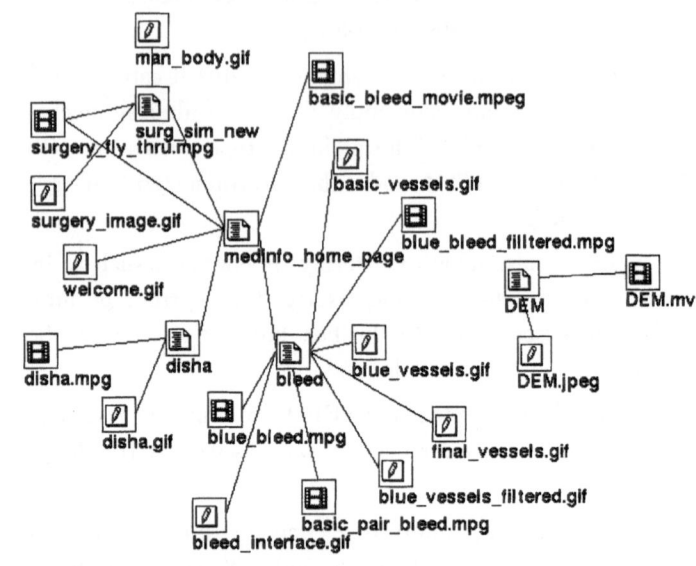

Reproduced with permission of Sougata Mukherjea, GVU Center, Georgia Institute
of Technology. Copyright 1996.

Figure I.70

3D tree view of
default hierarchy
of GVU
Research pages
http://www.cc
.gatech.edu/gvu/
people/Phd/
sougata/hier.gif

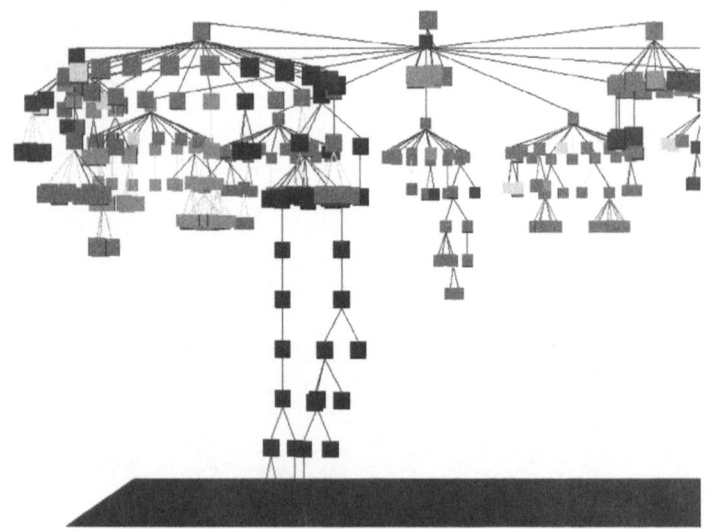

Reproduced with permission of Sougata Mukherjea, GVU Center, Georgia Institute
of Technology. Copyright 1996.

WebMapper are commercial products that allow users to modify graphically properties and linking structure of the HTML pages on a particular Web site (Figure I.71). NetCarta sees its products as being used for Web management, site analysis, structure-based search and retrieval, and concept-based publishing. The simpler CyberPilot Pro allows users to create and read WebMaps, which provide them with a visual representation of a Web site. It generates a hierarchical structure of the site and permits filtering out the pages a user is most interested in. Users can also compare different versions of WebMaps of the same site to discover changes on a site quickly.

NetCarta offers an enhanced version of CyberPilot, WebMapper, as a tool for Web administrators ("webmasters"). In combination with Lycos, WebMapper

Generates browsable NetCarta WebMaps that help users pinpoint information, save time, and decrease the load on the server.

Integrates with existing authoring tools, test tools, and compilers to provide a complete Web management suite.

Views are configurable to help focus your management efforts on one aspect of the site at a time.

Figure I.71

NetCarta WebMapper (from NetCarta data sheet)

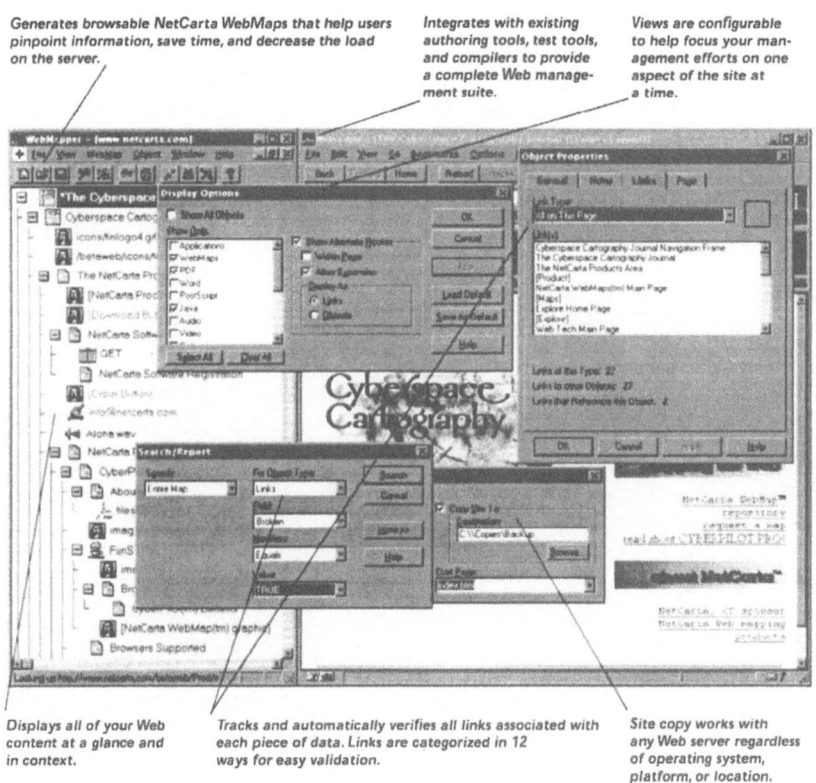

Displays all of your Web content at a glance and in context.

Tracks and automatically verifies all links associated with each piece of data. Links are categorized in 12 ways for easy validation.

Site copy works with any Web server regardless of operating system, platform, or location.

allows tracking links that point from other locations to the local site, thus enabling Web authors at other sites to fix stale or "dangling" links.

We can distinguish two types of mapping systems: (1) novel representations for hierarchical and nonhierarchical information such as fish–eye views, cone trees, perspective walls, and 3D hyperbolic space, and (2) systems for graphically representing links as some form of DAG (directed acyclic graph), eventually applying techniques of category 1, such as Intermedia's Web View, SOUR tools, maps of hyperspace, Navigational View Builder, CyberPilot, and WebMapper. What all of these systems have in common is an emphasis on the existing link structure—the most distinguishing feature of a hypertext document. Nevertheless, this is only part of the picture. The systems introduced in Chapter 10 as well as the Cybermap system presented later, address this other aspect of trying to generate information structure from contents.

Guides

and

Agents

Similarly to the mapping concepts already discussed, agents are orthogonal to the first five concepts of navigation in cyberspace, meaning that agent-based concepts can be used to assist readers in following links, conducting searches, constructing sequential paths, navigating in hierarchies, and recognizing similarities.

The cyberspace community distinguishes between guides and agents. Although both guides and agents assist readers in exploring large information spaces, agents embody a notion of autonomous behavior as well as "intelligence", while guides represent a human-like metaphor to assist in the navigation task. Contrary to guided tours (see Chapter 8), which take readers through a predefined path, guides are much more flexible. They simulate a human guide, which helps the user in orienting in unknown territory. The refined version of the guide, the agent, even tries to figure out the needs of the user and offer solutions based on this assessment. Guides and agents need not necessarily be represented on the computer screen by a virtual person, although for a computer-illiterate user, this interface may be more obvious than an abstract text-based representation.

Compared with agents, guides are more restricted and less autonomous (Table I.2). The guide idea stresses the human-like representation, but contrary

Table I.2	Guides	Agents
Agents versus guides	Simple form of agents	Autonomous software entities
	Present document selection based on index	Respond dynamically to user's goals, preferences, learning style, knowledge
	Assume role of guideposts and storytellers	Require some degree of "intelligence"

to agents, guides do not contain real content knowledge about the information they manage.

An agent is more powerful than a guide, but unfortunately the software technology to implement general–purpose agents is not yet commonly deployed. Although the foundations for implementing agents are in place, there are still many technical problems that need to be solved. In the meantime we can hardwire guides to show agent-like behavior. The enduser will not notice the difference as long as the underlying knowledge base remains static and is not modified by the user.

12.1 Guides: Orientation Assistants

Guides provide a familiar interface to readers by simulating a virtual creature on the screen that assists them in their orientation task. Guides can be as simple as Simon the storyteller in Brøderbound's animated children's book of Aesop's "The Tortoise and the Hare." The pictures in Figure I.72 display Simon introducing the different animated pages of the children's book. Simon exhibits hardwired behavior; in the opening sequence to each page, he introduces the story of the page in a canned movie. Nevertheless, Simon offers an easy-to-use navigation feature that can be understood even by three year olds.

Oren, Salomon, Kreitman, and Don describe an implementation of guides as the main interface to an educational hypermedia database [Ore90a][Ore90b]. The database contains material about American history from 1800 to 1850. The goal of Oren et al. was to find a way of structuring and providing information that avoided navigational overhead. The reader should always have a next, obvious choice instead of having to choose manually out of a large list of possible selections. The easy solution to this problem would have been to implement some sort of guided tour, but Oren et al. considered this approach too

Figure I.72

The guide Simon in [Brø94]

sequential and limiting for the user. Instead, they decided to offer navigation assistance through guides. Their guides are virtual personalities of the appropriate time period (e.g., preacher, slave, miner, settler, Indian). This historical look and feel of the guides has the additional advantage of putting the reader into the right historical context.

Oren et al. describe two versions of guides. The first version had simple, static guides. In a second implementation they added video guides, consisting of video clips where an actor dressed in contemporary clothing would give the navigation tips.

The first guide implementation (Figure I.73) was based on a hierarchical topic index of the articles. Each guide was characterized by a collection of

Figure I.73

Selection card for static guides of first implementation from [Ore90a:Fig. 6]

index entries. The "Sea Captain" guide was described, among other entries, by "Transportation," "Ships and Shipping," "Clipper Ships," and so forth. For each guide a ranked list of articles of interest was compiled. The first guides consisted only of a nested list of topics. Later each guide also got a life history to help choose topics and explain why certain topics had been selected.

In informal field testing of the first guide version, users preferred this form of navigation aid over more conventional ones like tours or maps. But users soon projected too many expectations onto the guides. They assumed a characterization behind the iconic figures. For example, they expected a personalized presentation of a story. They anticipated that the story about Andrew Jackson would be presented differently depending on whether they were guided by the slave or the Indian.

The second version corrected two main deficiencies of the first version. Users wanted to know why the guide had brought them to a particular article, and they also wanted to know whether the article would be presented from the guide's point of view. *Storytelling guides* included these two additional features. Navigation tips could be called from the guide card (Figure I.74). Storytelling guides were then brought up as video clips where a character told a short first-person story explaining why he or she would take a user to a particular article (Figure I.75).

`http://www`
`.abbedon.com/`
`Project/guides`
`.html`

In comparison, video guides differ from the simple guides in form, content, and function [Ore90 p. 374]:

The main goal of guides in Oren et al.'s project was to provide a simpler navigation interface than a complex hypertext map or a conventional query interface. Guides also succeeded in merging browsing and search into one single metaphor. Oren et al. conclude that the deliberate personification of the navigation interface seems to result in increased engagement of the user. Guides also offer an excellent way of exposing the biased view inherent in each article.

Table I.3		Simple Guides	Video Guides
Simple guides versus video guides	**Form**	generic historic characters	specific characters on pvideo
	Content	where should I go next	first-person stories
	Function	next-move generator	next-move generator and content provider

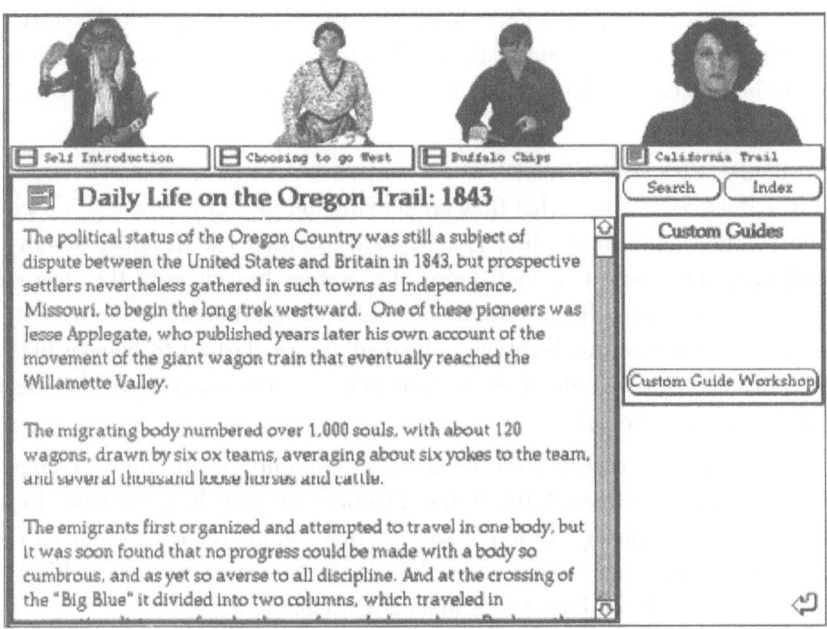

Figure I.74

Video guide: Daily life on the Oregon Trail

Figure I.75

Video guide: the settler gives a navigation tip from [Ore90a:Fig. 12]

By letting different guides with different viewpoints (e.g., Indian and settler) tell the same story, the reader gets a more balanced view of this particular story. This approach is very demanding for the document author, because the stories have to be broken down into single facts that can then be reassembled by the guides.

Particular care has to be taken not to annoy more experienced users, because once users know what they are looking for, they often see a guide as an obstruction rather than a help [Lau92]. This problem can be addressed by monitoring the user's behavior. Once the system has guessed the user's intention, guides can offer to provide the information they think the user is searching. Guides at this level of sophistication are starting to behave like agents as described in the next section and are thus on a gradual scale between the two concepts.

User testing also revealed the need for a different type of guide. *Frame guides* lead the user through the system functions by providing assistance for all those functions that are system related. A frame guide is analogous to a TV anchorperson with an overview of the whole broadcast who introduces reporters with in-depth knowledge about a particular story.

The guide metaphor solves the problem of where to go next in a large document collection. The implementation, on the other hand, is rather complicated. The guides implemented by Oren et al. have been hardwired for this particular application. To build more generally usable guides, a broader framework is needed. Agents, as described in the next section, generalize the notion of guide.

12.2 Agents

This section introduces the agent concept and its application to navigational tasks. It is impossible to give in-depth coverage to this field, as this is an ongoing area of research. Rather, we try to briefly illustrate the state of the art and to outline the potential of agent technology for the exploration of cyberspace.

The use of agents as a new interface model for human-computer interaction was first proposed by Alan Kay. He also called agents "soft robots."

The model-building capabilities of the computer should enable mindlike processes to be built and should allow designers to create flexible "agents." These agents will take on their owner's goals, confer about strategies (asking questions of users as well as answering their queries) and, by reasoning, fabricate goals of their own.

—Allan Kay, 1991

[Kay91]

In the literature three slightly redundant different types of agents are distinguished:

1. *Autonomous agents*—programs that travel between sites, deciding themselves when to move and what to do (e.g. General Magic's Telescript or Agent-Tcl agents). They can travel only between servers that are set up to handle agents and are currently not widespread in the Internet.

2. *Intelligent agents*—programs that help users interactively to accomplish a task, such as choosing a product, or guiding a user through form filling, or do a search. The wizards in Windows 95 are simple versions of such agents. Their intelligence is in fact quite limited, as they are best at doing a well-defined task in a limited domain. As with most AI applications, vaguely defined tasks requiring commonsense knowledge are ill suited for intelligent agents.

3. *User-agents*—programs that perform mostly networking tasks for a user, such as e-mail user-agents like Qualcomm's Eudora, which filter a user's mail based on her or his interests.

`http://www`
`.qualcomm.com/`

Table I.4 contains a partial listing of possible tasks that can be done by an agent on behalf of the human user.

		Table I.4
Information	**Filtering Work**	Types of tasks
Navigation and browsing	Reminding	suitable for an
Information retrieval	Programming	agent [Lau90]
Sorting and organizing	Scheduling	
Advising		
Learning	**Entertainment**	
Coaching	Playing against	
Tutoring	Playing with	
Providing Help	Performing	

One obvious use of the agent concept is for navigation and localization of information. Contrary to guides, agents are autonomous software entities that make choices and execute actions on behalf of the user. They incorporate the knowledge to find and present information by responding dynamically to the user's changing goals, preferences, learning style, and knowledge. To succeed in this task, agents need some sort of intelligence. In particular, they require knowledge about the structure and contents of the underlying information. This leads to the conclusion that structured information as in AI knowledge bases like CYC, is particularly well suited to being managed by agents. For agents to grant access to unstructured information, this information has to be structured at least internally. For the agent prototypes available so far, most of the document structure has either been generated by manually structuring unstructured documents, or by limiting the functionality of agents to semi-structured information (see the next section).

The behavior and properties of an agent must be made visible to the user. For some agents, a textual representation is completely sufficient—in Weizenbaum's ELIZA program [Wei76] its bodiless phrases may have been its greatest strength. Frequently, agents that have human-like traits are particularly well suited to make the internal properties of the agent obvious to the user. Dramatic characters are better suited than full-blown personalities, because they selectively represent only those traits that are important for the tasks the agent is supposed to support [Lau90]. Figure I.76 shows two representations of Phil, a semi-intelligent agent who appeared in the famous Knowledge Navigator videotape of Apple Computer. Although the two representations differ, the characteristic bow tie makes Phil recognizable in both representations.

The ALIVE project at the MIT Media Lab (Figure I.77) offers a new level of immersion to the user employing virtual reality (VR) technologies. The user can interact with autonomous, intelligent agents in the form of virtual creatures (such as the dog in Figure I.77) without being constrained by VR devices such as headsets, goggles, or special sensing equipment. The system is based on the so-called magic mirror metaphor: ALIVE users see their own image on a large TV screen as if in a mirror. Autonomous, animated characters join the user's own image in the reflected world.

The ALIVE project is one of the most advanced agent projects with respect to the human–computer interface. The next section introduces agents based on a textual interface; they are used to manage semistructured information. The Oval agents provide navigational cues based on semistructured content information.

Figure I.76

Phil, a fictive
agent for Apple's
Knowledge
Navigator
videotape
[Lau90:Fig. 2]

Figure I.77

Human
interacting with a
virtual creature
in MIT Media
Lab's ALIVE
project
http://alive.www
.media.mit.edu/
projects/alive

http://ccs.mit
.edu/

12.3 Oval: A Tool Kit to Build Information Exploration Interfaces

Thomas Malone has led the development of a series of systems—first called Information Lens, later Object Lens, and most currently Oval—that incorporate many of the features described above [Crow88] [Lai88] [Lai91] [Mal92]. Oval uses ideas from artificial intelligence and user interface design to represent information in a way that can be processed intelligently by human beings and computational agents. It integrates ideas from the fields of hypertext, object-oriented databases, electronic messaging, and rule-based intelligent agents [Lai88] [Mal92]. Its focus is on the development of applications for cooperative work, but most of the ideas can easily be applied to other domains. Malone calls his system *radically tailorable* [Mal92], because new applications can be built using the four basic building blocks *objects, views, agents,* and *links.* Oval is semiformal in the sense that it is well suited to process formally specified information, but the formal specification can easily be changed. Oval distinguishes between passive information, represented in semistructured objects with template-based interfaces, and active rules for the processing of the passive information. Views specify the interface of the object to the users and allow them to edit instances of the object; links represent the relationships between the objects. Radical tailorability allows users to

- Define new object types easily.
- Add fields to existing object types.
- Select views for objects and collections of objects.
- Specify the parameters for a view.
- Create new agents and rules.
- Insert new links.

Malone and Lai use the power of radical tailorability to reimplement other cooperative work applications easily.

Objects in Oval represent familiar things such as messages, people, meetings, tasks, manufactured parts, and software bugs [Lai88]. The information in the objects is semistructured in the sense that users are free to fill in as much information into the different fields as they want. Fields can also be in free-text format. Figure I.78 shows one instance of an object that can be edited in a template editor.

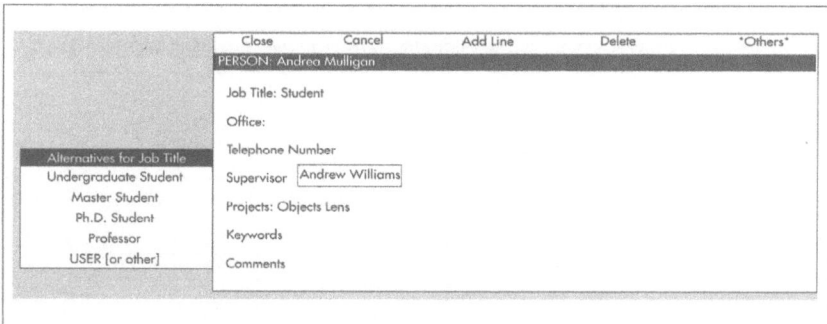

Figure I.78

Template editor
for objects
[Lai88:Fig. 1]

Objects and object hierarchies are defined by a set of templates. By clicking on the template of an object and selecting the appropriate command from a menu, users can modify an object (Figure I.79).

To perform an action on an object, the user creates an agent. The behavior of the agent is specified by a collection of rules that are created with a rule editor (Figure I.80). In this example, the rule specifies what has to happen to e-mail messages. Rules consist of "if" and "then" parts, which are applied to the current object.

The real power of the Oval system comes from the combination of objects and agents, where objects are displayed in views and manipulated by agents, and relationships between the objects are expressed by links. Oval is thus particularly well suited for manipulating *active information*—information that is accessed in different form by different persons, such as e-mail. Indeed, e-mail was one of the first applications of Information Lens, the first-generation predecessor of Oval.

Contrary to guides, agents react based on an analysis of the real contents of the document. As Oval illustrates, the behavior of agents is defined by rules. But there is still a long way to go until agents will take over our daily duties we do not want to do anymore, and will, for example, go out to search the Internet autonomously for the book that we did not find in our local library.

Figure I.79

Object hierarchy
defined by
templates
[Lai88:Fig. 3]

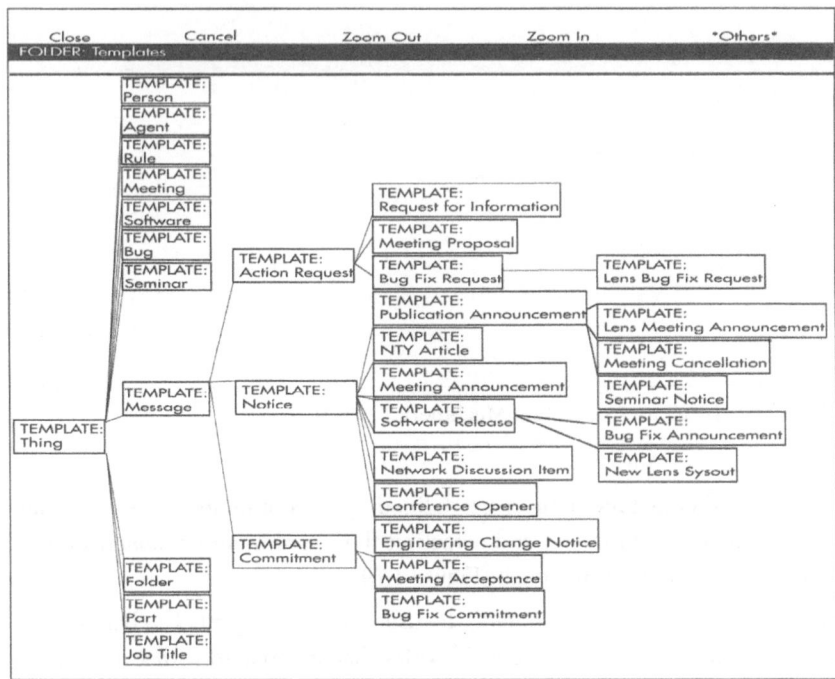

Figure I.80

Rule describing
actions on
objects
[Lai88:Fig. 6]

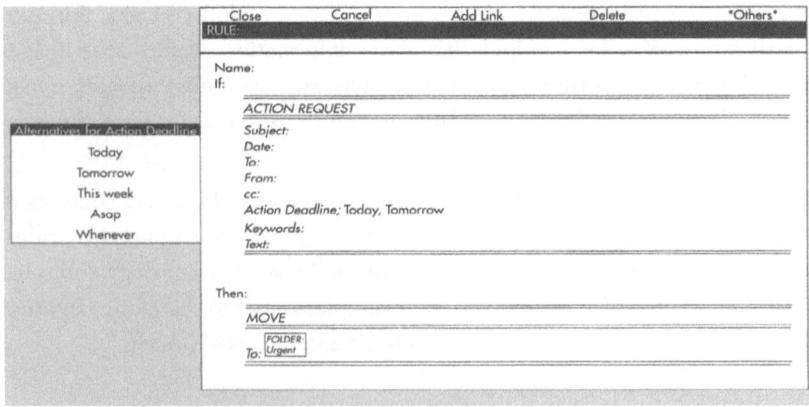

Conclusions

Chapters 5 to 12 presented the seven design concepts for navigation in cyberspace. The concepts have been introduced by giving an overview of the whole range of navigation tools and techniques in large information spaces. Obviously there is neither a single, all-encompassing navigation tool nor one predominant concept. Rather, we have shown a complementing collection of seven concepts and tools that cover different needs of different users with different goals. With the current growth rate of the Internet, the navigation issue will become even more important. We do not yet have the cyberspace envisioned by William Gibson in his science-fiction stories [Gib84], offering direct transparent access to all aspects of knowledge and entertainment. But there are many promising approaches available today, although on a small scale. We still have a far way to go to get final solutions workable in the scale that cyberspace suggests.

Some of the tools presented here demand already structured metainformation as input. This extends from static systems as IGD, where the document author has to create a hierarchically structured document, to knowledge bases such as CYC, where all information is stored as rules and frames. The knowledge bases containing the structured metaknowledge have been manually constructed. As the contents of the information space grow in scale and dimension, it will become increasingly harder to construct manually tools to navigate and explore this space. This means that the construction of metainformation will have to be supported by the computer to a much larger extent than it is today. Techniques based on automatic recognition of structure and contents of the information space will become increasingly important. The concepts introduced here, such as similarity, hierarchy, linking, and searching, lend themselves well to automation. Unfortunately, today's implementations of these systems still need too much human intervention and preprocessing.

The next part introduces Hiermap, Navigation Diamond, Viewfinder, and Cybermap, which address the issues raised in Part I. They provide innovative mechanisms for navigation in cyberspace by giving an automatic overview of an unstructured information space, offering guidance of what to do next, and putting a single node into a hierarchical context.

p a r t **II**

The Cyber-
Toolbox

Many of the tools and techniques introduced in Part I are based on some sort of manual preprocessing or are even constructed by hand. As the content of cyberspace grows in scale and dimension, it will become increasingly harder to construct manually tools to navigate and explore this information space. This means that their generation will have to be supported by the computer to a much larger extent than is the case today. Techniques based on automatic recognition of structure and contents of the information space will become increasingly important. Unfortunately, today's implementations of these systems still need too much human intervention. Our vision of the ideal system encompasses a tool set for navigating in cyberspace that operates on raw, unstructured documents, is capable of giving users an overview of their field of interest, offers guidance on what to do next and gives readers a graphical overview of their local and global context. The solutions offered here illustrate promising approaches for possible solutions.

The next eight chapters present tools and mechanisms for navigation and visualization of information structures. These tools represent the result of six years of work in this area done mostly at MIT and Dartmouth College, experimenting with tools and methods for navigation in cyberspace, but also testing those tools and concepts by building some large-scale hypermedia documents. We have implemented a hypermedia version of a computer science textbook *Introduction to Algorithms*[Cor90], as well as a series of hypermedia conference proceedings, both described in Parts III and V.

The issues raised in the previous chapters have been addressed in our own work in different ways:

Hierarchy. We have built a hypertext engine, the Gloor/Dynes hypertext engine, that is based on hierarchical navigation. This engine is particularly well suited for educational material as well as conversions of textbooks, because they are generally hierarchically structured.

Sequentialization. The Gloor/Dynes hypertext engine contains, among other tools, a path editor that allows authors to construct paths and guided tours easily and flexibly. We are in the process of porting the path editor to the World Wide Web.

Similarity. The Cybermap system computes similarities between hypertext nodes based on the vector space model introduced in Chapter 1. This structure is then visualized by clustering the nodes into so-called hyperdrawers. The hyperdrawers are displayed graphically based on similarity between hyperdrawers.

Mapping. Our tools Cybermap and Hiermap make heavy use of the mapping concepts described in Chapter 11 to visualize the semantic information structure (Cybermap) and the hierarchical document structure (Hiermap).

Cybertools:
from
Text To Hypertext

The Gloor/Dynes hypertext engine [Glo93b] has been developed as a hypertext shell on the Macintosh in HyperCard extended by XCMDs in C [Win90] (Figure II.1). It has been used for various hypertext projects, among others for the *Animated Algorithms* project and the DAGS multimedia proceedings series described later in the book. It embodies most of the popular concepts found in Web browsers on a stand-alone platform but also offers some features not commonly found in hypertext systems.

14.1 Hierarchical Navigation with the Gloor/Dynes Hypertext Engine

This section focuses on the main characteristic of the Gloor/Dynes hypertext engine: its support for hierarchical document structures. One of the core concepts that distinguishes our system from other hyperdocuments is the ability to examine ideas and concepts at different levels of abstraction, ranging from a broad and shallow level to a narrow but deep level. This feature allows the user to read the material first at an abstract level and to get an understanding of what the essential points of a certain section are. The capability to pop up

Figure II.1

Sample hyper-
text page of the
Gloor/Dynes
hypertext engine

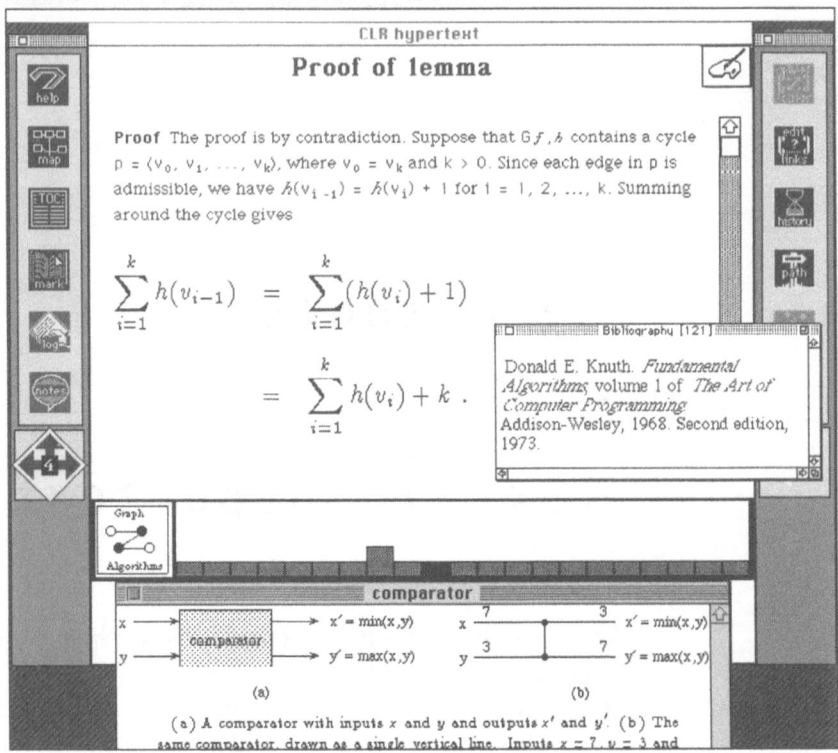

quickly to a high level of abstraction also lessens the chance that the reader loses the forest for the trees. For use as a reference, being able to browse the text at various levels of abstraction enables the user to filter relevant sections from those less important quickly.

The hyperdocument is composed of nodes with four different detail levels (Figure II.2):

1. A broad overview of each of the seven parts of the book; composed of nodes incorporating the text making up the preamble to each part.

2. The introduction to each chapter, detailing what each chapter is about.

3. The preambles to each of the chapter sections.

4. The actual text that makes up each chapter section, encompassing most of the text of the book.

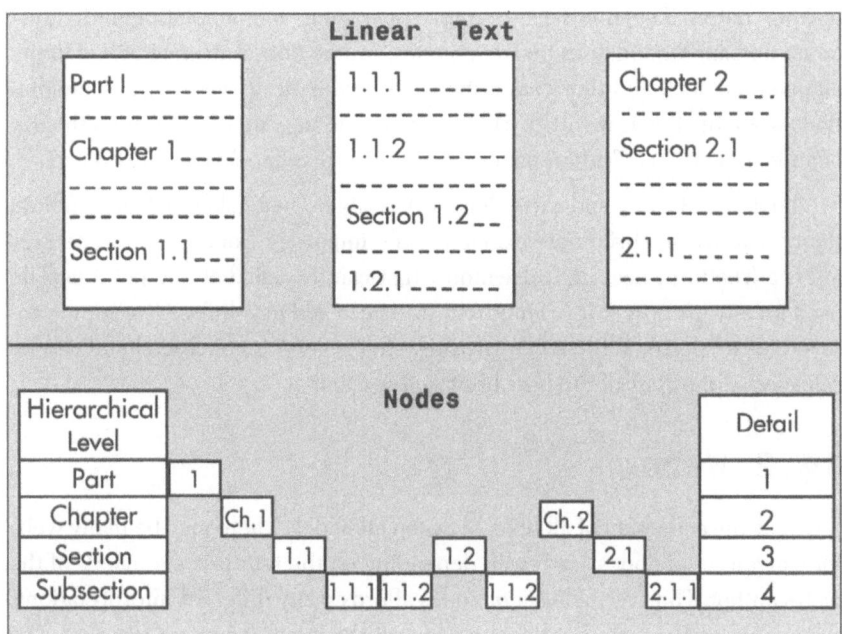

Figure II.2

Hierarchical
document hyper-
text structure

We offer multiple, partly redundant means of getting from one node to another. We distinguish between intrinsic and extrinsic means for navigation. Intrinsic means consist of hardwired links between nodes, generated automatically by the text-to-hypertext conversion. We also offer extrinsic means of browsing: key word search, booklike lists, the navigation diamond, and the viewfinder, discussed in the next chapter.

Nodes may also include references to graphics or to text contained in other nodes. Animations and figures are accessed in their own window. Also referenced are display equations, theorems, and pseudocode for describing algorithms. Each of these is available as a pop-up window where referenced.

Each hyperdocument consists of two part. The *hypertext* contains the full hyperdocument as one large HyperCard stack. A small file, the *personal file*, is a template for individual users to copy onto local storage (hard disk or floppy). The personal file stores individual modifications and other personalizations the user makes to the hypertext stack, which may be distributed on CD-ROM and thus may not be modifiable.

Some of the personalizations include methods for recording thoughts and making notes. The interface contains provisions for annotating individual nodes and annotating links between nodes. Annotations remain attached to the annotated object, and there are options for automatically viewing link annotations when the link is invoked. The node annotation is signaled through the use of an icon on the navigation panels of the hyperdocument (Figure II.3).

A bookmark facility and a user log are available. The bookmark facility allows the user to write a brief note explaining the importance of the node. The user log is a free-form floating text window that can be called at any point and be used for any purpose. More ambitious users can add new links. User inputs are saved to the personal file when the browsing session is concluded and can be reloaded at the start of the next browsing session.

14.2 Webs

A web is the collection of all links between all nodes. There may be many webs for a given set of nodes, each web depending on the interests and needs of the web's author. Thus, a single set of nodes affords many different interpretations, depending on the web that ties the nodes in the hyperdocument together. The hypertext comes with a predefined web, the *base web*, consisting of the index links, Cybermap links, animation links, definition links, reference links, and display links.

Figure II.3

Hypertext user interface with navigation panels

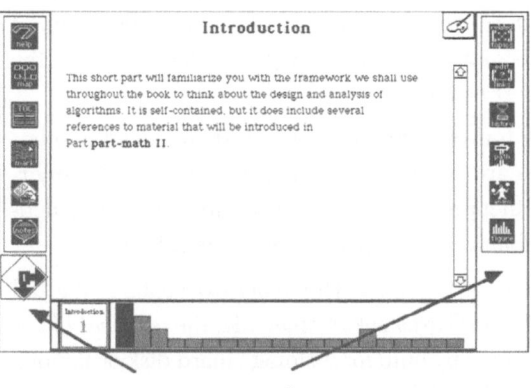

navigation panels

Because it is important for the user to be able to modify the contents and links in the hypertext, we added tools to allow users to create their own nodes and, in a limited sense, their own webs. Since we thought that no single user would want to create all the links needed to make sense out of hundreds of nodes, we decided that users could add links to the predefined web but not delete base web links. This also ensures that the work of the original author will be preserved. To create a link between nodes, the user chooses an anchor in the initial node. The anchor can consist of either highlighted text or an entry into the "related topics" field. The user then navigates to the destination node and completes the link. The information that defines the new link is written to the user's personal stack. To add their own nodes, users must create a new card in the personal stack, and link it to the main stack.

14.3 Guided Tour Through the Gloor/Dynes Hypertext Engine

After double-clicking on the hypertext stack, users are brought to the first text card (Figure II.4).

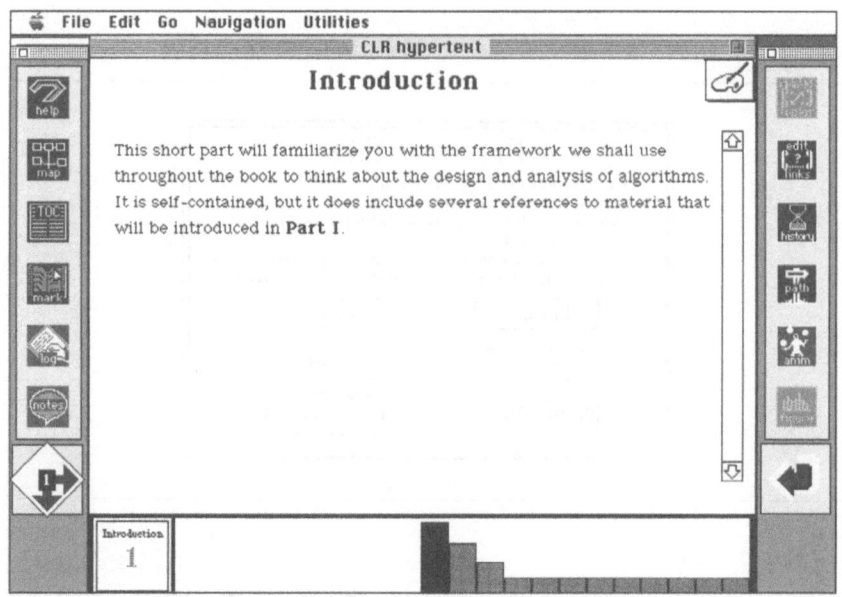

Figure II.4

First card of *Introduction to Algorithms* hypertext stack

To create a personal file, users have to select the command Personal File of the menu Utilities which brings up the personal file dialog box (Figure II.5). Clicking the Create button creates a new personal file. Without a personal file, personal bookmarks and links will not be saved, and it is impossible to create node annotations and a global log book entry.[1]

If users wish to create a bookmark, they click the 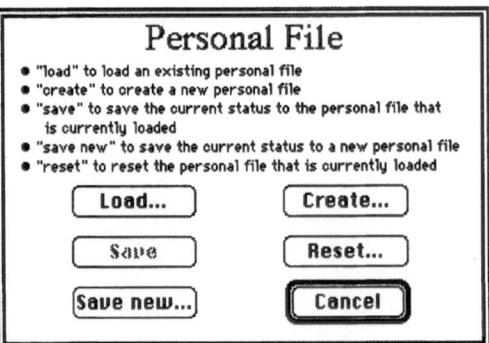-button on the left navigation panel. This brings up the Book Marks dialog (Figure II.6), where a new entry can be created using the Make Mark button. After being prompted for an annotation, a new entry is inserted into the list.

By calling the Book Marks dialog from any other node, selecting an entry, and clicking the Visit Node button, the user can return to the marked node.

New links can be created similarly using the -Edit Links button. On the Links selection dialog (top of Figure II.7), the Create Link button has to be clicked first.

A Create Link window (bottom of Figure II.7) is then opened and stays open while users can select the destination node using, for example, the navigation diamond. Once the button Mark Link Destination has been clicked, a new link is generated between the destination node and the node where the Create Link button has been clicked.

Figure II.5

Personal file
dialog

Personal File

- "load" to load an existing personal file
- "create" to create a new personal file
- "save" to save the current status to the personal file that is currently loaded
- "save new" to save the current status to a new personal file
- "reset" to reset the personal file that is currently loaded

[**Load...**]   [**Create...**]

[**Save**]   [**Reset...**]

[**Save new...**]   [**Cancel**]

---

1 This approach differs from most Web browsers that silently store user-specific information somewhere on the local hard disk.

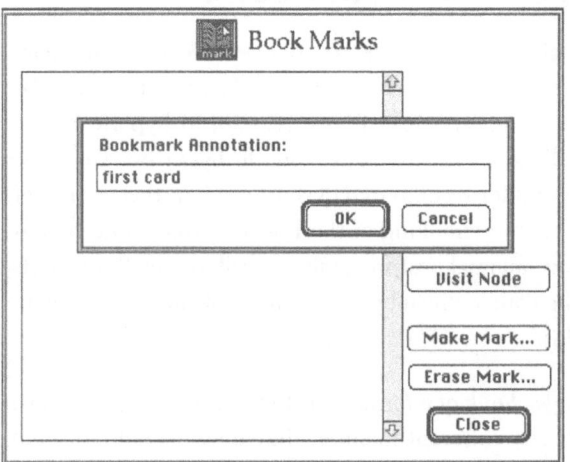

Figure II.6

Book Marks
dialog

Figure II.7

The two dialog
boxes for creat-
ing a link

14.4 Conversion to Hypertext

This section gives anecdotal evidence of our experience collected while converting the extensive university-level textbook *Introduction to Algorithms* by Tom Cormen, Charles Leiserson, and Ron Rivest [Cor90] to hypertext. The textbook is particularly well suited for the conversion to hypertext, since the text is organized in hierarchical form composed of short sections that are rather self-contained. Nevertheless, the chunking of the linear textbook into hypertext nodes required extensive manual postprocessing by subject-matter experts (students who had taken the course given by one of the book authors) to maintain the chunking principles:

1. *A node should be a single chunk of information.* To be effective, nodes must be expressed in a logically coherent manner; they must be able to stand alone and convey their information content without the need for constant reference to other nodes. Conversions of serial text that construct "nodes" by putting each succeeding 25 lines of text into a separate unit fail to meet this criterion.

2. *The node should be of a length short enough to fit within a single screen* but also long enough to contain a substantial thought or concept. The single screen concept is of value since all the information in a self-contained node is visually available without scrolling. This enables the user to relate concepts in the node without having to flip between separate chunks of text. The hypertext concept also tries to decompose larger concepts into smaller ideas. Because psychologists tell us that the human short-term memory is not able to store more than four to nine information items, even a small Macintosh 9 inch screen is of appropriate size to display one idea composed of four to nine sentences. Nodes larger than an individual screen are contained in a scrolling field. Although scrolling fields are aesthetically unappealing and not the most effective method of displaying large amounts of text, the alternative would have been to have parts of the node on separate screens, which would have made viewing separate parts of a node similar to viewing different nodes. The sense of a node as a unit was more important than the slight disadvantage caused by scrolling screens.

The original textbook was produced using the L_AT_EX macro package for T_EX [Lam85]. The sophisticated referencing facilities available in L_AT_EX, which were used extensively in the text source, offered major advantages in converting the text. As used, L_AT_EX enabled the abstraction of citations, index entries, definitions, Figures, and proofs. These methods associate one region of text with other regions of text, figures, index entries, or other elements. L_AT_EX also offers great control over the hierarchical structure of the document, which allowed a mapping of the text into detail levels. The smallest hierarchical structures used in the L_AT_EX source were subsections or subheadings, which were often of the right size and content to constitute a node.

In converting the L_AT_EX source text to nodes, the text making up each node was written to individual files, and references to that particular node were noted in lists according to the reference type. From these files, a utility program created nodes in the hyperdocument. Intrinsic links between nodes were generated automatically using relationships between nodes as defined in the L_AT_EX reference lists. In this sense, L_AT_EX enabled us to automate the generation of structural links in the same manner that SGML, HTML, or HyTime [New91] might.

One of the more difficult aspects of converting the text arose from the mathematical nature of the source text. Rather than laboriously recreate each mathematical expression, an interpreter was written in HyperTalk that translated most of L_AT_EX's in-line math and text formatting commands. Because the Macintosh and HyperCard do not support the wide range of symbols found in the source text, we developed two separate fonts to provide all the necessary math symbols. Additionally, we manually converted and edited 1230 formulas as bitmaps, because they could not be displayed on the screen using our custom fonts. Also, we scanned in and edited 327 Figures.

Cybertools: Hierarchy with Hiermap, Viewfinder, and Navigation Diamond

The Gloor/Dynes hypertext engine offers a unique way of browsing in a hypertext document on different levels of complexity using two new navigation tools: the *navigation diamond* and the *viewfinder*.

15.1 The Navigation Diamond

The navigation diamond (Figure II.8) consists of a set of buttons enclosed in a diamond-shaped border. The buttons contain arrows pointing left, up, right, and down. The center of the navigation diamond displays the detail level (see Figure II.2) of the current node. The navigation diamond allows the user to travel between nodes by level or by following a path.

Traversal by levels using the navigation diamond is tantamount to reading the text at various levels. Clicking on the left arrow will take readers to the previous node of the same level. Clicking the up arrow will take them up a level, and clicking the down arrow has an analogous effect. Using this tool, a user can step back to see an overview of what is being presented by just hitting the up-arrow button.

Figure II.8

Navigation
diamond

15.2 Viewfinder

The viewfinder is located at the bottom of the text card. It gives the reader a graphical overview of the hierarchical context of the actual node (Figure II.9).

The icon at the left side of the viewfinder depicts the chapter to which the node belongs. The long bar at the right shows the hierarchical context. The actual node is shown in white; the nodes to the right and to the left of the actual node are shown as horizontal gray bars. The left and right orientation is in relation to the main path, which is based on the original ordering of the nodes in the textbook. The height of a bar represents the hierarchy level of the node, with level 1 nodes having the highest bars.

Figure II.10 illustrates the use of the viewfinder for the Web version of this book on the Birkhauser Web site. As marked by the red arrow, the user is currently reading the third level 2 node in the book. Because this version uses advanced JavaScript features, it needs Netscape 3.0 to be fully functional, although it will also work in restricted mode with Netscape release 2.

Figure II.9

Viewfinder

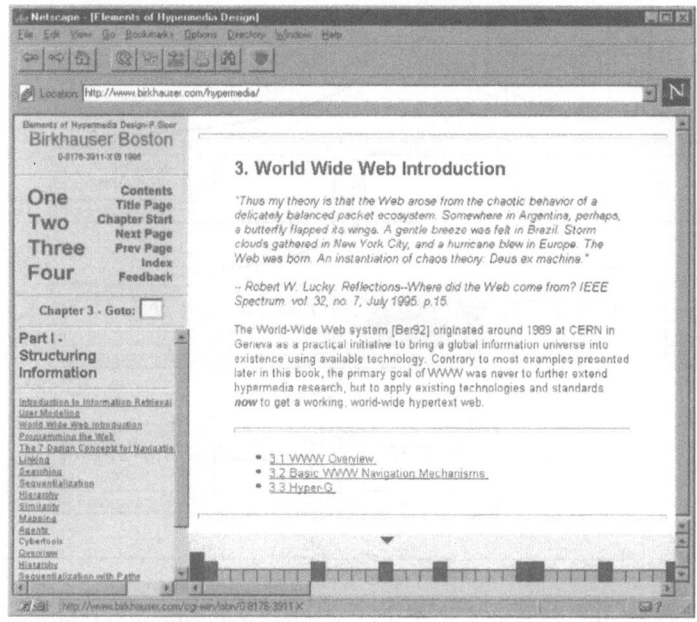

Figure II.10

Screen dump of
Web version of
this book. Note
the viewfinder in
the lower right
frame.

15.3 Hiermap

Overview maps are one of the most useful means for navigation in cyberspace
[Utt89]. The purpose of an overview map is at least twofold:

1. Readers see where they are in the document. The context of the actual
   node is displayed in a fish–eye view fashion [Fur86] to help in orientation.

2. Readers see where they can go from the actual location. They perceive
   which links are starting from their location in the document.

In our overview map implementation (Figure II.11), a node is represented
by a box enclosing the title of the node. The map consists of many boxes,
arranged hierarchically: there can be up to four rows of boxed node titles visible on the map, corresponding to the hierarchically structured hyperdocument. The current node is displayed in a highlighted box in the center of the
map. A vertical line is drawn from that node to its parent node in the next

Figure II.11

Hiermap of
Animated
Algorithms

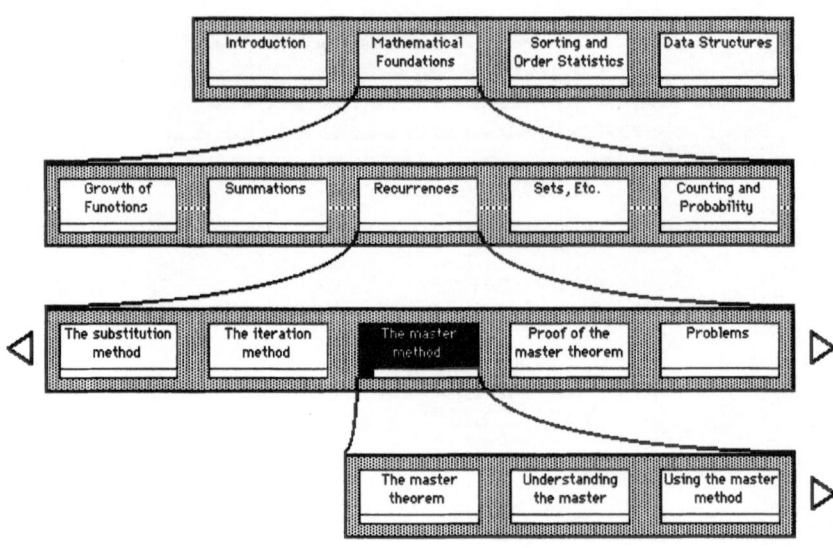

higher row. The remaining boxes in each row are filled with siblings of the corresponding node. For current nodes that are in levels 1 through 3, the result is a fish-eye view of the structure of the serial text, as viewed from the current node.

The map allows users to zoom in the hierarchical node structure in a fish–eye view fashion. If users wish to see the subnode structure of a particular node without actually jumping there, they can cause the display of the most prominent subnodes surrounding the particular node by clicking in the corresponding box.

In addition to displaying contextual information, the map serves another purpose: it displays nodes that have been visited. Beneath each box, a slider represents the fraction of *offspring nodes* that have already been read. Offspring nodes include all nodes that have that node as a parent, grandparent, and so on. Thus, the browser can tell at a glance which subjects have been explored.

Besides support for hierarchical navigation, the Gloor/Dynes hypertext engine includes sophisticated path editing and guided tour facilities.

CHAPTER 16

Cybertools: Sequentialization _with_ Paths

Although the Gloor/Dynes hypertext engine primarily supports hierarchical hypertext, care has been taken to give access to the sequential structure of underlying documents.

The path concept greatly expands the usefulness of a hyperdocument as a learning tool. One of the advantages of hypertext is the ability to browse through information space without restriction, each user impressing his or her own order on the information structure. While this is of great value in finding and following interesting threads, it is contrary to the method employed to teach students in the classroom. Teachers who are attempting to mold the knowledge of the students into a coherent representation of the subject matter usually have an ordered list of elements they believe are essential to the field. Traditional textbooks are merely expressions by various authors of this ordered list. To improve the usability of hyperdocuments for classroom use, the Gloor/Dynes hypertext engine contains path creation facilities by which the instructor can create a sequential ordering out of the hierarchically structured nodes in the hyperdocument.

The user can create paths by editing an existing path or creating a new path from scratch. The path editor consists of two parts: the large-scale path editor used for the copying of many sequential nodes from various sources, and the detail-level editor used to control the order of individual nodes. In either mode, the user has the ability to add path annotations to the path links in order to explain the ordering of information better.

The easiest ways to create a new path is to use the history list (Figure II.12) of the Gloor/Dynes hypertext engine.

Because the history list stores all locations that have been visited, prospective path creators just need to visit sequentially all the nodes they would like to include into their path. In the large-scale path editor (Figure II.13), they can then load the history for further editing.

The large-scale path editor represents sequential nodes as bars, the height of the bar representing the detail level of the node. This representation, similar to the viewfinder navigation tool, allows the user to select nodes easily from entire sections or chapters of the text and paste them into the path being edited. Clicking on the bars shows information about that node, and allows editing of the path annotation.

Figure II.12

History list of Gloor/Dynes hypertext engine

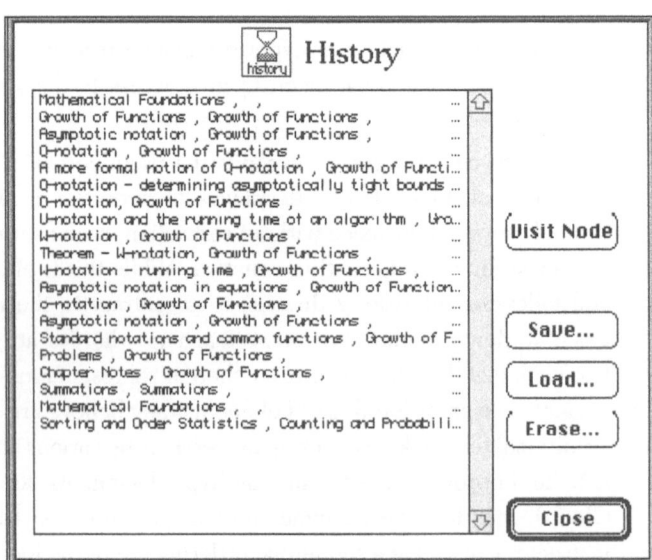

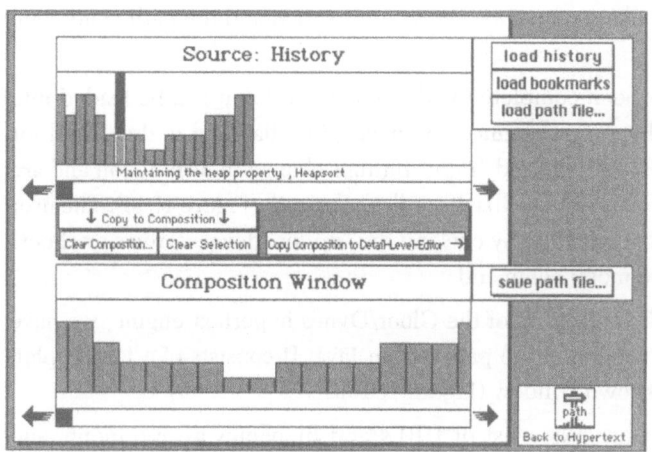

Figure II.13

The large-scale
path editor

The detail-level editor (Figure II.14) positions more detailed representations
of individual nodes along a path in the order they will be displayed. The order

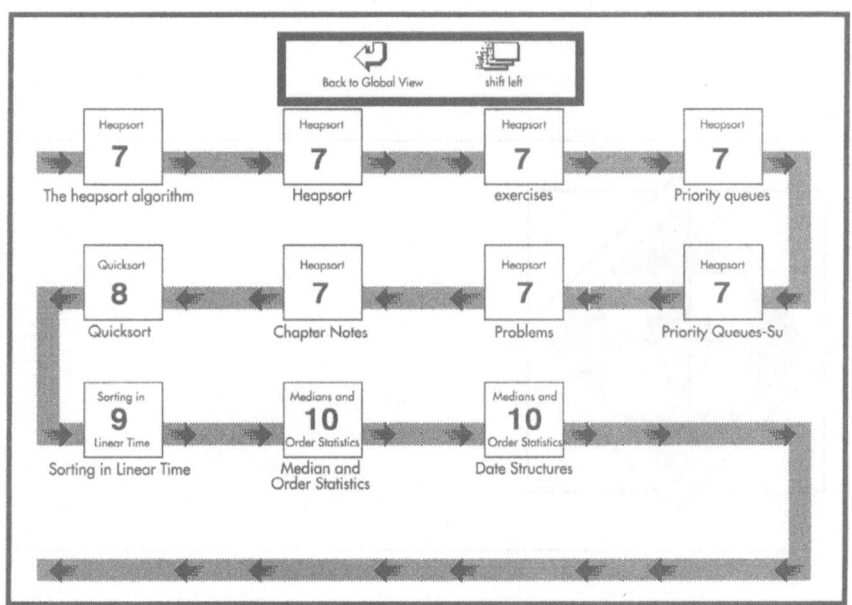

Figure II.14

The detail-level
path editor

of the nodes can be changed by dragging the nodes to the desired position on the path. Again, clicking on a node shows information and the path annotation for that node.

Once a path has been completed with the path editor, it can be loaded into the Gloor/Dynes hypertext engine. The navigation diamond is then used for following the path: the "left" and "right" buttons change their function and are used to navigate "forward" and "backward" on the path (Figure II.15). The user can leave the path at any time by clicking the "up" or "down" arrows or choosing the appropriate menu command.

In addition to the path tools of the Gloor/Dynes hypertext engine, we have developed a Web version of the path tool in Java. It consists of a Java applet, which resides in its own window (Figure II.16).

The path applet accepts a list of URLs and filenames as arguments and allows users to browse sequentially through the Web following a predefined path. The panel in the lower half of the path tool displays all URLs on the path and gives the reader the capability to jump directly to any location on the path.

Figure II.15

Use of navigation diamond to follow a path

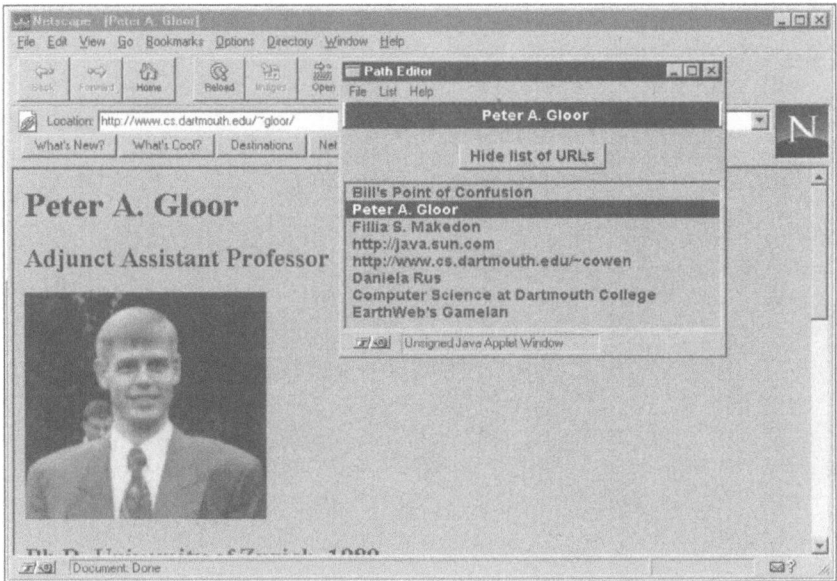

Figure II.16

Java-based path tool

Cybertools: Similarity *with* Cybermap

Not only is it easy to lie with maps, it's essential. To portray mean-ingful relationships for a complex, three-dimensional world on a flat sheet of paper or a video screen, a map must distort reality.

—Mark Monmonier
[Mon91]

In chapters 5 through 13 we surveyed existing tools for the navigation in cyber-space. Unfortunately, these tools, in particular the more sophisticated and pow-erful ones, need a substantial amount of manual preprocessing in order to transform the document structure into machine-readable format. In our own system, Cybermap, one of our main design goals was to eliminate the manual preprocessing phase. Cybermap automatically generates overview maps for textual documents. By integrating dynamic linking and automatic link genera-tion into the automatic generation of an overview map, we get a unique tool for navigation in cyberspace. Cybermap creates a tree-shaped graphical layout for a collection of nodes by clustering related nodes by content. The resulting overview map can be used for quick access to information and data filtering in large information spaces. Cybermap incorporates the concept of hyperdrawers to get a means for the partitioning of nodes into ordered sequences. Cybermap either complements existing navigational aids for hyperdocuments or provides a self-sufficient navigation tool for browsing in a document. In addition, Cybermap offers the capability of horizontal growth and easy hypertextualization of nonhypertextual documents without restricting the use of already installed browsing mechanisms.

17.1 Motivation

There are different systems trying to assist in IR, orientation, and navigation in huge collections of information. One of the best known examples is WAIS from Thinking Machines Corporation [Kah91]. WAIS allows full-text search in free-text databases. Although WAIS offers a flexible interface and does an excellent job in quickly searching huge data collections, it does not address some cognitive problems. As a motivation for our approach, consider Figure II.17 which shows a screen dump of the Macintosh WAIS interface.

In Figure II.17 users formulated a query in plain English in searching for background information on Kenya. Before submitting their query, the users had to decide which databases to search. Based on previous knowledge about the

Figure II.17

WAIS Macintosh
user interface

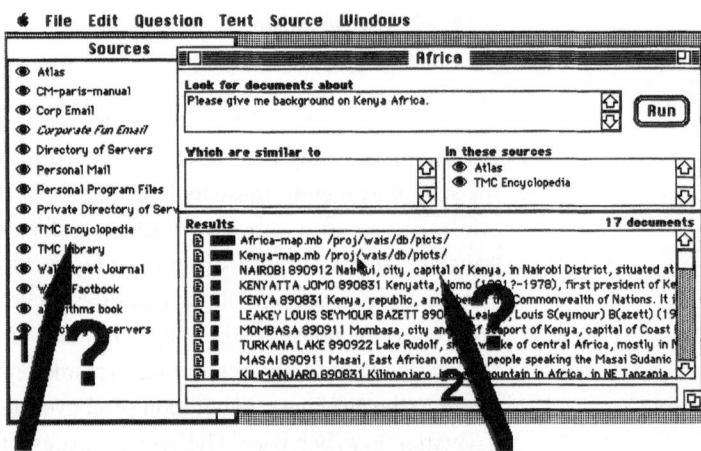

What is in TMC Encyclopedia?   What did I retrieve? From which source?

contents of the databases, their decision was to search the databases Atlas and TMC Encyclopedia. But how does a first-time user know what is contained in which database (arrow 1 in Figure II.17). Obviously it would be very helpful to get a self-explaining overview or a table of contents of the data contained in a particular database.

In Figure II.17 WAIS returned a large number of text files as answer to the query. Unfortunately the answer is presented as a textual list that can easily grow to a few hundred items (arrow 2 in Figure II.17). Although WAIS offers sophisticated mechanisms for narrowing or expanding the search, the general problem of representing the retrieved information in an easily understandable way persists. It would be very helpful to get a graphical representation of the answer that could be perceived at one glance.

The general problem we address in this chapter is the *automatic generation of navigational aids like structural overview maps* of large collections of unstructured data and the related problem of quickly presenting an *overview of retrieved data*. In this and the following chapters, we present the theoretical foundations of Cybermap, the algorithms used for the implementation, as well as sample applications based on actual prototype implementations of Cybermap in HyperCard on the Macintosh and in C* on the massively parallel supercomputer Connection Machine CM-2 [Hil87] as well as in C and Java for the World Wide Web.

17.2 Why Overview Maps?

Overview maps are one of the best tools for the orientation and navigation in hypermedia documents [Utt89][Fei88][Tri88]. Authors disagree, however, on whether these maps can be produced automatically. Although there are systems that offer automatically generated overview maps, including Intermedia and Hyper-G, as Bernstein claims [Ber88], it may be impossible to generate satisfactory and comprehensible maps without understanding the contents of the documents.

Bernstein's system does not automatically generate overview maps but instead shifts the burden of cartography entirely to the author. Bernstein lists two main reasons for the difficulty of the automatic generation of overview maps:

1. A suitable graph structure for a two-dimensional projection of the generally multidimensional hypertext network is hard to find. In particular, this task is impossible without knowledge about the contents of the document.

2. It is impossible to draw more than at most 20 node-icons on a screen. For every document that contains more nodes, many nodes must be suppressed to keep the screen from becoming a meaningless tangle. This requirement demands knowledge not only about the contents of the document but also about the intentions and goals of the reader.

We agree with Bernstein in the reasons that it is so difficult to generate an overview map automatically. But instead of shifting this task to the hypertext author, we try to solve the underlying problems. Our approach is different from the Intermedia and Hyper-G solution in that we do not use the actual linking structure of the document directly. Instead, we analyze the contents of the nodes and of the hyperdocument by using automatic indexing and clustering techniques described in Chapter 1. Based on this knowledge, we compute a structure graph for the overview map. This structure graph has nothing to do with the actual node-link structure of the hyperdocument.

We thus address the problem of automatic generation of structural overview maps of large collections of loosely structured data and the related problem of quickly presenting an overview of retrieved data. We first depict an ideal solution. We then address step by step the problems raised by the ideal solution and describe a possible implementation. We later extend our system to include hierarchies of Cybermaps for very large node sets. We also present cybertrees, a minimum-spanning-tree-based algorithm for the automatic generation of tree-shaped overview maps.

17.3 The Ideal Cybermap

The ideal Cybermap pops up every time users want to read a hyperdocument.[1] It accompanies them during the whole reading process. It can serve as a starting point by giving readers a graphical outline of the document, but it also shows them all the time where they are in the document by reflecting their navigational movements.

---

1 As our society shifts towards complete information linkage, we approach the cyberspace society described in the books of William Gibson [Gib84]. We hope that the society we get will be different from the one Gibson describes, but the concept of the tool described here fits well into Gibson's cyberspace; as Gibson's electronic agents do, our tool tries to help the reader to navigate in a complex virtual environment without the reader's having to understand the inner workings of the tool. Therefore we have titled our navigation tool Cybermap.

Figure II.18 shows a schematic sample screen of the use of Cybermap. The user reads a textual document in the lower left corner of the screen.[2] The Cybermap window in the upper right corner of the screen shows a graphic overview map of the document. The Cybermap window serves as the primary navigation aid. The fundamental idea is that the original hypertext document remains unmodified, while the Cybermap shows an organized view of the data.[3] Figure II.19 displays a screen dump of the actual system where the user is about to browse a document about dinosaurs. The Cybermap window is located in the upper left corner.

The purpose of Cybermap is threefold:

1. It gives an overview of the information contained in the document.

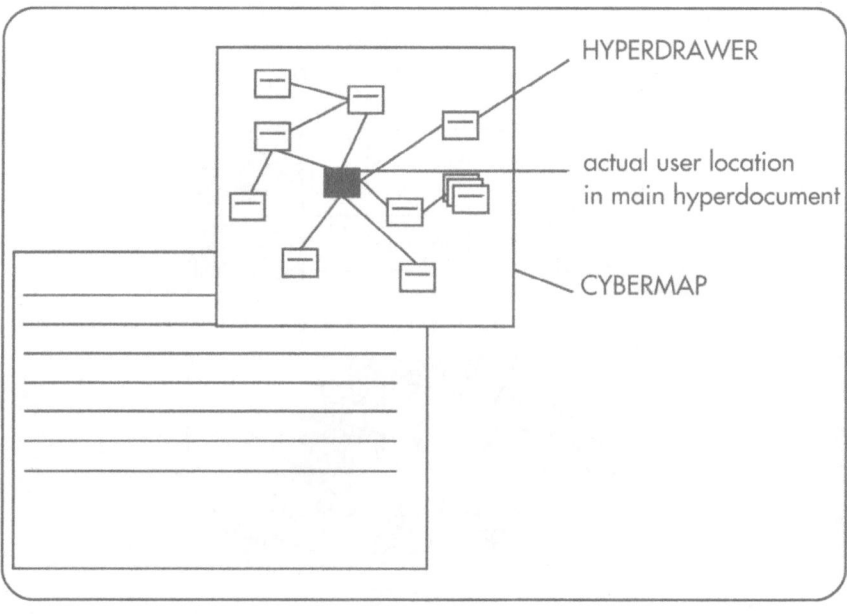

Figure II.18

Schematic view of the use of Cybermap

---

2 It is of no importance whether Cybermap is applied to a sequential document or a hyperdocument. Therefore the terms "document" and "hyperdocument" are used interchangeably to designate the basic document on which Cybermap is applied.

3 Cybermap can also be used to browse plain (non-hypertext) documents.

2. Users see where they are in the document. In Figure II.19 the location of the user is marked by the black rectangle in the middle of the Cybermap window.

3. Users see where to go next by perceiving which logical links are connected to their actual location.

One rectangle in the Cybermap window represents not only one node of the hyperdocument but a collection of related nodes. The Cybermap representation of such a collection of related nodes, a *hyperdrawer*, offers a means of partitioning the hyperdocument into a set of smaller, manageable fragments. This partitioning can be disjoint or overlapping: one node may belong to exactly one or to various hyperdrawers. In our work we restrict the distribution of nodes into hyperdrawers to the simplest case: every node belongs

Figure II.19

Screen dump of Macintosh Cybermap implementation

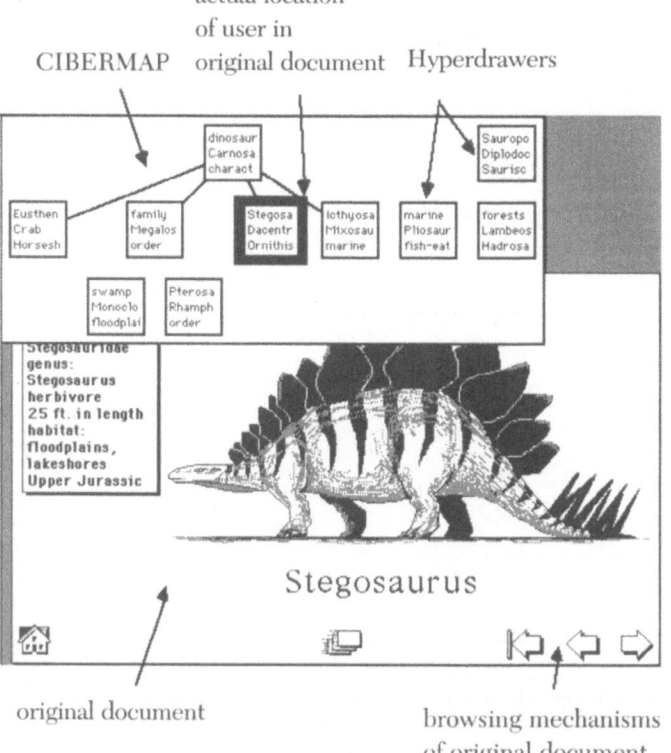

actual location
of user in
CIBERMAP   original document   Hyperdrawers

original document

browsing mechanisms
of original document

to exactly one hyperdrawer.[4] Therefore we get a disjoint partitioning of nodes into hyperdrawers (Figure II.20). The hyperdrawers are functionally equivalent to the notion of clusters in information retrieval. We coined a new term to add the notion of sequentiality inside the cluster because the nodes in a hyperdrawer have to be ordered meaningfully to offer some sort of guided tour through the hyperdrawer.

The algorithm for the automatic generation of the Cybermap is based on fish–eye view filtering. Cybermap can be used for the production of hyperdocuments written from scratch, but it is more useful for adding similarity links to existing hyper- and nonhyperdocuments. As has been mentioned by various authors [Fou90] [Irl90] [Ber90], the transformation of linear documents into hypertextual form, and particularly the automatic generation of links for related nodes, poses a serious problem. A shallow approach, which resembles the algorithm used in the link apprentice (see Chapter 6), is used to find the structure of the hyperdocument.

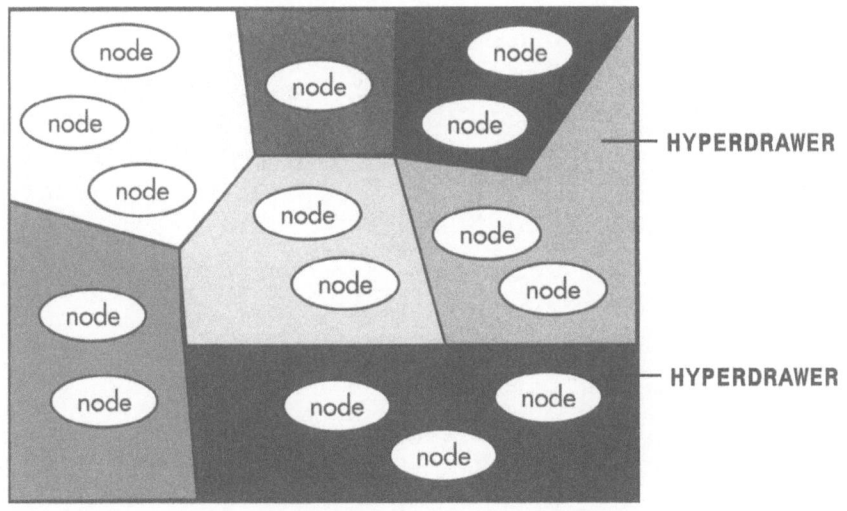

Figure II.20

Partitioning of nodes into hyperdrawers

HYPERDRAWER

HYPERDRAWER

---

4 It is straightforward to put a node into more than one hyperdrawer. Instead of putting the node into just one hyperdrawer, the node is placed into all hyperdrawers where the similarity of node and hyperdrawer is above a certain threshold.

CHAPTER 18

Cybermap:

System Architecture

This chapter identifies the main theoretical problems that need to be solved for an implementation of Cybermap: the identification of the hyperdrawers and the model of the user. It then describes the different Cybermap implementations built by our team over the past five years.

18.1 Identification of Hyperdrawers

To partition the nodes into hyperdrawers, three related problems have to be solved.

Problem 1 is to put related nodes into the same hyperdrawer. The hyperdrawers have to be identified, and related nodes have to be grouped together. An easy way to do this for textual nodes is to cluster the nodes by using automatic indexing techniques (described in Chapter 1).

In order to find an even distribution among the hyperdrawers, we have to identify a hash function F (Figure II.21) with the following *ideal* properties:

- Because of ergonomic and cognitive aspects F should distribute the nodes among the hyperdrawers as equally as possible. Ideally every hyperdrawer

Figure II.21

Hyperdrawer
hash function F

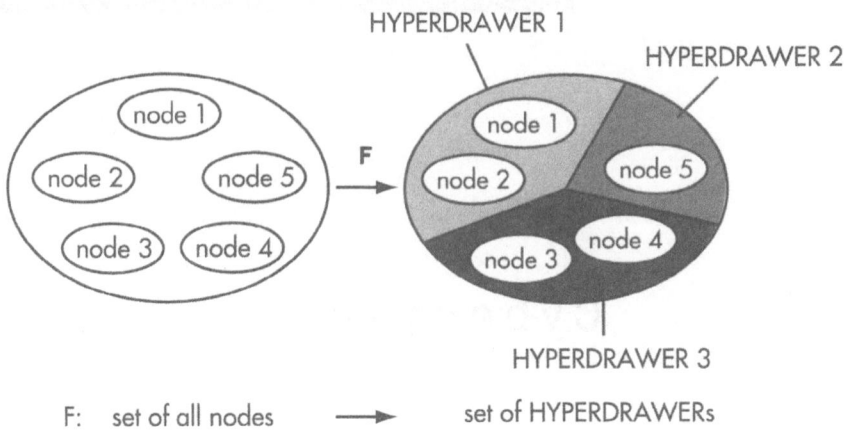

F: set of all nodes ⟶ set of HYPERDRAWERs

should contain the same number of nodes: $\forall$ i, k: **#** elements of hyperdrawer$_i$ = **#** elements of hyperdrawer$_k$.

- F should ensure that there are not more than about 20 hyperdrawers. If there are too many boxes on the screen, it gets too cluttered: number of hyperdrawers $\leq$ 20.[1]

- F has to group together in one hyperdrawer the most related nodes. This means that the contents of every node have to be analyzed and a measure for the affinity between nodes has to be defined.

Problem 2 is to name the hyperdrawers. Meaningful names for the groups, or hyperdrawers, have to be identified.

Problem 3 is to identify the topology. After the hyperdrawers and the partitioning hash function F have been found, the hyperdrawers have to be drawn in the Cybermap in as informative and aesthetically appealing a manner as possible. The easiest approach would be to distribute the hyperdrawers at random on the map. Ideally, however, one would like to put more information about the

---

1 The number 20 may seem somewhat arbitrary and in contradiction to the human user interface guideline of not using more than 5 to 9 different items at the same time. But 9 items are often insufficient to show the structure of a complex document. In our tests we got best results with up to 20 nodes.

structure of the document into the Cybermap. Therefore the document structure has to be identified based on an analysis of the contents of the document. The linking structure of the hyperdrawers has a priori nothing to do with existing links in the hyperdocument.

18.2 The Model of the User

The Cybermap offers not only a generic overview of the whole hyperdocument, but also a personalized view of the document based on the actual model of the user. This means that the system has to keep at least two knowledge bases about the user:

1. *User profile.* The user profile contains data about the user's interests and preferences. This data are manipulated directly by the user and can be changed during the whole session.

2. *Reading history of the user.* The Cybermap has to show to users at least where they have been in the document. An advanced version of the system should also try to update the model of the user concerning user capabilities and user preferences by analyzing the reading behavior. The system would then be able to make better guesses about the interests of the reader.

The user model is of fundamental importance for a flexible and informative overview map. In our prototype implementations, the user profile consists of only an interest list derived from the index. The user profile is used to reduce the number of nodes shown in the Cybermap. Only the nodes of interest to the user are shown in the hyperdrawers. The filtering is done by comparing the interest list with the contents of the nodes.

Following the taxonomy of Chapter 2, we currently have an analytical cognitive, individual explicit user model with long-term capabilities where the user is in the agent role. An obvious extension to the interest list would be the integration of a thesaurus to reduce the number of entries in the index for the specification of the interest list. A more sophisticated user model would also try to analyze the reading behavior of the user in order to make guesses about other nodes that have not been specified in the user profile but might be of potential interest to the reader. This means that implicit capabilities would be added to the user model.

18.3 Application Structure

Cybermap is used for two purposes:

1. The map is always *in relation to the actual location of the user* in the hyper-document; it shows users where they are in the document. This can easily be implemented by highlighting the actual hyperdrawer.

2. It shows the user where to go.[2] Based on the interests of the user Cybermap shows the user other nodes of potential interest. Using a DOI function (degree of interest)[3] the most interesting subset of nodes is selected.

The content analysis of the document is based on an index. Ideally an index is already available in the document. Otherwise an index is generated using automatic indexing techniques as described in Chapter 1 (Figure II.22).

The algorithm for the generation of the overview map has to satisfy the following basic requirements:

* Every node must have its place in the overview map. If the user jumps from any node to the Cybermap, there must be a well-defined place for the representation of this node on the map.

* Based on a content analysis of the nodes, related nodes are grouped together into the same hyperdrawer.

* Because of ergonomic and cognitive aspects, the distribution of the nodes into the hyperdrawers has to be approximately well balanced. Every hyperdrawer must have approximately the same number of nodes.

* Repeated runs of the algorithm must deliver the same Cybermap representation for the same set of boundary conditions *(repeatability)*. The algorithm must also be resistant to small changes in the boundary conditions *(stability)*. Small changes to the user profile should result in only small changes to the Cybermap.

---

2 An obvious extension would be to show users also where they have been by marking all read nodes on the Cybermap. A sort of "breadcrumb" mechanism [Ber88] has already partly been implemented in Cybermap. (See Figure II.29 for an example.)

3 For a detailed explanation of the fish eye view concept and the DOI function see Chapter 11.

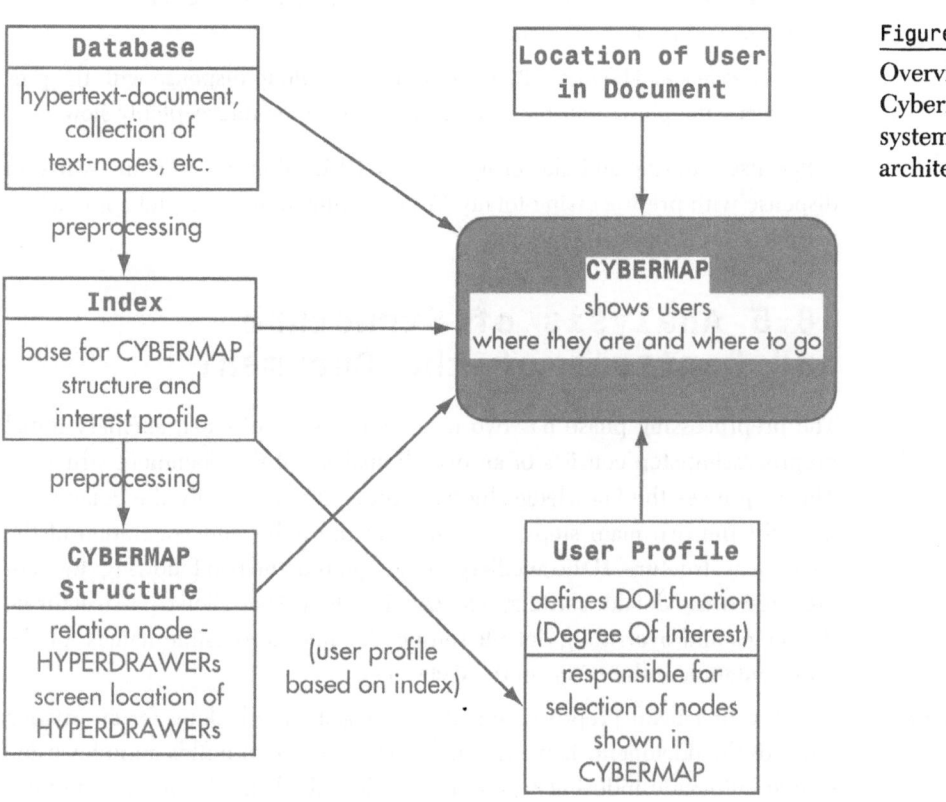

Figure II.22

Overview of the Cybermap system architecture

18.4 Preprocessing

In the preprocessing phase, the index and the Cybermap structure are generated so that the map can be updated at run time as fast as possible. If the user adds or deletes nodes in the original document, the preprocessing step has to be repeated for the following reasons:

- *Tailoring.* Often the preprocessing phase is done by somebody who is more knowledgeable than the final reader of the document. By introducing a preprocessing phase, the knowledgeable user is able to tune the run time generation of the overview map. To get an optimal overview map, the user can modify additional parameters and add knowledge about the internal structure of the document.

- *Performance*. Theoretically it would be possible to dispense with the preprocessing phase, but the updates would become unacceptably slow.

Because indexing and clustering are very CPU intensive, it is impossible to dispense with preprocessing totally. We are using an incremental approach to minimize the preprocessing phase.

18.5 Analysis of Structure and Contents of the Document

The preprocessing phase has two main steps. An additional, ancillary initial preprocessing step consists of an overall analysis of the document structure. This step gives the knowledgeable user the ability to modify the default settings for the two main steps: generation of the index and generation of the Cybermap structure. If the ancillary step is ignored, the two following steps are executed using default settings. The ancillary first steps allows prestructuring the nodes and overriding default settings for finding sensible names for the representation of the nodes in the Cybermap.

Generation of the Index

In the first main preprocessing step, the system is looking for an existing index of the document. If there is no index, the system builds an index using simple automatic indexing techniques as described in Chapter 1. The most recent Cybermap implementation is using the SWISH system to build the index. The index is used afterward for:

- The automatic generation of a structure graph of the document based on the occurrence of index terms in the nodes of the document.
- The generation of a list of index entries where users may select the terms most related to their interests. We call this list of index entries an *interest list*.

Generation of the Cybermap Structure

The second preprocessing step is more important. Here the Cybermap structure is generated. The generation of the Cybermap is based on the index. To find a suitable map structure, a two-step process is used:

1. Find the hyperdrawers. In this step, the nodes are clustered (Figure II.23). Similar nodes are identified using the index by assigning a key word vector $D_i = (d_{1i}, d_{2i}, d_{3i}, ...d_{ni})$ to every node n_i where d_{ki} represents the

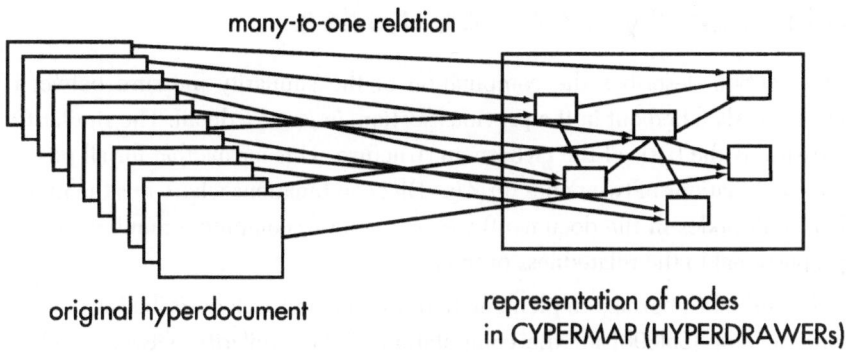

many-to-one relation

original hyperdocument

representation of nodes
in CYPERMAP (HYPERDRAWERs)

Figure II.23

Relation "nodes
in document–
hyperdrawers in
Cybermap"

weighted key word T_k assigned to node n_i. The weight for each key word is computed based on the key word frequency and the inverse document frequency of the key word. The similarity between two nodes is based on the similarity between the corresponding key word vectors [Sal89b] [Sal96]. It is defined as an inner vector product (dot product):

$$sim(D_iD_j) = \sum_{1 \leq l \leq n} d_{li}d_{lj}$$

Finally the most frequently used key word in all nodes of a particular hyperdrawer is selected as hyperdrawer label. (This process is described in detail in the next section.)

2. Find the relations between the hyperdrawers in the Cybermap. The drawing of these structural links is not mandatory, but it helps the reader to get a better overview of the structure of the document. All possible links between hyperdrawers are calculated first, using the similarity measure defined in step 1. Afterward the most related hyperdrawers are connected by links. The number of links is determined using a dynamically adjustable threshold value.

Once all structure links are calculated, the hyperdrawers for the nodes and the links between the hyperdrawers are drawn. To achieve a better hyperdrawer-link layout, the most frequently linked hyperdrawers are drawn as roots of a tree at the top of the screen. Less frequently linked hyperdrawers are arranged farther down.

18.6 Computing the Similarity Between Nodes

This section describes the computation of the similarity measure between nodes, as sketched out in the previous section, in greater detail. The similarity measure is the basis of the Cybermap structure. This means that for all possible combinations of two nodes ($[n \times (n-1)]/2$ combinations where n is the number of all nodes in the document) we are trying to compute a number that is proportional to the relatedness of the two nodes.

The initial Cybermap implementation uses an approach described by Salton and Buckley [Sal89b] for the computation of the similarity between nodes, based on a key word index of the whole document. We may use an index that is available from an external source or automatically generate one using automatic indexing techniques (see Chapter 1).

The subsequent computation of the similarities between nodes happens in five main steps (see Figure II.24 for an example):

1. Count the number of occurrences of each key word in each node (node frequency). Example: the key word "human-computer interaction" in Figure II.24 has node frequency 1 in nodes 1 and 2 and node frequency 2 in node 3.

2. Count the number of occurrences of each key word in the whole document. Each key word is counted only once per node (document frequency). Example: the key word "human-computer interaction" in Figure II.24 has document frequency 3.

3. Compute the weighted key word vectors of each node (column 2 in Figure II.24). The weight for each key word is calculated based on the node frequency, the inverse document frequency of the key word, and the total number of nodes in the document (see Chapter 1).[4] The exact formula used is:

   Weight of key word T_i in node k:

   $$d_{ik} = nodeFrequency_{ik} \times \log_2 \left(\frac{numOfNodes}{documentFrequency_i} \right)$$

   Example: the key word "human-computer interaction" in Figure II.24 has weight $1*\log(7/3) = 1.222392$ in nodes 1 and 2 and weight $2*\log(7/3) = 2.444785$ in node 3.

---

4 For a full motivation of the use of $\log_2$ and inverse document frequency, see [Jon72].

4. Assign a key word vector $D_k = (d_{1k}, d_{2k}, d_{3k}, \ldots d_{nk})$ to every node n_k, where d_{ik} represents the weight of key word T_i assigned to node n_k.

5. Compute the similarity between the nodes using the key word vectors D_k. The similarity between two nodes is based on the similarity between the corresponding key word vectors [Sal89b]. It is defined as an inner vector product:

$$sim(D_i D_j) = \sum_{1 \le l \le n} d_{li} d_{lj}$$

Example: the similarity between node 2 and node 3 in Figure II.24 is: $1.222392*2.444785 + 1.807355*1.807355 = 6.255018$. Note that in Figure II.24 the similarities are already sorted and listed in decreasing order of similarity.

18.7 Dynamic Linking with Cybermap

The Cybermap approach implements linking by similarity. Depending on the needs of the user, new links are calculated as the Cybermap is updated after either a modification of the user profile or the original document base. Cybermap complements the existing linking structure to offer another perspective to a user-specified subset of cyberspace. It is in this sense complementary to tools that visualize the linking structure such as our own Hiermap (see Chapter 15), and most of the mapping tools described in Chapter 11.

Cybermap does not make direct use of static links available in prefabricated hyperdocuments. These links are *not* used for the generation of the Cybermap for three reasons:

1. The implementation of links is extremely *system dependent*. Every system implements its links different. For example, it is almost impossible to write a filter procedure that extracts all hard- and softwired links from any HyperCard stack because there are too many possible ways to implement linking in HyperCard. Systems like Hyper-G make this task much easier because they store the links in external databases. On the Web, there are many different ways to implement links, and the use of CGI scripts and Imagemaps makes it nearly impossible to extract all links automatically. Because linking is now done on a worldwide scale, it also

Figure II.24 Example of computing similarities	1. Input data File	2. Weighted KeyWord Vectors	3. Similarities Between Nodes
	1 human-computer interaction ergonomics	1 ergonomics, 2.807355 human-computer interaction, 1.222392	2,3=6.255018 1,3=2.988486 6,7=2.797886
	2 human-computer interaction interactive computer systems user interface	2 human-computer interaction, 1.222392 interactive computer systems, 2.807355 user interface, 1.807355	4,6=2.607288 3,7=1.494242 3,6=1.494242 1,2=1.494242 5,6=1.303644
	3 human-computer interaction user interface human-computer interaction learning	3 human-computer interaction, 2.444785 learning, 1.222392 user interface, 1.807355	4,7=1.303644 4,5=1.303644
	4 neural networks neural networks network processing	4 network processing, 2.807355 neural networks, 1.61471	
	5 neural networks associative memory	5 associative memory, 2.807355 neural networks, 8.807355	
	6 neural networks memory neural networks learning neurophysiology	6 learning, 1.222392 memory, 2.807355 neural networks, 1.61471 neurophysiology, 2.807355	
	7 neural networks learning	7 learning, 1.222392 neural networks, 8.807355	

becomes prohibitively hard to keep a link database locally accessible and globally updated all the time.

2. In order to offer a *dynamically updated user-dependent view* of the document, the Cybermap structure is based on the concept of dynamic links.

3. Because Cybermap does not directly use the link structure of the hyper-document, the Cybermap concept is equally usable for hypertext documents and nonhypertext documents.

The current Web Cybermap implementation makes use of linking information in that key words within the <A HREF> tag can be weighted much higher to compute the similarities.

Of course, the reader is free to dispense with the Cybermap navigation mechanism at any time and to browse in a hyperdocument using the original linking mechanisms of the hyperdocument.

Cybermap:

Implementation Issues

This chapter describes a series of prototype implementations of Cybermap. The initial implementation was done on a Macintosh using HyperCard [Win90]. The first prototype worked only for HyperCard Stacks, but it could easily be generalized because it is straightforward to include plain text documents in HyperCard stacks. The application structure has been kept free from any hardware or software–dependent Macintosh or HyperCard particularities and has already been ported to different other environments. Table II.1 lists the various Cybermap ports that have been done.

We implemented the first Macintosh-only version according to the system architecture outlined in Chapter 18. The main problem with the Macintosh HyperCard implementation was its speed. The first Cybermap prototype on a Macintosh IIfx or Quadra took about 30 minutes to cluster moderately sized documents (up to 100 nodes with a few hundred words each). The Macintosh system thus works only as a proof of concept, and the amount of data processing required to generate an overview map for even a small document precludes its use as an interactive tool. It was clear that work on larger, more substantive documents would require a more powerful system.

	Name	GUI	Indexing & Clustering	Analyzed Documents
Table II.1 Overview of different Cybermap implementations	Macintosh only	Macintosh: HyperCard + XCMD	Macintosh: C	HyperCard stacks
	Macintosh with CM-2 back end	Macintosh: HyperCard + XCMD	Connection Machine CM-2: C*	Plain text, HyperCard stacks
	Web-enabled Macintosh with CM-2 back end	Macintosh: HyperCard + XCMD + Netscape	Connection Machine CM-2: C*, Macintosh: C	Web, HTML
	Web version	Java + Netscape	SWISH (C), Java	Web, HTML

The distributed and repetitive nature of the task, as well as the quantity of data, called for a parallel computer.

19.1 Implementing Cybermap on the Connection Machine

The port of algorithm to the supercomputer CM-2 allows us to generate Cybermaps of large documents (a few thousand nodes with a few hundred words each) in about 3 to 30 minutes.

The CM-2 is a massively parallel computer made by Thinking Machines Corporation [Hil87]. Contrary to other machines, such as the CM-5, its successor, the CM-2 is a SIMD (single instruction multiple data) machine, which means that the same instruction can be executed in parallel on thousands of data objects (as many as there are processors in the CM-2). The CM-2 is a fine-grained parallel computer with a maximum configuration of 65,536 processing elements. Each processing element contains 4096 bits of memory and a 1-bit-wide ALU (arithmetic logic unit). All elements are connected via a 12-dimensional hypercube network that contains 16 processing elements on each vertex. Any processor can communicate with any other processor on this network. The CM-2 uses a parallel disk array called the Data Vault mass storage system. Each Data Vault unit provides up to 40 GB of storage with a transfer rate of 25 MB per second. Data Vault files are vector structured; each location in the file stores 1 byte/word from each processing element in the machine.

Because of the enormous differences between the Macintosh and Connection Machine, we decided to start from scratch with the CM-2 implementation. As the implementation language, we chose C*, the parallel version of C on the Connection Machine containing additional constructs to use the data parallel features of the CM-2.

To address the problem of nonuniformity in the length of words, we abstracted the words away by giving each unique (i.e., lexicographically distinct) word in the database a numeric key or ID code. The determination of these word IDs would be the first step in processing any document, and any other structures such as the index would use these IDs to refer to words.

The abstraction of words into numeric codes provides certain advantages. The codes are uniform in size and on the average slightly more compact than the full text of the words for large databases. The numeric codes can easily be compared and operated on using fast integer operations. This makes certain tasks, like determining if two words are the same, easier by comparing the numbers rather than the full strings. Also, by carefully selecting the word ID generating function, one can maintain other properties within the word ID code. For instance, by sorting all the words and using the rank of the word in the sorted order, one can determine the dictionary order of two words by comparing their word IDs. Further, these numerical IDs can easily form an index into a vector, easing the construction of centroid vectors needed for the clustering algorithms.

The *textset* is a C* structure used to store information on a hyperdocument. The textset contains several parts: a linked list of *units*, which are discrete pieces in the document (normally the nodes in the hyperdocument); a dynamic set of all the words contained in the document called the *wordspace*; and an index of the document, containing information about which words appear in which units. The functions of the textset are to keep track of what units belong to the document it represents, keep track of any changes to the set of units, and ensure that the wordspace and index are maintained in accord with the contents of the set of units. Thus, the textset makes sure that the wordspace contains all the words in the document, adding words when new units are added. Then, using the word IDs generated by the wordspace, the index is built.

This method of using abstract codes for words has a drawback: to process a document, one must essentially repeat it twice—once to compute all of the word IDs and then again to compile index information using the word IDs as key information. In the current implementation, the wordspace has no convenient provision for the deletion of words; thus, removing words entails completely rebuilding the wordspace. The index also has no provision for incremental updates, which means that most changes to the wordspace require the index to be rebuilt. We did not make any efforts to improve this part of the system, as the speed of the Connection Machine allows us to rebuild the textset of a 0.25 MB document in about 30 seconds. (In comparison, processing time for a 10 KB document on a Macintosh IIci is about 15 minutes.) Because the development is still in a prototype stage, emphasis has been placed on developing a complete, working system that is effective enough to do the task yet sufficiently flexible to withstand continuous development and many incremental extensions. Certainly performance is a consideration in developing the algorithms, but the development has sought not to provide performance at the cost of developing maintainable and extensible code.

Although the Connection Machine implementation is a powerful tool, it was ultimately not the right direction for Cybermap. This implementation exhibits several faults that are fundamental to the CM-2 system. The many variations in the textual data (i.e., word and node sizes) demand careful consideration, as the CM-2's SIMD architecture favors very uniform data. Although the power of the CM-2 hides many of these problems, we have found instances of documents that cause the system to work inefficiently due to the granularity of the problem, thus defying an efficient mapping to the architecture. This problem can be overcome through further development. One problem that could not be overcome was access to the Connection Machine itself. The CM-2 was a scarce, nonshareable resource in high demand. Thinking Machines Corporation went out of the hardware business altogether in 1995, and we found reliance on a dedicated special-purpose parallel computer too restricting. We therefore developed the next version using C for indexing and Java for clustering and the graphical user interface.

19.2 Enabling Cybermap for the Web

Documents on the World Wide Web are an ideal area to apply the Cybermap concepts. We therefore wanted to be able to use Cybermap for navigation on the Web. The first Web port of Cybermap was straightforward, albeit limited to the Macintosh.

We maintained the CM-2 clustering back end and combined the HyperCard/C Cybermap GUI with AppleScript-aware Web browsers such as Netscape. It took only a few days to replace the HyperCard-browsing mechanism with a Web browser. Instead of calling a HyperCard stack, Cybermap sends a GetURL Apple event [Goo94] to the browser, which then loads the next HTML file.

Figures II.25 and II.26 illustrate browsing the Web using the original Web-enabled Cybermap on the Macintosh. The GUI part could be taken from the Mac implementation with minor modifications, and the generation of the Cybermap structure was done off-line on the CM-2 using the clustering back end.

This solution is not satisfactory, because the GUI is limited to the Macintosh. Also, because of the limited availability of the CM-2, we were planning on porting the clustering part to a more portable platform anyway. We therefore

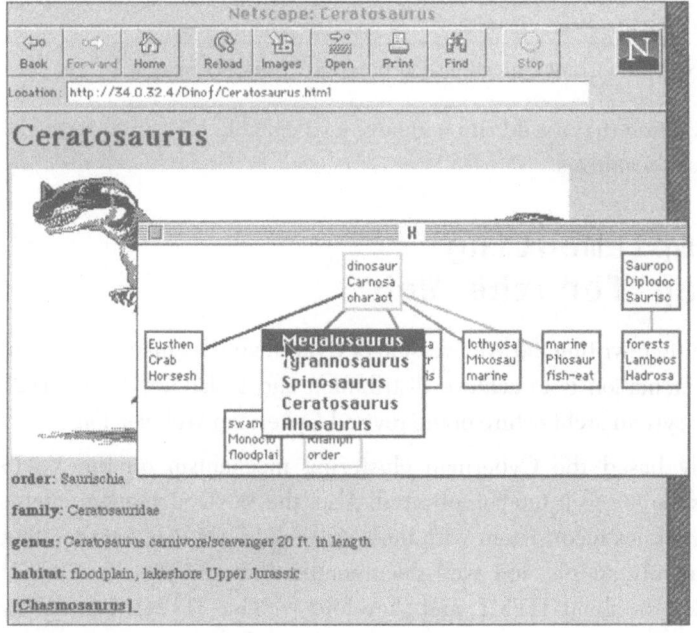

Figure II.25

Web-enabled
Mac Cybermap

Browsing the
Web on the Mac
using the
original
Cybermap

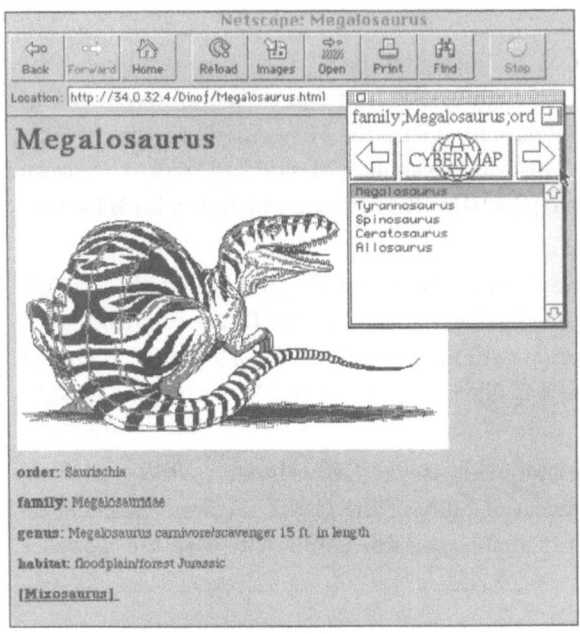

built a Web version that would run with any Java-capable Web browser on all
major hardware platforms.

19.3 Implementing Cybermap for the Web

We are currently rewriting the Web version of Cybermap. The main design goal
of this implementation is to achieve distribution and scalability. Figure II.27
illustrates the system architecture of the revised Cybermap Web version.

We initially based the Cybermap clustering mechanism on the WAIS
indexer but soon found it too complicated. Also, the WAIS documentation is
poor and sometimes inconsistent with the source code. SWISH, on the other
hand, is relatively simple and well documented (see Chapter 7). SWISH
specifically knows about HTML and therefore weights HTML-tagged key
words accordingly.

The SWISH index is used as input for a scatter/gather-based clustering algorithm. The scatter/gather algorithm [Cut92, Cut93] offers much faster clustering

Graphical User Interface Java/AWT		**Browsing** Java-capable Web Browser Netscape
Indexing SWISH C	**Clustering** Scatter/Gather Java	

Figure II.27

Cybermap Web implementation architecture

than the document clustering described in Chapter 18. Compared to the original Cybermap clustering algorithm that exhibits quadratic run time behavior because all pairs of similarities must be considered in each run, scatter/gather offers near linear performance. We are using a variant of the algorithm [Cut92] that works as follows:

1. Find k centers (centroids) by using the initial quadratic algorithm over the document set as described in section 18.6.

2. Assign all documents to the centers in a single pass by assigning each node to the most similar center.

To be able to manage large clusters, we apply this procedure recursively to large clusters, until our clusters have the desired node size. Clustering is implemented in Java. We were first considering implementing it in C but then opted for Java to allow for portable clustering at a client's machine without the need to recompile the clustering engine for every new CPU or operating system version. This also permits distributed clustering, such that new nodes can be flexibly added to clusters at the client's site.

The Web Cybermap GUI (Figure II.28) has been implemented using Java and the AWT [Van96], a portable API (application programming interface) and Java class library that implements user interface functionality on all Java platforms.

19.4 Evolution of the Cybermap GUI

There have been five iterations of the Cybermap GUI. In the first version we used a rectangular layout with the most frequently linked node in the upper left corner (Figure II.29). The only advantage of this approach was its easy implementation. There are many disadvantages, such as no easy discernible

Figure II.28

Java GUI of
Cybermap Web
version

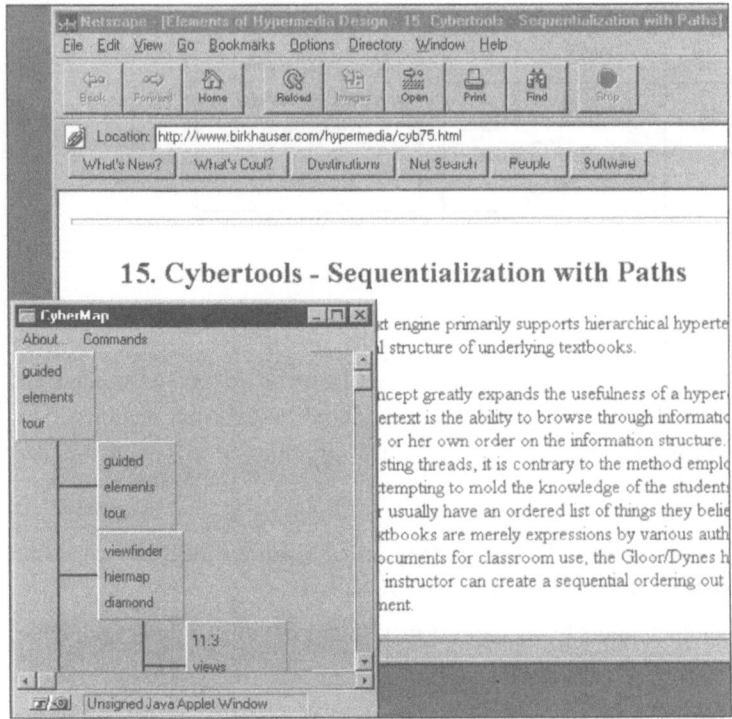

root and the fact that links that are between nodes in the same horizontal line cannot be distinguished.

We developed a history mechanism in the first version that was evaluated superior to others implemented in later versions in our user tests. We used partly blackened bars underneath the hyperdrawers, where the blackening of the bar indicated the number of already visited nodes of that particular hyperdrawer.

In the second version of the Cybermap GUI we replaced the grid layout of the hyperdrawers by vertically growing trees (Figure II.30). This eliminates the problem of indistinguishable links and also displays most significant hyperdrawers closer to the root of the trees. The thickness of the lines corresponds to the degree of similarity: the more similar two hyperdrawers are, the thicker is their connecting line. We also allowed multitrees (see section 9.4) in this version.

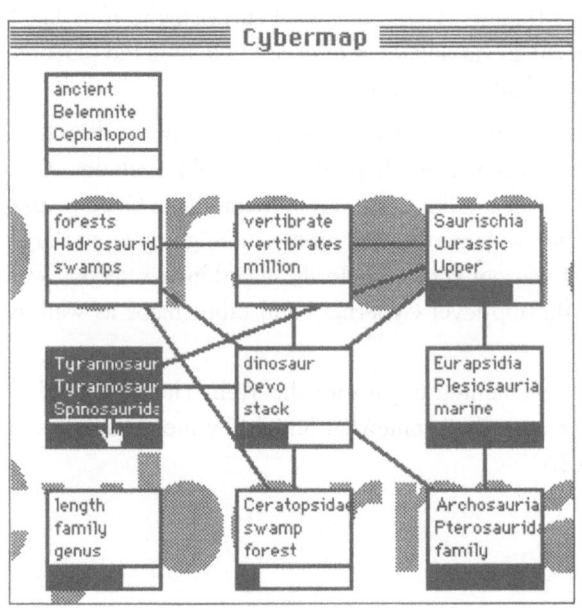

Figure II.29

First version
of Cybermap
user interface

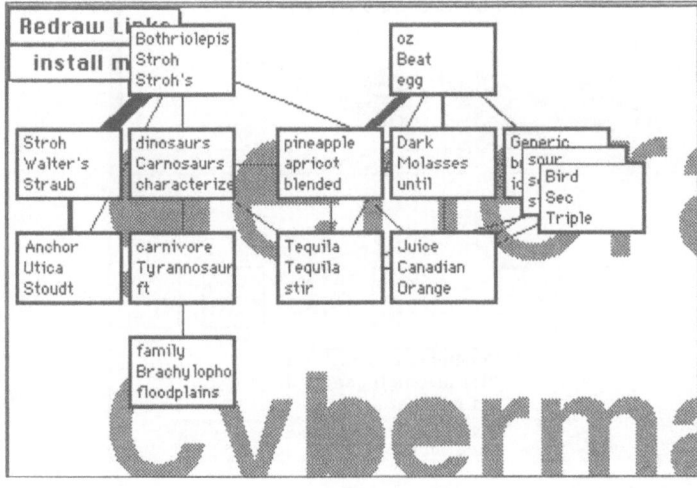

Figure II.30

Second version
of Cybermap
user interface

In the third version we used color coding to indicate the significance of links as well as browsing history (Figure II.31). Somewhat surprisingly, users liked the partly black bars better than varying degrees of red to denote the percentage of nodes read in a particular hyperdrawer.

The forth version of the Cybermap GUI was refined to permit the display of hierarchical hyperdrawers, where one hyperdrawer could include other Cybermaps (see Chapter 20 for a full description of hierarchical Cybermaps). This was judged very useful, as hyperdrawers otherwise might get very large quickly. One problem that was not yet satisfactorily solved in this version was the distinction between the top-level Cybermap and other maps as well as between lower-level maps.

The fifth version was implemented in Java for the Web. The GUI tried to improve on the fourth version, albeit somewhat limited by the capabilities of the AWT (see section 19.3).

Figure II.31

Third version of Cybermap user interface

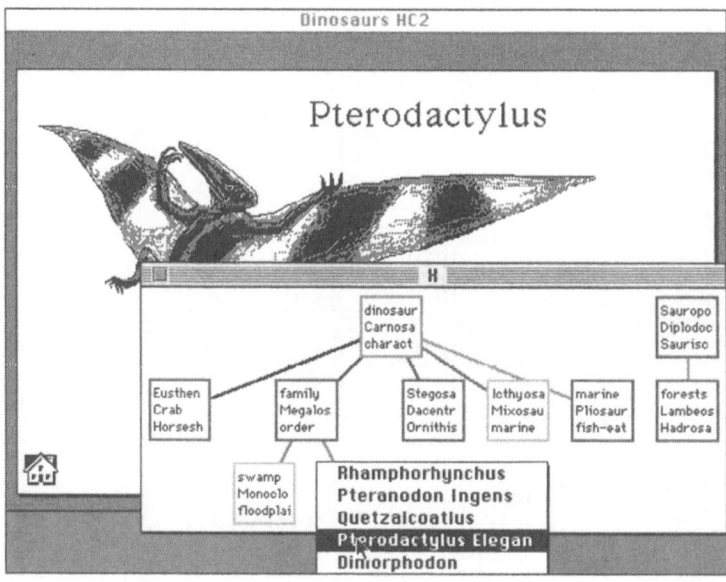

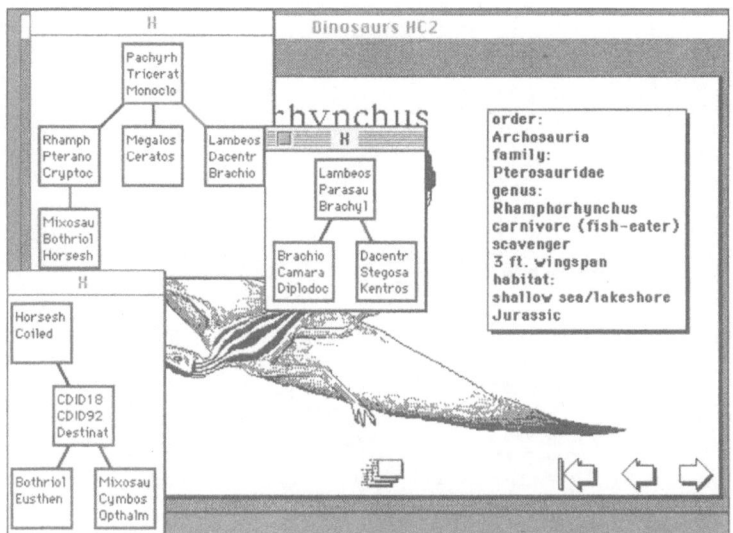

Figure II.32

Fourth
hierarchical
version of
Cybermap user
interface

19.5 A Sample Guided Tour

At run time, users set their profile by selecting the key words that interest them most and placing them in the interest list. After every modification of the user profile, Cybermap is newly computed. Once the map has been calculated and drawn, users are free to jump to any selected node in the hyperdocument and to browse at will in the document. This means that readers can use the original browsing mechanisms of the browsing environment while staying in the hyperdocument. There is no constraint on the following of links that have been produced by the original author of the hyperdocument. If the reader jumps back to the Cybermap, the most recently visited node in the document is shown in the map.

The screen shots in Figures II.33 through II.37 show a brief example of the use of Cybermap where the readers are about to browse in a HyperCard stack about dinosaurs. For this browsing example the original version of Cybermap was used. There have been many changes to the ways the hyper-drawers are presented, but the original browsing mechanism is still the same.

Figure II.33

The readers
selected the key
words that are of
interest to them
and are about to
compute a new
Cybermap.

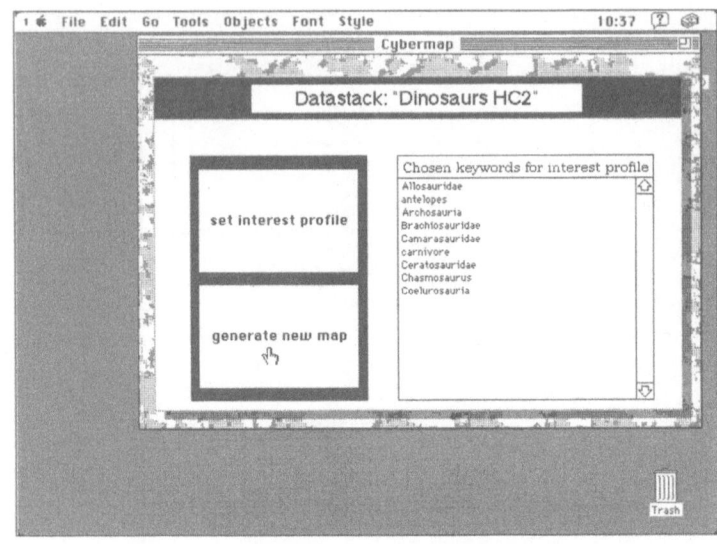

Figure II.34

Readers started
in the Cybermap
by clicking on
the hyperdrawer
containing
"Tyrannosauridae"
and selecting
"Spinosaurus".
The partly black
boxes beneath the
hyperdrawers
denote the per-
centage of
retrieved nodes
out of all nodes
of each
hyperdrawer.

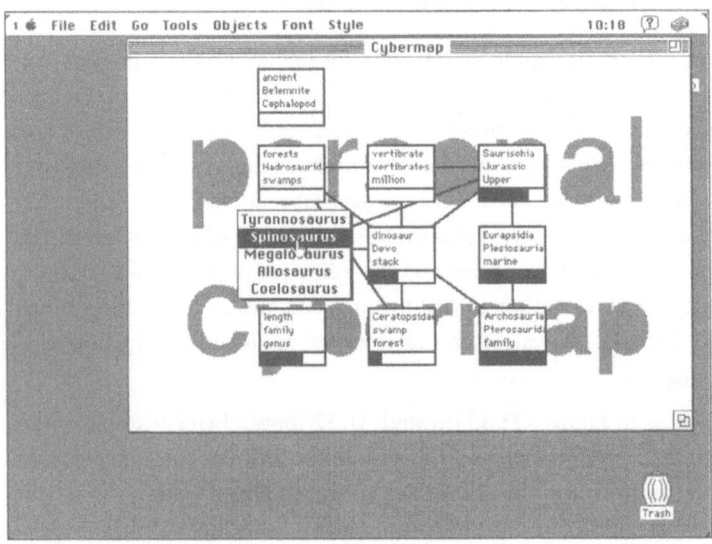

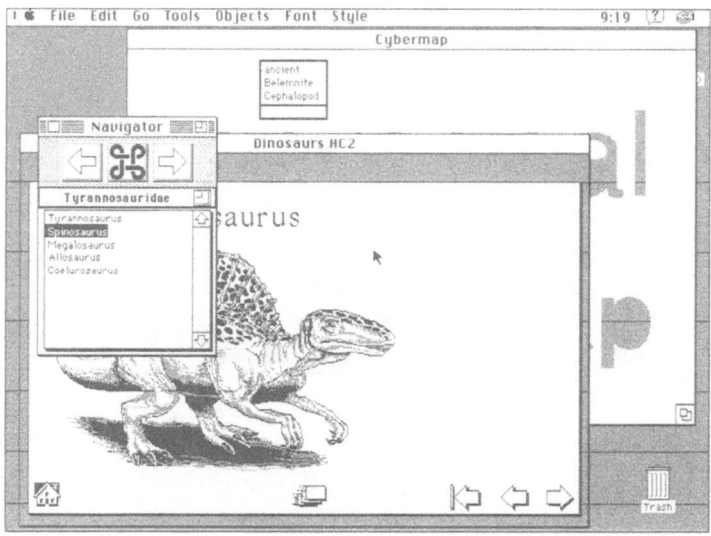

Figure II.35

The system jumped to the node titled "Spinosaurus." To ease further browsing, a navigator window popped up showing all nodes of the hyperdrawer.

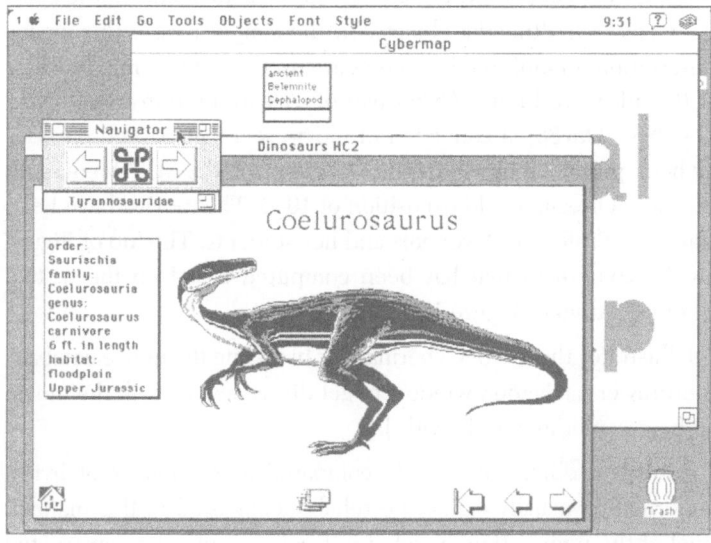

Figure II.36

Readers browsed sequentially to the Coelurosaurus node using the navigator window. The navigator window has been collapsed by the readers.

Figure II.37

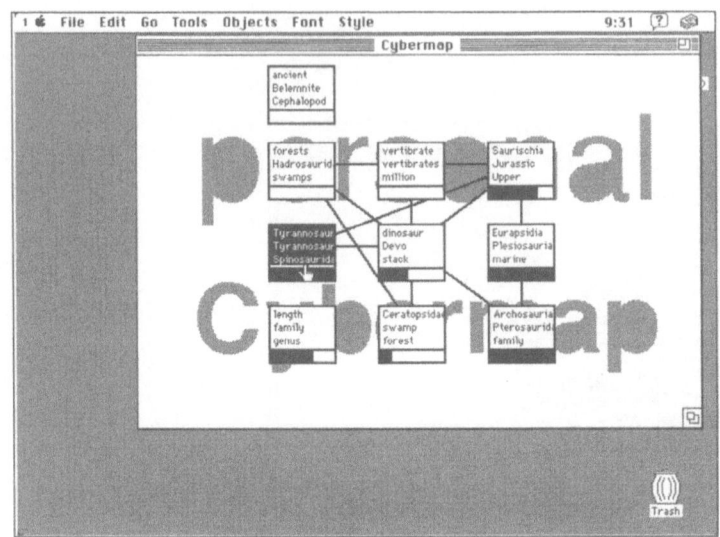

Finally the readers jumped back to the Cybermap by clicking on the button ⌘ (see previous screen shot). Their momentary location in the dinosaur stack is marked in the Cybermap by highlighting the rectangle representing the "Tyrannosauridae" hyperdrawer.

19.6 Cybermaps for Multimedia Data

It would be very useful to apply Cybermap not only to textual data but to compute overview maps of multimedia objects. In the simplest case, this means that textual descriptions of multimedia objects are used for clustering. In a first realization of this idea, we built a Cybermap of "A City in Transition—New Orleans 1983–1986" [Dav88], a collection of movie segments stored on laser disk that have been produced by Glorianna Davenport at the MIT Media Lab illustrating the New Orleans world exposition of 1986. The movies have been manually indexed by Professor Davenport and her students. The top of Figure II.38 displays the Cybermap that has been computed based on the textual index shown at the bottom of Figure II.38.

Figure II.39 illustrates the use of Cybermap for browsing the movie database using the hyperdrawer navigation window to get direct access to all the movie segments that have something to do with Jax.

In textual databases, objects are easily compared as sequences of bytes. Multimedia information usually cannot be reliably compared in this manner. Rather, a model of the information encoded in the bytes must be constructed to provide a basis for comparison.

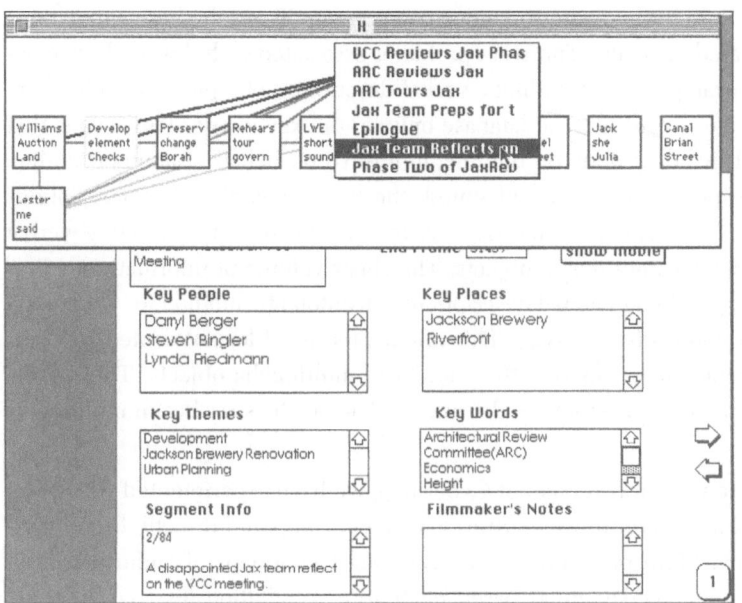

Figure II.38

Cybermap for collection of movie segments "New Orleans in Transmission"

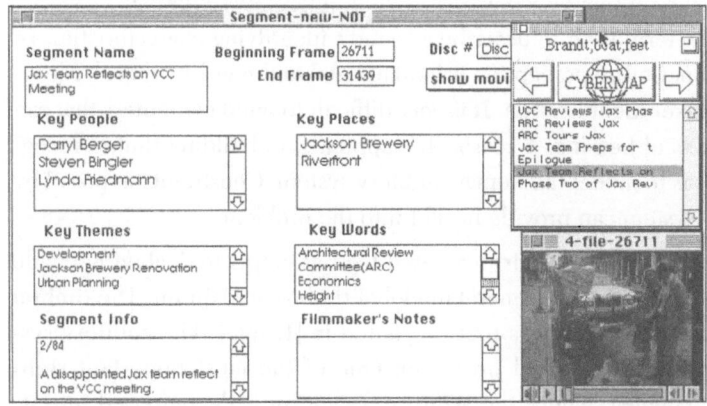

Figure II.39

Browsing in "New Orleans in Transition" stack using Cybermap

Our first multimedia Cybermap circumvented these issues by attaching annotative text to the audio and video components. Typically these annotations are generated manually. There are problems associated with this method, however. For example, by providing a verbal description of a piece of audio (e.g., explosion) one can query a database only on the key words. This means that the search is being done on one medium (text) on behalf of another (audio). Given the perceptual nature of sound, the limitations of verbal descriptions should be apparent. Another issue is the practicality of generating verbal descriptions for multimedia objects. The sheer volume of information is prohibitive to providing manual descriptions. An automatic method for generating these annotations is necessary. This implies the need for automated methods for analyzing and comparing the content of multimedia objects. These same methods could be used for conducting media-specific searches in multimedia databases.

In the newest Web version of Cybermap, we have experimented with maps of audio data where the similarities have been computed directly from multimedia data. More precisely, we are building Cybermaps of audio databases using an automated method based on timbre recognition for analyzing and comparing the contents of these audio objects.

Audio-only databases can be found in a number of fields. In the entertainment industry, for example, sound designers regularly use databases of thousands of sounds in the creation of soundtracks for movies and commercials. Invariably, designers use their ears, perhaps listening to dozens or hundreds of sounds. A browser for audio databases would improve this situation.

Timbre is the term used to describe a sound's identifying characteristics. In human audition, timbre perception is fundamental to things like speech recognition and speaker identification. It is very difficult to build computers that can simulate aspects of hearing. A reasonable approach in building timbre recognition systems is to model the human auditory system. Constraints imposed by the biological system can provide insight into the problem.

The method of audio analysis presented here attempts to deal with a wide variety of sounds by using a general model of timbre perception. The timbral representation being used was first presented in [Lan95]. The auditory system is a complex multistaged processor. One of the most important steps occurs in the cochlea, where the acoustic waveform is decomposed into its time-varying spectral components [Pic88]. In the present work, the cochlea is simulated by an algorithm developed by [Fit92] based on an algorithm by [Qua85]. Figure II.40 shows the output of the cochlear model for a trumpet tone.

Studies indicate that features like spectral envelopes (the shape of the spectral information) and amplitude envelopes (the shape of the amplitude information) are important in timbre perception [Bre90]. The current technique extracts 10 such features from the output of the cochlear model, which are stored as coarse-coded vectors. The shape-based representation allows easy calculation of sound similarity by comparing the similarity of corresponding sets of curves. A number of similarity measurements could be used, such as the correlation coefficient. However, since we are potentially interested in distances within the timbre space, we choose a metric similarity measurement. The particular measurement used here is the ordered linear direction metric (OLD) [Pol87], which compares the similarity in adjacent linear direction between two curves. Given a database of sounds we can now extract the timbre categories within the database. Clustering is one method of finding the categories. By calculating the combinatorial similarities between all files, we can make clusters of sounds that are highly similar. Based on this similarity, it is now straigthforward to compute a Cybermap.

The database used in this project consisted of 171 sounds representing 19 different timbre categories (bluejay, boat, camel, crow, chime, clarinet, "clink," cymbal, flute, glockenspiel, guitar, harp, organ, parakeet, piano, rooster, saxophone, trumpet, whistle). Each sound was approximately 1–2 seconds in

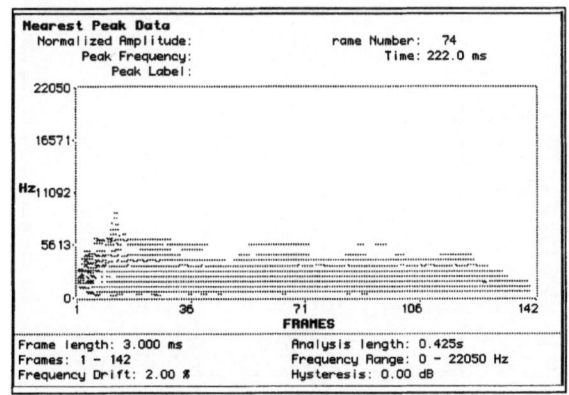

Figure II.40

Analysis of a trumpet tone

length. In the initial clustering operation, three thresholds were tested (0.2, 0.24, 0.26). The lower the threshold, the more timbre categories the clustering algorithm found. At the lowest threshold (0.2) the clustering algorithm found 31 categories; at a threshold of 0.24, 26 categories were found; at 0.26, 20 categories were found.

The Timbral Cybermap has been implemented in Java as an applet (Figure II.41). The user is presented with a partial tree representing the database. Each node is a timbral category. At each node the user can choose to play any of the sounds in that category. The user can also expand a subtree by pushing the Grow button.

The need for multimedia browsing tools seems clear. Toward that end, content-based methods of media analysis are needed to extract structure from the

Figure II.41

Timbral audio Cybermap on the Web

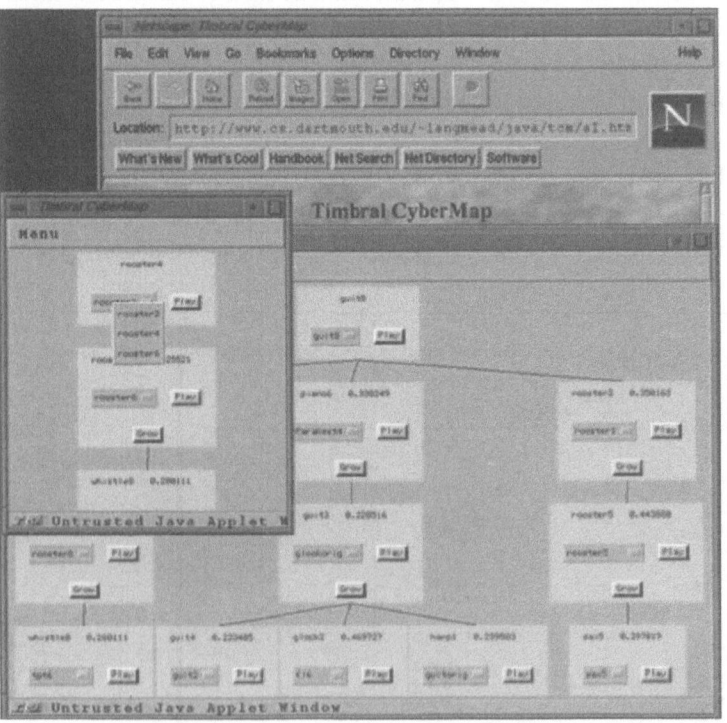

database. The project presented here demonstrates one such method for audio. The ultimate goal in that aspect is the creation of a system that can automatically classify sounds in a manner consistent with human perception.

Besides the issue of computing a structure for nontextual data, we also have the problem of visualizing extremely large information spaces. The next chapter introduces a way to visualize large information structures consisting of many nodes by permitting hierarchical nestings of Cybermaps.

CHAPTER 20

Building

Hierarchical Cybermaps

The model described so far is of only limited use for extremely large hyper-documents with thousands or even millions of nodes because there is only one Cybermap for the whole hyperdocument. This means that one hyperdrawer has to represent hundreds or even thousands of nodes. In this case, Cybermap offers a usable overview of the whole hyperdocument, but it can no longer directly be used for navigation purposes. The interest list still offers a viable mechanism to get direct access to the most interesting nodes. Fortunately, it is straightforward to extend our technique by introducing layers of Cybermaps where every sub-Cybermap describes only a small part of the document. Sub-Cybermaps then have to be subsumed in hyperdrawers of other Cybermaps, resulting in a hierarchy of Cybermaps.

20.1 Hierarchical Clustering Algorithms

The hierarchical Cybermap clustering algorithm starts with the similarities between nodes as defined in Chapter 18. For clustering, it uses the notion of *centroid* or average key word vector (see section 1.5).

centroid　　　　　　　The centroid C of a cluster is the vector $C = (c_1, c_2, c_3, \ldots c_n)$, where c_i is the average of all weights d_{ik} for key word T_i over all nodes n_k in the cluster. The algorithm now works as follows:

```
algorithm ClusterHierarchical MaxNumOfClusters, maxNumOfNodes
Put each node into a separate cluster;
Repeat while the actual number of clusters is larger than
MaxNumOfClusters and there are clusters that contain more nodes
than maxNumOfNodes
      Repeat for all clusters
        If current cluster contains more nodes than maxNumOfNodes
        then
          ClusterHierarchical MaxNumOfClusters, maxNumOfNodes;
        else
          Repeat for all nodes within current cluster
          Add node n to the cluster that has the highest similarity to n,
          based on the centroid C of the cluster, i.e., recompute the
          similarities between n and all clusters;
          Take precautions against strong fluctuations in the number
          of words per node:
            (1) define a threshold value for very large nodes, and start
            by clustering the smallest nodes first;
            (2) normalize the weights of the key word vector with
            respect to the number of words;
```

The output of this algorithm not only consists of a tree with the parent-child relation representing "parent-cluster contains child-clusters," but it also returns the similarities between the tree-nodes. The leaves of the tree are the single nodes. The algorithm allows one to specify in advance the number of hyperdrawers per Cybermap and the number of nodes per hyperdrawer. If there are too many hyperdrawers in a Cybermap during the execution of the algorithm, the Cybermap splits into multiple, lower–level Cybermaps. Similarly, if there are too many nodes in a hyperdrawer, the particular hyperdrawer is made a Cybermap, and its nodes are split into lower–level hyperdrawers. Unlike the original, nonhierarchical Cybermap, this algorithm allows the user to control the number of hyperdrawers at the highest hierarchy level while still clustering the most related nodes at the lower level.

20.2 Hierarchical Cybermap Example: News Selection

To test the hierarchical Cybermap, we have built a system for filtering news messages. The system is based on the CM-2 version of the Cybermap implementation. It automatically downloads the daily political news messages of the "clari.news...." news groups into a HyperCard stack. A single mouse click (and the availability of the Connection Machine) generates the hierarchical

Figure II.42

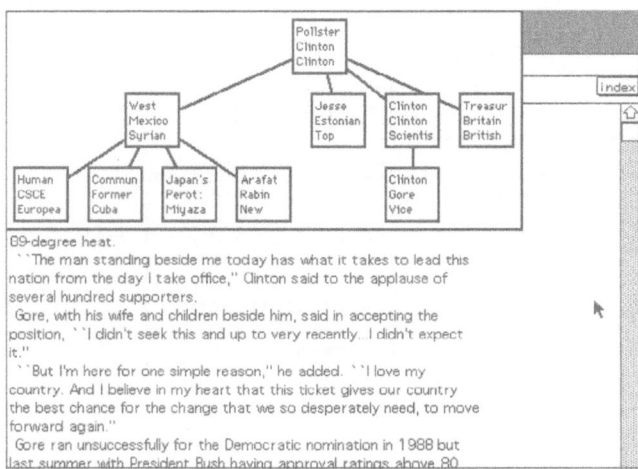

Cybermap. Figure II.42 displays the top-level Cybermap window of the news messages of a day (in the top left corner) and one article of the news stack in the background.

By clicking the hyperdrawers of the Cybermap, readers either get a pop-up menu listing all the nodes in the hyperdrawer (Figure II.43) or can bring up a new Cybermap (Figure II.44).

In Figure II.44 the lower-level Cybermap number 6 has been brought up. In Figure II.45 the reader selects a hyperdrawer about a European summit and turmoil. In II.46 the reader selects a particular article of the hyperdrawer.

Figure II.47 displays the article about the European summit, as well as browsing options for this hyperdrawer. Using the "right" and "left" arrows of the browsing window in the top left corner of Figure II.47, the user can sequentially browse all the articles of the current hyperdrawer.

This example illustrates the real-world usage of Cybermap. It would be very time-consuming for readers to select the messages they are interested in by sequential reading. Cybermap offers an easier way to get a quick overview. It allows either browsing, by examining a few articles per topic, or in-depth reading, by sequential reading of the articles in the hyperdrawers of lower-level Cybermaps.

Figure II.43

Top-level
Cybermap

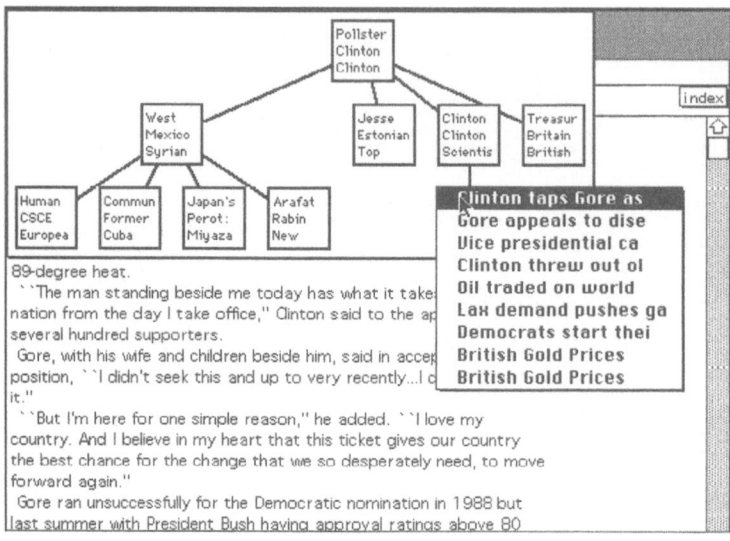

Figure II.44

Selecting lower-
level Cybermap
from top-level
Cybermap

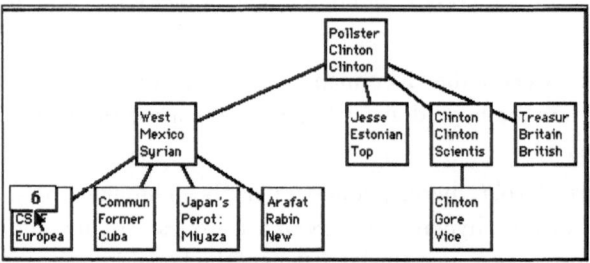

Until now we have concentrated on the clustering aspects of the Cybermap system. In the next chapter we focus on the problem of finding an optimal layout for hyperdrawers on the screen. We will present an algorithm based on minimum spanning trees, which can be used for either clustering related nodes or the layout of related nodes on the screen, or both. Compared to the original Cybermap system, the new algorithm, which we have called *cybertree*, offers better performance but less flexibility.

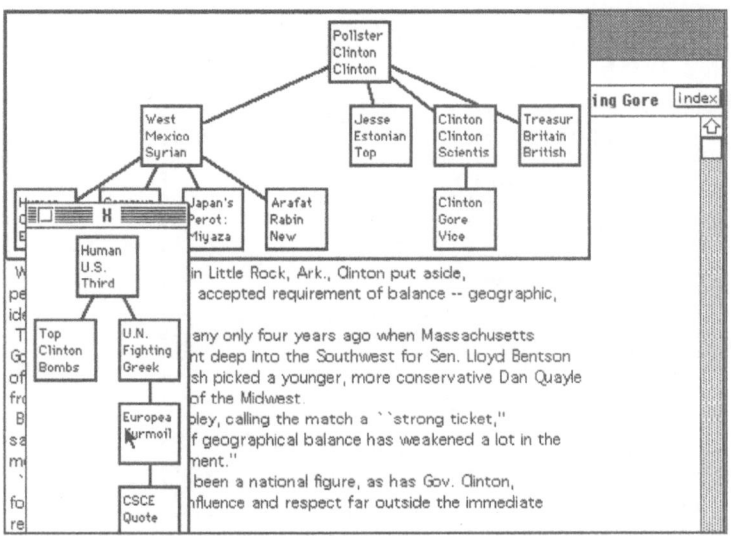

Figure II.45

Lower-level
Cybermap

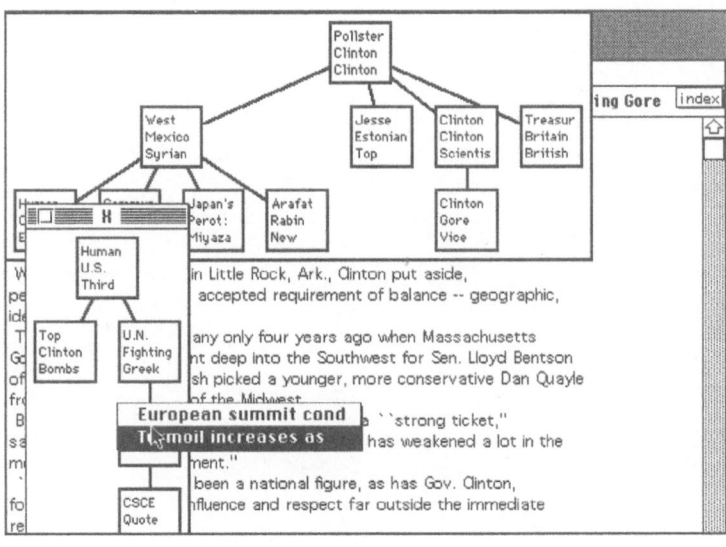

Figure II.46

Selecting a particular article of the hyperdrawer

Figure II.47

Browsing the
selected articles
of the
hyperdrawer

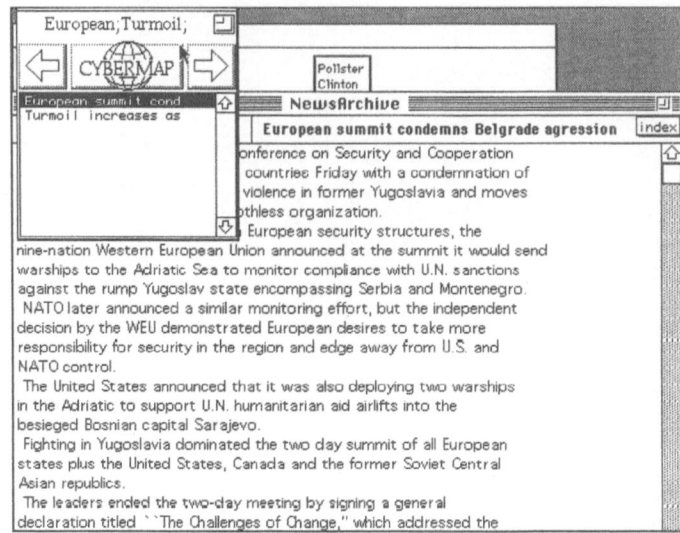

Cybertrees:Tree-Shaped

Overview Maps

This chapter introduces two algorithms, CREATE-LOCAL-TREES and CRE-
ATE-GLOBAL-TREE, based on Kruskal's minimum spanning tree (m.s.t.)
algorithm [Cor90]. Kruskal's algorithm builds an m.s.t. by growing a forest. It
adds unconnected edges with the heighest weight to the tree until all nodes are
connected. By omitting tree-connecting links in Kruskal's algorithm, we get a
clustering in local trees; inclusion of the tree-connecting links results in one
global tree.

21.1 Cybertree Algorithms

The algorithms described in this chapter are based on similarities between
nodes that have been computed as described in section 18.6. The computation of a global tree structure occurs in two steps. In step 1, algorithm CRE-
ATE-LOCAL-TREES computes a collection of local trees. The algorithm
divides and structures all nodes into multiple disjoint trees. As a side effect
of computing local trees, this partitioning also works as a computationally
cheap clustering algorithm. (We will compare the clustering properties of the
local tree generation with Cybermap clustering in the next chapter.) In the

optional second step, CREATE-GLOBAL-TREE merges the local trees into one global tree.

CREATE-LOCAL-TREES first sorts all possible links between the nodes by similarity. It then walks iteratively through the sorted similarity list and basically adds in each iteration of the loop one node to the tree containing a parent that is the most similar to the node being added.

```
CREATE-LOCAL-TREES
sort all link triples <similarity, node₁, node₂>
    descending by similarity;
treelist ← NIL;
for i ← 1 to number of links
    if node₁ᵢ ¬∈ treelist ∧ node₂ᵢ ¬∈ treelist
     create new tree with root node₁ᵢ and first child node₂ᵢ;
     add tree to treelist;
    if node₁ᵢ ∈ treelist ∧ node₂ᵢ ¬∈ treelist
     add node₂ᵢ to tree with parent node₁ᵢ;
    if node₂ᵢ ∈ treelist ∧ node₁ᵢ ¬∈ treelist
     add node₁ᵢ to tree with parent node₂ᵢ;
    if node₁ᵢ ∈ treelist ∧ node₂ᵢ ∈ treelist
     ignore this link triple;
```

Figure II.48 contains a practical example of the stepwise execution of CRE-ATE-LOCAL-TREES using the numbers from Figure II.24.

treelist(1) in Figure II.48 represents the state of the local trees after the first iteration through the similarity list. The second line of the similarity list adds node 1 to the first tree. Line 3 causes the generation of a second tree in **treelist(3)**. The subsequent iteration steps add nodes 4 and 5 to the second tree. The last three lines of similarity list are ignored for the creation of the local trees because all nodes already have been placed.

CREATE-GLOBAL-TREE merges the local trees into one global tree. Of course, the trees can be merged only if there is a similarity above 0 between at least two nodes of different trees. If there is no similarity between two trees (no nodes in the two trees have at least one common key word), the trees are completely unrelated with respect to our similarity measure and thus cannot be merged.

CREATE-GLOBAL-TREE starts with the tree that has been created last because this tree has the weakest similarities and is therefore a prime candidate to be merged with earlier created trees. The algorithm takes the similarity triple with the highest weight where one node of the triple is the root of the tree to be merged and the other node of the triple is not in the tree to be merged:

Similarity List:

2,3 = 6.255018
1,3 = 2.988486
6,7 = 2.797886
4,6 = 2.607288
3,7 = 1.494242
3,6 = 1.494242
1,2 = 1.494242
5,6 = 1.303644
4,7 = 1.303644
4,5 = 1.303644
5,7 = 0.651822

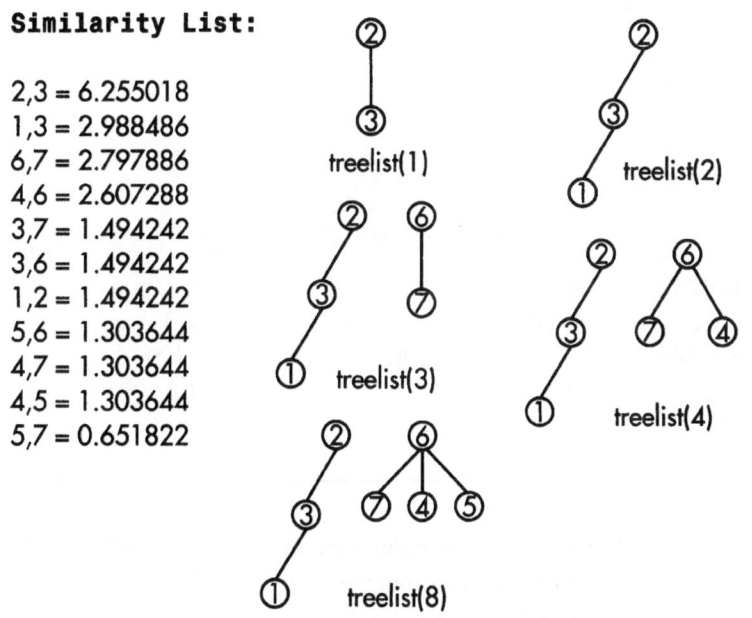

Figure II.48

Example of creating local trees

```
CREATE-GLOBAL-TREE:
treelist ← CREATE-LOCAL-TREES;
for i ← number of trees in treelist down to 1
    take triple <similarity, root_i, node_k> or <similarity, node_k, root_i>
      of similarity list with highest similarity where node_k ¬∈ tree_i;
    merge tree_i with tree_k using node_k as parent of tree_i;
    delete tree_i in treelist;
```

Figure II.49 shows the application of CREATE-GLOBAL-TREE for our previously used data set. Since there are only two subtrees to be merged, line 6 in the similarity list does the job, linking root 6 of tree 2 to node 3 in tree 1.

This algorithm can be refined by selecting the root of the local trees more flexibly. In Figure II.49 the second tree would then be rerooted, and node 7 would become the connecting root.

21.2 Comparison between Cybermap and Cybertree

The Cybermap algorithm of Chapter 18 offers a lot of flexibility concerning the total number of hyperdrawers and the maximum number of nodes in a

Figure II.49

Example of
creating a global
tree

Similarity List:

2,3 = 6.255018
1,3 = 2.988486
6,7 = 2.797886
4,6 = 2.607288
3,7 = 1.494242
3,6 = 1.494242
1,2 = 1.494242
5,6 = 1.303644
4,7 = 1.303644
4,5 = 1.303644
5,7 = 0.651822

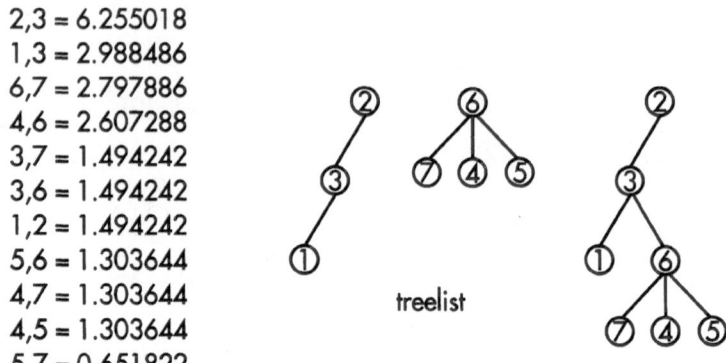

treelist

hyperdrawer. It is straightforward to reduce the number of hyperdrawers by merging them. Alternatively, one can remove some hyperdrawers and redistribute their contents throughout the rest of the document on a node-by-node basis. It is also easy to subdivide hyperdrawers by calling the clustering procedure recursively within a hyperdrawer to get a hierarchical separation of a hyperdrawer into subhyperdrawers. All this flexibility has its price: it takes a supercomputer such as a Connection Machine about 3 to 30 minutes to compute the Cybermap of a moderately large document collection.[1]

The Kruskal-based cybertree algorithm does not offer this flexibility. It is conceptually easy and computationally cheap once the similarity list is available. But the only way to reduce or increase the number of clusters is by splitting or merging trees. That means that there is only one way of arranging the inner structure of a cluster. In particular, there is no easy way of reducing the total number of local trees by distributing their elements among other clusters, a procedure that can easily be done with Cybermap. On the other hand, the Kruskal-based algorithm generates a graphical layout of the nodes and clusters them in one single pass. With Cybermap, figuring out the graphical layout demands an additional computation step that can be done, for example, with the Kruskal-based algorithm.

---

1 The Connection Machine CM-2 needs 5 to 10 minutes (depending on the number of attached processors ranging from 4 k to 16 k) to compute a Cybermap of the Bible.

Thus, Cybermap offers more flexibility concerning the clustering of nodes and generally results in better and more meaningful clusters. On the other hand, it is much more computing intensive and, without running on a supercomputer like a Connection Machine CM-2, works for only small document sets. The Kruskal-based algorithm offers a computationally cheaper way to get a first clustering approximation and delivers a tree representation of the nodes in the same step. It can also be used for quickly arranging a tree of hyperdrawers.

The scatter/gather clustering algorithm used for the Cybermap Web version offers the best of both worlds. It takes a Silicon Graphics Indy workstation using Java about 5 minutes to compute the Cybermap of a Web site with a few hundred documents. We are using a combination of Salton's algorithm and scatter/gather for clustering (see section 19.3). We employ hierarchical nestings of hyperdrawers (see Chapter 20) and use the cybertree algorithm for the layout of the hyperdrawer structure on the screen.

21.3 Cybertree Examples

The following four empirical examples of the Kruskal-based algorithm illustrate possible applications of cybertrees, although they are of practical use only for smaller document collections and are therefore of lesser use for the Web. Nevertheless, cybertrees offer a valuable tool to get an initial first overview and navigation instrument in unknown territory.

The accuracy of the algorithm has been measured manually by comparing the correctly placed nodes with (from a human viewpoint) misplaced nodes.

Example 1. A homogeneous collection of data nodes about dinosaurs. Each node contains some key words out of a limited vocabulary describing the particularities of the dinosaur pictured on that node (see also the guided tour starting on page 196). In addition there are three data nodes containing free-text background information about dinosaurs.

Example 2. A computer science books database. Each entry was indexed manually by a librarian. For the computation of the cybertrees, only these key words have been used (i.e., for the purpose of the algorithm, each node consists only of a short list of key words).

Example 3. A free text collection of e-mail messages. These messages come from a mailing list discussing how to connect the Mattel PowerGlove to a personal computer. In this example all words except stop words (*a*, *an*, *by*, *of*, *the*, etc.) have been indexed.

Example 4. Political news messages. This example consists of a one-day sampling of political news messages with indexing over all words except stop words.

In the first example, our database consists of a homogeneous collection of nodes where each node describes one dinosaur. In this homogeneous case, the algorithm works extremely well. Figure II.50 contains the local cybertrees of the dinosaur database. It has an accuracy of 95 percent, meaning that all but 2 out of 42 nodes have been put at meaningful places and that the clustering into groups of nodes has been meaningful. For example, the third local cybertree (with root "Mixosaurus Icthy") contains three nodes about dolphin-like dinosaurs.

Figure II.51 contains the global cybertree as a result of the execution of the algorithm CREATE-GLOBAL-TREE for the tree in Figure II.50. It exhibits the same accuracy as the local cybertrees (95 percent) and gives a meaningful overview of all data contained in the dinosaur database. It shows that there is an introductory node (CDID18052) and an overview node (titled "destination") and that there are four main groups of dinosaurs: Mixosaurus Icthy (dolphin–like beasts), Pteranodon (flying dinosaurs), Allosaurus (meat eaters and rhinoceros–like beasts of the same time period), Stegosaurus (big herbivores), and some entries that could not be grouped tightly like "coiled belemnite" (a snail-like animal).

The next example (Figure II.52) shows some of the local cybertrees of the catalog of the MIT computer science library. Here the tree algorithm uses the index generated manually by the librarians. We get an accuracy of 100 percent, meaning that each node in the trees has been placed meaningfully. Of course, this example is somewhat artificial because the tree generation was based on only a few key words per node (between two and five words) out of a well-defined set. It is a proof by example of our Kruskal-based algorithm, but there are few real-world examples that exhibit the characteristics of such a small, consistent, and carefully chosen key word index.

The algorithm does not work well for large, unordered document sets. One interfering factor is big differences in node size—document collections where some nodes contain many more words than others.[2] Another distorting factor

---

2 This effect can be corrected to some extent by normalizing the weights of the key word vector with respect to the number of words.

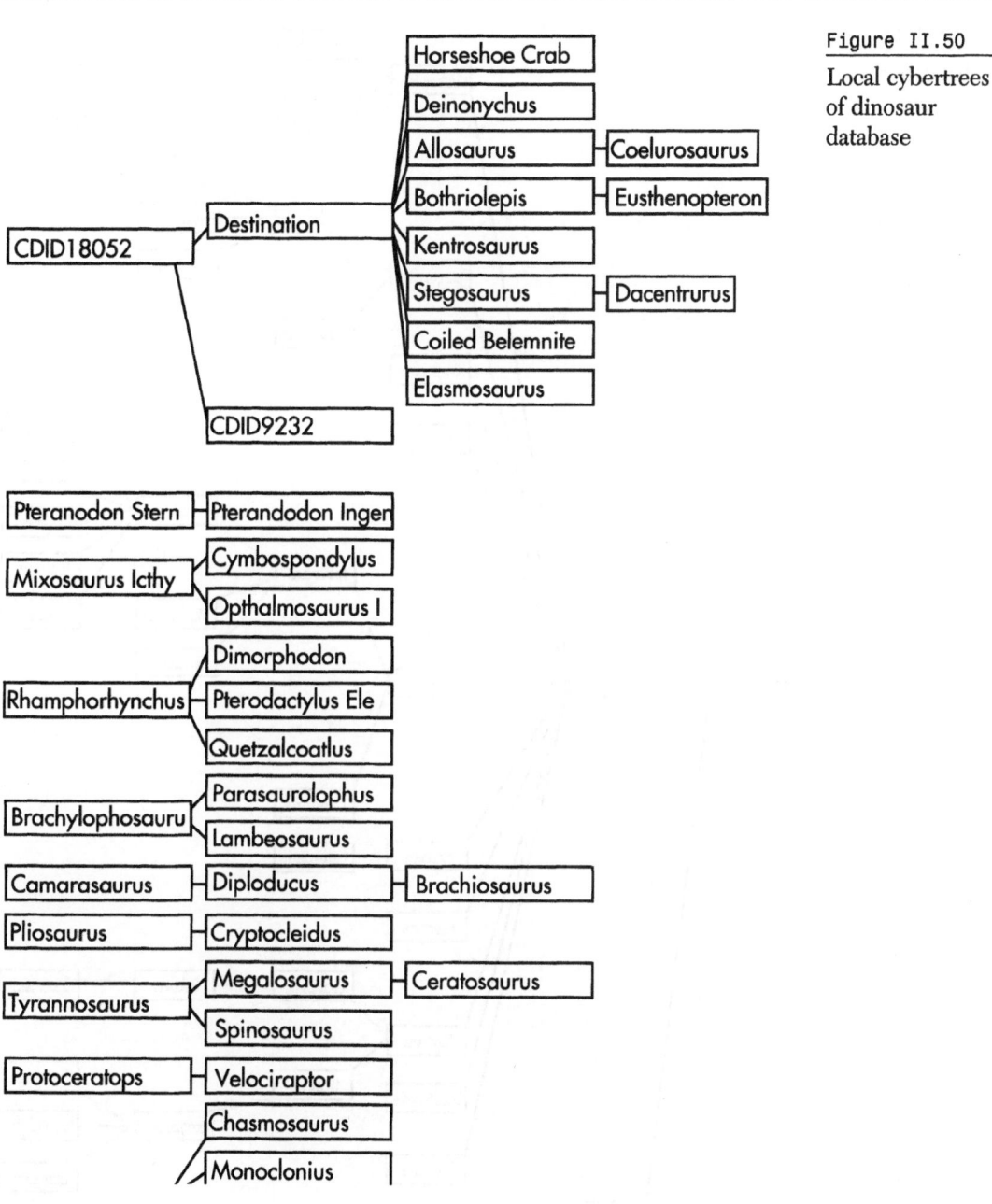

Figure II.50

Local cybertrees
of dinosaur
database

Figure I.51

Global cybertree
of dinosaur
database

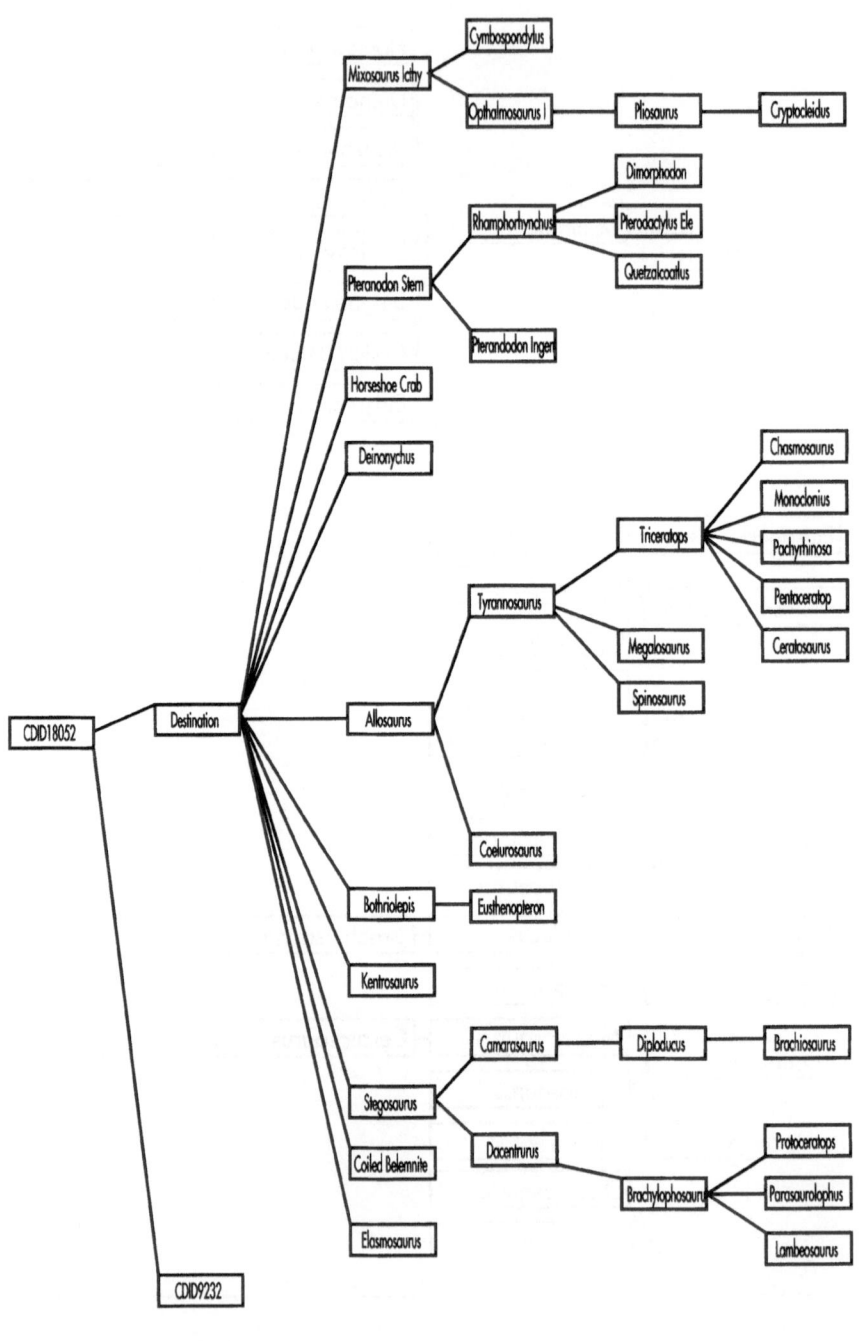

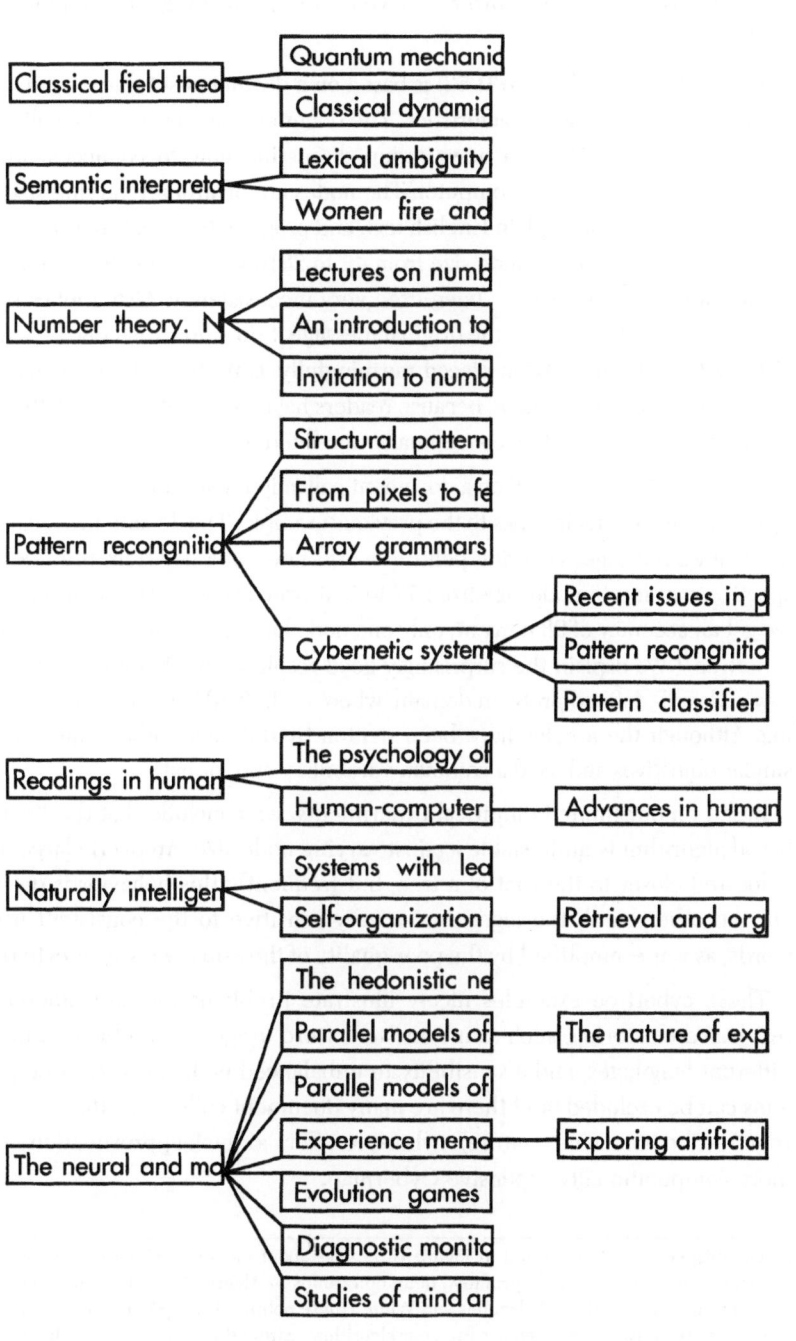

Figure II.52

Local cybertrees
for manually
indexed
computer
science database

is the fact that the same word can have different meanings depending on its context.

The next example (Figure II.53) is based on a document set that exhibits both of the other distorting characteristics. The document set consists of a collection of e-mail messages from a news group discussing how to connect a Mattel PowerGlove to a personal computer. The nodes are of strongly varying size and contain e-mail headers, plain English text, and program fragments in C or assembler language varying in node size from 44 to 2810 words. Due to the informal nature of e-mail, words have been used very inconsistently. Also, replies *sometimes* contain the full text of the original message. Still, approximately 50 percent of the 224 nodes have been placed meaningfully. Unfortunately this makes the cybertree useless in this case, because readers have to expect that a link they follow leads half the time to a conceptually unrelated node.

The last example is based on a document collection that exhibits, at least at first glance, similar characteristics to the previous example. The document set consists of 51 news messages covering political world news of a day from the U.S. perspective, varying in node size from 77 to 953 words (Figure II.54). Surprisingly we get an accuracy of 98 percent, only one node has been vastly misplaced in the cybertree.[3] We explain the surprisingly good result of our algorithm by the narrow and well–defined problem domain, where each word basically has one meaning. Although the articles have been written by different authors, they all had similar objectives and used a common vocabulary and format.

Based on our limited empirical experiments, we conclude that the Kruskal-based algorithm is quite stable against varying node size. An overly large node is located closer to the root of a tree, but frequently this behavior is desired. On the other hand, the algorithm is very sensitive to the consistent use of words, as was exemplified by the poor quality of the e-mail messages cybertree.

These cybertree examples nicely illustrate problems that are inherent in text-based clustering, such as inconsistent word usage, the problem of mixing different languages, and a sensibility to unbalanced node sizes. If those problems can be excluded (and there are many document collections that are of the required homogeneous nature), cybertree offers a quick approximation of the more computationally expensive Cybermap.

---

3 The misplaced node indicated in Figure II-54 talks about members of the Islamic Salvation Front being held hostage in primitive detention camps in Algeria. It has been put into a tree about the U.S. presidential elections and White House politics. It is up to the reader to decide whether the misplacement comes from our algorithm or from the nature of U.S. politics.

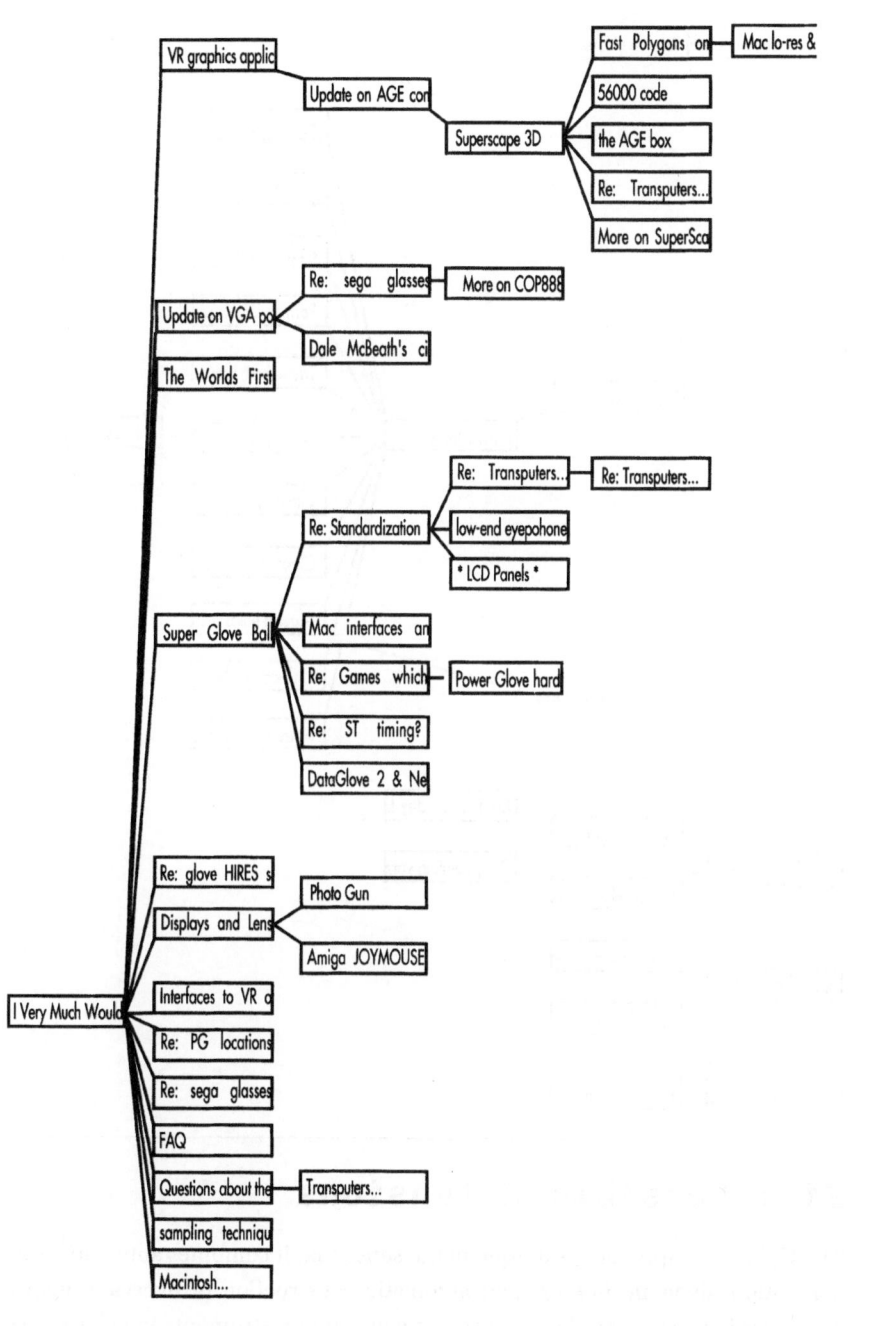

Figure II.53

Global
cybertrees for
collection of
e-mail messages

Figure II.54

Local cybertrees for collection of political news messages

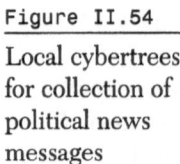

Release of check-
Release of check-
Polish finance min
Poll: Bush barely
Rudman will not s
Former foes have
Democrat race do
Triumphant Brown
Tsongas drops out
Brown throws mo
Bush refuses deal
House sustains Bu
Clinton praises Ts
Clinton" 'I just ha
Algeria holds men
misplaced node
Bush acknowledge
Americans rate C
Election Sunday li
French socialist F
Socialist defeat r
Disappointing vote
French election si
House postmaster
Special counsel na
A sticky question
Bush in 'good shap
Bush to get medic

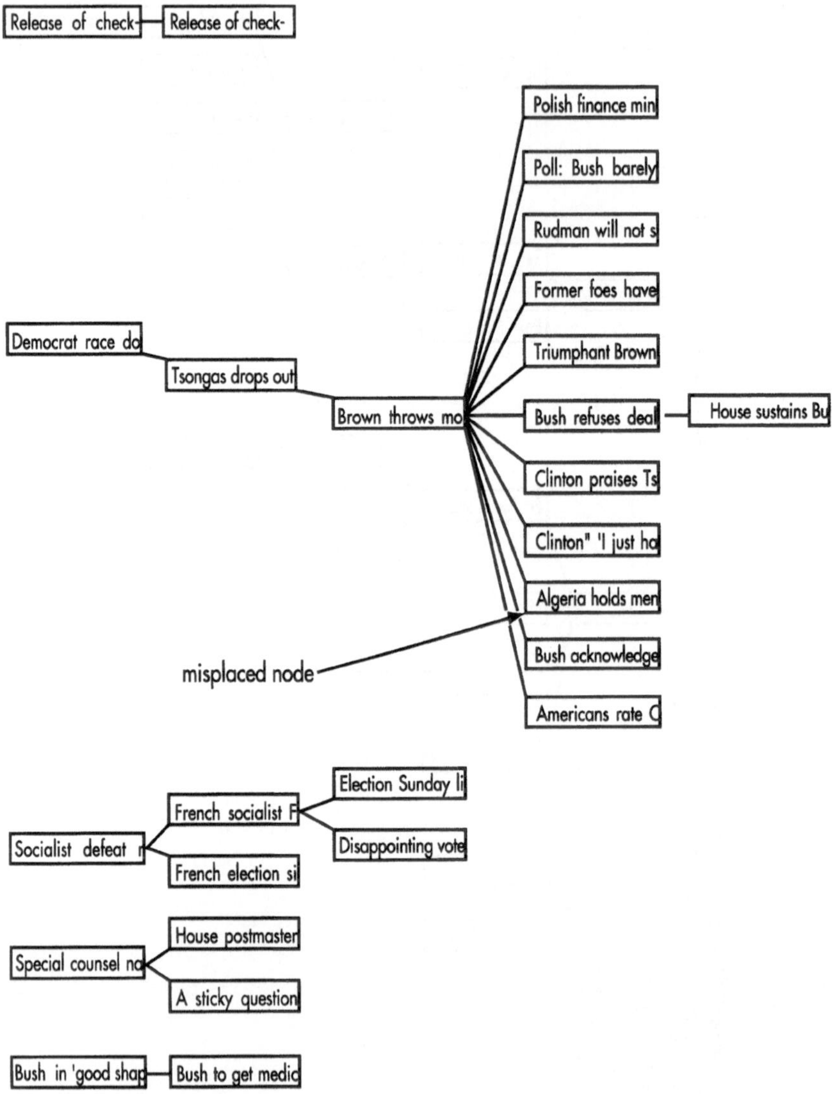

21.4 Possible Extensions

The Cybermap approach is unique in the sense that it combines automatic link generation, dynamic linking, and automatic construction of overview maps. The overview maps can then be used as navigation instruments in cyberspace and are also effective in filtering out information.

Cybermap so far makes only limited use of the link structure in that the Web version uses <A HREF>-tagged links as preferred key words. The direct inclusion of the actual document link structure into Cybermap introduces a whole set of new and interesting problems, such as how to extract this information and how to integrate the link information with the contents analysis.

Another extension is to use Cybermap for multimedia data. We plan to expand the timbral Cybermap to improve clustering of audio data. Also, we intend to investigate combining VideoScheme, which is described in Part IV, with Cybermap to be able to analyze audio and video on the fly for clustering.

A further component of Cybermap that can be improved is the graphical layout of the hyperdrawers. This means that other algorithms for the arrangement of the nodes need to be explored.

A last point is that the user model can be further refined by adding the ability to analyze the reading behavior of the user. Cybermap would then be able to include additional nodes that have not been specified directly in the interest list but might be of interest to the reader.

We are working on improving the dynamic clustering part in Java to allow for the user-specified addition of nodes to an existing Cybermap on the fly. The Cybermap Web version described here will be made available on the Web for noncommercial public domain use.

`http://www.cs`
`.dartmouth`
`.edu/~gloor/`
`CyberTools/`

Conclusions

In Chapter 1 we started by covering the basics of the information retrieval and navigation in cyberspace problem. We have subsequently given a broad overview over the field and have introduced the seven concepts of navigation in cyberspace: linking, searching, sequentialization, hierarchy, similarity, mapping, and agents. Our own Cybertools Hiermap, Navigation Diamond, Viewfinder, Cybermap, and Cybertree cover a broad range of promising new research directions in the hypermedia research community. By integrating dynamic linking and the automatic generation of an overview map, we have created a unique tool set that integrates the best of both worlds. We have extended Cybermap by allowing hierarchical nestings of hyperdrawers. We have also presented a broad range of Cybertool applications. The Cybertools complement existing navigational aids for hyperdocuments and provide a self-sufficient navigation tool for browsing in cyberspace. Finally, the Cybertools offer the capability of horizontal growth and easy hypertextualization of non-hypertextual documents without restricting the use of already installed browsing mechanisms. To the best of our knowledge, there is no other system like ours that combines hierarchy, similarity, and mapping concepts to give an overview and quick access to large collections of information.

In the introduction we outlined our vision of the ideal tool for navigating in hyperspace. It should be a tool that operates on raw, unstructured documents, is capable of giving users an overview of their field of interest, offers guidance on what to do next, and gives a graphical overview of the most relevant piece of information in reply to a query. Although the Cyber–Toolbox is not yet the ideal tool we envision, it nevertheless addresses our requirements: it operates on structured as well as unstructured data without the need for manual pre-processing, creates an overview map of the information collection to be explored, filters out the most relevant information based on the user's interests and provides sequential and hierarchical navigation, and offers options of what the reader can do next. The Cyber-Toolbox thus illustrates that our ideas can be realized and are extremely useful for navigation and information explo-ration. While there is still a long way left to go to Gibson's cyberspace, we think that our Cyber-Toolbox can provide at least a small step toward making cyber-space more hospitable.

Part III addresses the second element of hypermedia design: presentation. We introduce a particular concept for presenting and visualizing complex abstractions: algorithm animation.

p a r t **III**

Visualization

You do not understand

anything until you

understand it in more

than one way.

—Marvin Minsky

authors have frequently tried to explain and visualize complex concepts and ideas by means other than the printed word. The proverb, "A picture is worth more than a thousand words," still holds true in the multimedia age. Additionally, the computer provides more sophisticated ways to visualize complex facts, concepts, and algorithms. Scientific visualization, program visualization, and algorithm animation are well–known concepts in computer science, although their use is only slowly starting to emerge outside the academic community. Part III describes one aspect of scientific visualization, algorithm animation, that has been around for some decades but has only rarely been used apart from the computer science domain. Using algorithm animation at its best offers a prospective multimedia author a unique way to explain complex concepts that are very hard to convey by other means.

After a short survey of algorithm animation, Part III focuses on the Animated Algorithms project, a large-scale attempt to create an educational hypermedia product based on the textbook Introduction to Algorithms by Tom Cormen, Charles Leiserson, and Ronald Rivest [Cor90]. Animated Algorithms consists of three interactive components: a hypertext version of the book itself, animations of the most important algorithms, and movies explaining the use of the hypertext interface and the animations. On the example of Animated Algorithms, Part III illustrates design criteria, user interface issues, and the creation process for the production of algorithm animations. Special emphasis is put on the educational aspects. Later chapters of Part III introduce advanced concepts of creating algorithm animations by using an animation-specific scripting language and animating proofs of algorithms.

CHAPTER 23

Introduction
to
Algorithm Animation

algorithm animation

An algorithm animation allows visualizing the behavior of an algorithm. Although algorithm animations have mostly been used in computer science, potential applications in other scientific domains, such as mathematics and economics, abound. An algorithm animation creates an abstraction of both the data and the operations of the algorithm. First it maps the data (the current state of the algorithm, i.e., the current values of the variables used in the algorithm) into an image, which then gets animated based on the operations between two succeeding states in the execution of the algorithm. Animating an algorithm allows for better understanding of the inner workings of the algorithm; furthermore it makes apparent its shortcomings and advantages, thus allowing for further optimization.

algorithm animation system

An algorithm animation system is composed of an integrated set of multimedia tools (such as graphics, animation, text, video, and code) that simulate how the algorithm works using abstractions of the data, operations, and semantics of the program behind the algorithm. Algorithm animation may involve views that have no direct correspondence to the algorithm's data or execution.

http://hcrl
.open.ac.uk/
jvlc/JVLC-
Body.html

Price, Baecker, and Small [Pri93] distinguish in their survey paper, "A Principled Taxonomy of Software Visualization," between *program visualization*

229

(the use of various visualization techniques to enhance the human understanding of the actual implementation of computer programs) and *algorithm animation* (a visualization of the high-level concept or algorithm that is later implemented in software). Collectively, they define both of them to be part of *software visualization*, which is the "use of the crafts of typography, graphic design, animation, and cinematography with modern human-computer interaction technology to facilitate both the human understanding and effective use of computer software."

Efforts to develop algorithm animation systems started as early as the late sixties and early seventies [Bae69]. One of the most famous systems is Balsa-II [Bro88a][Bro88b], a standalone system based on a kernel running on Macintoshes (Figure III.1). Views for new algorithms are constructed in Pascal using an animation library. The algorithm is also specified in Pascal. Synchronization between the algorithm and the view is achieved by adding interesting events that trigger an action in the animation.

http://www
.research
.digital.com/
SRC/zeus/
home.html

Marc Brown has completed a successor to Balsa-II, called Zeus [Bro91a], in the DEC System Research Center in Palo Alto, where he has investigated the use of color and sound for algorithm animation [Bro91b] [Bro91c] (Figure III.2). Zeus runs on special multiprocessor machines and has been used to animate a variety of algorithms for teaching and research purposes.

In his latest system, *Collaborative Active Textbooks*, [Bro96] Brown goes one step further by directly integrating algorithm animations into the Web. He is addressing similar goals as our *Animated Algorithms* project but allows users to view and customize the same algorithm simultaneously. Instead of HyperCard

Figure III.1

Balsa screen dump illustrating Dijkstra's shortest-path algorithm

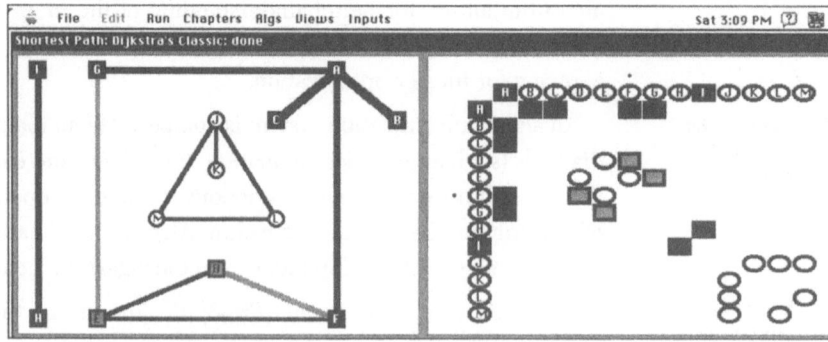

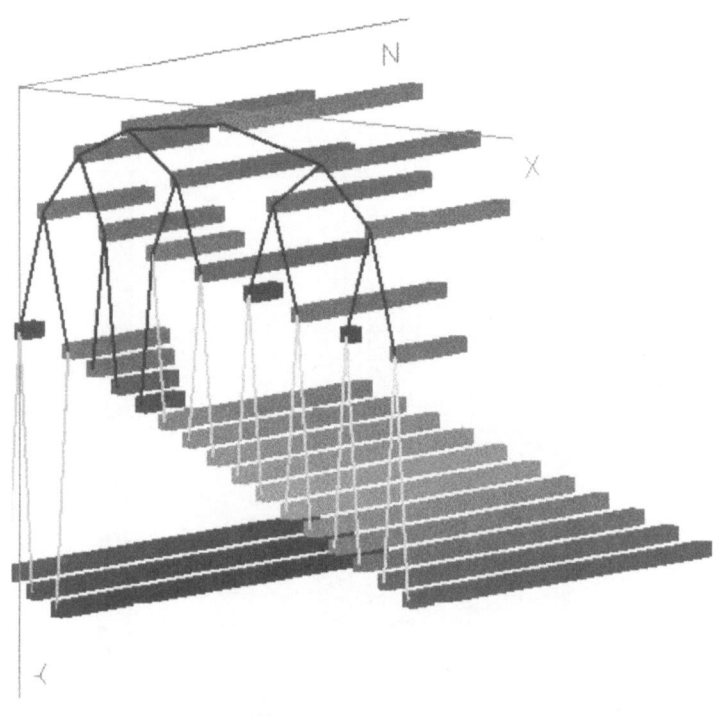

Figure III.2

Screen dump of Zeus heapsort animation (http://www .research.digital .com/SRC/zeus/ heapsort3D.4.gif)

he is using a Java-like Web programming system called Obliq developed at the DEC System Research Center.

John Stasko [Sta89] [Sta90] implemented a system called Tango (short for "Transition based ANimation GeneratiOn") that can be used to create algorithm animations (Figure III.3). In newer versions of his system, the emphasis is on developing animations integrating three-dimensional views of data and on the integration of direct manipulation programming techniques into the animation development [Sta91]. Extended versions of XTango named Polka are being developed at Georgia Tech.

http://www.cc .gatech.edu/ gvu/softviz/ algoanim/ algoanim.html

Gruia-Catalin Roman and his concurrent systems group at Washington University in St. Louis are developing a system called Pavane [Cox94] (Figure III.4). Visualizations in Pavane are specified abstractly as a mapping from computational states to images on the screen. This declarative approach is favored by the Pavane team because visualizations can be specified and

http://swarm .cs.wustl.edu/ pavane.html

Figure III.3

Screen dump of
XTango first-fit
bin-packing
animation
(http://www.cc
.gatech.edu/gvu/
softviz/algoanim/
bpack.gif)

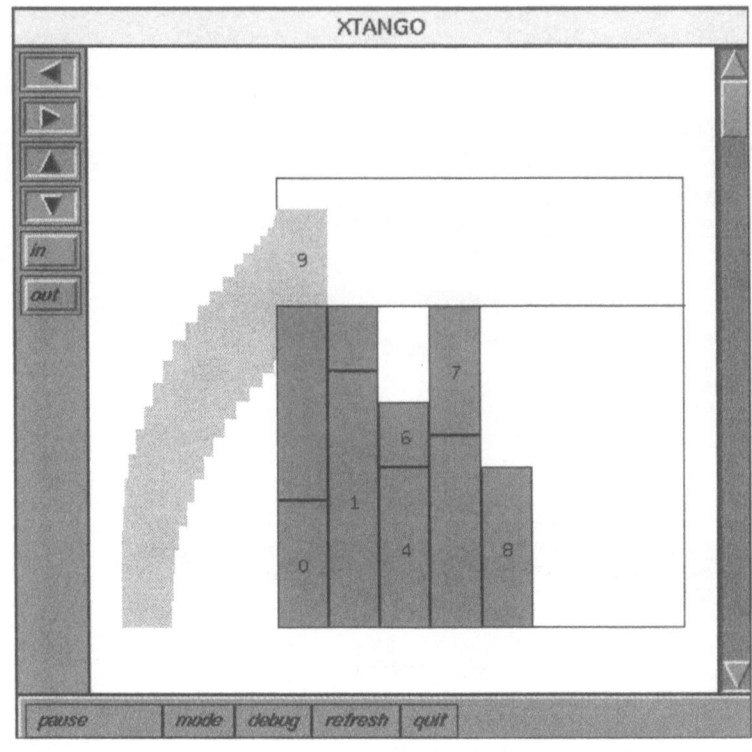

modified more easily and because visualization is decoupled from the program code. Duisberg pursued a similar approach about ten years ago based
on temporal constraints [Dui86].

Another animation system is Anim by Jon Bentley and Brian Kernighan
[Ben91]. Anim was used at Bell Labs, running under UNIX and X windows, to
produce simple program animations. Contrary to Balsa-II, XTango, and
Animated Algorithms, Anim is not interactive but is more like a Camcorder and
VCR [Ben91]. Anim's advantages lie in the wide availability of the underlying
hardware and software and in its reliance on general-purpose UNIX tools like
AWK [Aho88]. In this aspect, it is similar to Animated Algorithms, which relies
on the HyperCard run time environment. But Anim has disadvantages in that

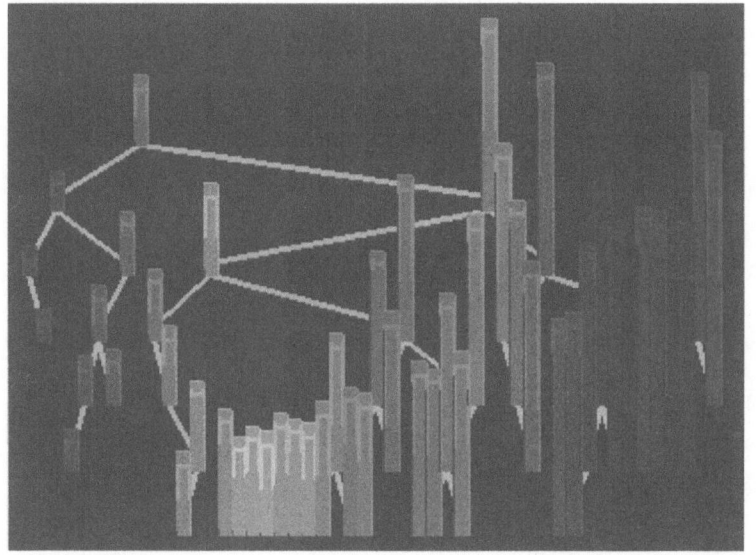

Figure III.4

Screen dump of Pavane quicksort animation (http://swarm.cs .wustl.edu/ vislab/gallery/ pics/quicksort2 .Gif)

it is not interactive, its user interface is relatively crude, and it demands an experienced UNIX programmer to do more than just run the movies.

Compared to these algorithm animation systems, Animated Algorithms uses far less expensive hardware and less sophisticated software. It is less a vehicle for research than a generally usable hypermedia learning environment, allowing the teacher to develop new animations of well-known algorithms quickly using a simple but powerful scripting language. The student gets an interactive system affording intimate exploration of the run time behavior of algorithms unobtainable with more conventional means. Animated Algorithms exhibits some unique features in that it is based on a general–purpose run time environment like HyperCard, covers a broad range of computer science algorithms with an easy–to–use interface, and is interactive.

Animated

Algorithms

Animated Algorithms is a multimedia system for computer science education that illustrates a new class of educational multimedia applications characterized by a seamless integration of different multimedia data types. The combination of hypertext, computer animation, and digital video results in an interactive hypermedia learning environment impossible to realize before the advent of multimedia technology. *Animated Algorithms* is an integrated hypermedia learning environment for teaching and studying computer science algorithms. It tries to aid in the understanding of core algorithmic concepts that are especially difficult for students to comprehend. Algorithms are a complex subject to teach and understand. One of the difficulties in understanding an algorithm is the development of a sophisticated conceptualization of the algorithm from written explanations and pseudocode. Our system applies the concepts of algorithm animation, hypertext, and digital video to facilitate this task.

24.1 System Overview

Animated Algorithms [Glo93a] is intended to be used to complement a conventional textbook for the Introduction to Algorithms course. It assists in the

235

understanding of core concepts, like the O- and Ω- notation and the comprehension of advanced subjects, like Fibonacci-Heaps. The algorithm animations can be used for classroom teaching or for the individual to study new algorithms and deepen the understanding of known ones. The hypertext part provides individual access to a vast reference book covering the whole field of algorithms.

The system has been implemented on the Macintosh. As multimedia authoring system we used HyperCard [Win90]. Apple's digital video architecture QuickTime [App91] allowed us to integrate digital video segments into multimedia documents without needing additional hardware.

The goal of Animated Algorithms is to offer an integrated hypermedia learning environment for computer science algorithms. It contains three complementary components: A full hypertext version of the book *Introduction to Algorithms* by Thomas H. Cormen, Charles E. Leiserson, and Ronald L. Rivest [Cor90], interactive animations of the most important algorithms, and movies explaining the use of the hypertext interface and the animations.

The screen dump in Figure III.5 displays the main components of Animated Algorithms: the window in the lower right corner shows a "talking head" digital movie explaining the features of the algorithm, the top half of the screen

Figure III.5

Screen dump of
*Animated
Algorithms*

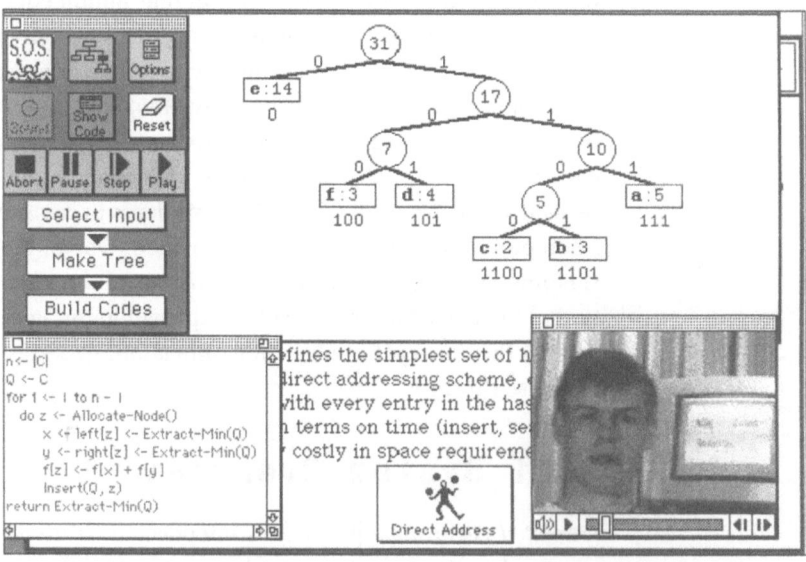

depicts an animation of the "Huffman Tree" algorithm, and in the background there is some hypertext visible that explains the fundamentals of Huffman Trees.

The hypertext, including the figures, is stored in HyperCard stacks. It contains tools for instructors and students to facilitate navigation, text annotation, tracking of preexisting links, full-text search, and the adding of links and paths through the document. The algorithm animations implemented in HyperCard are linked with the hypertext and can be controlled interactively by the user. They also include extensive on-line help to make them self-contained. Some animations include scripting facilities allowing users to program animations of specific data structures. The movies ("talking heads" and demonstrations) provide a way to view noninteractive versions of the algorithm animations.

The hypertext, consisting of 1850 text nodes and figures, is implemented in HyperCard stacks. It contains tools for navigation, text annotation, tracking of preexisting links, full-text search, and the adding of links and "paths" through the document. (Innovative hypertext concepts pioneered in Animated Algorithms are described in Chapters 14–16.)

The animations, which are implemented in HyperCard, are linked with the hypertext and can be controlled interactively by the user. This interactivity not only includes the ability to single-step through the pseudocode but also (in certain animations) the ability to choose initial conditions and the specification of assumptions the algorithm makes, enabling the user to affect the action of the algorithm. Some animations include scripting facilities allowing users to program animations of specific data structures. Animations also include extensive on-line help, making them self-contained.

24.2 Project Goals

Most of the animations for the Animated Algorithms system have initially been developed by students as homework assignments for algorithm animation classes or as thesis work. The students had taken algorithm classes before and thus already had knowledge of the subject. It was our goal to make them productive in developing animations as fast as possible. Therefore the development environment needed to fulfill stringent boundary conditions:

- *Rapid development.* The development environment should allow for early student integration into the development process. That means that the students should become productive developing animations very quickly. In particular, the system should be easy to learn for computer science majors (and not for graphics designers). We therefore favored an approach based on a programming language over a strictly mouse– or menu–based animation development system. Basic programming languages, such as C or Pascal, had to be excluded because of productivity limitations. We also excluded the option of developing a dedicated animation shell from scratch. Instead we looked for an appropriate off–the–shelf scripting language animations package.

- *Portability.* We wanted to create a system that we could distribute easily without having to pay tremendous royalties. The software should also run on a broad hardware base.

- *Homogeneity.* We not only wanted to have a collection of algorithm animations, but also a usable and homogeneous system at the end of the course. In particular, the user interface should be uniform and easy to use on different algorithms.

- *Color and sound.* It would be nice to have not only black–and–white silent animations but also color and sound. On the other hand, algorithm animations need not be high–quality Gouraud–shaded, ray–traced computer animations.[1] We therefore decided to have as much graphic quality as possible, but that all other aspects mentioned here should have preference. In particular we gave interactivity preferential treatment over sophistication in output quality.

- *Speed.* The animations should run at a comfortable speed. Ideally they should be independent from hardware and degrade gracefully if the system ran on slower hardware. This requirement contrasts to the demand for high-quality color animations.

- *Hypertext.* It was our goal to get not only algorithm animations but also a hypermedia environment explaining them. We needed an extendible application development system exceeding bare animation capabilities. Ideally the system should offer built-in hypertext linking capabilities.

We soon decided to use the Macintosh as the hardware base because of its wide availability and acceptance among schools and universities. We investigated HyperCard [Win90], MacroMedia Director [Vau94], and AddMotion [Add90] for development environment.[2] To our surprise we finally ended up

---

1 Gouraud shading is a computer graphics procedure to get smoothly shaded surfaces of three-dimensional objects. Ray tracing is another process that allows for more than one light source with mirroring of the light sources.

using HyperCard almost exclusively, adding some simple color animations with AddMotion. The frame-based structure and clumsy scripting language made MacroMedia Director a poor choice for computer scientists developing algorithm animations.

24.3 The Animation System

We defined a simple uniform framework for all animations with each algorithm animation having an animation window and an algorithm window (Figure III.6).

The algorithm window shows the code for whatever algorithm is currently in progress. The current line of the code (that is, the line being animated) is highlighted to emphasize which part of the algorithm is running. We employ a VCR–type controller (see Figure III.6) as the basic user interface metaphor for all of the algorithms. Frequently this controller is augmented by buttons emphasizing the main steps of an algorithm. This interface allows for a better in-depth understanding of the algorithm. Obviously these extra commands are sometimes difficult to define or are even inappropriate and can be applied only if the algorithm lends itself well to substructuring.

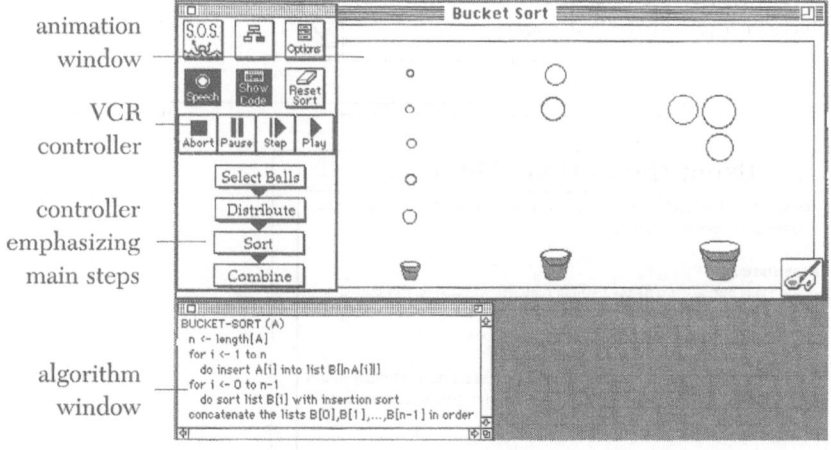

animation window

VCR controller

controller emphasizing main steps

algorithm window

Figure III.6

Basic animation screen layout

---

2 MacroMedia Director is a powerful standalone animations package with a built–in scripting language, Lingo. It is based on the cast, score, and stage movie maker metaphors. AddMotion is an animation package embedded within HyperCard that extends HyperCard's built–in animation capabilities.

Our goal is not to produce a monolithic collection of algorithm animations but to implement an integrated learning environment. Because each topic should be self–contained, it has its own, hierarchically structured overview map. Figure III.7 shows the overview map for the hashing animations.

The overview map presents all options currently available. In Figure III.7 the student has the following possibilities:

- Getting help for using the stack.
- Reading an introduction to hashing.
- Interactively executing the hashing algorithms.

Figure III.7

Overview map
for hashing
chapter

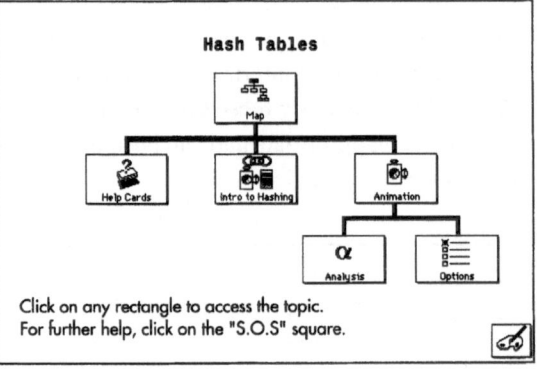

Figure III.8

Help card for
options menu

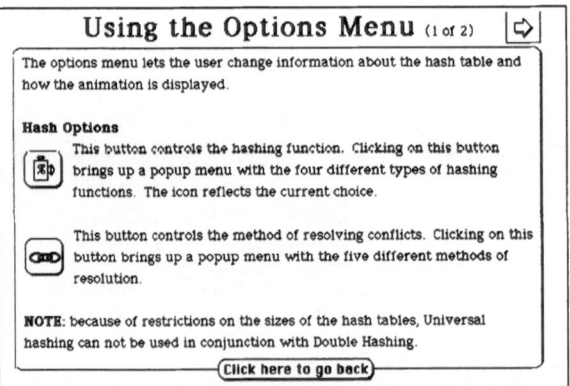

- Going to an analysis card for comparison of the different hashing algorithms.
- Reviewing animation options.
- Returning to the global animation overview map card.

Figure III.8 shows the help card for the options menu. It illustrates our efforts to offer extensive on-line help making animations as self–explaining and easily usable as possible.

CHAPTER 25

User Interface Design *for* Algorithm Animation

consistency of object and motion

Because a system must be both easy to use and quick to learn, the design of the user interface is of fundamental importance. Two aspects of the user interface require standardization: the consistency of object and motion and the consistency of the control interface. The first aspect means that animation objects should always move the same way (consistency of motion) and that similar algorithm variables should be represented uniformly (consistency of object). To address the second aspect, Animated Algorithms offers a consistent control interface employing the VCR controller metaphor (Figure III.9).

consistent controller interface

The VCR controller is always the frontmost window on the screen and allows control over the stepping through or playing through of algorithms. Where appropriate, we have added controller elements that emphasize the main steps of the algorithm and allow the student to proceed consciously from one logical algorithm step to the next (Figure III.10).

These added controller elements emphasize the main steps of the algorithm and allow the student to step consciously from one logical algorithm step to the next.

Figure III.9

VCR controller for sorting animations

Based on our experience with Animated Algorithms, we have come up with the "ten commandments of algorithm animation":

```
1.    Be consistent.
2.    Be interactive.
3.    Be clear and concise.
4.    Be forgiving to the user.
5.    Adapt to the knowledge level of the user.
6.    Emphasize the visual component.
7.    Keep the user interested.
8.    Incorporate both symbolic and iconic representations.
9.    Include analysis and comparisons.
10.   Include execution history.
```

These points have been identified while making many mistakes and rebuilding many different versions of the Animated Algorithms user interface and animations. Obviously they range from general concepts to very algorithm animation–specific requirements. Let us look at them in detail:

1. *Be consistent.* This aspect, true for the user interface of any system, is especially important for educational algorithm animations. We request consistency of object and motion and consistency in the control interface.

Figure III.10

Controller emphasizing the main steps of bucket sort

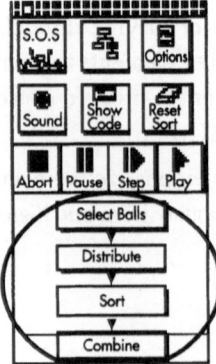

2. *Be interactive.* A high degree of interactivity is necessary to keep users interested and improve their understanding of the inner workings of an algorithm. Basically users should be forced to interact with the system at least every 45 seconds.[1] Additionally, users should be able to select their own input. For novice users, on the other hand, a predefined input data set should be offered. In Animated Algorithms, controller elements emphasizing the main steps (Figure III.10) force the user to interact with the animation by starting the next logical step of the algorithm.

3. *Be clear and concise.* The essential points of the algorithm have to be presented clearly and to the point. Complexity can be hidden by a hierarchical substructure. Access to this substructure is made possible by a "Step Into" button.

Figure III.11 illustrates the "Step Into" button for the heap sort algorithm where the user is about to step into the `heapify` procedure. This technique permits the user to learn fundamental concepts first and then expand into complexity. By highlighting the currently executed pseudocode line, the user is always able to see exactly how the animation relates to the algorithm. It is also important to demonstrate where the algorithm breaks—to show under which boundary conditions the algorithm is inefficient or will not work.

Important logical algorithm steps can be emphasized not only by means of a separate controller (see Figure III.10), but they should also be accentuated in the animation by transitions from one step to the other. The student

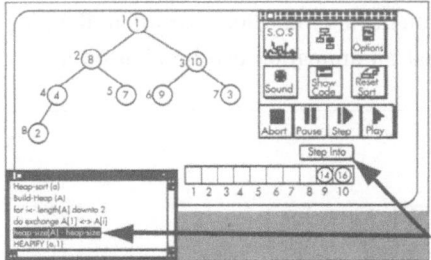

Figure III.11

"Step Into" button for heap sort

---

1 This means that no animation step should last longer than 45 seconds. We came to this number by conducting informal user tests during the development of Animated Algorithms.

can get explicit pointers to the logical steps by hypertextual or voice annotations.

4. *Be forgiving to the user.* The system has to be generous and forgiving to erroneous user manipulations. This means that it allows only meaningful actions and alerts users if they are in the process of executing a meaningless action. Users are, for example, only allowed to define an input set that makes sense for the current algorithm. Also, the system should make sure that controller elements may only be used in correct order.

5. *Adapt to the knowledge level of the user.* The system has to be adaptable to the knowledge level of the user. We allow users to set the animation speed themselves. We also provide extensive built-in on-line help and permit stepping into or out of an algorithm where appropriate.

6. *Emphasize the visual component.* Since animation is a graphical process, visualizations should be as self-explanatory as possible. This means that elements should not needed to be interpreted further. For example, elements to be sorted could be differently sized bars or balls instead of letters of the alphabet (Figure III.12); one should use slider bars for setting the animation speed or employ colored arrows in a hash table to indicate its fullness.

The requirement for consistency of motion means that similar actions should always be animated in similar ways. This allows students to recognize repetitive steps more quickly, even when they choose to perform a previously unseen action. Figure III.13 shows the animation of the generic insert operation for the hashing algorithms, which is animated similarly independent of the particular addressing method.

7. *Keep the user interested.* An animation should not only capture the initial interest but keep the user's attention during the whole execution. Keeping the user interested also means that an animation can be aborted at any

Figure III.12

Different visual representation of data elements

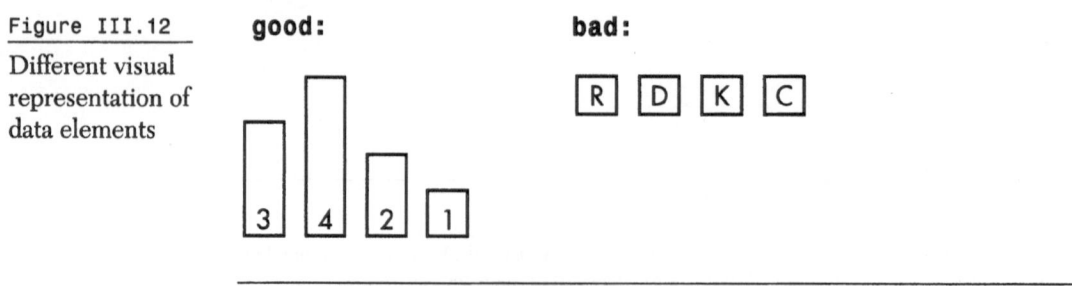

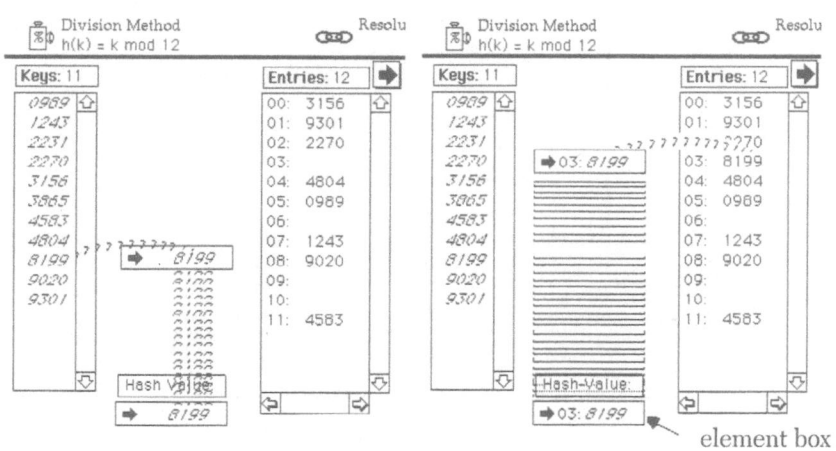

Figure III.13

Generic animation of the insert operation for the hashing animation

element box

time. This is advantageous if, for example, a large data set would keep the algorithm executing for a long time while the user has already understood all concepts. It means also that frequent stopping points for single stepping have to be foreseen. Voice annotations are another useful means of keeping the user interested.

An animation should definitely not offer humor at any price, but good real–world examples for the explanation of theoretical concepts help keep the user interested and improve the learning effect.

Figure III.14 demonstrates a real–world example of how to find the convex hull of a set of points in a plane using an elastic rubber band.

8. *Incorporate both symbolic and iconic representations.* The user should have the option of watching the execution of an algorithm in parallel as

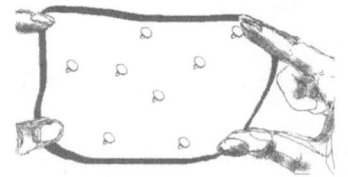 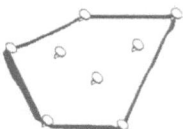

Figure III.14

Real–world example explaining the convex hull

Figure III.15

Longest common
subsequence
animation
containing both
symbolic and
iconic
information

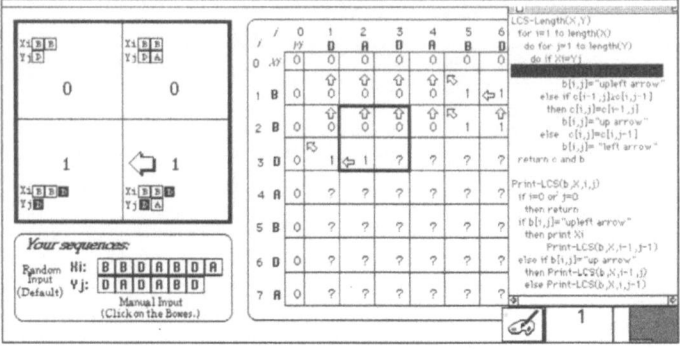

animation and as pseudocode. Figure III.15 shows the animation window
of an animation of the longest common subsequence algorithm.

The right side of the figure is a symbolic representation of the algorithm
in execution, and the left side is the iconic representation of the same
action.

9. *Include algorithms analysis.* Wherever appropriate, analysis of the algorithm's behavior should be included. Once an algorithm is run several
   times, it would be useful for the student to be able to see how different
   options affect the operation of the algorithms. These options can be parameters to the algorithms itself or variations in the input to the algorithm.
   Analysis information can be collected during the execution of the anima-

Figure III.16

Hashing analysis
card

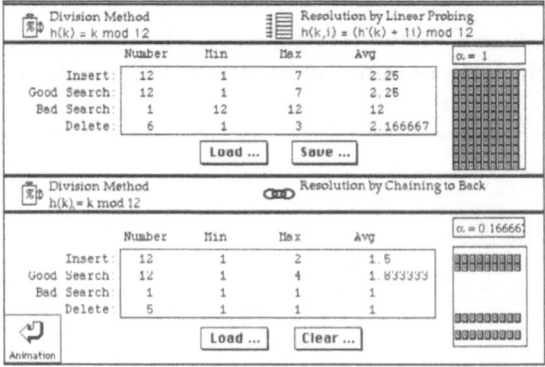

tions. Figure III.16 displays the hashing analysis card allowing the student to view the collected data .

Visual comparisons between different similar algorithms further deepen the student's understanding. Figure III.17 displays the sorting comparison animation of Animated Algorithms, allowing comparison of the different sorting algorithms with different input data sets.

10. *Include execution history.* One of Brown's three dimensions of algorithm animation (see Figure III-27) demands that the animation give a temporal context for the momentary action. Ideally an animation always keeps some sort of history that shows why the current action is happening based on a snapshot of past actions.

The snapshot of the radix sort animation in Figure III.18 illustrates the history concept. The fourth digit is currently being sorted, but the sorting sequence of all previous digits is still visible in the animation window.

Of course, an algorithm animation should also be implemented in a way such that it does not overstretch the built-in limitations of the hardware and operating system. This means, for example, that it was impossible to have full-color three–dimensional animations on the Motorola 68000-based Macintosh line that Animated Algorithms was designed for. It is more important for the student to have a system that runs at acceptable speed smoothly

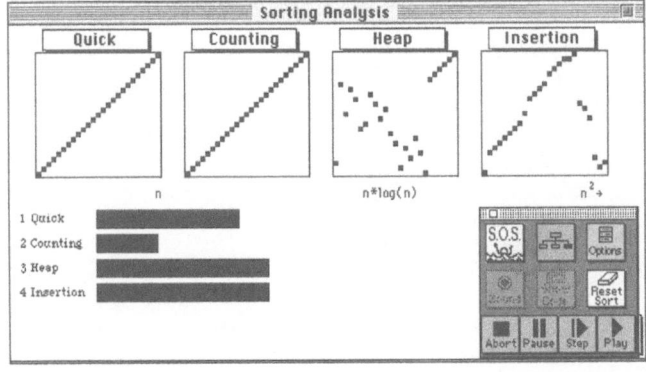

Figure III.17

Comparison of sorting algorithms

Figure III.18

Radix sort
containing
history of actions

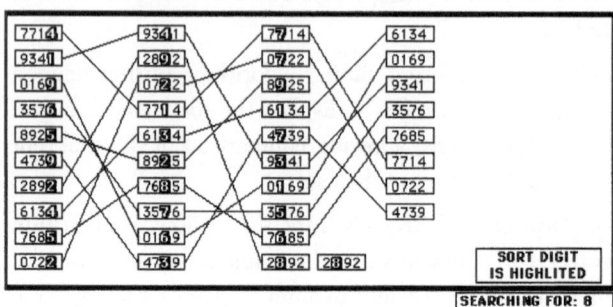

than a potentially dazzling system that is capable of only jerky motion on not top-of-the-line systems.

The ultimate requirement, of course, is to optimize the learning effect. Applying the "ten commandments", algorithm animation system designers should be capable of designing educational systems that avoid the perils and pitfalls that our team ran into while developing Animated Algorithms.

CHAPTER 26

Educational

Aspects

Everything should be made as simple as possible, but not simpler.

—**Albert Einstein**

26.1 Educational Benefits of Algorithm Animation

Algorithm animations support students in various learning situations:

- *Motivation enhancement.* Through appealing presentation of the complex material, students are better motivated to study complicated subjects. In addition, the ease of access to cross-references by hypertext removes barriers to an in-depth understanding of the topic being studied [Ste91].

- *Skill mastery through additional practice opportunities.* Students get a new way to experience algorithms. In addition to doing paper exercises and writing programs, they can perceive algorithms visually and study their features by watching and interacting with animations [Law94].

- *Development of analytic skills.* Algorithm animations assist in the development of analytic skills, as students are asked to collect their own data for algorithm analysis and subsequent design of improved algorithms.

251

- *Provision of additional context knowledge.* The hypertext reference provides easy access to the whole field of algorithms. By offering linking and path mechanisms, it encourages the student to browse in related topics and to explore additional subjects.

Algorithm animations offer distinct advantages compared to traditional teaching aids, such as textbook and blackboard:

- *Presentation aid in the classroom.* Animations support the teacher in explaining the dynamic behavior of an algorithm during the lecture. If computer screen projection is available in the classroom, the teacher can run algorithm animations interactively to compare, for example, the relative search times of red-black trees and binary search trees using the same data sets.

- *Individual improvement of student's understanding.* Using the algorithm animations interactively, the student can playfully and without stress explore the peculiarities of an algorithm. By manipulating the algorithm and its input and then studying the resulting actions of the algorithm, students can form a conceptual model of the algorithm in addition to learning the code. They also can modify parameters and analyze algorithms empirically. As has been verified by Lawrence, Badre, and Stasko in an experiment [Law94], this interactivity adds a new level of effectiveness to a hypermedia learning environment, making it an even more effective tool in teaching concepts, as it forces learners to take part in the lesson, as opposed to simply watching a movie.

- *Reference library for the student.* Using the exhaustive search and navigation capabilities of an integrated hypermedia learning environment, a student can easily access the vast information contained in systems like Animated Algorithms or the Web [Bro96].

Animated Algorithms version 1.0 was finished in January 1993. It has been thoroughly tested in the development lab and has been used repeatedly in MIT's Introduction to Algorithms course on a voluntary basis, with students asked to complete questionnaires concerning their reactions to the learning environment. The main benefit reported has been improved student motivation, as students used particular animations to get a better understanding of the algorithm.

The hypertext part has been tested by volunteers (students and computer science professors), who were particularly impressed with the "path" feature and the capability to traverse the document on various levels of complexity. Also the reference capabilities of the hypertext—full-text search, for example—were appreciated.

26.2 Structure-Based Algorithm Animation

In most systems, algorithm animators define a view suited for a certain class of algorithms. They then adapt the view for each particular algorithm of this class but try to keep the individual adaptations as small as possible. In the following discussion, this approach is called *unified view-based*. We have selected for Animated Algorithms a slightly different approach, which we call *structure-based*. Our approach stresses the particularities of each algorithm and tries to emphasize its main points. Each of the two types has advantages:

- *Unified view-based animation.* The animator tries to animate different but related algorithms in a similar way by using generic views. This approach has two main advantages. (1) The algorithm animator is more productive because, once the animation view has been established for the first algorithm, the view can easily be adapted to accomplish the other related algorithms. (2) The behavior of related algorithms can be compared more easily because of the common base.

- *Structure-based animation.* With this approach, the animation for each algorithm is developed from scratch. It takes more effort to animate algorithms this way because the algorithm has to be understood thoroughly before a meaningful representation can be found. This approach emphasizes the particularities of an algorithm. Fortunately we were well supported in this task by *Introduction to Algorithms* [Cor90], which already contains excellent graphical representations of most of the algorithms.

Figure III.19 illustrates our approach by comparing unified view-based with structure-based animated sorting algorithms. The unified view-based animated examples are from an earlier experiment in algorithm animation undertaken by L. Richter and the author at the University of Zurich [Glo89]. Obviously the unified view-based animated algorithms allow the user an easier comparative analysis of the different sorting algorithms, but we feel that it is well worth expending the additional effort for structure-based animations because they communicate much more information about the intrinsic working of the particular algorithm. To compare structurally animated algorithms, some additional effort has to be made, but these comparisons are then much better

Figure III.19

Unified
view–based
versus
structure–based
algorithm
animation

Unified View Based   # Structure Based

Bubble Sort

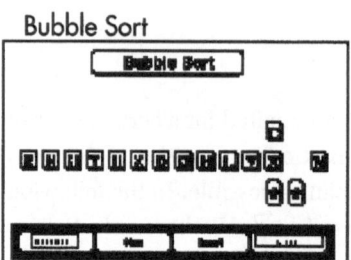

Bucket Sort

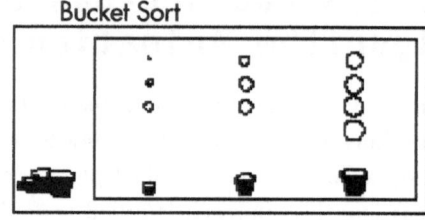

Insertion Sort

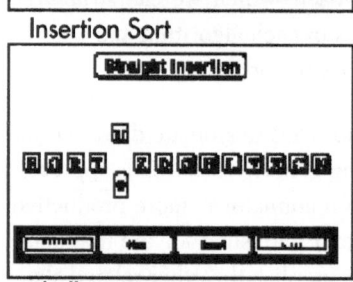

Counting Sort

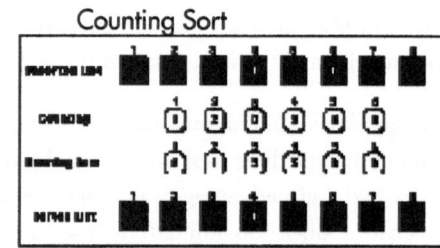

Shell Sort

Radix Sort

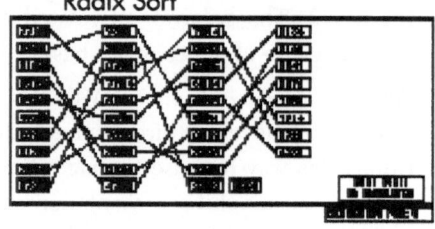

Quick Sort

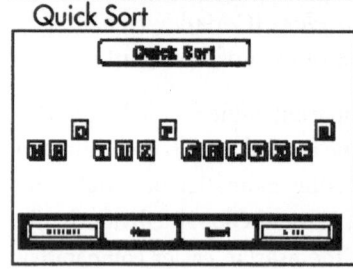

Quick Sort

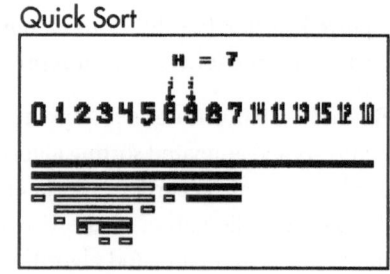

tailored to the actual algorithm comparisons. For an example comparing algorithms, see Figure III.17, which depicts an analytical comparison of sorting
algorithms in Animated Algorithms.

26.3 Find "the Best" Pseudocode

The pseudocode representation is the most precise and mathematically correct
description of an algorithm. But obviously there are many different
pseudocode representations for the same algorithm. How do we find the
pseudocode description that is best for our educational purpose?

To illustrate our point, consider two possible pseudocode descriptions of the
"bucket sort" algorithm:

1. Full pseudocode, mathematically correct:

```
n ←length[A]
for i ← 1 to n
  do insert A[i] into list B[⌊nA[i]⌋]
for i ← 0 to n-1
  do sort list B[i] with insertion sort
concatenate the lists B[0],B[1],...,B[n-1] together in order
```

2. Abbreviated pseudocode, emphasizing the main steps:

```
select input
distribute elements into buckets
sort buckets
concatenate elements from buckets
```

The first pseudocode description, from [Cor90], describes very clearly and
compactly what the algorithm does. But for the student's understanding of
what bucket sort is really about, the second description is quite helpful also. It
is not mathematically exact, and it would be impossible to generate executable
code automatically out of it, but it teaches the fundamental concept. First the
elements to be sorted are distributed into buckets; then the elements in each
bucket are sorted separately; and finally the sorted elements of each bucket are
concatenated into the sorted output list.

Because of educational reasons, both descriptions are necessary. To specify
exactly what bucket sort is, we need the first description. But every effort should
also be made to find a commonsense description of the actions in the algorithm.
By complementing each other, the two descriptions give the student an intuitive
and mathematically sound understanding of the inner workings of the algorithm.

Animating

Proofs

Visualizing the proof of an algorithm is different from visualizing the algorithm itself, as is done by various systems described in Chapter 23. Visualization of a proof is an algorithm animation that goes one step further: It can be composed of an algorithm animation extended by a proof-dialog that exhibits in a temporal fashion and with visual means the correctness of the algorithm. In this chapter we describe a framework that defines three primary components for a proof visualization system: (1) the definition of the abstract operations necessary for a proof of correctness visualization, (2) the design of operations for the proof process or dialog, and (3) the correspondence between the proof visualization and the algorithm visualization. A detailed description of this system can be found in [Glo92b].

The correctness proofs we consider are at the level that such proofs are customarily done in a classroom and thus should not be confused with program verification. The latter usually refers to a formal proof that examines the actual code implementing some algorithm step by step and shows that the program actually achieves the goal. Our endeavor is to illustrate why the algorithm works; we introduce an interactive system that deals with the algorithm at a high level and with the fundamental ideas underlying the algorithm.

27.1 Components of the Proof Visualization System

The lack of previous work in this area is partly due to the fact that proofs often involve hypothetical and abstract objects created for the purpose of the proof. Such objects are difficult to visualize. The proof visualization system therefore tries to provide such objects. It is composed of:

1. Abstract graph objects, for example graphs, subgraphs, and paths that are hypothetical, of indefinite size, or structure.

2. Concrete graph objects, such as vertices and edges of a given graph.

3. Descriptions of theorems to be proved and invariants examined for validity during the proof.

4. Dynamic hypertext help providing updatable information about the objects appearing on the screen.

5. The proof-dialog description.

Although our system could be standalone, we suggest that it be used in conjunction with a proof orientation (introduction) describing the problem and the algorithm through pseudocode that explains the important steps, and an integrated animation of the algorithm. The term *integrated* refers to an animation that operates on the same pseudocode and uses the same concrete objects as the proof system. Users are urged to examine and understand the animation first, such that they have some intuition of how the algorithm works. As we mentioned, the aim of the proof system is to show why the proof works.

A typical session begins with users' going through the introduction and the interactive visualization of the algorithm. When they are familiar with the algorithm and the pseudocode that implements the algorithm, they are told the theorem along with a set of invariants that should be satisfied during the run of the algorithm. This means that if the invariants are satisfied during the run of the algorithm, the theorem is true.

Users are then guided through the proof step by step. The proof visualization is controlled by the proof-dialog. A sequence of statements is presented to the users, and they can either accept them or ask for more explanation of any statement. In the latter case, the system gives further explanation. Moreover, at any time users can jump back into the algorithm animation and examine more examples to improve the understanding of the algorithm, before resuming the proof session. The session ends when a complete set of statements has been presented and has been understood by the users. Users can go through the proof–dialog as many times as they wish. They also have the option of stepping backward to take a closer look at some concepts presented earlier.

The programmer who implements a proof visualization has to provide the following:

1. The *introduction part*, in which the definition of the problem, its significance, and other similar information appear.

2. An *animation of the algorithm* that solves the problem. This animation can be used as a repository for the concrete and abstract proof objects. In addition the animation contains an educationally suitable pseudocode description of the algorithm that is employed in the theorem.

3. The *proof-dialog* in terms of a text file having a special format. This text file contains the theorem, a set of invariants, and a set of expandable statements.

4. The *animation* of the basic and inductive *proof* steps.

5. A *help file* that contains information about the objects.

27.2 Master Teaching

To present complex concepts, we are applying a three-step process, called *master teaching*, that has already been put to use successfully in other educational multimedia projects at the Dartmouth Interactive Media Lab. The three steps are defined as follows:

http:// griffith .dartmouth .edu/iml/iml .html

1. *Master teaching.* A teacher who is a master in teaching as well as a master in the methods she or he teaches presents the subject to the students. Ideally, this is done interactively by the human teacher. Unfortunately, master teachers are a scarce resource, and it is often desirable to replace or augment the master teacher. In the simplest case, this is done by a text provided by the master teacher, but with today's multimedia capabilities, this can be done much more effectively using video segments showing the master teacher teaching.

2. *Experiential learning.* Students practice the concepts taught by the master teacher. "Learning by doing" is still one of the most effective ways to understand new ideas. The learning effect can be improved if the new ideas are presented and can be practiced in different ways.

3. *Reflective learning.* This step provides for an in-depth understanding of the taught and practiced concepts. By combining their own experiences with the methods taught by the master teacher, students build their own mental model of the concepts.

This three-step learning process can easily be adapted for multimedia-enhanced teaching of computer science algorithms. It is particularly well suited for teaching proofs of theorems.

Figure III.20 displays the overview map of an animated learning environment for Prim's algorithm for finding a minimum cost spanning tree (m.s.t.) [Pri57]. It illustrates the three main parts of our learning environment. These correspond directly to the three steps of master teaching. The Introduction part explains the basic concepts as they would be explained by the master teacher. The Algorithm part contains an interactive animation environment corresponding to the "experiential learning" step in the master teaching method. Finally, the Proof part provides the "reflective learning" step.

Figure III.21 shows a screen dump of the animation of Prim's algorithm. The interactive environment allows the student to experiment with Prim's algorithm, while the animation is running synchronously with different pseudocode representations. This visual-with-code representation of the algorithm affords an intuitive and thorough understanding of the algorithm, which leads to a better understanding of how the proof works.

Figure III.20

Overview map of Prim's algorithm

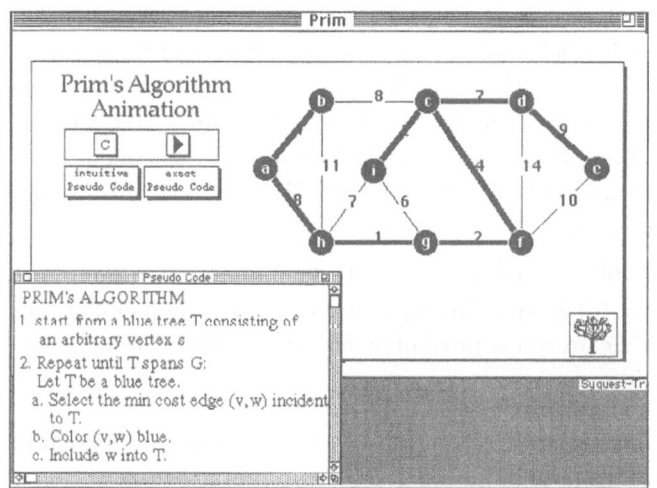

Figure III.21

Animation of
Prim's algorithm

Figure III.22 displays one sample step in the animated proof–dialog of the proof of Prim's algorithm. The presentation of the proof corresponds to the "reflective learning" step in the master teaching method. In this step the student is expected to understand the proof based on an understanding of the algorithm gained in the previous two steps.

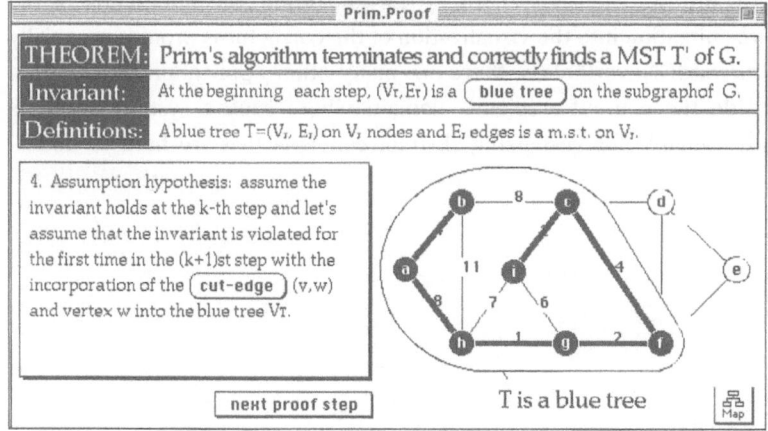

Figure III.22

Step 4 in the
visualization of
the proof of
Prim's algorithm

Obviously the set of expandable statements in the presentation of the proof represents the core of our animation system. This means that our system still is based on a textual description of the text. But the usefulness of the text alone gets vastly expanded by adding hypertext links on a microlevel, as shown in the Animated Algorithms project. The hypertext links allow direct access to any points the teacher thinks that a student might have difficulties in understanding, but they do not interrupt the flow of the proof because the student is not forced to follow the links.

There is considerable research activity in the field of algorithm animation, but so far nobody has tried to combine hypertext concepts with algorithm animation to visualize a correctness proof of an algorithm. The following points summarize our experience:

- The method for animating proofs is basically a guided walkthrough of slides to be shown one after the other.

- Emphasis is on the hypertext aspect of the system because access to additional information can be given at the location where it is actually needed.

- The animation for the proof is based on an animation of the algorithm to be presented before the proof. Although it is rather simple, it vastly improves the student's understanding of the complex subject matter.

- Color is very useful for emphasizing the actual and important points of a slide.

The method described can be used to visualize any proof. Because graph algorithms are particularly well suited for animation, the integration of the algorithm animation into the visualization of the correctness proof is especially straightforward. Nevertheless, there are many other application areas within and outside the computer science domain where such a system could be extremely valuable for visualizing abstract concepts that are hard to understand.

The Art

of

Algorithm Animation

To emphasize a specific action or reaction, the animator can exaggerate the movement with a take, sneak, or stagger.

—Tony White
The Animator's Workbook [Whi86]

Algorithm Cormen, Leiserson, and Rivest describe an algorithm informally as any well-defined computational procedure that takes some value, or set of values, as input and produces some value, or set of values, as output. An algorithm is thus a sequence of computational steps that transform the input into the output [Cor90]. But although the algorithm is a well-defined procedure, the animation of the algorithm is much less well defined. Rather, animating algorithms is much more of an art than of a science.

28.1 How to Animate Algorithms

Somewhat surprisingly, we found that the steps for producing algorithm animations are still basically the same as originally identified by Walt Disney for conventional (noncomputer) animation [Tho91]. The following seven-step

263

process illustrates, using a practical example—the list–ranking algorithm to compute the distance from the end of a list for each object in a linked list [Cor90]—how to get from the pseudocode description of the algorithm to the full animation.

1. *Script*

   The first stage in any film production is the creation of a script. In contrast to a live film, where the dialogue is at the center, the algorithm description in pseudocode describes the high-level action happening in the animation. Figure III.23 gives a pseudocode description of the list-rank algorithm described in [Cor90] used to compute the distance from the end of the list for each object in a linked list.

2. *Storyboard*

   From the script, the animation director produces the storyboard, a series of drawn images that graphically illustrate the action described in the script. A similar process also applies to algorithm animation. The animation storyboard graphically visualizes the main steps during the execution of the algorithm. Figure III.24 shows a sample storyboard of the list-rank algorithm directly taken from the illustration in the textbook [Cor90].

2. *Layout*

   Once the storyboard defines the main course of action, the film designer produces visual interpretations of all the characters featured in the film. Similarly, for an algorithm animation, the main elements (usually data structures) to be animated have to be specified graphically. Figure III.25 displays the main character of the list-rank animation: a processor element

---

Figure III.23

List-ranking algorithm to compute the distance from the end of the list for each object in a linked list (from [Cor90])

```
LIST-RANK(L)
1 for each processor i, in parallel
2    do if next [i] = NIL
3        then d[i] ← 0
4        else d[i] ← 1
5 while there exists an object i such that next [i] ≠ NIL
6    do for each processor i, in parallel
7        do if next [i] ≠ NIL
8            then d[i] ˜ d[i] + d[next [i]]
9                next [i] ˜ next [next [i]]
```

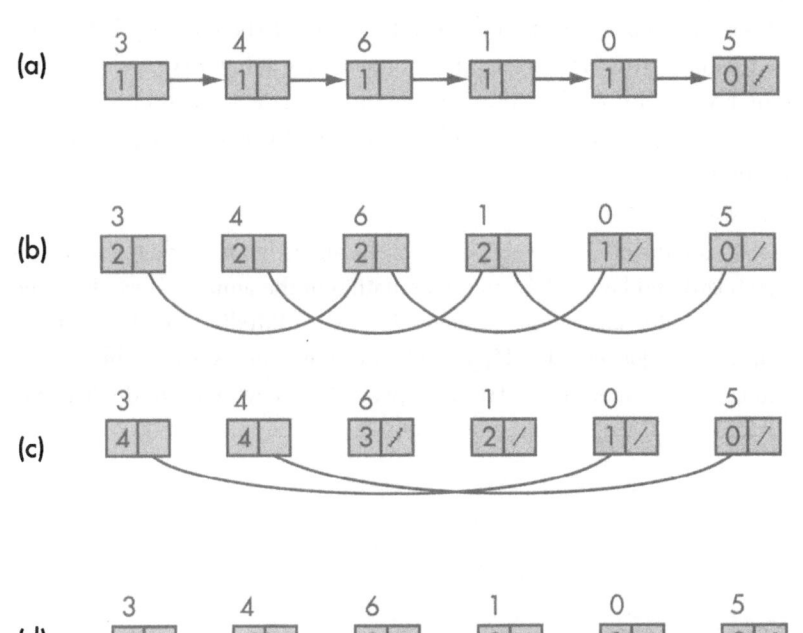

Figure III.24

Graphical
visualization of
the list-rank
algorithm in
[Cor90]

Finding the distance from each object in an *n*-object list to the end of
the list in *O* (lg n) time using pointer jumping. (a) A linked list represented
in a PRAM with *d* values initialized. At the end of the algorithm, each *d*
value holds the distance of its object from the end of the list. Each object's
responsible processor appears above the object. (b)—(d) The pointers and *d*
values after each iteration of the while loop in the algorithm **List-Rank**.

including a box storing the computed distance of the element from the list
end.

Figure III.25

Sample layout of
main element for
list-rank
animation

4. *Sound Track*

   If there is a sound track for the animation, it has to be recorded before the final animation is produced. This fundamental animation producer wisdom applies also to algorithm animation; for perfect synchronization the sound track has to be completed first, and then the animation produced to fit the sound track.

5. *Animation*

   In this step the computer animation of the algorithm is produced based on storyboard and layout. The implementation of the animation can be done with computer animation packages like MacroMedia Director [Vau94], scripting languages like HyperTalk, or animation systems like Zeus, XTango, or Pavane. Figure III.26 displays three keyframes of the list-rank

Figure III.26

Keyframes for
list-rank
animation

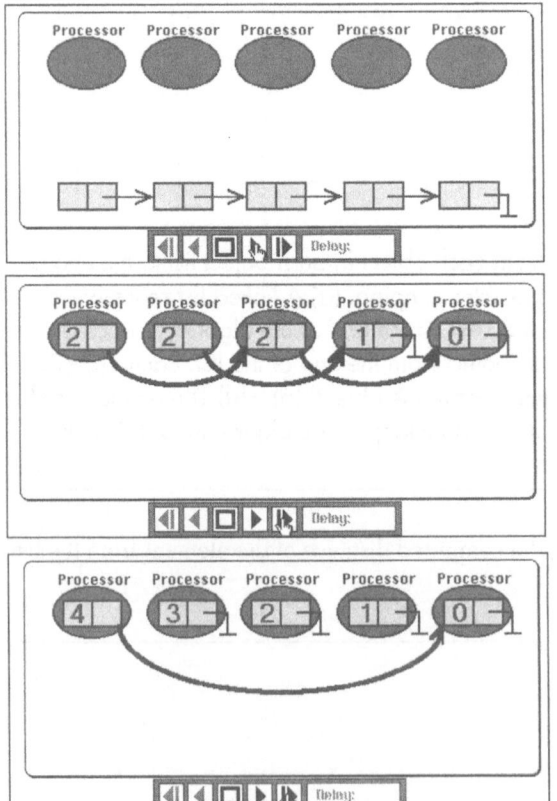

animation. This animation was done with AddMotion [Add90], a computer animations package that allows the creation of animation elements graphically and then a way to control them through HyperTalk scripts.

6. *Inbetweening*

   Once keyframes have been defined (as in Figure III.26) in the animation authoring environment, the inbetweening is done automatically by the animation authoring system.[1] The end product is a smoothly running animation.

7. *Editing*

   The last step in conventional animation, careful editing of the completed animation, should never be omitted. The quality of the final product can easily double if a last deliberate editing process is applied to the completed algorithm animation.

Some steps that Walt Disney used for producing his animated movies— *Xeroxing, Inking, Painting*, and *Camera*—can here be omitted due to the capabilities of the computer that is automatically generating the final movie.

28.2 Requirements of the Algorithm Animator

Marc Brown [Bro88a] makes a distinction between the view designer and the algorithmmathematician. The view designer understands the programming environment and knows how to implement new views. The algorithmmathematician is a theorist with a mathematical background who understands algorithms. In Brown's system, the algorithmmathematician takes the work of the view designer and synchronizes it with the algorithm by annotating the algorithm with interesting events that trigger an animation action in the graphical representation.

While developing Animated Algorithms, we found that almost every group of associated algorithms (e.g., algorithms that find the convex hull of a set of points) requires a different view. It also became obvious that to specify a meaningful view of an algorithm, the view designer needed to have a thorough understanding of the algorithm. The people developing the animations were algorithm experts and therefore fit into Brown's category of algorithmmathematician. But contrary to Brown's functional job division, every

---

1 Inbetweening is the menial step of adding all the frames between the keyframes to get a smooth animation.

algorithmathematician developed her or his own views from scratch. Based on this experience, we conclude that the two functions of algorithmathematician and view designer should be unified in one person. To produce educationally appealing animations, the combination of both roles delivers optimal results: the algorithmathematician's own visualization of a process provides the insight necessary to make the animation a valuable teaching tool.

In contrast to systems like Balsa where animations are built with predefined views that can be extended by a procedural programming language, we prefer a scripting language–based approach as provided by the HyperCard/HyperTalk environment where animation primitives like objects for sorting can be controlled by the scripting language. The scripting language gives the algorithmathematicians the flexibility to implement their own views and does away with the need for specialized view designers.

28.3 Automatic Algorithm Animation

Because of the large collection of algorithms to be animated in the Animated Algorithms project, we initially investigated the possibility of automatically generating animations based on pseudocode. We used Brown's "three dimensions of algorithm animation" to determine the requirements for the ideal algorithm animation. These requirements explain why it is almost impossible to produce educationally appealing algorithm animations automatically.

Brown [Bro88a] defines the three dimensions of algorithm animation as *transformation, persistence,* and *content* (Figure III.27). The instructionally best animation is placed in the upper right quadrant of Figure III.27. This ideal animation displays changes in the state of the variables incrementally (transformation), shows a history of the evolution in the execution state from the beginning until the actual moment (persistence), and not only contains a direct mapping of variables to objects on the screen but also shows synthetic metastructures of the algorithm as a performance analysis (content).

Knowing about the difficulties of automatic algorithm animation generation, we nevertheless decided to try developing our own system. We facilitated the task by narrowing the problem domain. A student wrote a HyperCard prototype of an automatic system for sorting algorithms. But although he did an impressive job and delivered a workable system, its animations were far inferior to the manually developed ones.

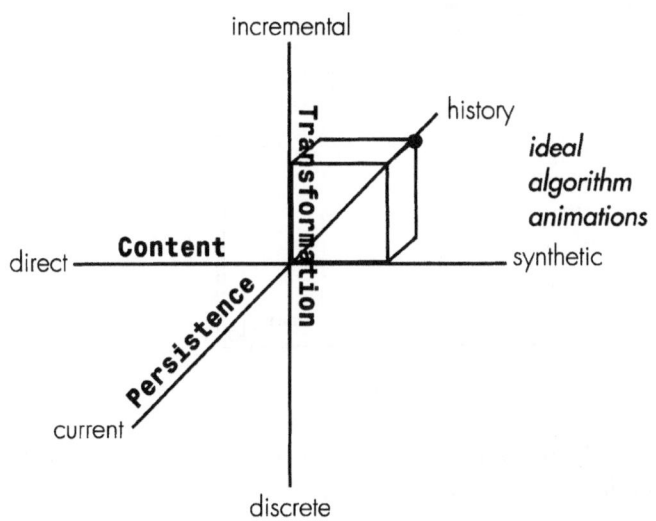

Figure III.27

Brown's
dimensions of
algorithm
animation
[Bro88a]

Figure III.28 shows the main control card of the automatic animation generation system and a bubble sort animation that has been generated automatically, based on the executable HyperTalk description of the algorithm in Figure III.29. The left side of Figure III.28 also illustrates the control flow of our automatic algorithm animation system. After programming the algorithm in HyperTalk, the system parses the algorithm and identifies variables that can be animated. It is then up to the user to link selected variables to predefined display elements, which are then mapped into so-called regions (i.e., predefined views).

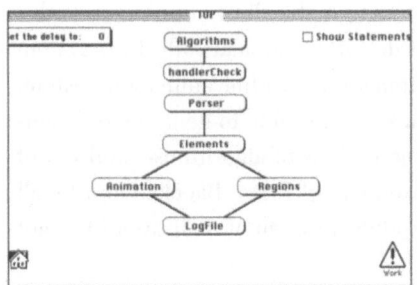 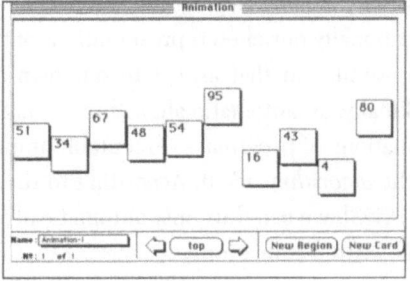

Figure III.28

Automatic
algorithm
animation:
general control
card (left) and
automatically
generated
animation of
bubble sort
(right)

Figure III.29

Bubble sort in
HyperTalk as a
basis for
automatic
algorithm
animation

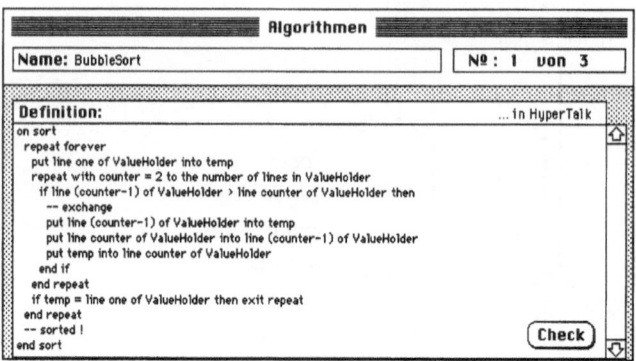

This system works only for animating directly displayed variables. The animation is updated each time the displayed variable is accessed by the program. Because of its internal structure, the automatic animation generation system delivers usable unified view-based animations (see section 26.2), but the results are insufficient for our more ambitious structure-based approach. Obviously, it is almost impossible to produce animations of upper right quadrant quality in Figure III.27 automatically, as these require in-depth knowledge of the inner workings of the algorithm. Additionally, the run time performance is poor because the algorithm is interpreted and animated at run time. We therefore decided not to use automatic algorithm animation for the Animated Algorithms project but to concentrate on the manual generation of instructive, appealing animations that contain a maximum of desirable qualities as defined in the three dimensions of algorithm animation. We were confirmed in our decision by Lin [Lin91], who describes a framework for automatic algorithm animation. Lin explicitly states that a system like the one he implements is only able to display internal data structures graphically, but not to add educationally enriched representations of the algorithm automatically. Lin's system is similar in that aspect to our own automatic algorithm animation system. Finally, an automatic algorithm animation system is able to generate only animations of *programs*—executable implementations of algorithms—and not of the *algorithms* itself. According to the taxonomy of Price, Baecker, and Small [Pri93], we can thus only automatically produce program visualizations but not algorithm animations.

CHAPTER 29

Algorithm Animation

by

Scripting

Algorithm animation systems are normally implemented with either procedural or object-oriented programming languages or with an interactive animation system. In the first case, implementers usually add an algorithm animation–specific library package to the programming language, containing routines for the display of the screen elements and the synchronization of the algorithm with the animation. Balsa-II is a typical representative of this type of system [Bro88a]. In the latter case, animators either adapt an existing computer animation system to their needs or build their own, as exemplified by XTango [Sta89] or Pavane [Cox94]. In this chapter we suggest a third approach, based on an algorithm animation scripting language.

Some animations in Animated Algorithms have been implemented based on this approach, although the scripting language interface has been hidden to the end user in order to keep the user interface simple and easy to use. In particular, hashing algorithms [Vel92], binary search trees, and red-black trees [Has92] have been implemented in that fashion. In the following we illustrate the general principles with examples of the red-black tree animation. For an introduction to the algorithmic basics of red-black trees, see [Cor90].

A scripting language for algorithm animation facilitates three different tasks:

1. *Playback of animations that have previously been recorded interactively.* This is the most obvious use of a scripting language. This allows, for example, recording algorithm animations for different, specific input data sets that produce "special cases."

2. *Use of the scripting language to build the animations.* The scripting language can be used to build new animations as any other programming language could be used. The goal is, of course, to be much more productive by using an animation language targeted toward algorithm animation.

3. *Use of the scripting language for interactive quizzes and exams.* The idea is to have the student manually reconstruct algorithmic operations. The system records a script of the student's actions. After students have completed their task, the system compares the recorded script with the correct solution. (Example: The student does a red-black-tree-insert (RB-insert) for a red-black tree [Cor90] by manually inserting the node in the tree on the screen with the mouse and rearranges the tree to maintain the RB property.

The use of an algorithm–specific animation language has the additional advantage that it takes away from the teacher or application programmer the burden of having to implement algorithmically correct animations. Instead, the system is responsible for correct execution of the algorithm. This means, for example, that an RB-insert command automatically inserts the node at the correct position in the red-black tree. It is up to the system to make sure that the red-black properties of the tree are not violated.

In Animated Algorithms, the WYSIWYG direct manipulation interface is closely coupled with the scripting language in the sense that the interactive actions of the user directly call the commands of the scripting language. For the red-black tree animation, for example, a click on the Insert button calls the command RB-Insert. Optionally, the command Insert can also be recorded to a log to be replayed later. The whole animation system thus is implemented based on the scripting model.

The scripting language consists of two layers (Figure III.30):

1. *Primitive layer.* The lower–layer primitive language elements provide the functionality for the graphical animation of the screen elements. For example, for graphs, the command `insertNode position value` displays the node at the desired location.

2. *Semantic layer.* The higher layer includes the algorithm–specific language elements. Using these commands, it is very easy to modify existing

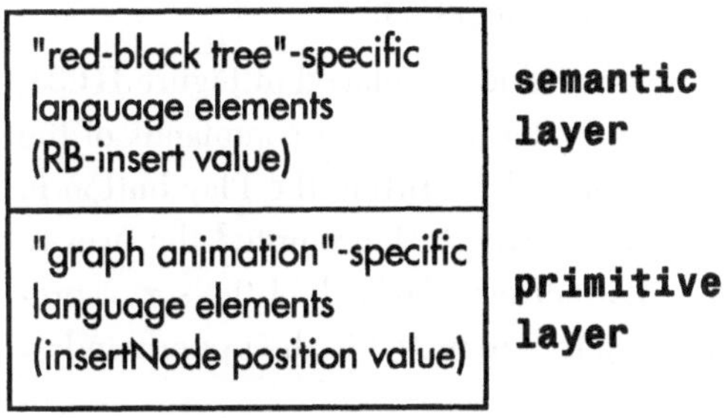

"red-black tree"-specific language elements (RB-insert value)	**semantic layer**
"graph animation"-specific language elements (insertNode position value)	**primitive layer**

Figure III.30

Two-layered scripting language architecture

animations or to construct new ones. For example, `RB-insert value` inserts an element at the correct position in an RB tree.

Table III.1 shows the low-level primitive command set for the animation of tree graphs. The language already contains commands colorRed and colorBlack. Note that these commands do nothing but actually color the node on the screen. In particular, the low-level language elements do not know about the algorithm, which means that invalid red-black trees can easily be constructed by a sequence of algorithmically wrong commands. The advantage of this approach is that the same low-level primitives can be used for animations of any graph algorithms. In Animated Algorithms the graph manipulation command set has been used for red-black trees and binary trees.

Command	Arguments	Action
insertNode	position and value	Insert a node
deleteNode	position	Delete a node
moveNode	position 1, position 2	Move a node from one position to another
linkNodes	position 1, position 2	Draw a link between two positions
deleteLink	position 1, position 2	Delete a link between two positions
colorRed	position	Color a node red
colorBlack	position	Color a node black

Table III.1

Low-level graph manipulation language for trees

Figure III.31 shows a screen dump from the red-black tree animation of Animated Algorithms using the low-level command set.

Normally the user does not see the commands displayed in Figure III.31, as these are being called transparently by the high-level commands of the semantic language layer as listed in Table III.2. Hitting the Play button in the palette in the lower left corner of Figure III.31 prompted the user to load the script shown in the lower right corner. Playback of the script produced a movie resulting in the red-black tree depicted in the upper window of Figure III.31.

Table III.2 High-level red-black tree commands	Command	Arguments	Action
	RB-insert	value	Insert a new node into the tree
	RB-delete	position	Delete a node from the tree
	RB-rightRotate	position	Rotate a node in the tree to the right
	RB-leftRotate	position	Rotate a node in the tree to the left

Figure III.31

Red-black tree animation created with low-level commands

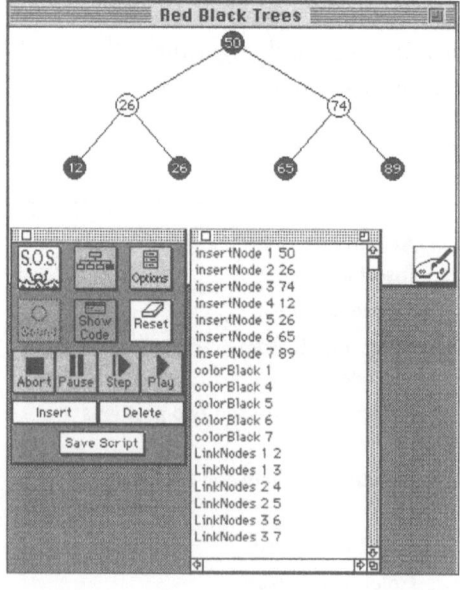

In contrast to the low-level primitive commands, the red-black-tree-specific commands listed in Table III.2 will always produce correct red-black trees. These commands "know" about the red-black tree algorithm and thus make it very easy for the teacher or algorithm animator to produce animations.

Figure III.32 shows a red-black tree that has been created interactively by clicking subsequently on the Insert and Delete buttons on the palette in the lower left corner. The script window in the lower right shows a recording of the commands. The user can now save the script and play it back by clicking the Play button and reloading the script. This offers an extremely convenient and rapid way to create animations of various red-black tree cases (e.g., for play-back in the classroom).

Figure III.33 displays an overview map of various interesting cases of red-black tree inserts for different data sets. If users click on any of the cases, the system jumps to the animation viewer and loads the appropriate script for play-back.

Using such a scripting mechanism affords a very effective way of producing many similar animations. Of course, there is some initial overhead in that the low- and high-level command sets first need to be implemented. Nevertheless, we are convinced that this approach offers tremendous gains in productivity and flexibility once this initial hurdle has been overcome.

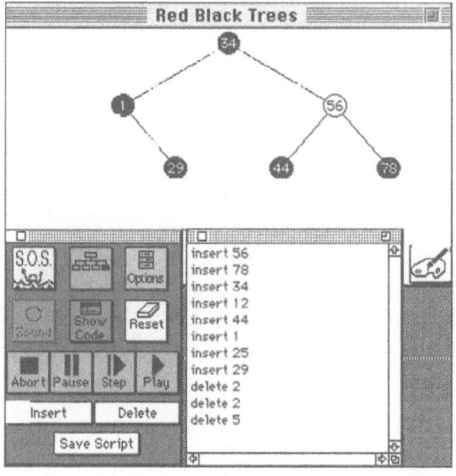

Figure III.32

Red-black tree animation created with high-level commands

Figure III.33

Overview map of
various red-black
tree animations
in Animated
Algorithms

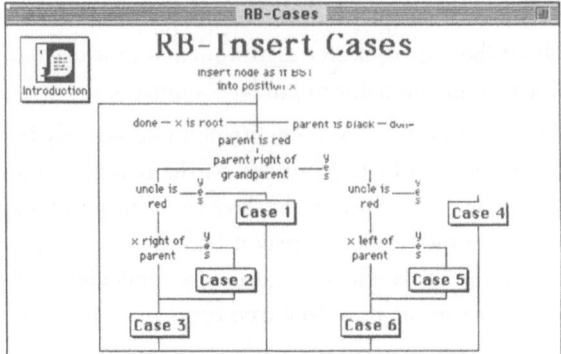

Conclusions

This part has propagated the utilization of algorithm animation for much broader use than this has been done until now. We have described the state of the art and given recommendations to readers on how to build algorithm animations, based on our own experience implementing Animated Algorithms.

Algorithm animation remains a highly labor–intensive process, even using sophisticated tools and techniques. Lack of time and resources restrain authors from implementing animations of all the algorithms they would like. Even with powerful animation tools like HyperCard and MacroMedia Director, it still takes days or weeks to animate an algorithm of intermediate complexity. One obvious solution is to implement the set of scripting commands described in Chapter 29 to get a more comfortable algorithm animation environment for faster development. Of course, this entails implementing low-level and high-level command sets for different types of algorithms and views.

For Animated Algorithms, we produced animations covering a broad spectrum of computer science algorithms. Using a simple programming language like HyperTalk and based on a general-purpose application development system like HyperCard, we were able to implement structure-based animations. For educational systems like Animated Algorithms, we recommend animations adapted to each algorithm instead of animations based on general views. The greater development effort is more than compensated for by the increased educational quality of the animations. Special emphasis should be put on finding alternate pseudocode descriptions, accentuating the main logical steps of algorithms, because this restatement considerably improves student understanding of complex procedures.

The user interface is of utmost importance. Users want a consistent animation system without the need to learn a new interface for each new animation. Embedding the animations in an integrated hypermedia learning environment like Animated Algorithms makes it easy to locate related concepts without having to change media types.

Although there are some algorithm animation systems available for visualizing and teaching computer science algorithms, and although the initial technology is here for creating algorithm animations in any domain, widespread application is still in its infancy. Even the most sophisticated hypermedia learning environment will never be able to replace human teachers, but it should assist them in teaching complex subjects. In numerous situations a human instructor is not readily available, be it for classwork assignments or for the self-tutoring student. We are convinced that algorithm animations provide a useful tool that aids the teacher in explaining and the student in understanding complex subjects. Algorithm animation is a concept that can be applied in almost any application domain, to the great benefit of students.

Part IV turns to the next element of hypermedia design: content. It introduces a novel way of multimedia editing based on a combination of direct-manipulation editing with a programming language–centered approach.

part

Multimedia Editing

You know you have

achieved perfection in

design,

Not when you have

nothing more to add,

But when you have

nothing more to take

away.

—Antoine de Saint Exupéry

The electronic dissemination of multimedia contents involves previous editing of this material for presentation. With the emergence of powerful yet reasonably priced hardware, most of the video and audio editing is now done digitally. Most digital multimedia authoring tools, such as Adobe Premiere [Pre93], are based on visual, easy-to-use direct-manipulation interfaces. This is not surprising; most movie editors, producers, and graphic editors are visually thinking people. Nevertheless, there are many tasks that can be much better supported by a language-based multimedia authoring approach. Visual direct-manipulation user interfaces are limited by their manual nature and cannot easily accommodate algorithmically defined operations. We suggest a melding of the common direct-manipulation interface with a programming language that has been enhanced to manipulate digital audio and video. The result is a system that can automate routine tasks as well as perform tasks based on sophisticated media recognition algorithms.

Introduction

The advent of affordable multimedia has made possible the development of new forms of communication and interaction. Just as film was originally used to present stage plays, digital multimedia initially has been a new technology for dealing with older media using well-established techniques and methods. But just as film eventually spawned forms of storytelling worlds removed from the theater stage, multimedia can be put to uses previously unimagined—taking advantage of interactivity, networked communication, hypermedia, automatic media analysis, and other departures from the linear, start-to-finish, sender-to-receiver model of current video communication.

In the restricted domain of digital video manipulation, easy-to-use tools have been developed to enable what has been termed "virtual video editing"—the editing of computer representations of video [Mac89]. Personal computer programs such as Adobe's Premiere [Pre93] allow users to edit video data in much the same way that popular word processors allow users to edit text. Video is represented by visual proxies, typically thumbnail images and graphic representations of audio waveforms. Users can employ a mouse to click on desired movie clips and drag them into place. VCR-style buttons can be used for playback, and a collection of other metaphorical tools (e.g., scissors, magnifying glass, trash can) is available (see Figure IV.1), on page 288.

In one sense these tools take the video editor back to the time before videotape, when film editors held the medium in their hands and edited it without the intermediate presence of video decks and time codes. But the new digital systems offer advantages beyond a more direct interaction with the media. Thanks to random access storage devices, these systems let the editor manipulate many sections of video simultaneously, with quick jumps to any point in the source material. There is no penalty to repeated editing, since the digital information does not degrade. The user interface can be tailored to use common metaphors and standard commands for the computer platform in question. The result is an environment where casual experimentation is encouraged, and beginners can quickly produce acceptable results.

The direct manipulation nature of these systems, however, also limits user options. Some repetitive or complex functions cannot be expressed with the provided tools. A user can visually select and delete a period of silence in an audio track, but in a pure direct–manipulation interface, there is no way to abstract that specific operation into a more general command ("if there is silence, delete audio data") that can be applied repetitively. The ability to evaluate conditions (e.g., "Is this audio data silent?" "Is this a scene transition?") is left to human eyes and ears, when the computer might be able to do the job more quickly or accurately. And the user is limited to the operations that the system designer considered important; an unusual function or combination of functions may be completely out of reach, and no designer can imagine or implement all the functions that might prove to be useful.

Systems like Premiere exploit the high bandwidth of the visual computer interface to deliver a more concrete and approachable experience to its users. But this emphasis on the concrete comes at the expense of tasks that are by their nature abstract. A user can manually select a period of silence from a sound track, but there is no way to make the leap to a more general command ("if a segment of the audio track is silent, delete it"). Similarly, repetitive tasks or unforeseen combinations of tasks cannot be readily automated.

The shortcomings of direct-manipulation systems are particularly costly in a field such as digital multimedia, where the range of interesting operations is undergoing rapid expansion and no canned software package can anticipate the user's needs. We therefore endorse an approach that combines direct manipulation with computer programming, yielding systems that are flexible enough to tackle new tasks. Such systems can be of particular use in multi-media authoring, research, and education. In this part we describe a proto-type of such a system, called VideoScheme, and discuss a number of promising applications.

Related

Work

Adobe Premiere® is currently considered the state–of–the–art low-end video editing system [Pre93]. Figure IV.1 displays a sample screen illustrating the various features available in this application. The WYSIWYG interface offers intuitive ways of arranging movie and audio segments and inserting transitions between segments or adding filters.

Adobe Premiere® 4 also includes limited user programming capabilities. It allows modifications of video segments using so-called transition and filter factories (e.g., to make one video segment redder, amplify a channel, or mix multiple channels). Additionally, the command palette (on the right in Figure IV.1) gives the user the capability to define new commands interactively. Unfortunately, the user is limited to adding only the commands to the command palette that are already available in the Premiere® application. A real scripting language for defining new editing actions composed of predefined commands is missing.

Researchers have attempted to address such shortcomings, in both the wider domain of direct manipulation software and the specific area of video editing systems. Eisenberg's SchemePaint system combines a simple painting program with a Scheme interpreter [Eis91]. The result is an immediately usable

Figure IV.1

Adobe Premiere® sample screen

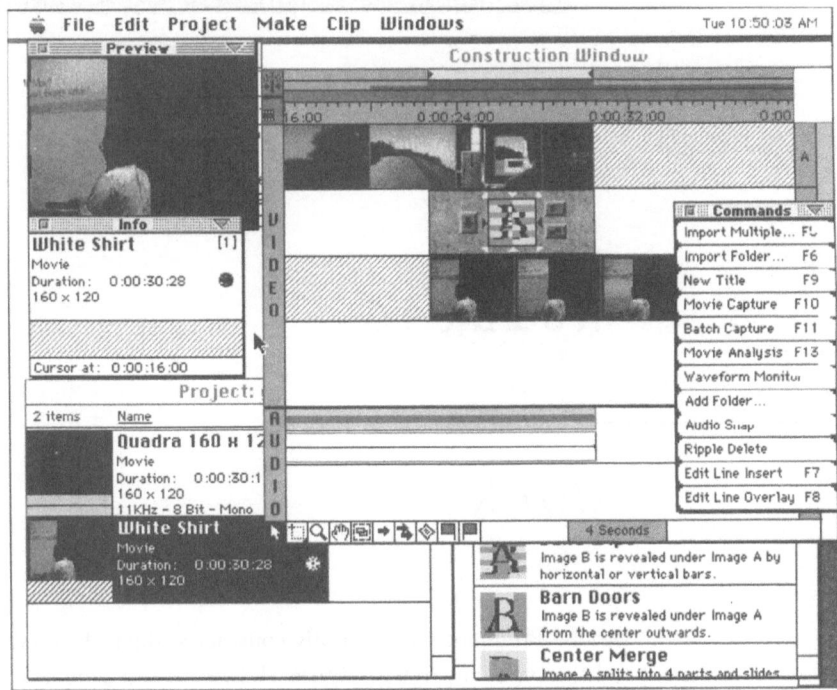

Adobe® and Adobe Premiere® are trademarks of Adobe Systems Incorporated.

system that can also be programmed to produce results impossible with a strictly manual interface. Eisenberg argues for the incorporation of domain-enriched programming languages into a wide variety of direct–manipulation systems, including video editing systems.

Ueda, Miyatake, and Yoshizawa's IMPACT system attempts to enrich the video editing interface from another direction. Rather than making it programmable in a general way, they supplement the direct–manipulation interface with powerful functions that exploit image processing and analysis algorithms [Ued91]. The IMPACT system includes functions to identify cuts in a stream of video, to classify cuts (e.g., as a zoom in or pan left), and to extract moving objects from scenes.

http://www .tns.lcs.mit .edu/

The VuStation system developed at MIT [Lin96] is a programming environment that facilitates the development of compute-intensive multimedia applications that combine intelligent media processing with traditional capture and display. Although the VuSystem was initially developed for proprietary ATM hardware, it now runs on a variety of commercially available systems. It is implemented as a UNIX application that interprets an extended version of Tcl [Ous94]. A collection of so-called in-band modules is linked into the application shell, providing extended functionality such as media capture, file storage, and media display. The application developer can either use existing modules from within Tcl or develop new modules in C++.

Figure IV.2 describes a sample VuSystem application integrating predefined modules using Tcl. The VuSystem has also been extended with an interactive graphical environment to develop VuSystem applications based on a flow graph representation of the running program, providing end users with programming capabilities [Wet94].

Rivl is a Tcl language extension for audio, video, and image manipulation [Swa95]. Rivl extends Tcl with image and sequence (video, audio) data types. It allows for geometric manipulation, media assembly, conversion and transformation. The Rivl interpreter stores operations in a directed acyclic graph (DAG) whose edges correspond to images and whose nodes correspond to primitive operations such as scale or overlay. It is available on various UNIX system. Rivl is still under development at Cornell, with the goal of building a rapid prototyping environment for exploring video contents processing.

```
http://www.cs
.cornell.edu/
Info/Projects/
zeno/rivl/
rivl.html
```

ImageTcl is an Image and Video Software Development Environment currently under development by Charles Owen at the Dartmouth Experimental Visualization Laboratory. It is designed to provide a highly modular, rapid prototyping environment for image processing and incorporates features for

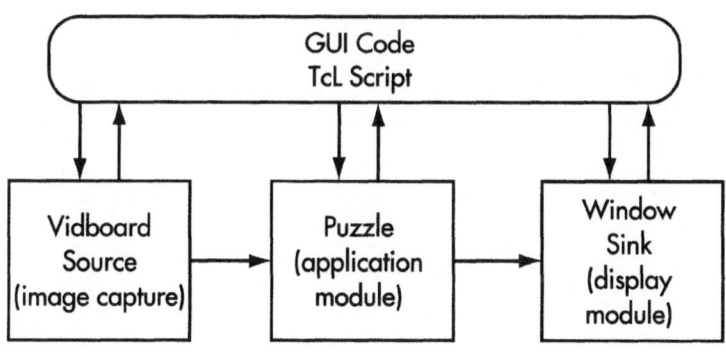

Figure IV.2

Sample
VuSystem
application

temporal control. ImageTcl has been developed primarily as a mechanism for research in information retrieval in compressed digital video.

Our effort, VideoScheme, is similar to these examples. Compared to the VuSystem, our venture is much more restricted in scope, while the Rivl system, contrarily to our approach, omits the visual editing part. VideoScheme has been conceptually influenced mostly by the SchemePaint system in that we have built an extensible video editing system that provides the user with programming capabilities. By embedding a program interpreter into a direct–manipulation video editing system, we hope to achieve the flexibility and expressiveness demonstrated by SchemePaint. In particular, we hope to make it possible to implement the dedicated media analysis functions of systems like IMPACT in this programming language, yielding advantages in both power and flexibility.

VideoScheme:

System Overview

There are only five musical notes, yet the combination of these five give rise to more melodies than can ever be heard.

—**Sun Tzu (500-200 B.C.),**

The Art of War

VideoScheme is implemented as an application for the Apple Macintosh, written in C and totaling approximately 100 KB of executable code. It provides a visual browser for viewing and listening to digital movies, using Apple's QuickTime system software for movie storage and decompression [Qui92]. The browser displays video and audio tracks in a time-line fashion, at various levels of temporal detail. Clicking on the video tracks displays individual frames in a "flip book" fashion; clicking on the audio track plays it back; clicking twice in rapid succession plays back both audio and video.

The concept of providing additional power in an editing program through the use of programmability is not new [Ten93]. Common text editing programs such as Microsoft Word and Emacs provide a programming engine and build complex functions in their associated languages. Emacs, in fact, has a very

Figure IV.3

The
VideoScheme
system

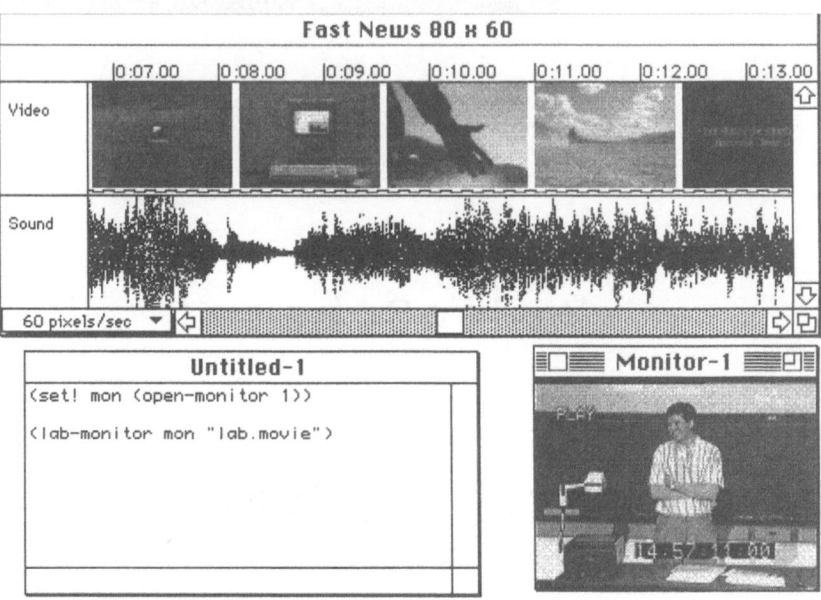

LISP-like programming language. VideoScheme is the first video editor to implement this concept. Of course, programming is an advanced skill, and many users will not have the necessary experience or knowledge to utilize the programming features of VideoScheme. In such normal cases, VideoScheme allows a skilled developer to write potentially complex editing functions in the Scheme programming language, while still providing simple capabilities for the naive user. Once a program is developed and tested, it can be mapped to menu or keystroke options for the normal user. Hence, the capabilities of the editor can be easily extended. VideoScheme includes an interpreter for the LISP-dialect Scheme, built on the SIOD (Scheme-in-One-Defun) implementation, along with text windows for editing and executing Scheme functions [Sio92]. Functions typed into the text windows can be immediately selected and evaluated. The text windows coexist with the video windows, allowing very quick switches between manual editing operations and programming (Figure IV.3). The environment, while deficient in debugging facilities, offers such standard LISP/Scheme programming features as garbage collection and a context-sensitive editor (for parentheses matching). In addition, it offers a full complement of arithmetic functions for dynamically sized arrays, an important feature for handling digital video and audio.

Scheme was chosen over other alternatives (such as Tcl, Pascal, and HyperTalk) for a number of reasons. It treats functions as first–class objects, so they can be passed as arguments to other functions. This makes it easier to compose new functions out of existing ones and adds greatly to the expressive power of the language. Scheme is also easily interpreted, a benefit for rapid prototyping. Scheme includes vector data types, which map naturally to the basic data types of digital multimedia—pixel maps and audio samples. Finally, Scheme is easily implemented in a small amount of portable code, an advantage for research use. The most significant drawback to using Scheme is the programming syntax, which nonprogrammers (and even some programmers) find difficult to use. Desirable alternative languages include Logo and Dylan, which have the positive properties of Scheme but with more attractive syntax.

We chose the SIOD Scheme interpreter for its small size, support of array data types, and extendibility. This last feature made it possible to add new built-in functions that bridge the gap between the Scheme environment and video editing. The functions are designed to be independent of the lower-level QuickTime-based implementation. They could be reimplemented on another platform, to allow for portability of VideoScheme programs (Figure IV.4).

The fact that Scheme is an interpreted language makes it ideal for a distributed environment. VideoScheme can be considered as having two major components: a graphical front end and a Scheme back end. These two components need not always run in the same system. The graphical front end can run on a local machine, and the interpreter back end can be run on a remote video server. The common component of the two, the Scheme programming language, is interpreted and as such is common to the two environments, though they may be totally disparate architectures and operating systems.

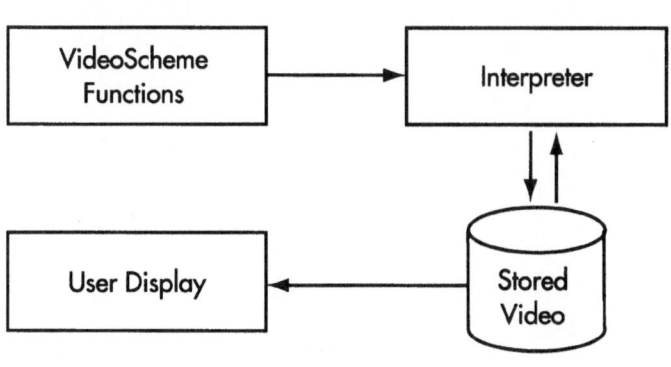

Figure IV.4

VideoScheme's functional layout

VideoScheme

Language Overview

VideoScheme extends the Scheme language to accommodate digital media. In this section selected VideoScheme data objects and functions specific to video and audio editing and manipulation are described in order to illustrate the design of the program. In addition to the standard number, string, list, and array data types, VideoScheme supports objects designed for the manipulation of digital video, such as:

movie—a stored digital movie, with one or more tracks.

Track—a time-ordered sequence of digital audio, video, or other media.

monitor—a digital video source, such as a camera, TV tuner, or videotape player.

Image—an array of pixel values, either 24-bit RGB or 8-bit gray level values.

Sample—an array of 8-bit Pulse Code Modulation audio data.

These objects are manipulated by new built-in functions. Movies can be created, opened, edited, and recorded:

```
(new-movie)
     ; creates and returns a reference to a new movie
(open-movie filename)
     ; opens a stored movie file
(save-movie filename)
     ; saves a movie file
(cut-movie-clip movie time duration)
     ; moves a movie segment to the system clipboard
(copy-movie-clip movie time duration)
     ; copies a movie segment to the system clipboard
(paste-movie-clip movie time duration)
     ; replaces a movie segment with the segment on the clipboard
(delete-track movie trackno)
     ; removes a movie track
(copy-track movie trackno target)
     ; copies a movie track to another movie
(record-segment monitor filename duration)
     ; records a segment of live video from the monitor to a file
```

Images and sound samples can be extracted from movie tracks or monitors, and manipulated with standard array functions:

```
(get-video-frame movie trackno time image)
     ; extracts a frame from a video track
(set-video-frame movie trackno time duration image)
     ; inserts a frame into a video track
(get-monitor-image monitor image)
     ; copies the current frame from a video source
(get-audio-samples movie trackno time duration samples)
     ; extracts sound samples from an audio track
(get-color-histogram64 sub-pixels histogram
     ; compute color histogram of an array of color
     ; pixels using 64 buckets
     ; (i.e., 2 bits each for red, green, blue)
```

With this small set of primitive objects and built-in functions, we can rapidly build a wide variety of useful functions with applications in research, authoring, and education.

One point to be made about VideoScheme is that it is a passive editing system. Edits are made by creating new reference lists of existing data or deriving new data. This structure is necessitated by the large volumes of data in a typical video segment. An advantage of this approach is that VideoScheme is an ideal test bed for information retrieval concepts since it does not directly modify files it manipulates.

VideoScheme

Applications

With powerful computers and digital media, it is possible to build systems that perform automatic analysis of video and audio data. The results of this analysis can be used to make existing applications (such as indexing, retrieval, and editing) more efficient or to enable entirely new applications [Nag92] [Ued91] [Zha93]. It would certainly be desirable if computers could perform these analytical tasks as well as a trained human, but short of such a breakthrough in artificial intelligence, there are numerous less ambitious goals to be pursued by researchers in this field.

35.1 Automating Repetitive Tasks

Splitting a movie

The automation of repetitive, well-defined tasks can be accomplished with simple programming language constructs. A video editor may want to divide a long video sequence into smaller, equal-sized chunks. By hand this would be a tedious, error-prone process, but in VideoScheme it can be performed with a simple program:

```
(define split-movie
 (lambda (movie chunk-size)
  (let
```

```
((time 0.0))
(while (< time (get-movie-duration movie))

  ; copy the next chunk of the movie
  (copy-movie-clip movie time chunk-size)

  ; paste it into a new movie
  (paste-movie-clip (new-movie) 0.0 0.0)

  (set! time (+ time chunk-size))))))
```

With the function thus defined, splitting the frontmost movie into 1-minute sections is as simple as evaluating the expression (`split-movie` (`get-front-movie`) `60`).

Speeding up a movie

A single new movie can be created by choosing multiple excerpts from an existing movie. Indeed, by this simple formula we can achieve the effect of speeding up the movie:

```
(define speedup
 (lambda (movie factor)
  (let
   ((time 0.0)
    (new (new-movie)))
   (while (< time (get-movie-duration movie))

     ; copy a fraction of the next tenth of a second
     (copy-movie-clip movie time (/ 0.1 factor))

     ; paste it at the end of the new movie
     (paste-movie-clip new
      (get-movie-duration new)
      (get-movie-duration new))

     (set! time (+ time 0.1)))
   new)))
```

The expression (`speedup` (`get-front-movie`) `2`) returns a version of the frontmost movie that appears to run at double speed, since every other twentieth of a second has been removed from it. An analogous function could be written to duplicate information in a movie rather than removing it, yielding a slow-motion effect.

Reversing a movie

We can make these mechanical functions sensitive to the structure of the movie with the aid of VideoScheme's built-in functions. One of these, `get-next-frame-time`, returns a list consisting of the time stamp and duration of the next frame in a video track. With this function we can copy a movie on a frame–by–frame basis, reconstructing it in reverse order:

```
(define reverse
 (lambda (movie trackno)
  (let
   ((time 0.0)
    (frame-info nil)
    (duration 0.0)
    (new (new-movie)))
   (while (< time (get-movie-duration movie))

    ; find out when the next frame starts,
    ; and how long it lasts
    (set! frame-info
     (get-next-frame-time movie trackno time))
    (set! time (car frame-info))
    (set! duration (car (cdr frame-info)))

    ; copy the next frame
    (copy-movie-clip movie time duration)

    ; paste it at the beginning of the new movie
    (paste-movie-clip new 0.0 0.0)

    (set! time (+ time duration)))
   new)))
```

Simple, repetitive functions are called for in some circumstances, but their power is clearly limited by their simplicity. Most video editing decisions must take the content of the video data into account, and more powerful VideoScheme functions can be created when the medium itself is consulted. VideoScheme includes two built-in functions for accessing the movie data: `get-audio-samples` and `get-video-frame`. Each of these returns arrays of integers: 8-bit sound samples in the case of `get-audio-samples` and 24-bit color pixel values in the case of `get-video-frame`. These arrays can then be analyzed and the results used to create new editing functions.

One straightforward application is to search through video data for periods of silence. We can characterize silence as a period where none of the audio samples has an amplitude greater than 10 (out of a maximum amplitude of 128). The returned samples are in the range of 0-255, where the sample value 128 has an amplitude of zero. Therefore our silence predicate looks like this:

Searching for silence

```
(define silence?
 (lambda (movie trackno time interval)
  (let
   ((samples (cons-array 0 'long)))
```

```
; get an array of audio samples
(get-audio-samples movie trackno time
 interval samples)

; compute their absolute amplitudes
(adiff samples 128 samples)
(aabs samples samples)

; is the loudest sample less than 10?
(< (amax samples) 10))))
```

This predicate may prove unreliable with noisy audio sources. In that case examining the median amplitude or a certain percentile might prove more effective. These possibilities can be explored easily with VideoScheme.

35.2 Authoring with Programming

Digital media technology has enabled more than the creation of movies on computers; it has also made possible new sorts of information systems. One example is the DAGS '92 multimedia proceedings CD-ROM (introduced later in Part IV) that integrates digital video, audio, animation, and hypertext to communicate the proceedings of an academic conference [Che96]. The unusual nature of the system posed numerous challenges to the development staff, challenges that were only partly addressed by existing authoring tools. For example, the centerpiece of the proceedings is eight 45-minute synchronized audio–video presentations of speech with overhead slides. It was sometimes necessary to move audio tracks independently of the accompanying video, to accommodate sound editing software. Our commercial tools did not provide a way to do this without recompressing 6 hours of animations, but VideoScheme was quickly adapted to the task. Earlier in the process we needed to remove silences from the original 12 hours of sound tracks, a painstaking manual process. Had VideoScheme been available at that time, it would have been a simple function:

```
(while (< time (get-movie-duration movie));
            loop through whole movie
 (if (silence? movie trackno time 0.1)
            ; if there is 0.1 seconds of silence
  (cut-movie-clip movie time 0.1)
            ; then remove that segment
  (set! time (+ time 0.1))))
            ; otherwise move on to next segment
```

We also removed noise words (such as "um" and "ahh") by hand, and we believe that VideoScheme could be extended to assist in this step as well.

It was clear from our experience that while existing tools offer high-quality solutions for problems in their domain, they are often poorly suited to the ad hoc tasks that arise in innovative multimedia authoring. In such cases a programmable system may provide the necessary flexibility to turn a tedious, manual process into an automatic operation. It may also permit entirely novel operations. In his work on a programmable graphics editor, Eisenberg noted that such an editor can produce effects such as fractals and recursive Escher-like designs that would be nearly impossible with manual tools [Eis91]. We can imagine VideoScheme programs to implement algorithmically defined effects, such as fades and wipes, that could hardly be achieved any other way.

A critical concern with authoring tools is the speed with which new applications can be developed. Traditional programming environments (featuring compiled languages such as C and C++) offer complete access to the computer hardware and data but can require months or years of effort to produce a usable tool. Object-oriented frameworks accelerate the process somewhat, but even then many details must be coded by hand. By contrast, a rapid-turn-around interpreted language like VideoScheme makes it possible to write applications in minutes or hours. Tool authors do not need to master the low-level details, and powerful operations can be composed from high-level primitives and previously written functions.

35.3 Cut Detection

One important use of VideoScheme is the implementation of an automatic system for dividing digital video into segments, by detecting the "cuts" that divide one shot from another. There is no perfect definition of a cut, but generally the term refers to a sharp discontinuity in a video stream, such as the break between two recording bursts in unprocessed video or the point where two clips were concatenated in the editing process. Once cuts are found, the segments they define can be represented by a subset of the segment's data (e.g., the first and last frames), since the continuity of the segment ensures a great deal of information redundancy. This reduction of a potentially long segment to a few frames is a significant boon to a number of applications, such as indexing, logging, navigation, and editing, since those tasks may be performed on a greatly reduced set of data.

A number of algorithms have been proposed for automatic cut detection, and one of the advantages of VideoScheme is that such algorithms can be implemented as compactly as their mathematical formulation. For example, a simple measure of visual continuity is a sum of pointwise differences in gray value or color. Such a test can be performed by the following fragment of VideoScheme code:

```
(adiff frame1 frame2 delta)
            ; subtract arrays of gray value
(aabs delta)
            ; compute absolute difference values
(atotal delta)
            ; sum differences
```

Scene changes trigger large pointwise differences, but this measure is also very sensitive to camera motion and zooming, which may change every pixel without introducing a new scene. Refinements of this algorithm, such as one that counts the differences that exceed a threshold, have a similar weakness. So there appears to be some value in a test that is not so spatially sensitive, such as the difference between summed gray values:

```
(- (atotal frame1) (atotal frame2))
            ; subtract summed gray values
```

This measure is insensitive to camera pans and zooms, but it is also insensitive to actual cuts, since the average gray level may not change dramatically across the cut. A more reliable indicator is the gray level or color histogram. Using VideoScheme's built–in color histogram function, we can easily compute this measure:

```
(get-color-histogram64 frame1 histogram1)
            ; compute 64-bucket color histograms
(get-color-histogram64 frame2 histogram2)
(adiff histogram1 histogram2 delta)
            ; subtract histograms
(aabs delta)
            ; compute absolute differences
(atotal delta)
            ; sum differences
```

This test can be refined by breaking each frame into a number of subframes and discarding the ones with above-median changes, or counting the number of changes that exceed a threshold. Either modification is quickly implemented in VideoScheme, and each makes the algorithm more robust against local phenomena such as object motion.

While histogram comparison is widely considered a robust solution to detection of simple camera breaks, the general problem remains a fertile area for new approaches. In recent years novel algorithms have been proposed for detecting gradual transitions and for using motion–sensitive measures in conjunction with a projection–detecting filter [Ued91] [Nag92] [Ots93].

Nagasaka and Tanaka have investigated automatic cut detection algorithms, obtaining the best results with a test that measures the differences in color distributions between adjacent frames [Nag92]. Following their algorithm, we can write a function to compute the normalized difference between two histograms:

```
(define histogram-difference
 (lambda (hist1 hist2)
  (let
   ((hist-diff (cons-array 0 'long)))

   ; subtract the two histograms
   (adiff hist1 hist2 hist-diff)

   ; square the difference
   (atimes hist-diff hist-diff hist-diff)

   ; normalize by one of the histogram arrays
   (aquotient hist-diff hist1 hist-diff)

   ; sum the squared, normalized differences
   (atotal hist-diff))))
```

This function makes use of VideoScheme's built-in array functions to subtract, square, normalize, and sum the histogram differences. We can compute the histograms themselves using a built-in function, making it a simple matter to compute the visual continuity at any point:

```
(define full-frame-diff
 (lambda (movie trackno time1 time2)
  (let
   ((pixels (cons-array 0 'long))
    (hist1 (cons-array 64 'long))
    (hist2 (cons-array 64 'long)))

   ; get the histogram for one frame
   (get-video-frame movie trackno time1 pixels)
   (get-color-histogram64 pixels hist1)

   ; get the histogram for another
   (get-video-frame movie trackno time2 pixels)
   (get-color-histogram64 pixels hist2)

   ; compare the histograms
   (histogram-difference hist1 hist2))))
```

Figure IV.5

Comparison of
subframes for
Nagasaka-Tanaka
Algorithm

Nagasaka and Tanaka found this function to be sensitive to momentary image
noise, which typically affected only parts of the image but created undesirable
spikes in the color continuity. They eliminated this effect by dividing the
frames into 16 subframes, comparing the subframe histograms, and discarding
the 8 highest difference totals (Figure IV.5).

We can implement this improved algorithm in VideoScheme:

```
(define nagasaka-tanaka-diff
 (lambda (movie trackno time1 time2)
  (let
   ((pixels1 (cons-array 0 'long))
    (pixels2 (cons-array 0 'long))
    (sub-pixels (cons-array 0 'long))
    (hist1 (cons-array 64 'long))
    (hist2 (cons-array 64 'long))
    (diffs (cons-array 16 'long))
    (frame1 nil)
    (frame2 nil)
    (index 0))

    ; get the two frames in question
    (set! frame1 (get-video-frame movie trackno time1
    pixels1))
    (set! frame2 (get-video-frame movie trackno time2
    pixels2))

    (set! index 0)
    (while (< index 16)
     ; histogram one 16th of frame1
```

```
(get-sub-frame16 frame1 index sub-pixels)
(get-color-histogram64 sub-pixels hist1)

; histogram one 16th of frame2
(get-sub-frame16 frame2 index sub-pixels)
(get-color-histogram64 sub-pixels hist2)

; remember the difference
(aset diffs index (histogram-difference hist1 hist2))
(set! index (+ index 1)))

; order the subframe differences and discard the 8
highest ones
(asort diffs)
(asetdim diffs 8)

; total the remaining differences
(atotal diffs))))
```

A number of applications can be built using this measurement of visual continuity. A simple function can search a movie for the beginning of the next cut:

```
(define next-cut
 (lambda (movie trackno time)
  (let
   ((diff 0))
   (while
    (and
     (< diff 10000)
     (< time (get-movie-duration movie)))

    (set! diff
     (nagasaka-tanaka-diff movie trackno time
       (+ time 0.1)))
    (set! time (+ time 0.1)))
   time)))
```

We can modify the split-movie function presented earlier to split a movie on scene boundaries rather than at a fixed interval:

Splitting movies by cut

```
(define split-movie-by-cut
 (lambda (movie trackno)
  (let
   ((time 0.0)
    (cut 0.0))
   (while (< time (get-movie-duration movie))

    ; find the next cut
    (set! cut (next-cut movie trackno time))

    ; copy up to the next cut
    (copy-movie-clip movie time (- cut time))
```

```
; paste the segment into a new movie
(paste-movie-clip (new-movie) 0.0 0.0)

(set! time cut)))))
```

The results of executing the `split-movie-by-cut` function on a 15-second TV commercial are shown in Figure IV.6. The movie "Fast News 80 x 60" has been split into nine segments, seven of which are shown. In one case the cut detection algorithm has performed better than the naked eye: the cut between segments Untitled-7 and Untitled-8 is almost undetectable when the movie is viewed at normal speed, but close examination and the Nagasaka-Tanaka algorithm reveal the cut.

Using other knowledge of how video is sometimes structured, we can detect even higher-level boundaries, such as television commercials (which can be

Figure IV.6

Results of split movie by cut

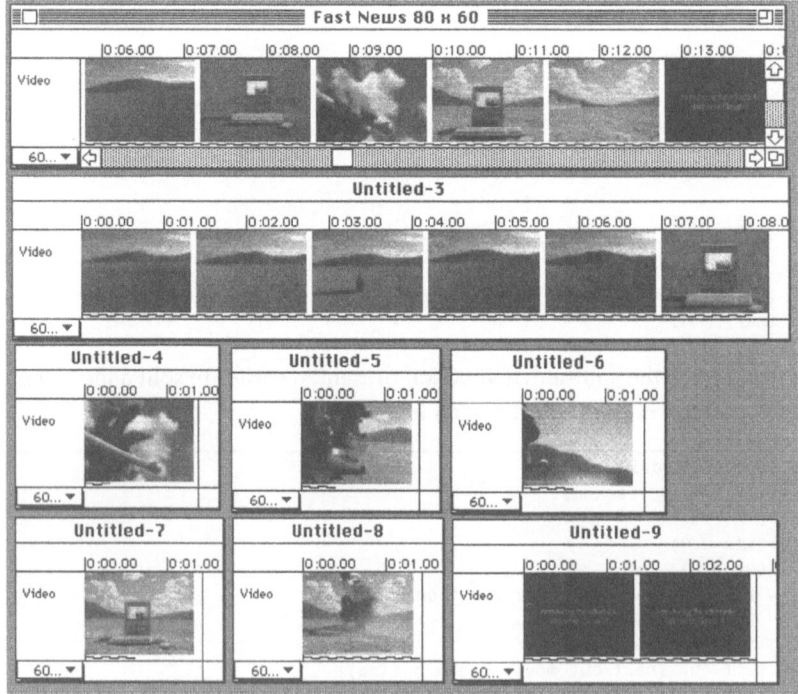

characterized by scene changes exactly 15, 30, or 60 seconds apart). We can also detect common editing idioms; the expression (`nagasaka-tanaka-diff movie track time (next-cut movie track time)`) evaluates the visual continuity between the frames that bracket a cut. A high degree of continuity suggests that the editor is cutting back and forth between two video segments, for example, footage of two different characters who are speaking.

35.4 Automatic Video Analysis

Another area of research is the application of automatic video analysis to interactive multimedia. Chris Lindblad has termed this "computer–participative multimedia" since the computer is actively involved, reacting to the content of the video data [Lin93]. VideoScheme's monitor object makes it possible to implement such applications easily. For example, this VideoScheme code fragment implements the core of a video room monitor:

```
(set! camera (open-monitor 1))
            ; create a monitor object for a camera
(get-monitor-image camera baseline)
            ; capture a baseline image
(while t
 (get-monitor-image camera new-image)
            ; capture a new image
 (if (image-diff baseline new-image)
            ; compare to baseline
  (record-segment camera "monitor-movie" 5.0)))
            ; record 5 seconds of video
```

With a camera pointed at a door, this fragment keeps a running log of all the people who enter and leave the room. With the addition of a sound playback command, this function could also serve as a video answering machine: people approaching a closed door could be automatically prompted to leave a video-taped message. This fragment assumes that any significant change in the image striking the camera represents a person. More sophisticated analysis functions could look for more specific phenomena. For example, they could automatically record television programs with a certain opening screen or on-screen logo.

Conclusion

The future is bound to bring more proposed algorithms, targeted at specific video sources and applications. We believe that VideoScheme's flexibility makes it a useful vehicle not only for research but also for rapid application development and prototyping. VideoScheme's high-level primitives and rapid turnaround programming environment make programs compact and prototyping very rapid.

We have implemented a prototype of VideoScheme and have demonstrated the usefulness of our system on some real-world editing tasks. We have seen that it is possible to achieve some of the results of dedicated video authoring systems such as IMPACT in a programmable editing system with a small number of special-purpose video functions. VideoScheme offers the further advantage of flexibility: it is a simple matter to experiment with new algorithms and to build new operations by combining previously written functions. These are the classic advantages of programming, and we believe that we have shown them to be equally valid in the domain of interactive video editing.

VideoScheme is a unique attempt at achieving the best of both worlds: the ease of use of direct manipulation and the flexibility and expandability of an interpreted programming language.

Part V will now put together the pieces of the puzzle of hypermedia design by presenting issues and obstacles that arise when building complex hypermedia systems. We discuss our experience in publishing a series of multimedia conference proceedings over four years using a variety of systems and technologies.

part **V**

Hypermedia
Publishing

Writing a book is like

creating a wave you

can surf on; writing a

CD-ROM is more like

making a box of

chocolates . . . . Like

the chocolates, in the

end, the taste and the

texture matter more

than words.

—The Economist
[Eco95a]

It should be obvious by now that hypermedia publishing is a multifaceted task that involves activities in many different domains. As an exemplary application involving the whole spectrum of the hypermedia creation and authoring process, the last part of this book presents issues and obstacles encountered while producing a series of multimedia conference proceedings. The Dartmouth Institute for Advanced Graduate Studies (DAGS) conference proceedings were initially produced for dissemination on CD-ROM; with the advent of the information superhighway, the latest proceedings have been published on the Web. We believe that multimedia conference proceedings provide an exceptional test bed for hypermedia publishing, highlighting many pending research issues that must be resolved before similar projects can be quickly and inexpensively accomplished.

Introduction

Academic conferences are a well-established and effective form of communication. Conference participants communicate by sight and sound, that is, by viewing individuals, text, and graphics and by hearing the spoken word. This same-time, same-place communication is sufficiently valuable to justify large investments in time and travel funds. Traditional printed conference proceedings and session videotapes are attempts to recapture the value of a live conference participation, but they are an insufficient substitute for having personally experienced speakers giving their presentations. Although multimedia conference proceedings are no replacement for interpersonal communication at the conference, they offer an integrated hypermedia environment combining printed proceedings with the audiovisual experience of listening to the speaker that would be impossible with audiotapes or videotapes and printed proceedings.

As Figure V.1 suggests, hypermedia conference proceedings include much more than just papers and talks. Obviously, implementing such proceedings offers an exceptional test bed for addressing a broad range of research and development topics in the field of hypermedia publishing.

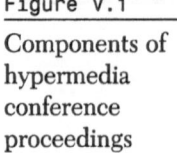

Figure V.1

Components of
hypermedia
conference
proceedings

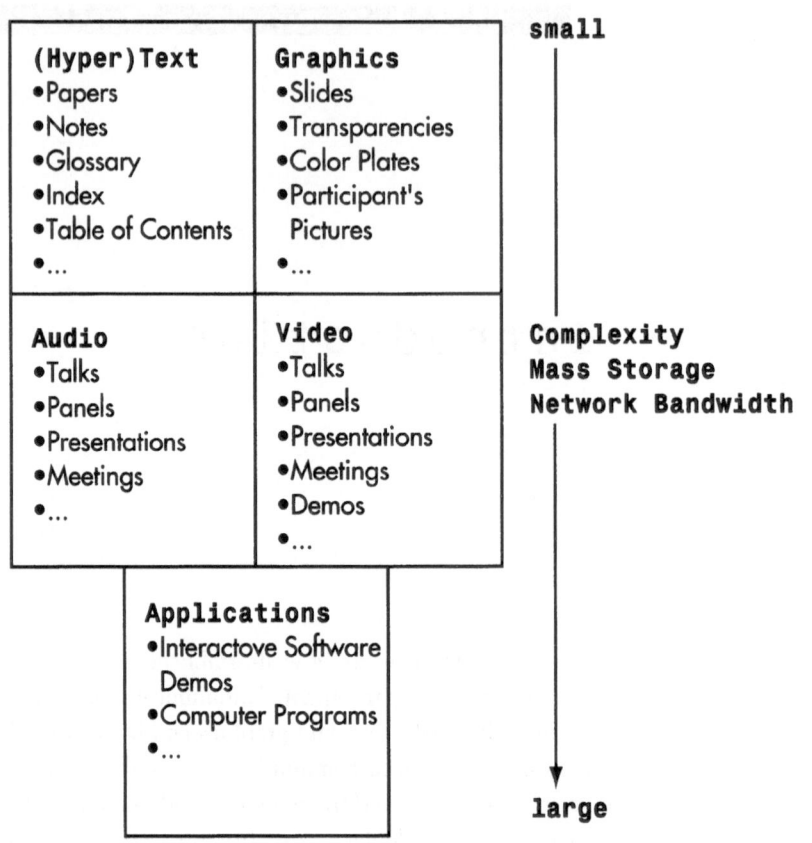

Our work on the DAGS Multimedia Conference Proceedings series
addresses these open issues. One of our immediate goals is to deliver more of
the value of an academic conference to the audience. Recently, the potential of
multimedia proceedings has been recognized by conference organizers, and
some first efforts at multimedia proceedings on CD-ROM and on the Internet
have been published. The results are, however, mostly a collection of papers in
two or three different formats that can be used mainly as "digital microfiche,"
along with a few digitized movies. Their main problems are a lack of interaction between the components and a lack of fast searching mechanisms. They
were produced to serve as an alternative to printed proceedings, yet printing
the articles reveals many missing pictures or graphics. These are efforts in the
right direction, but they fall short of the capabilities of multimedia.

The DAGS multimedia proceedings deliver text, graphic, audio, and video information in an integrated hypermedia learning environment, with extensive provisions for random access and hypermedia linking. This project provides a model for future conference publications and highlights some of the pending research issues that must be resolved before similar publications can be quickly and inexpensively produced. The experience gained from this effort is equally valid not only for multimedia conference proceedings of the future but also for multimedia textbooks and learning environments.

37.1 Related Work

Their aim is to ensure that when a paper refers to another paper, a click on the reference will bring up the second paper, along with a list of all other papers that cite it. In this way the interdependent web of the scientific world reveals itself: each discovery built on the bricks of hundreds before it, all now connected by a trail of mouse clicks.

—*The Economist*
[Eco95b]

Electronic proceedings are not a new idea. For nearly as long as there have been computer networks and conference papers written on the computer, researchers have found ways to make their conference papers available on the network. The first electronic proceedings in either CD-ROM or on-line format were restricted to offering printed documentation in electronic form. Main advantages were cheaper mass production and improved search facilities. Talks, lectures, panel discussions, and audiovisual presentations remained an experience reserved to conference attendees. As time has passed, new interfaces for retrieving and searching papers have been implemented, and a variety of proceedings have been created. The following listing of multimedia conference proceedings is a representative overview of the field, with no claim on completeness. For a broad comparison of multimedia conference proceedings see [Reb95].

- *Official SEAM'92 CD-ROM*, Proceedings of the 1992 MacSciTech Conference on Scientific and Engineering Applications for the Macintosh [Mac93]. This was one of the first multimedia conference proceedings on CD-ROM, combining hypertext presented in HyperCard, images, and video. Its early appearance and diverse content make it an interesting first attempt at interactive electronic proceedings, although the limited technology of the time and some user interface decisions make it less useful than it could be.

http://
superbook
.bellcore.com/
SB/IWANNT/
iwannt93

- *1993 International Workshop on Applications of Neural Networks to Telecommunications* implemented in SuperBook, accessible on the Internet under X-windows [All93]. The proceedings are presented with SuperBook, a sophisticated hypertext system. They provide a rich navigation structure and sophisticated annotation facilities that are built into SuperBook. Because the proceedings are networked, participants can add annotations that other participants can view and extend.

- *Proceedings of the ACM 1993 Conference on Multimedia* on CD-ROM [Rad93]. This CD-ROM product is based on Adobe Acrobat, displaying distilled PostScript documents in PDF format. It also includes some QuickTime and MPEG movies. As with the SuperComputing'93 proceedings (see below), the greatest drawback of these proceedings is their fixation on the printed page. The lack of sophisticated searching and annotation makes this type of proceedings seem like little more than an electronic viewer of printed pages.

- *Proceedings of SuperComputing'93* on CD-ROM [Ieee93]. The proceedings are distributed on a multiplatform CD-ROM for UNIX, Macintosh, and Windows containing text and graphics from the conference. Similarly to the ACM'93 Multimedia proceedings, the viewer directly displays an image of the printed page in PostScript format.

http://ada
.computer.org/
conferen/sc94/
SC94Home.html

- *Proceedings of Supercomputing'94: The Conference on High Performance Computing and Communications* on the Web [Ieee94]. These are rather straightforward WWW proceedings containing mostly abstracts and the option of downloading PostScript versions of the talks.

http://www.acm
.org/sigchi/
chi95/
Electronic/
documnts/top
.html

- *Proceedings of the ACM 1995 Conference on Human Factors in Computing Systems* [Mac95]. The CHI'95 Conference Proceedings and Companion CD-ROM combine CD-ROM and WWW. The multimedia proceedings on CD-ROM include electronic versions of the papers linked to digital movies. The size of the available movies varies from 1 to 20 MB. The Internet download time for such files seems prohibitive. The primary intention for users that have Internet connection is therefore to use the CD-ROM as a means to play back movies more efficiently. The HTML version has been revised and offers the full papers in HTML format.

- *Deborah Estrin, RSVP*, Web talk on the Internet University. The WWW version of a talk by Deborah Estrin on the Cisco NetWorkers'94 conference is one of the first implementations of multimedia presentations over the Web. Although the system exhibits some design flaws, it is an early experiment on Web talks that gave us valuable hints for our own work implementing the DAGS '95 talks.

  `http://town`
  `.hall.org/`
  `university/`
  `network/estrin`

All of the above listed multimedia conference proceedings exhibit some common weaknesses:

- Text is normally delivered rather straightforward. It is either displayed as a PostScript image or, for the papers on the Web, the whole paper is directly converted to HTML. The capabilities of the hypertext concept allowing nonlinear browsing and searching are mostly neglected.

- The network bandwidth is still considered too narrow to allow the transmission of video or audio versions of talks over the Web. The talk by Deborah Estrin illustrates these shortcomings: although the audio track has been broken into separate clips, each belonging to one slide, those clips are still prohibitively large for downloading over a modem connection. (The RealAudio system, described in section 41.4 offers a proprietary solution.)

- Normally it takes a long time to develop multimedia versions of conference proceedings. With the exception of the SuperComputing '93, the ACM Multimedia '93, and the CHI'95 proceedings, all of the proceedings appeared well after the conference. Since conferences present new results, timeliness is a very important feature requiring new methods for speeding up the multimedia proceedings development process.

Our own work on the DAGS multimedia conference proceedings series specifically addresses these shortcomings and offers possible solutions.

37.2 Background

The Dartmouth Experimental Visualization Laboratory (DEVLAB) and the Dartmouth Institute for Advanced Graduate Studies (DAGS) at Dartmouth College have been collaborating to build electronic proceedings for the annual DAGS conferences. The yearly construction of electronic proceedings allows researchers and students to conduct experiments in electronic publishing and multimedia authoring. The DAGS/DEVLAB proceedings teams have built electronic proceedings for the DAGS 1992 conference on parallel computing

`http://www.cs`
`.dartmouth.edu/`
`devlab/devlab`
`.html`

`http://www.cs`
`.dartmouth.edu/`
`dags/`

[Glo93c], the DAGS 1993 conference on parallel I/O [Mak95], and the DAGS 1995 conference on electronic publishing and the information superhighway [For95]. While the DAGS '92 proceedings provided a simple navigation system for digital talks, the DAGS '93 proceedings extended the talks navigation features. The DAGS '95 proceedings simplify the interface but provide networked access to presentations. All electronic DAGS conference proceedings put special emphasis on including multimedia presentations of distinguished speakers.

DAGS '92:

CD-ROM

In June 1992 Dartmouth College hosted the first annual DAGS symposium, Issues and Obstacles in the Practical Implementation of Parallel Algorithms and the Use of Parallel Machines. The symposium program consisted of 8 talks by invited speakers plus 13 contributed talks, presenting a total of 22 papers (one invited talk spanned two papers). The topic is a central problem in the area of parallel computation today. It was therefore our intention to make the results as widely available as possible to the parallel computing community. In addition to the usual printed proceedings [Joh92], it was decided to publish multimedia proceedings that should try to capture some of the conference atmosphere.

38.1 System Description

The multimedia proceedings on CD-ROM contain the 22 papers in hypertext format integrated with the 8 invited talks in Apple's QuickTime movie format. Hypermedia links and random access are used extensively in this integrated system. The CD-ROM includes:

- A navigation shell (Figure V.2) that facilitates hierarchical navigation in hyperspace. The navigation shell is based on the Gloor/Dynes hypertext engine (see Chapter 14).

- Hypertext versions of the 22 papers presented.

- Digitized movies of the eight invited speakers delivering the conference talks.

- Speaker's transparencies, including marks added during the talks.

- Hyperlinks connecting relevant parts of the proceedings.

- Bibliography.

38.2 DAGS '92 Sample Guided Tour

In a typical session, users can get a quick overview of the contents of the CD-ROM. Then they can follow a talk on a particular topic that seems interesting by watching the movies of the transparencies and the speaker. They can get an overview of the talk by using the pop-up menu containing the section titles of the talk (by pressing the button "Jump to Highlights") or by skimming through

Figure V.2

Article screen of navigation shell

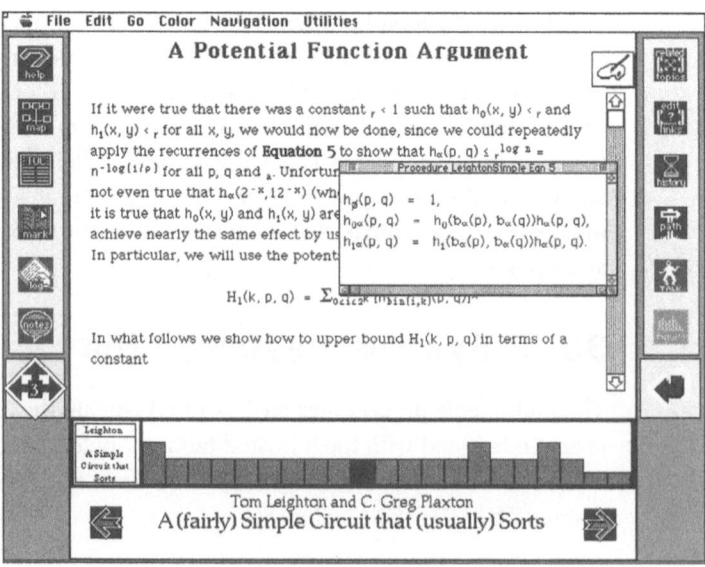

the transparencies. If at some point the speaker mentions a theorem without proof, as is usually the case in conferences, users can jump into the hypertext to read the omitted proof in detail. Then they can go back to the talk or continue reading the hypertext. They can also do a search on some key word to find out who else mentioned this key word during the conference. Assuming that the search brought up several candidate sections of papers, users can jump into another paper and continue reading from there, or even jump into the video movie of the second speaker and see how the material was presented during that talk. Thus, they can compare opinions on the speaker's view on a particular topic or simply see different presentation techniques on the same subject.

We will now describe a possible tour through the hypermedia document to give the reader an impression of the features of our system.

The system starts with a title animation and then presents a table of contents (Figure V.3) which gives users direct access to the eight invited talks. In this example, the user decides to study the talk by Charles Leiserson, "The Network Architecture of the Connection Machine CM-5." The user clicks on the title of this talk on the contents screen, and the system jumps to the speaker screen.

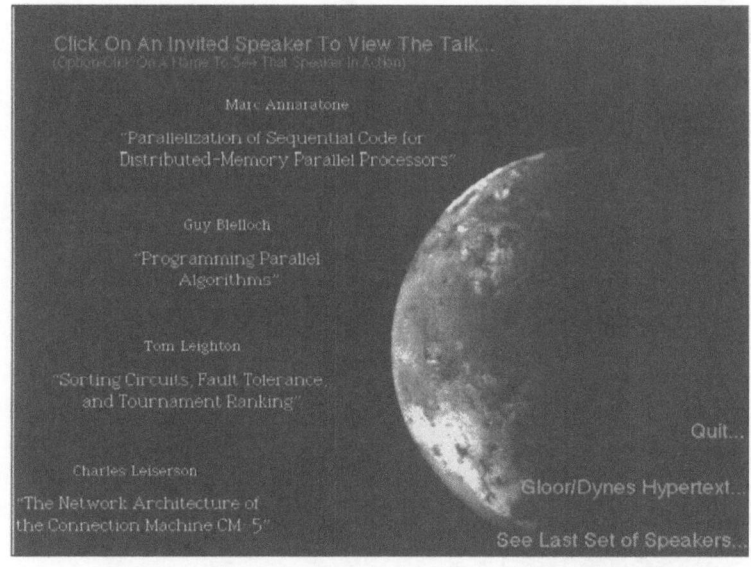

Figure V.3

Table of contents screen

On the speaker screen (Figure V.4) users can get background information about a particular talk by reading a short biography of the speaker, obtain a list of the talk's highlights, read the hypertext version of the paper related to the talk, or watch the talk. Another button can take them back to the previous "Table of Contents" screen. The user here decides to view the talk and clicks on the "View Talk" button.

The system now switches to the Talk screen (Figure V.5) where users can watch the actual talk from the beginning by clicking the "Start Talk" button, or they can go back to the Speaker and Contents screen by clicking the appropriate buttons. They can jump to any position within the talk using the slider controls on the left panel underneath the transparencies.

Another useful feature is the option to jump directly to the beginning of a subsection within the talk using the "Jump to Highlight" button. Upon pressing that button, the user is presented with an ordered pop-up list of the highlights of the talk (Figure V.6). In this example the user chooses to watch Charles Leiserson explain the CM-5 Data Network.

When the user releases the mouse button, the system jumps directly to the "CM-5 Data Network" section within Charles Leiserson's talk (Figure V.7). After

Figure V.4

Speaker screen

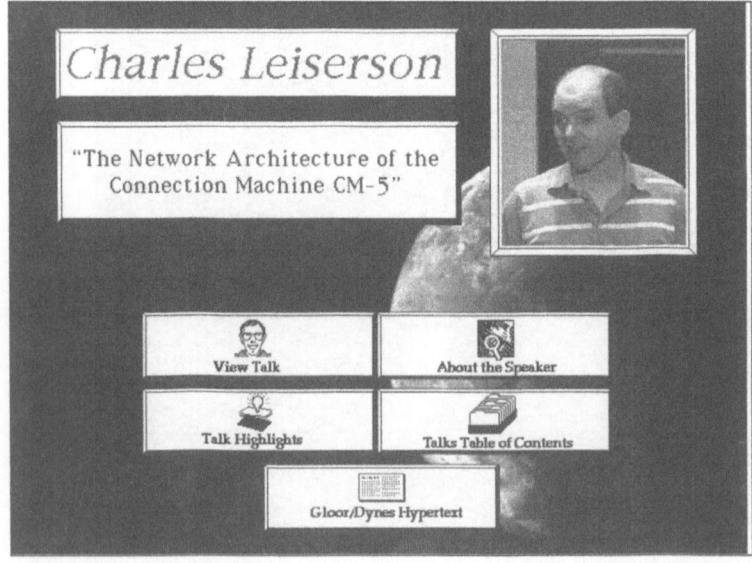

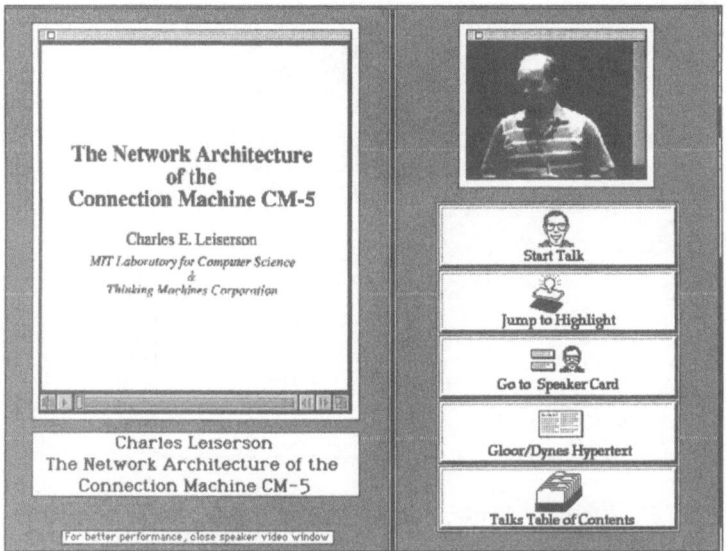

Figure V.5

Talk screen

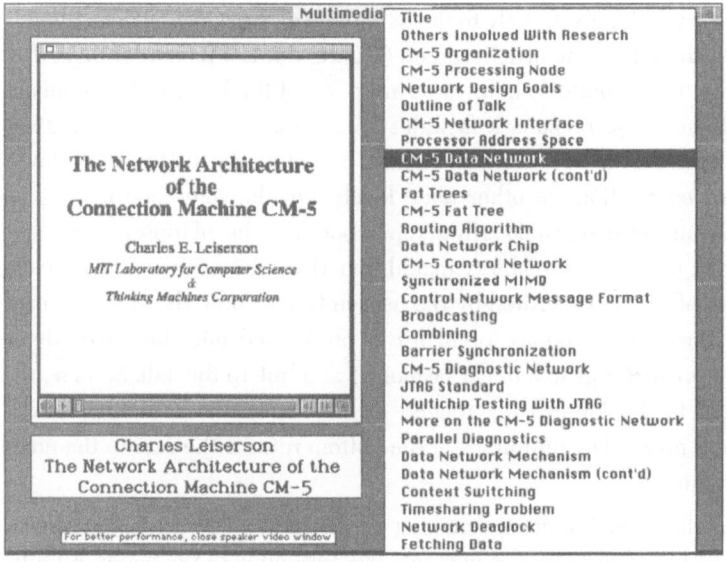

Figure V.6

Highlights of the talk

Figure V.7

Charles
Leiserson talks
about the CM-5
Data Network

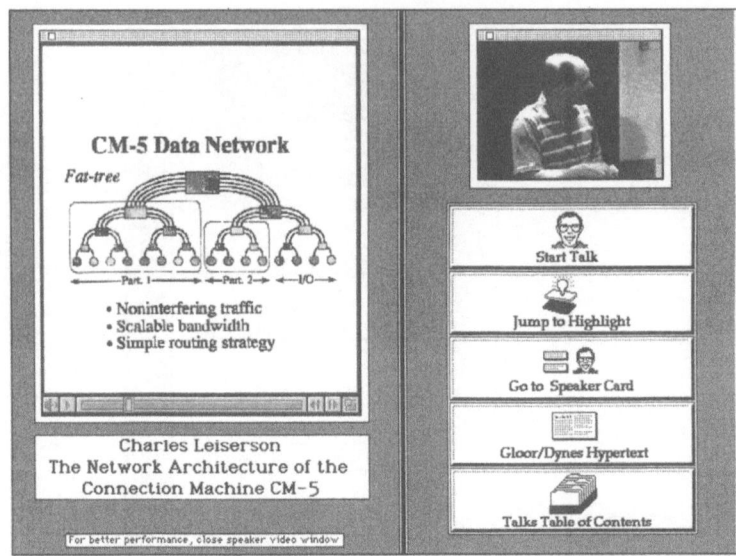

following the talk for awhile, users might want to read the paper associated with the talk. They can do that by clicking at the "Gloor/Dynes Hypertext" button.

The system now jumps directly to the beginning of the paper associated with the talk. On the left of the article screen (Figure V.8) is a palette of tools that provide (from top to bottom) help , a map of the hypertext contents, a table of contents , bookmark facilities , a notebook , and marginal notes . Below is the navigation diamond that marks the hypertext node level and its connections to other node levels. On the right side is another palette with buttons that provide (from top to bottom) a list of topics related to the current text node, the ability to add hyperlinks between text nodes, a history of the nodes visited by the user in this session, the ability to create a path through the nodes (or to use a predefined one that takes them through the proceedings in a linear fashion) , a link to the Talk Screen , and a button to the Figures related to the current node (dehighlighted when there is none). The button at the bottom returns the user to the node previously visited.

Following the level 2 nodes by clicking on the right arrow of the navigation diamond, the user brings up the next introductory node of the paper. A bibliographical reference or a figure mentioned in the paper can be opened by

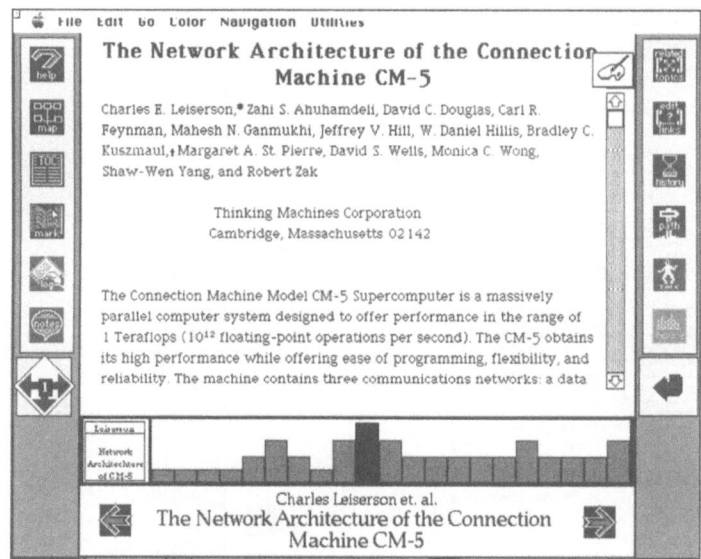

Figure V.8

The hypertext version of the paper

clicking on the word (Figure V.9). To get a feeling of the structure of this paper, the user can also bring up the overview map by clicking the Map button.

The system brings up the overview map that shows a graphical structure of the whole hypertext document in relation to the actual viewpoint of the user (Figure V.10). Users learn that they are on the section entitled "The CM-5 Data Network" of the "The Network Architecture of" paper. Information about previous and next sections also appears, along with information about the subsections of the current section. Clicking on another box makes this box the new center of the map; by "option-clicking" a box, the user can jump to any node in the hypertext.

There are numerous other features in the system. Readers are referred to the user's manual of the Parallel Computation CD-ROM [Glo93c] for a more detailed description of the user interface.

38.3 DAGS '93: CD-ROM

The DAGS '93 conference on parallel computation and parallel I/O was held in the summer of 1993 at Dartmouth College. Because of the success in developing multimedia proceedings for DAGS '92, a successor was planned based on the original. As in the earlier effort, it was chosen to provide a rich

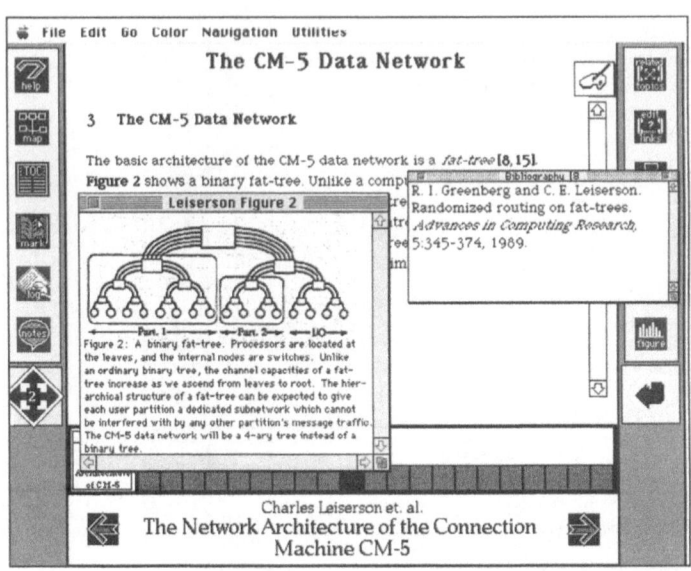

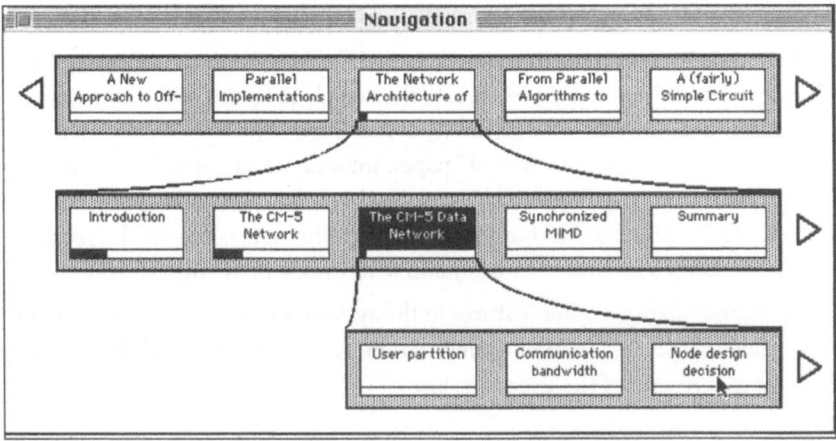

set of features to allow the readers of the electronic proceedings to manipulate them in various ways. The original plan had been to reuse the previous interface (which was Macintosh specific) with some modifications. However,

to allow for broader distribution, it was decided to develop a version that
would run on both Macintoshes and PCs. Although the original version was
based on HyperCard (which can be ported to ToolBook on the PC), it also
used many XCMDs (extensions to HyperCard). A direct port to ToolBook
would have required reimplementing all of these XCMDs. Therefore, it was
decided to reimplement the interface without XCMDs in HyperCard and
ToolBook.

Figure V.11 displays a screen shot of the DAGS '93 hypertext interface. The
GUI is much simpler, as it has to run on two platforms, and does not make use
of advanced Macintosh user interface features (e.g., floating palettes). On the
other hand, the search capabilities have been greatly extended based on
requests of DAGS '92 users.

Figure V.12 shows the redefined and extended talks interface for the
DAGS '93 proceedings. Because some users only want to watch and not to
interact, the interface includes low-interactivity controls as well as advanced
features like random talk access, where users can bring up a contents list for
the talk and quickly jump to any section or scroll through the slides using the
progress bar or the arrow keys.

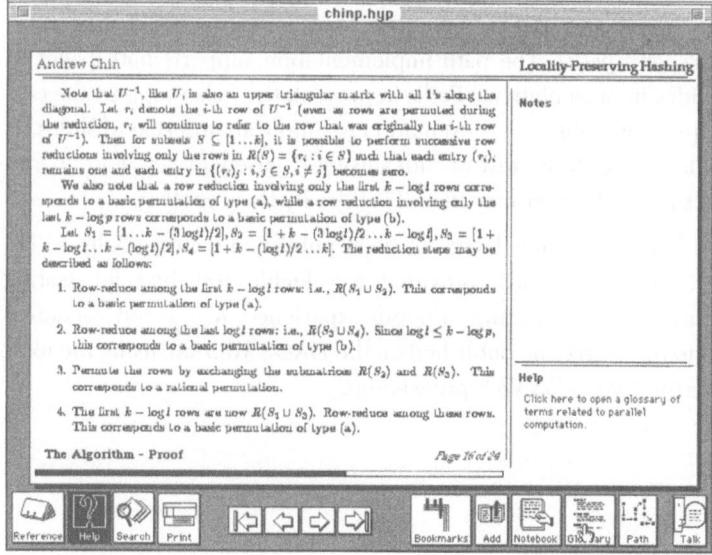

Figure V.11

Hypertext
interface of
DAGS '93

Figure V.12

DAGS '93 talks
screen

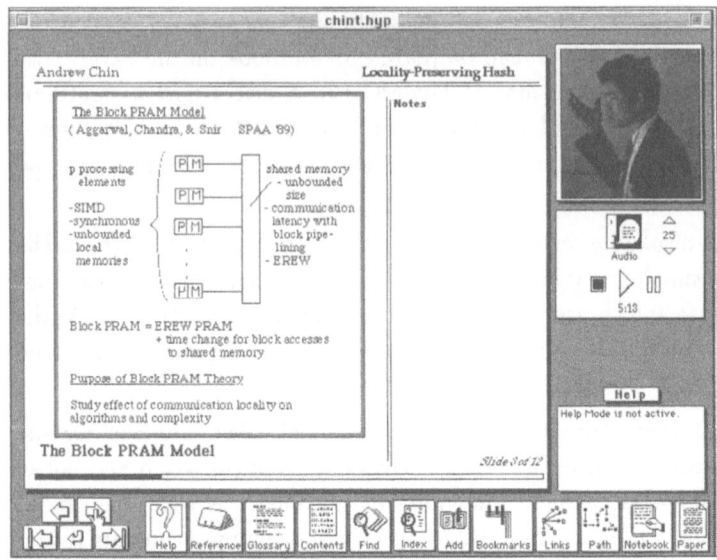

For users wishing to interact more closely with the proceedings, there are numerous other features. Users are able to add marginal notes to slides. The interface also supports a variety of hypertext links, including bookmarks, user-definable links, and paths. The path implementation supports both pages in papers and slides in presentations. Paths in presentations also support the creation of new presentations, as a presentation is simply an ordering of slides. It is also possible to search the text of slides using a variety of key word–based mechanisms, such that a user may identify slides by their content.

The DAGS '93 proceedings have not been published commercially so far. Nevertheless, the proceedings provided a valuable test bed for testing advanced concepts and collecting in-depth experience. A reduced version is being ported to the Web to be published on the DAGS Web site using the tools developed for the DAGS '95 Web proceedings.

DAGS '95:

On the Web

The DAGS '95 Conference on Electronic Publishing and the Information Superhighway brought together a broad audience to discuss issues, applications, and underlying technologies for electronic publishing. The conference was held at the Boston Park Plaza Hotel in Boston, Massachusetts, from May 30 to June 2, 1995. Given the topic of the conference, there was a lot of interest in the announced multimedia conference presentations on the Web. The distinguished speakers were Tim Berners-Lee, Peter Denning, Barbara Simons, Andries van Dam, and Brewster Kahle. The proceedings include presentations given by these five invited speakers. The last of the five talks was made available on the Web on June 23, 1995.

39.1 System Description

As the DAGS CD-ROM interface offers particularly powerful features for navigation and searching, concepts from this interface, in particular the random access feature allowing users to jump to a highlight within a speech, have been integrated into the user interface for the DAGS '95 talks on the Web.

At the core of the proceedings is the talks user interface (Figure V.13).

Figure V.13

DAGS '95 Talks
user interface

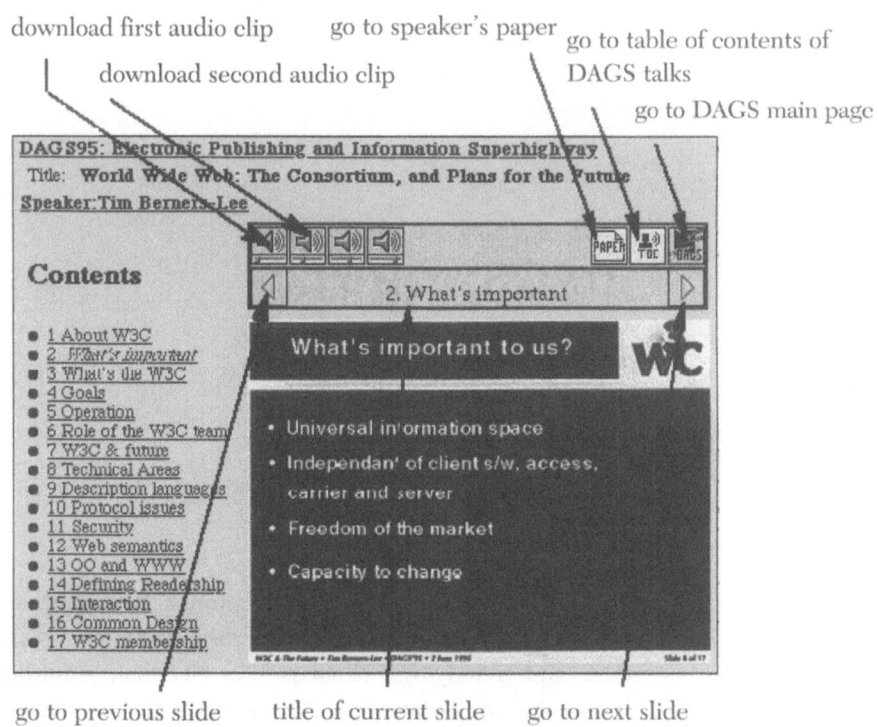

download first audio clip   go to speaker's paper
download second audio clip   go to table of contents of
                                               DAGS talks
                                               go to DAGS main page

go to previous slide   title of current slide   go to next slide

Each slide has a control panel above it containing clickable buttons and the title of the selected slide. The slide title in the panel provides the user with an additional navigational cue. The Previous and Next buttons, represented by a left and a right arrow, allow the user to navigate sequentially through the talk without having to click on an item in the table of contents. The first audio clip available for downloading can be accessed via the leftmost sound icon on the control panel. Since the duration of the audio sample for each slide varies, the number of sound clips (i.e., the number of sound icons per slide) also varies. In order to download the succeeding audio clips, the user must click on each of the presented sound icons one after the other.

Control panel design   Dealing with the graphical layout of the interface presented an interesting obstacle imposed by the limitations of HTML. To implement the control panel at the top of each slide, we were initially planning on having a basic background, while the button set and the text label would have been overlaid for each slide. This would have allowed for caching of the image resources such that moving to a different slide would not have required loading a new GIF file for the control panel. Unfortunately, we found that our ability to control detailed formatting information with HTML was too limited. Therefore we opted for a "one control panel per slide" approach. This solution required keeping the control panel very small, such that the download speed for new slides would be only marginally affected by also having to download the control panel for each slide.

We first considered converting text-only slides to HTML format, which **Slide design** would have offered the best download performance. On slides with figures and other complicated graphics, those would then have been inserted as smaller GIF files. We soon discovered that this approach would have prohibitively increased the complexity of creating WWW proceedings and decided to show all slides as images because this allowed us to retain the graphic quality of the overhead transparencies without additional editing.

Browsers use various helper applications to present nontext data like sound **Sound track** or movies. A common format for voice or talk audio files for all platforms using WWW browsers is 8 bit, 8 MHz, "AU" format. Since there is no general standard for audio compression, we stored the files in uncompressed AU format.

Each page of the talks also includes a link from the header of the page to the main entry point of the DAGS '95 proceedings, as well as a link to the speaker's home page or, if no such page is available, to a page containing a summary of the speaker's profiles.

39.2 DAGS '95 Sample Guided Tour

This section describes a sample guided tour of the Web-based DAGS '95 proceedings. The proceedings are available on-line on the Addison-Wesley-Interactive Web site.

After selecting the DAGS '95 URL, users get to a title screen offering vari-   `http://awi.aw` ous options (Figure V.14):   `.com/ DAGS95`

* Following the Invited Speakers link brings users to the digitized talks of the invited speakers.

Figure V.14

DAGS '95
proceedings title
screen
http://awi.aw
.com/DAGS95

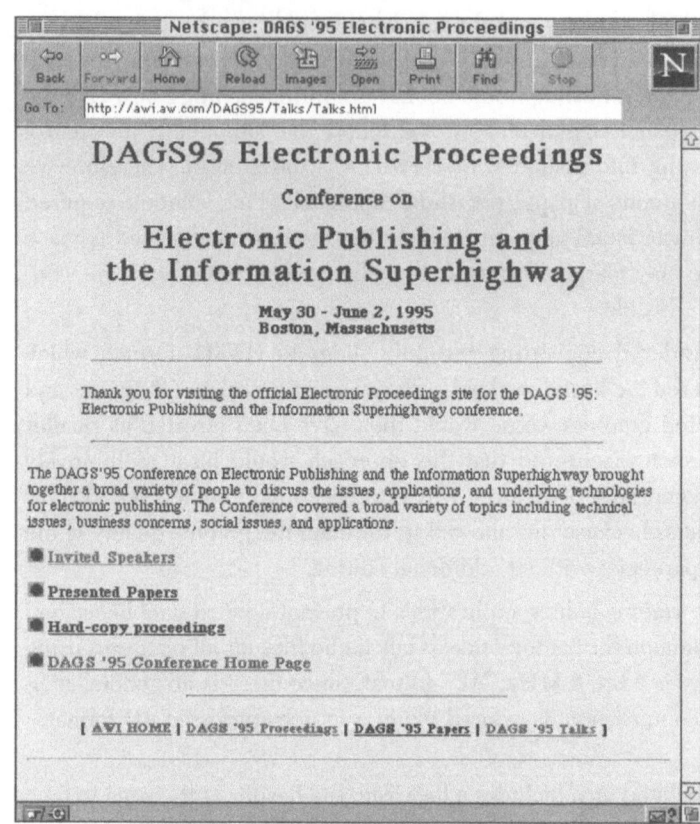

- The Presented Papers link leads users to a directory of the papers and on-line versions of most of the papers.

- The link to Hard–copy Proceedings allows users to buy a printed version of the proceedings. Even in the emerging cyberspace society, a printed document may be superior to any hypertext.

http://www.cs
.dartmouth
.edu/ dags/

- The DAGS '95 Conference Home Page leads to the official DAGS home page on the DEVLAB server at Dartmouth College.

If users choose to click on "Invited Speakers," they are presented with a table of contents of the names and titles of available presentations (Figure V.15). Clicking on a presentation title brings them to the first slide of a talk.

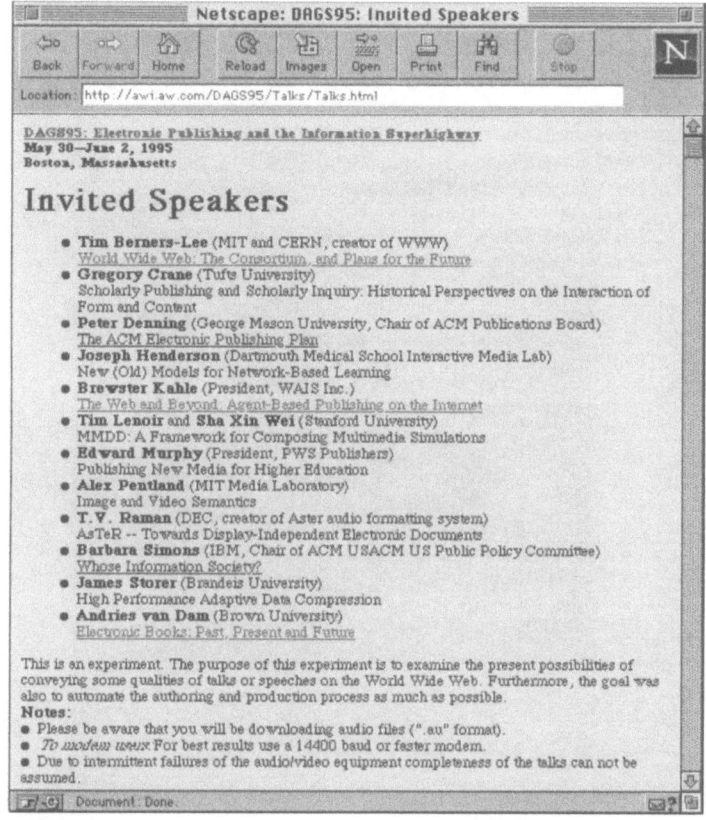

Figure V.15

DAGS '95 table
of contents for
digital talks
http://awi.aw
.com/DAGS95/
Talks/ Talks
.html

On the Talks screen (Figure V.16), a table of contents of all slides used in the talk is presented alongside the slide. Users can browse sequentially through the talk or jump to any slide by clicking on a slide title. The selected slide in the slide table of contents appears in italics to indicate the selected slide's title. In Figure V.16 users are on slide 6 of Tim Berners-Lee's talk.

Due to the restricted bandwidth of the Internet, the audio portion belonging to a slide has been cut into chunks of normally at most 300 KB. The sound track of slide 6 consists of three pieces, indicated by the three ▦ icons. By clicking on one of the icons in the control panel, users can download and play the sound

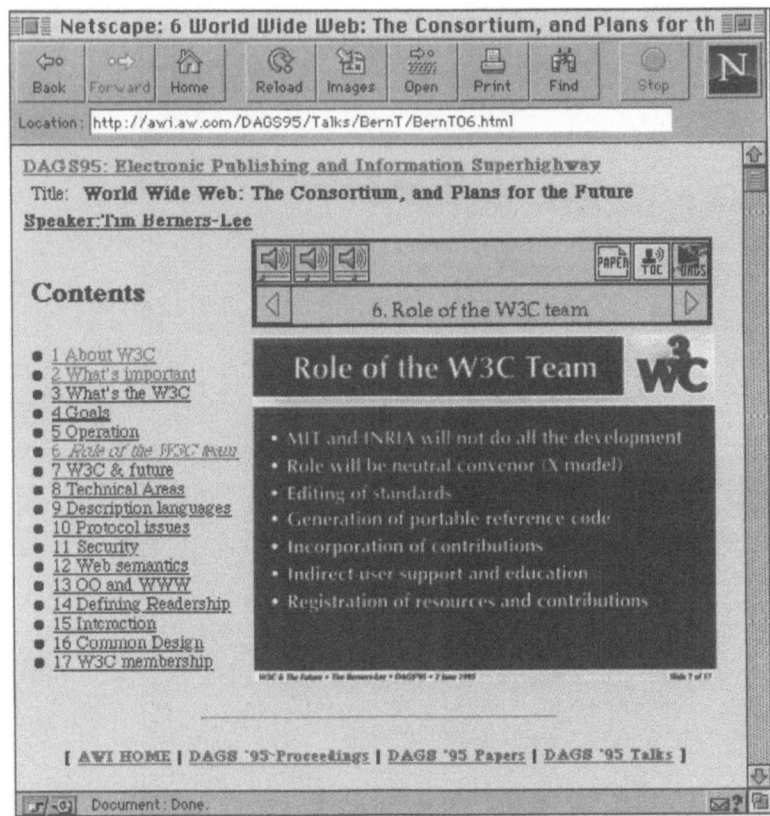

track of the talk piecewise. In Figure V.17 they clicked on the first sound icon to download the first sound clip.

Figure V.18 illustrates playback of the sound track for slide 6 playing back all three of the audio files sequentially, using the helper application SoundMachine.

During the talk, the user can get background information about the speaker at any time by clicking on the speaker name in the upper left corner of the Talks screen. Clicking on "Speaker:Tim Berners-Lee" leads to Tim Berners-Lee's home page at the MIT W3 consortium. In contrast to CD-ROM-based

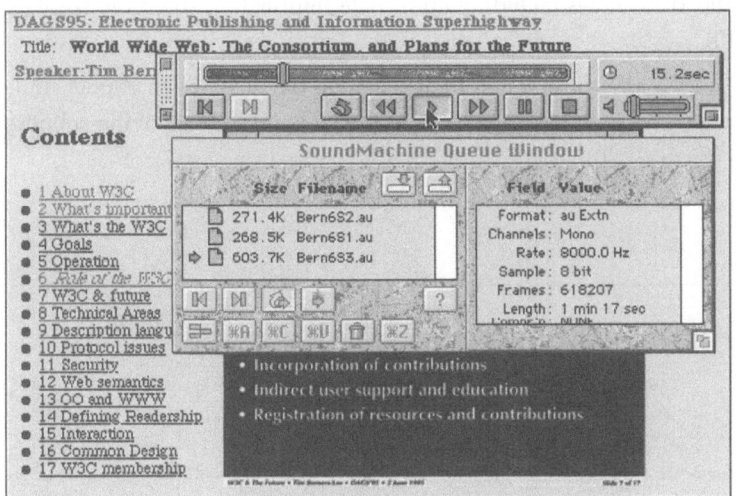

Figure V.17

Downloading part 1 of the sound track for slide 6 of Tim Berners-Lee's talk

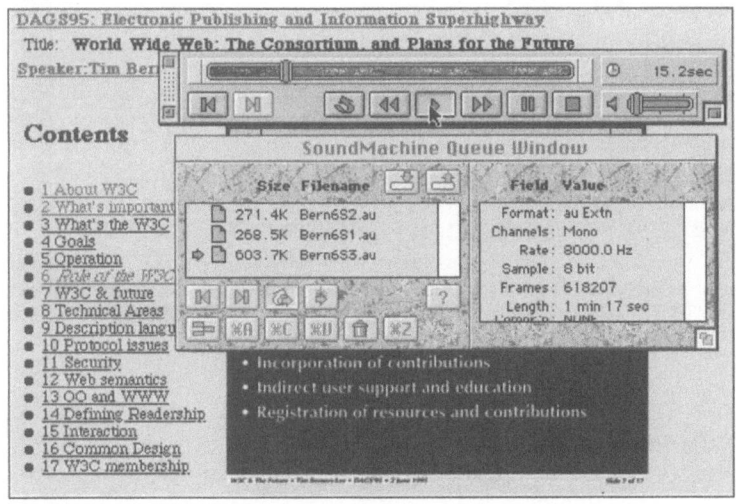

Figure V.18

Playing back the sound track for slide 6 of Tim Berners-Lee's talk with

proceedings, where only a canned version of the speaker's biography can be provided, the Web allows including up-to-date information about the speaker (Figure V.19).

Clicking on 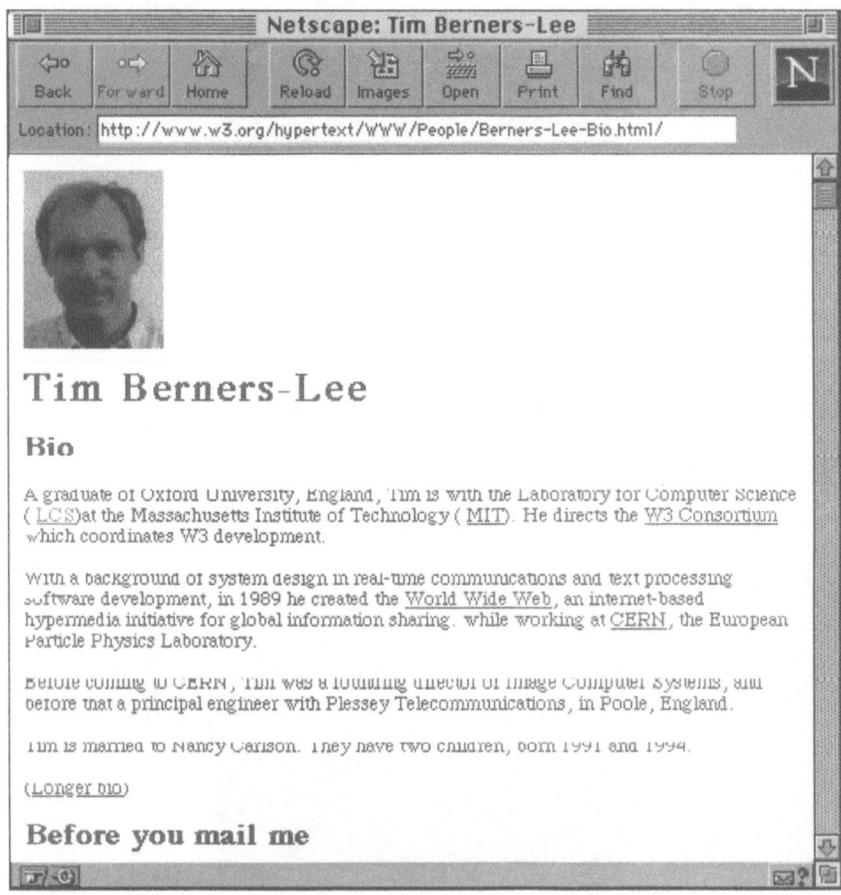 the -button and then selecting the "DAGS '95 Papers" link at the bottom of the previous page leads to the table of contents of the submitted papers (Figure V.20).

Figure V.19

Tim Berners-Lee's home page

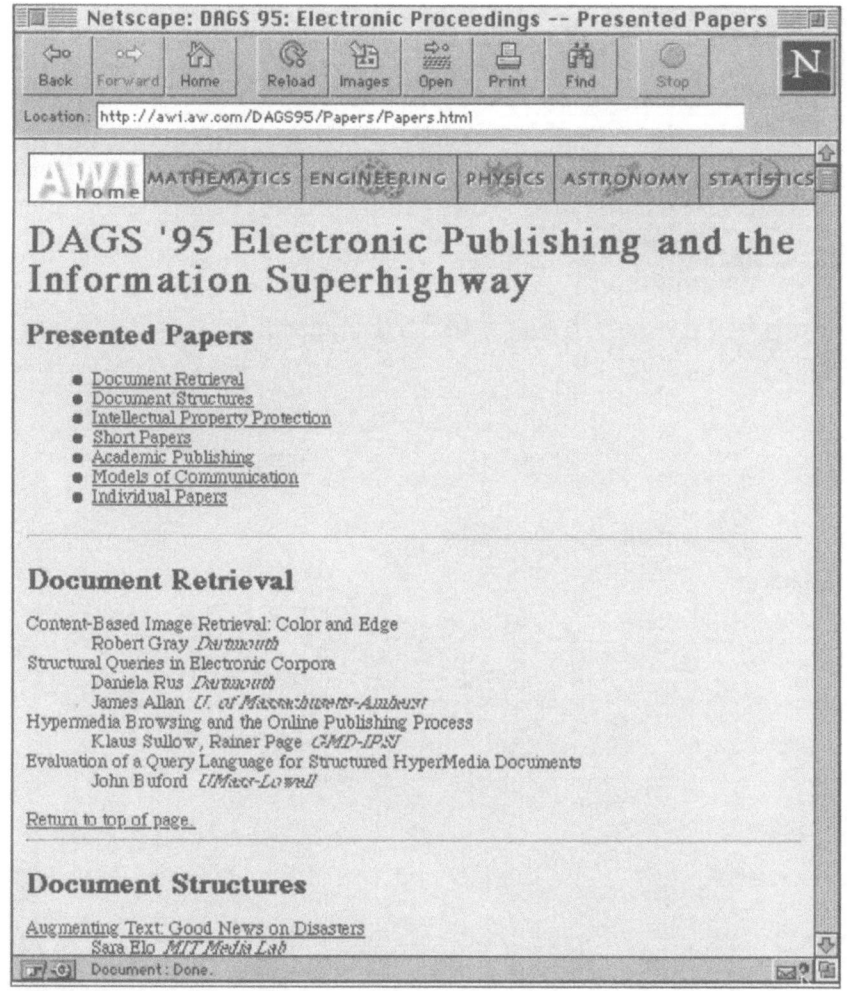

Figure V.20

Table of contents
of the DAGS '95
papers

Not all presenters also submitted their papers in HTML format, such that only a subset of the presented papers is available on-line on the AWI server. Clicking on "Augmenting Text: Good News on Disasters" leads to a full paper in HTML (Figure V.21).

On-line papers are available in a standardized HTML format, starting with an abstract and a table of contents (Figure V.21).

Figure V.21

Sara Elo's paper
in the DAGS '95
proceedings

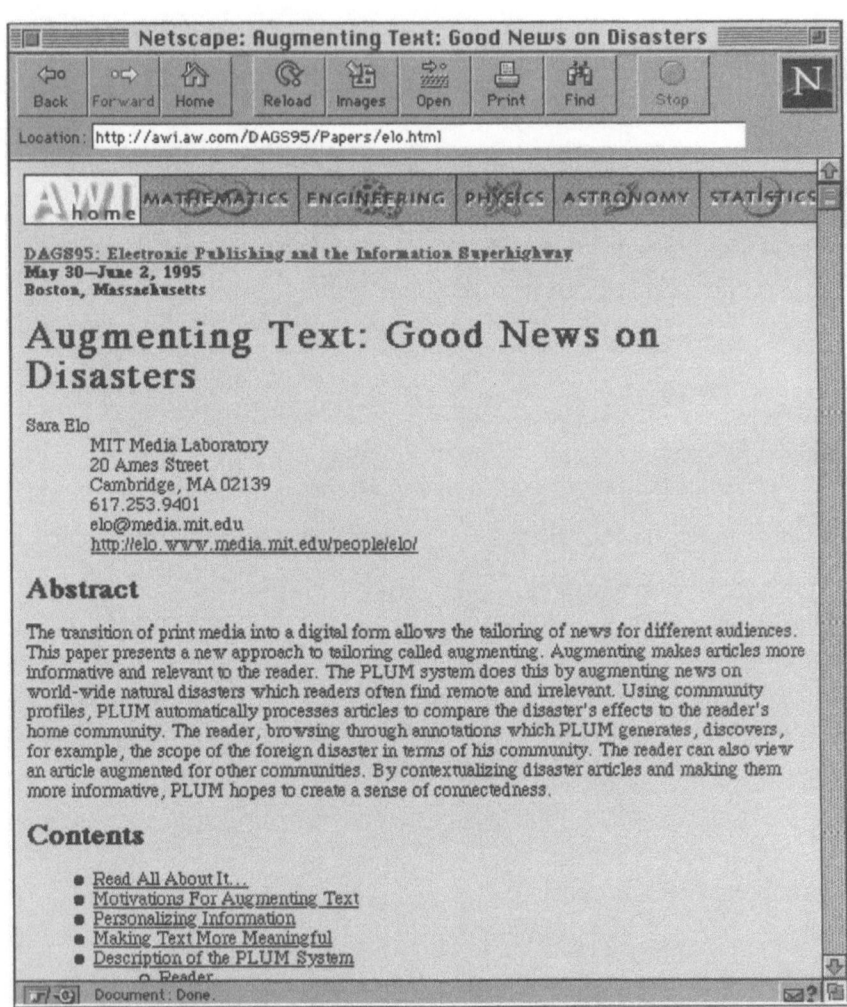

CHAPTER 40

The Development

Process

The first step in producing multimedia proceedings is always to collect the raw material (video, sound, text) in a format suitable for further processing. It is well worth spending substantial effort in making sure that the raw material is complete and of sufficient quality. The subsequent editing steps take much more time if low–quality slides, papers, and audio files have to be enhanced by software.

40.1 Producing Digital Talks for CD-ROM

Experiences during the development process for the DAGS '92 proceedings greatly influenced the design and development process of later multimedia and Web-based proceedings. To acquire the video footage for the digital talks, a procedure was developed for DAGS '92 that was refined for subsequent conference proceedings. During the conference, the speakers' presentations were videotaped, their overhead transparencies were copied, and their papers were collected. To make it easier to resynchronize transparencies and speech in the next editing step, we used two video cameras for videotaping; one focusing on the speaker and one on the projected transparencies (Figure V.22, step 1). In contrast to our initial expectations, it turned out that the videotape focusing on the transparencies was far more useful. After the collection, these materials were converted to digital form for computer-based processing (Figure V.22, step 2). Due to the space constraints of the CD-ROM, we decided to deliver only the eight invited talks in full audiovisual format.

Despite the huge storage provided by the CD technology, we knew that we could not fit the full 8 one-and-a-half hour video tracks on a CD-ROM. However, most of speakers are usually standing next to the projector so that they can change transparencies, mark them, and point to them. The audience gets most of the information by looking at the transparencies. Therefore, we displayed a short video loop of each speaker by selecting a piece of the video

Figure V.22

DAGS '92 development process

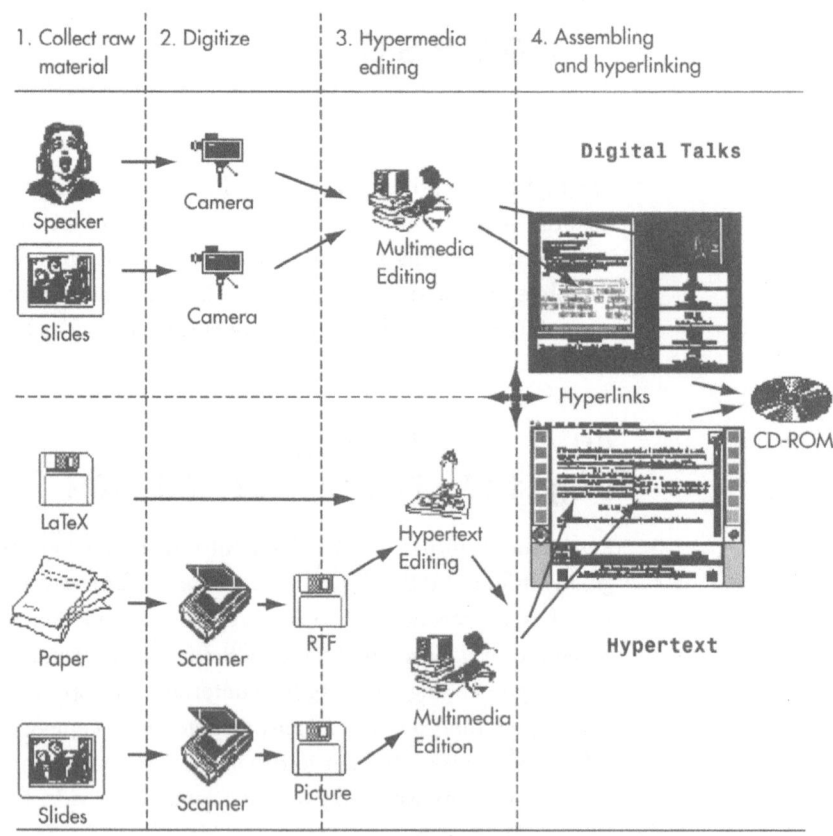

with similar beginning and ending frames so that the loop transition would not be distracting to the viewers. User feedback confirmed us in this decision because little valuable information was lost in this way; it turns out that about 2 minutes of video is sufficient to convey a sense of a speaker's appearance and mannerisms. Some users even preferred turning off the speaker video loop, to concentrate on the transparencies. Given the small size of the video capture screen, one can see the movement of the speaker and his or her overall appearance, but not tiny details like the movement of the lips. Somewhat surprisingly, we found that most users could not distinguish a loop of a few minutes of the speaker video from the whole video.

The video loops were digitized with a low-end video capture board and compressed to provide efficient playback from a CD-ROM. The loops were kept small to enhance playback performance. Due to the low resolution of the 120-by-180 pixel QuickTime video window, the user has to look closely to notice the missing synchronization between lip movement and the voice track.

The audio track of each talk was digitized and then edited to remove pauses and noise words such as "umm" and "ahh" (Figure V.22, step 2). The edited talks were roughly half as long as the originals, and much more listenable. To improve the quality, we amplified most of them using the SoundEdit Pro [Mac91b] sound processing application.

The overhead transparencies were scanned and edited for clarity and contrast; they were also made smaller to fit into the talks window of the user interface. After diminution, poorly handwritten transparencies were almost unreadable and had to be retyped.

Then, using the original videotapes with the transparencies as guides, we synchronized the transparencies to the edited audio tracks using the Adobe Premiere video editing program [Pre93]. The resulting "movie" reproduced the most important features of a talk, the speaker's words and transparencies, and preserved their temporal connection. These "movies" were indexed to allow random access to a list of primary topics and to allow more sensitive linking between the papers and the talks.

Given the variety of the playback speeds of the commercial CD-ROM drives available, single-speed CD-ROMs and slow CPUs have a hard time displaying both the transparencies video and the speakers' video loops on the screen at a comfortable speed. For that reason, we have given the user the option to stop the speaker video loop and replace it with a static color picture of the speaker.

40.2 Producing
Digital Talks for the Web

The basic design process of the Web-based DAGS '95 proceedings is similar to the one for the DAGS '92 CD-ROM proceedings, although some details had to be refined due to improved video processing technology, limitations in network bandwidth, and previous experiences with DAGS '92 and DAGS '93 [Glo96]. Not much could be done to improve the initial information gathering and documentation steps, still a mostly manual process, although we noticed that most of the speakers were now using presentation software to prepare their slides or transparencies, which made it easier for us to digitize their material. We had to make sure to collect the material not only on paper or foils but also in digital format.

http://town.
hall.org/
university/
network/estrin

Dealing with limited chunks of audio is still the only realistic continuous media approach for Web access. Due to the limited network bandwidth available on the Web, it is important to avoid forcing users to download huge sound files, something that may make an application unusable. It is obviously impractical to store entire files since the size of the sound of an uncompressed 30 to 45 minutes sound file digitized in low–quality 8 kHz AU format can easily take up to 40 MB. To address this problem, digitized talks have been offered as one large sound file per slide (e.g., Estrin's talk, see section 37.1).

In the development of the DAGS '95 conference proceedings, the audio files were cut into 200–300 KB pieces. Restricting the average file size of the audio clips to 200 KB implies that transmission via a 14,400–baud modem should generally take less than 2 minutes. This means that frequently the sound track belonging to one slide had to be broken into multiple sound clips. Given the common transfer rate achievable for modems, we nevertheless expect modem users to employ the "listen to audio" feature very selectively.[1] However, the trade-off here was that avoiding chopped sentences required intensive human postprocessing and defining all sound-clip boundaries manually. The target duration of the available audio clips was set at 40 seconds. Because there were different factors to consider in the audio editing process, the audio clip size varies considerably.

The numbering in the following sequential description of the creation process corresponds to the graphical representation of the process in Figure V.23:

---

1 The use of proprietary compressed audio file formats such as RealAudio [Rea95] allows authors to change the design of the audio part, because it permits real-time continuous download. RealAudio was not available when the DAGS '95 proceedings were built. RealAudio is discussed in section 41.1.

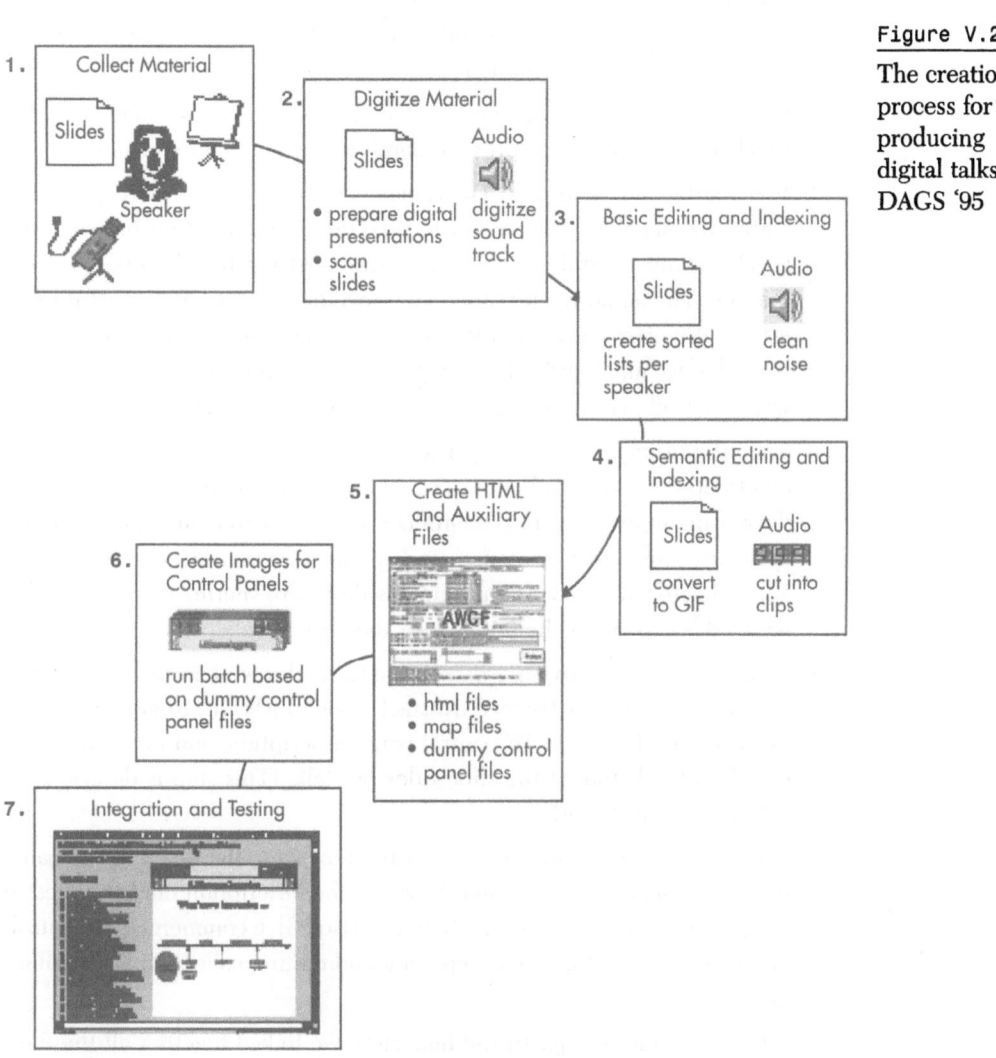

Figure V.23

The creation process for producing digital talks for DAGS '95

1. *Collect material.* Each talk was filmed with HI-8 video. Based on previous experience we made a movie not of the speaker but of the slides or transparencies. The audio input was taken from a microphone that speakers were requested to carry. Speakers had been asked to give us a slide set after the talk, preferably in both paper and electronic format. Slide originals were collected from the speakers after the talk. Last–minute

corrections or annotations by the speakers could be included in this way. The slide formats included hand-written slides, color transparencies, and files produced by presentation programs.

2. *Digitize material.* Transparencies were scanned and screen shots from the speakers' software-based presentations were converted to images.

3. *Basic editing and indexing.* The speakers were videotaped to capture the audio (the speakers' voice) and to provide synchronization between the speaker's voice and the slides. Slides were ordered based on the video of the talk. The audio track of the video was digitized using SoundEdit and Adobe Premiere. The samples were manually cleaned from noise and superfluous "ums" and "ahs" using the same applications. Unused slides were omitted, while some others were concatenated into one image.

4. *Semantic editing and indexing.* The sound track for each slide was cut into 30– to 50–second sound clips. The audio edit guidelines were (sorted by decreasing priority) (1) to synchronize the slides and audio clips, (2) to let speakers complete a sentence, and (3) to have sound clips of at most approximately 300 KB. Sound samples that were shorter than 20 seconds were added to either the previous or the next sample.

5. *Create HTML and auxiliary files.* Once the slides were available as sorted GIF files, we used a HyperCard stack (named AWCF) to generate automatically the HTML, GIF control panel description, and imagemap files based on the listing of the slide titles per talk. (This step is described in detail in the next section.)

6. *Create images for control panels.* In the next step, the GIF control panel image files had to be generated based on the description file generated in the previous step. We used DeBabelizer[Eqi93], a commercial Macintosh graphics program that allows creating and editing collections of graphics files in batch mode.

7. *Integration and testing.* In the final step, we linked together all the files, placed them on the server, and tested the validity of the links.

40.3 Automation of the Development Process

Timeliness is a critical feature for conference proceedings, as conference attendees are used to getting printed proceedings at the beginning of the conference.

This means that talks should be published weeks or at most months, after the conference. Turnaround time for the CD-ROM-based DAGS '92 and DAGS '93 multimedia proceedings was at least one year. For DAGS '95 it was possible to speed up the development process to 3 months past the conference because of three main factors: (1) experience with what material to collect and parallel processing of these, (2) placing the burden of hypertext (HTML) authoring on the author rather than on the production team, and (3) development of new production tools.

To emulate the "random talk access" feature of the DAGS '92 and DAGS '93 proceedings, we considered both static and dynamic approaches. The dynamic approach would have included the use of CGI/Perl scripts to generate HTML on the fly to display a particular slide. The CPU load on the server would have increased with the number of users accessing the talks, thus slowing response times. The static approach, on the other hand, entails advance generation of many short HTML files, one per slide. Because the HTML files are easily computed in advance and performance on the Web is usually poor anyway, we opted for placing static short documents on the server instead of relying on dynamic page generation.

Talks screen design: static versus dynamic approach

Our final screen design required that each slide be mounted on a separate page (see Figure V.16), that is, a different HTML file. The HTML file displays the actual slide title in the list of contents in italics and also brings up appropriate control panel and slide images. The control panel (an image in interlaced GIF format) has to be produced for every slide because the correct number of sound buttons and the title of the slide have to be displayed. Besides HTML files, a WWW page relying on an imagemap also requires a ".map" file to react correctly to clicks within the image. For the generation of HTML, imagemap references (text), and dummy control panel files, we developed the "AWCF" HyperCard stack (Figure V-24).

Talks screen design: final implementation

A typical 1-hour talk in which 30 slides are shown requires the following:

- Around 90 sound clips.
- 30 interlaced GIF images of slides (our screen design allowed for a maximal image width of 287 pixels with at most 256 different colors).
- 30 control panel GIF images.
- 30 HTML files.
- 30 map files (which contain individual sets of URLs for each slide).

Out of the 210 files, 30 HTML, 30 map, and 30 dummy control panel files are generated by AWCF ("A Web Conference Factory"). This means that AWCF relieves electronic proceedings editors from having to edit HTML text manually and from having to use an imagemap tool to assign links manually to clickable areas of an image. Furthermore, it associates each slide with a set of sound clips.

To generate the GIF control panel image files demands the extra step of using dummy files created by AWCF to compute the final images. The dummy files contain the slide title, the number of sound icons required for the slide, and the slide number. The actual control panel images are generated in an additional batch process using the commercial graphics manipulation program DeBabelizer.

AWCF requires the following input:

- Title of the talk.

- Full name and home page URL of the speaker.

- Table of contents of the slide titles.

- Number of sound files for each slide.

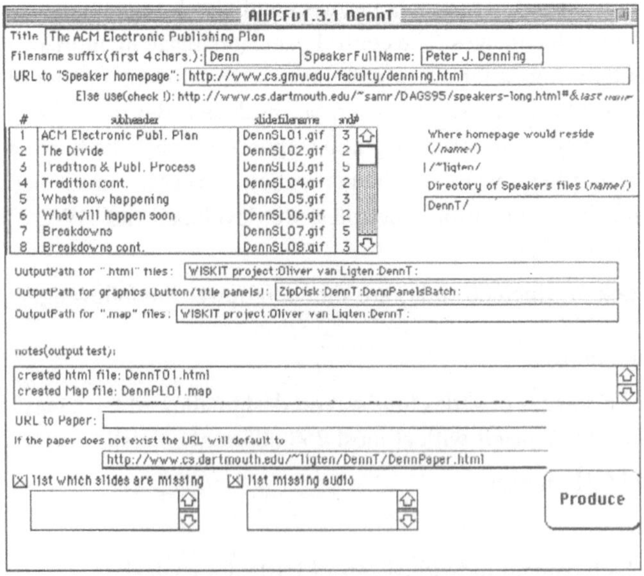

Figure V.24

AWCF user
interface

- File name suffix for the files to be generated.

- Path information to define an appropriate directory structure on the designated server.

- Path information to tell AWCF where to place the generated files.

The output path can be selected individually for the HTML files, the map files, and the graphics files. Final production preparation requires the slide images to be resized to fit below the control panel and the format to be changed to interlaced GIF. This process can also be executed automatically by DeBabelizer.

40.4 Producing the Hypertext for CD-ROM

Design objectives and creation process for the hypertext part have been much streamlined during the development of the various DAGS multimedia conference proceedings.

We wanted the DAGS '92 multimedia proceedings to be a real hypermedia product. We therefore decided to present the papers in hypertext form, using an advanced hypertext engine. We used the Gloor/Dynes hypertext engine [Dyn92], developed at MIT for the CD-ROM version of the *Introduction to Algorithms* textbook [Cor90] and based on Apple's HyperCard software. The Gloor/Dynes engine is described in detail in Chapter 14. Somewhat surprisingly, it turned out that the conversion of the22 papers into hypertext format took about two-thirds of the total DAGS '92 one man-year developing time.

We first broke the 22 papers into hypertext nodes and assigned each node a "node level" that reflected its degree of generality (see Figure V.22). For example, all the abstracts of the papers are on level 1. Thus, a user can quickly become familiar with the themes of the presented papers by visiting all the first-level nodes of the proceedings. All beginnings of sections within a paper are on level 2, such that a user can get an overview of the paper by following all level 2 nodes.

The "chunking" process was handled manually by computer scientists with expertise in the subject area. It appears that one cannot automate this process unless the authors have written their papers following predefined specifications. Since we did not anticipate this problem, we did not provide any specifications during the writing of the papers. The result was that each paper was written in a way that reflected the personal style of the author, not the expectations of a node-based hypertext. We tried to have authors provide chunking information afterward, but the results were not sufficiently consistent from paper to paper, so in the end all chunking was performed by the experts of our team.

In the next step we converted all the papers to HyperCard format. Every author provided PostScript versions of the papers and half of them provided electronic versions in T_EX or L^AT_EX format; the latter were converted to HyperCard using our own utilities. Unfortunately, we could not use PostScript files for the hypertext engine; therefore, the remaining papers were scanned, processed by optical character recognition (OCR) software, and then manually corrected. A great number of errors were introduced by the scanning and recognition process, and some pages were retyped. A number of text features required special treatment. HyperCard does not support mathematical text—not even subscripts or superscripts; therefore, special fonts were used instead. Special symbols were similarly provided by custom fonts. This still leaves out very complex equations, which were scanned and displayed as in-line graphics using the capabilities of the Gloor/Dynes hypertext engine.

Figures were scanned and edited for clarity. The text was manually marked to provide links to citations, tables, and figures. Each hyperlink in the text appears as a boldfaced word. The system supports multiple windows containing scanned figures, tables, or bibliographic information. Finally, hyperlinks leading to referenced sections were introduced.

The final step was to integrate all these elements into a single user interface and to test the resulting system. Extensive color graphics and on-line help facilities were built into the navigation shell. The system was tested on a number of machines with different capabilities and configurations. Special care was taken to optimize the transfer data rate so that it would perform reasonably well even on single-speed CD-ROMs.

40.5 Producing the Hypertext for the Web

Compared to the DAGS '92 proceedings, the hypertext part of DAGS '95 required much less postprocessing effort. This was mostly due to the fact that authors got an HTML template well before turning in the final version of their paper. All the authors who submitted their paper in electronic format

respected our editing guidelines. The only activity on our side was to link the
HTML files into the DAGS '95 proceedings directory structure. While the
DAGS '92 proceedings offer much more hypertext functionality, this functionality came at the price of manual postprocessing, resulting in much higher production cost and a longer production cycle. Shifting the burden of hypertext
editing to the author relieved the editors of hypermedia proceedings of their
biggest task. The price that we had to pay is the incompleteness of the proceedings, since we had no resources to convert manually to HTML the papers
that we got only on paper. Using OCR technology as we had done it for the
DAGS '92 proceedings would have overstretched our project budget.

The structure of a DAGS '95 paper on the Web is less than ideal in that each
paper is implemented as one, large HTML file with a table of contents in the
beginning. This structure makes it harder to add links within a paper and to
offer hierarchical navigation as available in the Gloor/Dynes hypertext engine.
Additionally, downloading one large text file may take some time on a slow network connection. Nevertheless, our experiment shows that publishing proceedings on the Web offers a valuable extension of printed proceedings at
much lower cost than CD-ROM publishing.

Extensions

and

Improvements

Then, as if planning an exhibition, the designer must chart the details of what to animate, what to film, who to interview, how to arrange the information in the space they have built and so on.

—Economist

[Eco95a]

41.1 Obstacles in the Creation of Digital Talks

Designing an interface and specifying a creation process general enough to cover all eventualities is nearly impossible. We ran into the following perils and pitfalls while implementing the digital talks part of the DAGS multimedia proceedings:

- *Missing or extra slides* or *wrong slide numbering* forced us to rely on the video to determine the slides used and the order in which they were presented. This means that the video of the overhead screen not only served as a cue to index and edit the audio, but also as a final record of the slides actually used during the talks.

- It was sometimes necessary to *concatenate a series of slides* because they were important but shown without much comment by the speaker. The legibility of digitized slides that were resized to fit beneath the control panel and next to the table of contents also had to be enhanced manually at times.

- We had to reconstruct *meaningful slide titles.* Slide titles were used as index items. Thus, the assumption was made that the slide name provides meaningful index information. This was not always the case. Slide titles like "strategy point 1," "strategy point 2," and so on, are rather meaningless as index information. This means that even if the creation process is automated, there is still no replacement for the human expert, who needs to do the last check to make sure that the system produces meaningful output.

- Intermittent *audiovideo equipment failures at the conference* caused sporadic losses of video material. A strategy had to be devised that would allow for gaps in the material. We manually inserted the missing sound track, displayed the slides without comment, or omitted slides without sound track, depending on the context.

- Presentations where speakers just showed *lengthy videos* had to be omitted from the digital talks because they did not fit the slide-with-audio model.

- Advanced animation features like animated titles and transitions in *software–supported presentations* in systems like PowerPoint posed additional problems because current Web browsers and HTML do not support this style of animation. Such presentations had to be coerced into the static slide-with-audio model by using screen shots of screens once they were complete (i.e., once the last animated title on a screen had appeared).

41.2 Improving the Development Process

Two related issues need to be addressed to improve the development process: automation and time to delivery. Developing multimedia products is still a very labor-intensive process. To reduce manual efforts, as many activities in the development process as possible have to be executed automatically by the computer. Automation also leads to shorter production cycles, as single steps in the development process can be executed faster or iteratively, if some hidden bug discovered late in the software life cycle makes it necessary to redo earlier steps. Following are areas for further improvement:

- *Minimize production turn-around.* When designing and implementing systems like the DAGS multimedia proceedings, there is always a trade-off between timely delivery and sophistication of provided features. In contrast to publishing on CD-ROM, publication on the Internet can be an ongoing creation and improvement process that may even preclude the conference for some sections. It is much easier to publish conference proceedings on the Web in a piecewise fashion, bringing additional proceedings parts on-line as soon as they are completed.

- *Improve production time by restricted functionality.* Compared to the hardwired functionality of Web browsers, CD-ROM authoring tools offer much greater flexibility—at a price: Because the layout of the DAGS '95 proceedings was limited by the features available in HTML 3.0, production time for Web proceedings was reduced, as there simply was no temptation to support additional elaborate graphic features.

- *Use advanced multimedia authoring tools.* Editing audio for clarity can be supported by tools like VideoScheme described in Part IV. We have already made some encouraging experiments using VideoScheme to remove pauses and noise words from audio sources automatically.

- *Convert linear text to a hypertext hierarchy.* Converting linear text to a hierarchy of hypertext nodes such that the semantic structure of the original document is maintained is a complicated and domain-knowledge-intensive process. This process can be automated only if authors follow the guidelines of the publishing editors in hierarchically structuring their document in advance. This hierarchical structure can then be exploited to allow for hierarchical navigation.

- *Collect raw material.* Besides identifying technical improvements for future CD-ROM and Web-based proceedings, working on the DAGS proceedings also taught us lessons for content gathering. Provisions should be made such that speakers themselves reliably submit slides and other material used. Using volunteers to collect slides from speakers after the conference is difficult, especially if many talks are held simultaneously. Furthermore, speakers are often distracted by discussions with participants after the talk and are then inaccessible to volunteers collecting the slides. Our solution, which worked only partially, was to notify speakers in advance of this requirement and to ask session chairs to collect a copy of the slides before the presentation.

41.3 CD-ROM versus WWW

One of the first design decisions that needs to be made when developing a new hypermedia product is the target platform. The capability to include large multimedia files and the low unit costs of mass production of the disks have made CD-ROM the prominent candidate as a delivery form for multimedia electronic proceedings. The Internet is a better platform for distributing information more widely, but it makes it harder to include large audio or video files or to synchronize the presentation of multiple objects. The choice between CD-ROM and WWW does not have to be exclusive, as is demonstrated by the CHI '95 Conference Proceedings and Companion CD-ROM (see section 37.1). Table V.1 compares CD-ROM and WWW for the publication of multimedia conference proceedings.

HTML browsers are available for almost any hardware and software platform, while CD-ROM authoring tools are still mostly platform specific. On the other hand, creators of hypermedia versions of presentations must be able to include large audio and video files in multiple, synchronized, multimedia data

Table V.1		Audio/ video	Fast access	Worldwide links	Publication turnaround	Multi- platform	Extend- ibility
Comparison of features required for multimedia talks on CD-ROM and WWW.	**CD-ROM**	good	good	by WWW	poor	difficult	poor
	WWW	poor	poor	good	good	good	good

formats. While CD-ROMs offer fast data access to large multimedia files, the advantage of Internet proceedings is their capability to include live worldwide links. Since researchers are interested in swift dissemination of their findings, shorter turnaround times as supported by the Internet are highly desirable. Furthermore, extending, adapting, and improving Internet publications can be an ongoing process. CD-ROM publishers, on the other hand, burn one final 600 MB volume for mass production and distribution. Increasing network data transfer rates, advances in data compression, and emerging support for multimedia on Web pages improve prospects for hypermedia proceedings on the WWW. Obviously, there are both advantages and disadvantages for using either CD-ROM or Internet as the distribution medium. Therefore, we assume that both will coexist peacefully for quite some time as platforms of choice depending on production time, budget, application area, contents, and audience.

41.4 Improving the Product Design

There are certain common points that need to be considered when designing the interface and functionality of a hypermedia product. Although the points listed here have been identified based on our work on the DAGS multimedia proceedings, they are valid for any other hypermedia publishing effort.

Improved linking

Currently digital Web talks are not yet fully linked to HTML papers. Since there is usually some correspondence between a submitted paper and the talk held at the conference, linking fragments of the talks to different sections of a paper is an obvious extension. Eventually it would be meaningful to reference multiple HTML documents from within a talk. Users could read relevant sections of a paper and listen to the speaker simultaneously. The AWCF application could be extended to automate linking individual slides to specific sections of various papers. If each slide were to be linked via an individual URL, papers could be submitted as a collection of hypertext files instead of one long piece of text. Providing such links between the paper and the talks would either involve human experts to do the indexing and linking or the use of automatic indexing methods as described in Chapter 1.

Support for multimedia synchronization

An interface like the one of the DAGS '92 talks requires synchronization of audio and slides (e.g., to support the transition from one slide to the other). Unfortunately, HTML was not designed with sufficient support for such multimedia synchronization, and it is not likely that HTML will support it in the near future. The best solution seems to be to enforce synchronization by segmenting the audio and explicitly requiring users to reload the next audio clip upon encountering the next slide, as we did for the DAGS '95 talks. Java and JavaScript now offer an alternate solution by allowing tighter control on the loading of new frames.

Audio over the Internet

http://www.
realaudio.com

The biggest disadvantage of the AU audio file format chosen for DAGS '95 is the long download times that modem users experience. Audio on demand for Internet delivery is a recognized need and market opportunity. For instance, encoder, player, and server software using RealAudio technology by Progressive Networks enables users to access RealAudio sound files and play them back instantaneously [Rea95]. Using a RealAudio player helper application or Netscape plug-in allows downloading an (almost) continuous audio stream over a 14,400-baud modem. RealAudio bypasses HTTP and directly relies on the underlying UDP protocol. Among other improvements, Progressive Networks developed a new protocol for time-based media that supports bidirectional communication between clients and servers allowing RealAudio users to pause, fast forward, and skip to particular sections. Progressive Networks also came up with a loss-correction system that minimizes the impact of lost packets over the less reliable UDP protocol and even degrades gracefully when there is packet loss.

RealAudio players are available for most of the popular target platforms for free; however, RealAudio servers come at substantial cost.[1] Nevertheless, the advent of RealAudio and other "sound over the Internet" products will certainly have far-reaching implications for the interface design and audio file format for future digital talks and other Internet publishing products.

Extending browsers

There are many different software tools available for CD-ROM-based multimedia editing. Authoring tools on the Web are far more limited. Tools for CD-ROM software development like HyperCard, MacroMedia Director, ToolBook, SuperCard, and Apple Media Tool allow easy implementation of custom features such as annotation, search, navigation, and layout. Using WWW as a delivery platform means that some features that might have to be programmed explicitly when creating an application for delivery on CD-ROM are hardwired into the WWW browser. Predefined features that add to the quality of the talks interface include the ability of browsers to keep track of

---

1 The price of a RealAudio server license is about $2,000 to $14,000 (February 1996) depending on the number of concurrently available audio streams.

locations visited and to add bookmarks. A significant pitfall of WWW browsers is missing support for user annotations. General functionality that goes beyond those provided by the browser can be provided through CGI or Java/JavaScript programming. Our own Java applets that provide additional navigation functionality extending Web browsers are described in Part II.

Given the preeminence of annotations and linking in the hypertext community, it is somewhat surprising that neither HTML nor current WWW browsers provide real support for shared annotations or user links being added to existing documents. This lack makes HTML inconvenient at best for true hypertext publishing. Fortunately, researchers are developing extended browsers and support systems for shared annotations [Roe95].

Support for annotations

The ultimate question concerns the effectiveness of the final result. We believe that the multimedia proceedings provide most of the content of live talks and linear papers, with the advantage of random talk access and hypertext linking. Although there are many situations where the printed book still surpasses any hypermedia document, there are obvious advantages to hypermedia publishing, demonstrated by the exponential growth of the Web and the rapidly growing number of CD-ROM titles available.

Usability testing

Conclusions

The DAGS multimedia proceedings series is a step toward academic publications that more fully reproduce the experience of a live conference or classroom. Currently such publications are still one of a kind, expensive to produce, and with clear but unmeasured advantages over their traditional counterparts. Our experience highlights some shortcomings but also suggests that improved systems can be built with less effort and greater rewards.

The usefulness of hypermedia products is greatly enhanced by tightly linking different media types such as digital talks and hypertext papers, implementing an integrated hypermedia environment where the sum is greater than its parts. On the other hand, there is no use in introducing a new media type for its own sake if a simpler representation completes the task as well. The talks interface can be reduced to a view of synchronized slide images combined with audio of the speaker's voice (rather than offering video of a gesturing speaker), without substantially compromising the overall experience of the talk.

For multimedia publishing to take off, the authoring and editing process needs to be greatly improved. Obvious improvements are to automate repetitive tasks and optimize the initial content–gathering process to collect raw material in a format suitable for further processing. The DAGS multimedia proceedings projects showed that the turnaround time of the creation process for hypermedia products can be reduced significantly by using tools such as the AWCF application and VideoScheme, which facilitate the integration of different multimedia objects and automate basic hypertext and multimedia authoring.

Hypermedia publishing will not replace the printed book in the near future. Rather, different media types will coexist peacefully for quite some time. Nevertheless, as we are finally getting close to the environment envisioned by Vannevar Bush [Bus45] 50 years ago, hypermedia documents offer a uniquely integrated environment that cannot be simulated on paper. We hope that our experience collected with various hypermedia projects described in this book will assist others in creating similar hyperdocuments with less effort but as much fun and pleasure as we had.

Glossary

Algorithm Animation System Composed of an integrated set of multimedia tools (graphics, animation, text, video, code, etc.) that simulate how the algorithm works using abstractions of the data, operations, and semantics of the program behind the algorithm. Algorithm animation may involve views that have no direct correspondence to the algorithm's data or execution.

Boolean Queries Using the boolean operators AND, OR, and NOT, Boolean queries such as "return me all documents that contain (("apple" AND "orange") OR "banana")" can be constructed. Boolean queries can return only true or false and are thus incapable of handling partial similarities.

Centroid A dummy average document at the center of the document space of a document collection.

Cyberspace On the Internet there are currently at least three slightly different definitions of the term *cyberspace* in use:

`http://edge`
`.stud.u-szeged`
`.hu/xanner/`
`cybdef.html`

1. "Cyberspace: A new universe, a parallel universe created and sustained by the world's computers and communication lines. A world in which the global traffic of knowledge, secrets, measurements, indicators, entertainments, and alter-human agency takes on form: sights, sounds,

presences never seen on the face of the earth blossoming in a vast electronic night."

http://www
.panix.com/
userdirs/
clays/Space/
place2.html

2. "The simplest definition of cyberspace is the space where electronic entities interact. In other words, digital actors need an electronic space to operate in. These various electronic spaces range from the literary to the architectural, which is to say from spaces created entirely with words to spaces which are intentionally modeled on architectural ideals."

http://www.s2
.sonnet.com/
bullock/def3
.html

3. "Cyberspace is used in this document to mean the Internet and other networks accessible from the Internet."

In this book we define cyberspace as a new parallel universe created and sustained by the world's computers and communication lines, most prominently the Internet.

Database Management System Stores and manages structured information by adding a layer between the user and the file system through special data processing languages, thus preserving data correctness and consistency.

http://www.w3
.org/pub/WWW/
MarkUp/

HTML HyperText Markup Language. A common data format for hypertext documents, currently available in version 3.0. It is specified as a SGML DTD (document type definition).

http://www.w3
.org/pub/WWW/
Protocols/
http://forum
.swarthmore
.edu/dr.math/
problems/
buhler20.html

HTTP HyperText Transfer Protocol. A common network access protocol for accessing Web servers.

Hypermedia Usually defined as hypertext—nonsequential text—where the hypertext nodes may contain multimedia contents [Nie90]. A more elegant definition is given by Halasz [Hal91]: "Hypermedia is a style of building systems for information representation and management around a network of multimedia nodes connected together by typed links."

Hyperspace In the science-fiction literature, an area in the fourth dimension but not in our three-dimensional universe. Science-fiction authors generally conceive of our three-dimensional universe as some convoluted shape in the fourth dimension. An analogy would be to draw something looking like a small intestine on a piece of paper and declare that in normal movement a spacecraft has to stay in the boundaries of this shape. To get from one end to another could take a very long time. When a spacecraft "goes into hyperspace", it crosses this boundary.

Since the shortest distance between two points on the piece of paper is a line, going through hyperspace can save a lot of time.

Information Retrieval System A system used to store items of information that need to be processed, searched, retrieved, and disseminated to various user populations" [Sal83]. An IR system normally stores unstructured information.

Internet definition The Federal Networking Council (FNC) defines the term *Internet* in its resolution of October 24, 1995 as follows

"Internet" refers to the global information system that—

http://www.fnc
.gov/
Internet_res
.html

(i) is logically linked together by a globally unique address space based on the Internet Protocol (IP) or its subsequent extensions/follow-ons;

(ii) is able to support communications using the Transmission Control Protocol/Internet Protocol (TCP/IP) suite or its subsequent extensions/follow-ons, and/or other IP-compatible protocols; and

(iii) provides, uses or makes accessible, either publicly or privately, high level services layered on the communications and related infrastructure described herein.

Inverted Index Lists all the document addresses of the terms that might be searched for. This means that normally each row in the inverted array specifies the documents corresponding to a particular term.

Java Applet Small application written in the Java programming language that is loaded over the network and runs within the environment of the Web browser.

PDF Portable Document Format. A device-independent page description language based on PostScript and developed and marketed by Adobe. Primarily intended for the exchange of preformatted pages over a network. Includes hot links, thumbnail icons of pages, chapter outlines, and page annotations.

Program Visualization The use of various visualization techniques to enhance human understanding of the actual implementation of computer programs.

Relevance Feedback Allows users of an information retrieval system to define their search by example (i.e., by using relevant documents as search input).

SGML Standardized Generalized Markup Language. A text formatting language standardized by the International Standardization Organization (ISO/IEC 8879-1986). It allows the description of documents independent of any platform in terms of their logical structure. SGML provides a metasyntax for expressing agreed-on syntaxes for individual documents. Each such syntax, called a "document type definition" (DTD), consists of a set of tags for coding a particular type of document, together with the allowable contents and attribute sets. Starting with HTML 2.0, HTML is specified as a SGML DTD.

http://www.w3
.org/pub/WWW/
Addressing/
Addressing
.html

URL Uniform Resource Locator. Implements a common naming scheme for documents accessible through the World Wide Web.

VRML Virtual Reality Modeling Language. A developing standard for describing interactive three-dimensional scenes delivered across the Internet. It allows textual description of three-dimensional virtual worlds for execution over the WWW.

References

[Add90]   AddMotion User Guide. Motion Work, Vancouver BC, Canada, 1990.

[Aho88]   Aho, A. Kernighan, B. Weinberger, P. *The AWK Programming Language*. Addison-Wesley, Reading, MA, 1988.

[Aks88]   Akscyn, R. Yoder, E. McCracken, D. The data model is the heart of interface design. *CHI Proceedings*, 1988, 115-120.

[All93]   Allen, R. B. (electronic proceedings editor). *Proceedings of the International Workshop on Applications of Neural Networks to Telecommunications*. http://superbook.bellcore.com/SB/IWANNT/iwannt93.eprocs .html.

[And95]   Andres, K. Kappe, F. Maurer, H. Serving information to the web with Hyper-G. *Proceedings of the Third International World-Wide Web Conference. Computer Networks and ISDN Systems*, 27, no. 6, 1995, 919-926.

[App91]   Apple Computer. *The QuickTime Architecture*. Apple Computer, Cupertino, CA, 1991.

[Bae69]   Baecker, R. M. Picture driven animation. In *Spring-Joint Computer Conference 34*, AFIPS Press, 1969, 273-288.

[Bel87]   Belkin, N. Croft, W. B. Retrieval techniques. *Annual Review of Information Sciences and Techniques (ARIST)*, 22, 1987, 109–145.

[Ben91]   Bentley, J. L. Kernighan, B. W. A system for algorithm animation. *Computing Systems*, 4, no. 1, Winter 1991.

[Ber88]   Bernstein, M. The bookmark and the compass. *ACM SIGOIS Bulletin*, October 1988.

[Ber90]   Bernstein, M. An apprentice that discovers hypertext links. *Hypertext: Concepts, Systems and Applications. Proc. European Conference on Hypertext*. Versailles, France, November 1990, 212-223.

[Ber92]   Berners-Lee, T. Cailliau, R. Groff, J. Pollermann, B. *World-Wide Web: The Information Universe*. CERN, Geneva, Switzerland, 1992.

[Bow95]   Bowman, C. M. Danzig, P. B. Hardy, D. R. Manber, U. Schwartz, M. F. Wessels, D. P. *Harvest: A Scalable, Customizable Discovery and Access System*. Technical Report CU-CS-732-94, Department of Computer Science, University of Colorado, Boulder, 1995.

[Bra79]   Brachman, R. J. On the epistemological status of semantic networks. In *Associative Networks: Representation and Use of Knowledge by Computers*. Academic Press, New York; 1979, 191-215.

[Bra87]   Brajnik, G. Guida, G. Tasso, C. User modeling in intelligent information retrieval. *Information Processing & Management* 23, no. 4, 1987, 305-320.

[Bre90]   Bregman, A. S. *Auditory Scene Analysis*. MIT Press, Cambridge, MA, 1990.

[Bro85]   Brown, M. H. Sedgewick, R. Techniques for algorithm animation. *IEEE Software*, January 1985, 28-39.

[Bro88a]   Brown, M. H. *Algorithm Animation*. MIT Press, Cambridge, MA, 1988.

[Bro88b]   Brown, M. H. Exploring algorithms using Balsa-II. *IEEE Computer* 21, no. 5, May 1988.

[Bro91a]   Brown, M. H. Zeus: A system for algorithm animation and multi-
            view editing. *Proc. 1991 IEEE Workshop on Visual Languages*;
            October 8-11, 1991.

[Bro91b]   Brown, M. H. Hershberger, J. *Color and Sound in Algorithm
            Animation*. Research Report 76a, DEC Systems Research Center,
            Palo Alto, CA, 1991.

[Bro91c]   Brown, M. H. (ed.) *An Anthology of Algorithm Animations Using
            Zeus*. Research Report Videotape 76b, DEC Systems Research
            Center, Palo Alto, CA, 1991.

[Bro96]   Brown, M. H. Najork, M. A. *Collaborative Active Textbooks: A
            Web-Based Algorithm Animation System for an Electronic
            Classroom*. Research report draft, DEC Systems Research
            Center, Palo Alto, CA, 1996.

[Brø94]   *The Tortoise and the Hare*. Brøderbound's Living Books, Novato,
            CA, 1994.

[Bru90]   Bruza, P. D. Hyperindices: A novel aid for searching in hyperme-
            dia. *Hypertext: Concepts, Systems and Applications. Proc.
            European Conference on Hypertext*. Versailles, France, November
            1990, 109-122.

[Bus45]   Bush, V. As we may think. *Atlantic Monthly* 176, no. 1, 1945.
            Reprinted in Greif, I. (ed.) *Computer-Supported Cooperative
            Work: A Book of Readings*. Morgan Kaufmann Publishers, San
            Mateo, CA, 1988.

[Car91]   Card, S. K. Robertson, G. G. Mackinlay, J. D. The information
            visualizer, an information workspace. *Proc. CHI '91*, New
            Orleans, April 27-May 2, 1991, 181-188.

[Car94]   Carr, L. Hall, W. Davis, H. De Roure, D. Hollom, R. *The
            Microcosm Link Service and its Application to the World Wide
            Web*. Presented at the 1994 WWW Conference, Geneva,
            http://bedrock.ecs.soton.ac.uk/Microcosm/conference94/
            www94.html

[Che96]   Cheyney, M. Gloor, P. Johnson, D. Makedon, F. Matthews, J.
            Metaxas, P. Towards multimedia conference proceedings. *CACM*
            39, no. 1, January 1996.

[Chi89]   Chin, D. C. KNOME: Modeling what the user knows in UC. In Kobsa, A. Wahlster, W. (eds.), *User Models in Dialog Systems*. Springer, Berlin, 1989, 74-107.

[Cli89]   Clitherow, P. Riecken, D. Muller, M. VISAR: A system for inference and navigation in hypertext. *Hypertext '89 Proceedings*. Pittsburgh, November 1989, 293-304.

[Con87a]   Conklin, J. Hypertext: An introduction and survey. *IEEE Computer* 20, no 9, September 1987.

[Con87b]   Conklin, J. *A Survey of Hypertext*. MCC Technical Report No. STP-356-86, Rev. 2. December 3, 1987.

[Cor90]   Cormen, T. H. Leiserson, C. E. Rivest, R. L. *Introduction to Algorithms*. MIT Press, Cambridge, MA, 1990.

[Cox94]   Cox, K. C. Roman, G.-C. A characterization of the computational power of rule-based visualization. *Journal of Visual Languages and Computing* 5, no. 1, March 1994, 5-27.

[Cro89]   Crouch, D. B. Crouch, C. J. Andreas, G. The use of cluster hierarchies in hypertext information retrieval. *Hypertext '89 Proceedings*, Pittsburgh, November 1989. 225-237.

[Cro95]   Croft, W. B. NSF Center for Intelligent Information Retrieval. *CACM* 38, no. 4, April 1995, 42-43.

[Crow88]   Crowston, K. Malone, T. W. Intelligent software agents. *Byte* 13, no. 13, December 1988.

[Cut92]   Cutting, D. Karger, D. Pedersen, J. Tukey, J. Scatter/Gather: A cluster-based approach to browsing large document collections. *Proceedings SIGIR 92*, Denmark, 1992.

[Cut93]   Cutting, D. Karger, D. Pedersen, J. Constant interaction-time scatter/gather browsing of very large document collections. *Proceedings SIGIR 93*, Pittsburgh, 1993.

[Dam95]   Damashek, M. Gauging similarity with n-grams: Language-independent categorization of text. *Science* 267, February 1995, 843-848.

[Dav88]   Davenport, G. *A City in Transition—New Orleans 1983-1986* (set of four laserdisks). MIT Media Lab, Cambridge, MA, 1988.

[Dey90]   De Young, L. Linking considered harmful. *Hypertext: Concepts, Systems and Applications. Proc. European Conference on Hypertext*. Versailles, France, November 1990, 238-249.

[Dui86]   Duisberg, R. A. Animated graphical interfaces using temporal
            constraints. In *Proceedings of the ACM SIGCHI '86 Conference
            on Human Factors in Computing Systems*. Boston, MA, April
            1986, 131-136.

[Dyn92]   Dynes, S. B. Gloor, P. A. *Using Hierarchical Knowledge
            Representation for an Animated Algorithm Hypertext Learning
            Environment*. MIT LCS/TNS Internal Report. 1993.

[Eco95a]   *Economist*. Making a CD-ROM: Back to the surfing board.
            December 16-23, 1995, Special Section: Review of Books and
            Multimedia, 12-13.

[Eco95b]   *Economist*. Electronic science journals—Paperless papers.
            December 16-23, 1995, 100.

[Ega91]   Egan, D. E. Lesk, M. E. Ketchum, D. Lochbaum, C. C. Remde,
            J. R. Littman, M. Landauer, T. K. Hypertext for the electronic
            library? CORE sample results. *Proceedings ACM Hypertext '91*,
            San Antonio, TX, December 15-18, 1991. 299-312.

[Eis91]   Eisenberg, M. *Programmable Applications: Interpreter Meets
            Interface*. MIT Artificial Intelligence Memo 1325, October 1991.

[Emt92]   Emtage, A. Deutch, P. Archie—an electronic directory server for
            the Internet. *Proceedings Usenix Conference*, 1992.

[Eqi93]   Equilibrium. *DeBabelizer Reference Guide*. Equilibrium,
            Sausalito, CA, 1993.

[Fai88]   Fairchild, K. M. Poltrock, S. E. Furnas, G. W. SemNet: three-
            dimensional graphic representations of large knowledge bases. In
            Raymonde Guindon (ed.), *Cognitive Science and its Applications
            for Human-Computer Interaction*, Erlbaum, Hillsdale, NJ, 1988,
            201-233.

[Fai89]   Fairchild, K. Meredith, G. Wexelblat, A. The tourist artificial real-
            ity. *CHI'89 Proceedings*, May 1989. 299-304.

[Fei88]   Feiner, S. Seeing the forest for the tree: Hierarchical display of
            hypertext structure. *Proceedings ACM Conference on Office
            Information Systems*, Palo Alto, March 23-25, 1988, 205-212.

[Fer94]   Ferrari, D. (ed.). *ACM Multimedia 94: The Second ACM
            International Conference on Multimedia*, October 15-20, 1994,
            San Francisco. ACM Press, New York, 1994. (CD-ROM)

[Fin89]   Finin, T. W. GUMS - A general user modeling shell. In Kobsa, A.
             Wahlster, W. (eds.), *User Models in Dialog Systems*, Springer,
             Berlin, 1989.

[Fit92]   Fitz, K. Time and Frequency Scale Modification of Audio Signals
             Using an Extended Sinusoidal Model. M.S. thesis, University of
             Illinois at Urbana-Champaign, 1992.

[For95]   Ford, J. Gloor, P. Makedon, F. Rebelsky, S. A. (eds.). *Electronic
             Publishing and the Information Superhighway*. Addison-Wesley
             Interactive, Reading, MA, 1995.
             http://awi.aw.com/DAGS95

[Fou90]   Fountain, A. M. Hall, W. Heath, I. Davis, H. C. MICROCOSM:
             An open model for hypermedia with dynamic linking. *Hypertext:
             Concepts, Systems and Applications. Proceedings European
             Conference on Hypertext*. Versailles, France, November 1990,
             298-311.

[Fri90]   Frisse, M. E. Cousins, S. B. Guides for hypertext: an overview.
             Artificial Intelligence in Medicine 2, 1990, 303-314.

[Fur86]   Furnas, G. W. Generalized fisheye views. *CHI Proceedings*, 1986,
             16-23.

[Fur89]   Furuta, R. Plaisant, C. Shneiderman, B. A spectrum of automatic
             hypertext constructions. *Hypermedia* 1, no. 2, 1989.

[Fur94]   Furnas, G.W. Zacks, J. Multitrees: Enriching and reusing hierar-
             chical structure. *Human Factors in Computer Systems CHI '94
             Proceedings,* Boston, 1994, 330-336.

[Ghe95]   Ghedini Ralha, A. Cohn, A.G. Building maps of hyperspace.
             WWW National Conference, Internet Multimedia Information,
             July 6-8, Minho University, Portugal, 1995.

[Gib84]   Gibson, W. *Neuromancer*. Ace Books, Berkeley Publishing Group,
             New York, 1984.

[Gir92]   Girill, T. R. Luk, C. H. Hierarchical search support for hypertext
             on-line documentation. *International Journal on Man-Machine
             Studies* 36, 1992, 571-585.

[Glo89]   Gloor, P. A. Algorithmen-Animation mit HyperCard. *Proceedings
             GI-19. Jahrestagung*. Informatik-Fachberichte 222, Springer,
             Berlin, 1989, 460-473.

[Glo90]   Gloor, P. A. *Hypermedia-Anwendungsentwicklung*. Teubner,
            Stuttgart, 1990.

[Glo91]   Gloor, P. A. Cybermap, Yet another way of navigation in hyper-
            space. *Proceedings ACM Hypertext 91*, San Antonio, TX,
            December 15-18, 1991, 107–121.

[Glo92a]   Gloor, P. A. AACE – Algorithm animation for computer science
            education. *Proceedings IEEE International Workshop on Visual
            Languages*, Seattle, 1992.

[Glo92b]   Gloor, P. A. Johnson, D. B. Makedon, F. Metaxas, T. A visualiza-
            tion system for correctness proofs of graph algorithms. *Computer
            Science Education* 3, no. 3, 1992.

[Glo93a]   Gloor, P. A. Dynes, S. Lee, I. *Animated Algorithms*. MIT Press,
            Cambridge, MA, 1993. (CD–ROM)

[Glo93b]   Gloor, P. A. Dynes, S. Animated algorithms, teaching computer
            science with hypermedia learning environments. *Proceedings
            IEEE Conference on Frontiers in Education FIE 1993*,
            Washington, DC, 1993.

[Glo93c]   Gloor, P. A. Makedon, F. Matthews, J. *Parallel Computation:
            Practical Implementation of Algorithms and Machines*.
            TELOS/Springer–Verlag, Santa Clara, CA, 1993. (CD–ROM)

[Glo93d]   Gloor, P. A. Hypermedia–Lernumgebungen für den
            Informatik–Unterricht, *it+ti* (Informationstechnik und
            Technische Informatik) 93, no. 3, June 1993.

[Glo96]   Gloor, P. A. Makedon, F. Van Ligten, O. Obstacles in multimedia
            publishing on the web: Bringing conference proceedings on line.
            Proceedings ED–Media 96, Boston, June 17–22, 1996.

[Glu89]   Glushko, R. J. Design issues for multi–document hypertexts.
            Hypertext '89 Proceedings, Pittsburgh, November 1989, 51–60.

[Gol90]   Goldfarb, C. F. *The SGML Handbook*. Clarendon Press, Oxford,
            1990.

[Goo94]   Goodman, D. *Danny Goodman's AppleScript Handbook*. 2d ed.
            Random House, New York, 1994.

[Hal86]   Halasz, F. G. Moran, T. P. Trigg, R. H. NoteCards in a nutshell.
            CHI Proceedings, 1987, 45–52.

[Hal88]   Halasz, F. G. Reflections on NoteCards: Seven issues for the next generation of hypermedia systems, *CACM* 31, no. 7, July 1988.

[Hal91]   Halasz, F. *"Seven Issues": Revisited.* Slides of Hypertext '91 Keynote Talk, *ACM Hypertext 91*, San Antonio, TX, December 15–18, 1991.

[Ham88]   Hammond, N. Allison, L. Travels around a learning support environment: Rambling, orienteering or touring. *CHI'88 Proceedings*, 1988, 269–273.

[Has92]   Haseltine, M. Hypermedia Algorithm Animation—Red–Black Trees. B.S. Thesis, MIT, 1992.

[Hel89]   Helttula, E. Hyrskykari, A. Raiha, K. Graphical specification of algorithm animations with Alladin. In *Proceedings of the 22nd Hawai International Conference on System Sciences*, Januar 1989, 892–901.

[Hil87]   Hillis, W. D. The Connection Machine. *Scientific American* 256, June 1987, 108–115.

[Htm95]   HTML 3.0: http://www.w3.org/hypertext/WWW/MarkUp/html3

[Hyt91]   *Information Technology –Hypermedia/Time–based Structuring Language (HyTime)*. ISO/IECJTC1/SC18/WG8 N1331 Draft International Standard. ISO, 1991.

[Ieee93]   Institute of Electrical and Electronics Engineers. *SuperComputing'93*. IEEE Computer Society Press, New York, 1993.

[Ieee94]   Institute of Electrical and Electronics Engineers. *Supercomputing '94: The Conference on High Performance Computing and Communications*. http://ada.computer.org:80/conferen/sc94/sc94home.html

[Int95]   Project Interact. Project Interact Home Page. http://gorgon.eng.cam.ac.uk/

[Irl90]   Irler, W. I. Barbieri, G. Non–intrusive hypertext–anchors and individual color markings. *Hypertext: Concepts, Systems and Applications. Proceedings European Conference on Hypertext*, Versailles, France, November 1990, 261–273.

[Jac91]   Jackson, S. Yankelovich, N. InterMail: A prototype hypermedia mail system. Technical Briefing *Proceedings ACM Hypertext 91*, San Antonio, TX, December 15–18, 1991, 405–409.

[Jai88]   Jain, A. K. Dubes, R. C. *Algorithms for Clustering Data*. Prentice
           Hall, Englewood Cliffs, NJ, 1988.

[Jai95]   Jain, R. Editor–in–chief's message. *IEEE Multimedia* 2, no. 3,
           Fall 1995, 3.

[Joh91]   Johnson, B. Shneiderman, B. Tree–maps: A space–filling
           approach to the visualization of hierarchical information struc-
           tures. *Proceedings Visualization '91*, San Diego, CA, 1991,
           284–291.

[Joh92]   Johnson, D. B. Makedon, F. Metaxas P. (eds.) *Proceedings of the
           1992 DAGS Conference*, Hanover, NH, June 23–27, 1992.

[Jon72]   Jones, K. S. A statistical interpretation of term specificity and its
           application in retrieval. *Journal of Documentation* 28, no. 1,
           March 1972.

[Jon89]   Jones, K. S. Realism about user modeling. In Kobsa, A. Wahlster,
           W. (eds.), *User Models in Dialog Systems*. Springer, Berlin, 1989.

[Jut88]   Jüttner, G. Güntzer, U. *Methoden der künstlichen Intelligenz für
           Information Retrieval*. K. G. Saur, Munich, 1988.

[Kah88]   Kahn, P. Information retrieval as hypermedia: An outline of
           Interbrowse. *Proceedings of the 9th National Online Meeting*,
           New York, May 10–12, 1988, 131–139.

[Kah89]   Kahle, B. *Wide Area Information Server Concepts*. Thinking
           Machines, Cambridge, MA, 1989.

[Kah91]   Kahle, B. *WAIStation*. Technical Report TMC–203. Thinking
           Machines Corporation, Cambridge, MA, 1991.

[Kas89]   Student modeling in intelligent tutoring systems – Implications
           for user modeling. In Kobsa, A. Wahlster, W. (eds.), *User Models
           in Dialog Systems*. Springer, Berlin, 1989.

[Kaz96]   Kazman, R. Al–Halimi, R. Hunt, W. Mantei, M. Four paradigms for
           indexing video conferences. *IEEE Multimedia* 3,no. 4, Spring 1996.

[Kay91]   Kay, A. Computers, networks and education. *Scientific American*
           265, no. 3, September 1991, 138–148.

[Kem95]   Kemp, Z. Multimedia and spatial information systems. *IEEE
           Multimedia* 2, no. 4, Spring 1995.

[Kir83]   Kirkpatrick, S. Gelatt, C. D. Vecchi, M. P. Optimization by simu-
           lated annealing. *Science* 220, 1983, 671–680.

[Knu73a]   Knuth, D. E. *The Art of Computer Programming, 2d ed.* Vol. 1. Addison–Wesley, Reading, MA, 1973, 309–310.

[Knu73b]   Knuth, D. E. *Sorting and Searching.* Addison–Wesley, Reading, MA, 1973, 561–562.

[Knu84]   Knuth, D. E. *The TEXbook.* Addison–Wesley, Reading, MA, 1984.

[Kok91]   Kok, A. J. A formal approach to user models in data retrieval. *International Journal on Man–Machine Studies* 35, no. 6, 1991, 675–693.

[Lai88]   Lai, K. Malone, T. W. Yu, K. Object lens: A "spreadsheet" for cooperative work. *ACM Trans. on Office Information Systems* 6, no. 4. October 1988, 332–353.

[Lai91]   Lai, K. Malone, T. Object lens: Letting end–users create cooperative work applications. *Proceedings CHI '91*, 1991, 425–426.

[Lam85]   Lamport, L. *LATEX : A Document Preparation System.* Addison–Wesley, Reading, MA, 1985.

[Lam88]   Lamdan, Y. Wolfson, H. J. Geometric hashing: A general and efficient model–based recognition scheme. *Proceedings of the Second International Conference on Computer Vision*, Tarpon Springs, FL, 1988, 238–249.

[Lan95]   Langmead, C. J. A Theoretical Model of Timbre Perception Based on Morphological Representations of Time–Varying Spectra. M.A. thesis, Dartmouth College, 1995.

[Lau90]   Laurel, B. Interface agents: Metaphors with Character. in Laurel, B. (ed.)*The Art of Human–Computer Interface Design* . Addison–Wesley, Reading, MA, 1990, 355–365.

[Lau92]   Laurel, B. Oren, T. Don, A. Issues in multimedia interface design: Media integration and interface agents. In Blattner, M. M. Dannenberg, R. B. (eds.) *Multimedia Interface Design.* ACM Press, New York, 1992, 53–64.

[Law94]   Lawrence, A. W. Badre, A. N. Stasko, J. T. *Empirically Evaluating the Use of Animations to Teach Algorithms.* Technical Report GIT–GVU–94–07. Graphics, Visualization, and Usability Center, College of Computing, Georgia Institute of Technology, Atlanta, 1994.

[Len90]   Lenat, D. B. Ramanathan, V. G. Pittman, K. Pratt, D. Shepher, M. Cyc: Towards programs with common sense. *CACM* 33, no. 8. August 1990, 30–49.

[Let96]   Letsche, T. A. Berry, M. W. Large–Scale information retrieval with latent semantic indexing. Submitted, 1996.

[Lew96]   Lewis, P. Davis, H. Griffiths, S. Hall, W. Wilkins, R. Media–based navigation with generic links. *Proceedings ACM Hypertext '96*, Washington, DC, March 16–20, 1996, 215–223.

[Lin91]   Lin, Yi–Jing. *A Framework for Automatic Algorithm Animation.* Technical Report CS–91–37. Brown University, May 1991.

[Lin93]   Lindblad, C. Wetherall, D. Tennenhouse, D. *The VuSystem: A Programming System for Visual Processing of Digital Video.* TR–590. MIT Laboratory for Computer Science, 1993.

[Lin96]   Lindblad, C. The VuSystem: A programming system for compute–intensive multimedia. to appear in *IEEE Journal of Selected Areas in Communication*, 1996.

[Luc95]   Lucky, R. W. Reflections—where did the Web come from? *IEEE Spectrum* 32, no. 7, July 1995, 15.

[Mac89]   Mackay, W. Davenport, G. Virtual video editing in interactive multimedia applications. *CACM* 32, no. 7, July 1989.

[Mac91]   Mackinlay, J. D. Robertson, G. G. Card, S. K. The perspective wall: Detail and context smoothly integrated. *Proc. CHI '91.* New Orleans, April 27 – May 2, 1991, 173–179.

[Mac91b]   Macromind Paracomp. *SoundEdit Pro User Guide.* Macromind Paracomp, San Francisco, 1991.

[Mac92]   MacSciTech. *Proceedings CD–ROM of the 1992 MacSciTech Conference on Scientific and Engineering Applications for the Macintosh.* San Francisco, January 15–17, California. 1992. (CD–ROM)

[Mac95]   Mack, R. Marks, L. Collins, D. (production editors). *CHI'95 Conference Electronic Proceedings and Companion CD–ROM,* May 7–11, 1995, Denver, ACM Press, New York, 1995. http://www.acm.org/sigchi/chi95/Electronic/chi95cd.htm

[Mak94]   Makedon, F. Rebelsky, S. A. Cheyney, M. Owen, C. Gloor, P. Issues and obstacles with multimedia authoring. In Ottmann, T. and Tomek, I. (eds.). *Educational Multimedia and Hypermedia, 1994*, June 25–30, 1994, Vancouver, BC, Canada. AACE, Charlottesville, VA, 1994, 38–45.

[Mak95]   Makedon, F. Metaxas, P. T. Rebelsky, S. A. (eds.). *Parallel Computation and Parallel I/O*. Forthcoming.

[Mal92]   Malone, T. W. Lai, K. Y. *Experiments with Oval: A Radically Tailorable Tool for Cooperative Work*. Technical Report. Center for Coordination Science, MIT, March 1992.

[Mar89]   Marshall, C. C. Irish, P. M. Guided tours and on–line presentations: How authors make existing hypertext intelligible for readers. *Hypertext '89 Proceedings*, Pittsburgh, November 5–8, 1989, 15–26.

[Mat93]   Matthews, J. Gloor, P. A. Makedon, F. VideoScheme: A programmable video editing system for automation and media recognition. *Proceedings of ACM Multimedia 93*, Anaheim, CA, August 1–6, 1993, ACM Press, New York, 1993.

[Mat94]   Matthews, J. Makedon, F. Gloor, P. A. VideoScheme: A research, authoring and teaching tool for multimedia. In *Educational Multimedia and HyperMedia*, AACE, Charlottesville, VA, 1994.

[Mau96]   Maurer, H. *HyperWave: The Next Generation Web Solution*. Addison-Wesley Longman, 1996. Draft available at http://www.iicm.edu/hgbook/

[McC83]   McCune, B. P. Tong, R. M. Dean, J. S. Shapiro, D. G. RUBRIC: A system for rule–based information retrieval. *Proceedings COMP-SAC 83, 7th Intl. Conference on Computer Software and Applications*, Chicago, November 7–11, 1983, 166–172.

[McC92]   McCahill, M. The Internet Gopher: A distributed server information system. *ConneXions – The Interoperability Report* 6, no. 7, July 1992, 10–14.

[Met94]   Metaxas, T. Cheyney, M. Gloor, P. Johnson, D. Makedon, F. Matthews, J. Conference on a Disk: An Experiment in Hypermedia Publishing. *Proceedings ED–MEDIA '94*, Vancouver, Canada, 1994.

[Met95]   Metaxas, P. T. Zhao, K. *A LATEX to HyperCard Translator.*
          Technical Report CSD–TR11–1995. Wellesley College, Wellesley,
          MA, 1995.

[Mon91]   Monmonier, M. *How to Lie with Maps.* University of Chicago
          Press, Chicago, 1991.

[Muk95]   Mukherjea, S. Foley, J. D. Visualizing the World–Wide Web with
          the Navigational View Builder. *Proceedings 3rd International
          World Wide Web Conference. Computer Networks and ISDN
          Systems* 27, no. 6, 1075–1087.

[Myk95]   Myka, A. Güntzer, U. HyperFacs – Building and using a digitized
          paper library. *ACM SIGLink Newsletter* 4, no. 2, September 1995,
          4–5.

[Nag92]   Nagasaka, A. Tanaka, Y. Automatic video indexing and full–video
          search for object appearances. *IFIP Transactions A (Computer
          Science and Technology)* A–7, 1992.

[Nel90]   Nelson, T. H. *Literary Machines.* Version 90.1. Mindful Press,
          New York, 1990.

[Nev95]   Neves , L. Oliveira, J. *Classifying Internet Objects with SOUR.*
          http://www.w3.org/pub/Conferences/WWW4/ Papers/ portugal

[New91]   Newcomb, S. R. Kipp, N. A. Newcomb, V. T. The "HyTime"
          hypermedia/time–based document structuring language. *CACM*
          34, no. 11, November 1991.

[Nic95]   Nicol, D. Smeaton, C. Slater, A. Footsteps: trail–blazing the Web.
          *Proceedings 3rd International World Wide Web Conference.
          Computer Networks and ISDN Systems* 27, no. 6, 879–885.

[Nie90]   Nielsen, J. *Hypertext & Hypermedia.* Academic Press, San Diego,
          1990.

[Obr93]   Obraczka, K. Danzig, P. Shih–Hao, L. Internet Resource
          Discovery Services. *IEEE Computer* 26, no. 9, September 1993,
          8–22.

[Ore90a] Oren, T. Salomon, G. Kreitman, K. Don, A. Guides:
          Characterizing the interface. In Laurel, B. (ed.), *The Art of
          Human–Computer Interface Design.* Addison–Wesley, Reading,
          MA, 1990, 367–381.

[Ore90b]   Oren, T. Laurel, B. Don, A. *Guides 3.0*. Videotape. Apple
            Computer, Cupertino, CA, 1990.

[Ots93]   Otsuji, K. Tonomura, Y. Projection detecting filter for video cut
            detection. *Proceedings ACM Multimedia '93*, Anaheim, CA, 1993.

[Ous90]   Ousterhout, J. Tcl: An embeddable command language . *Winter
            1990 USENIX Conference Proceedings*, 1990.

[Ous94]   Ousterhout, J. K. *An Introduction to Tcl and Tk*. Addison–Wesley,
            Reading, MA, 1994.

[Par89]   Parsaye, K. Chignell, M. Khoshafian, S. Wong, H. *Intelligent
            Databases*. Wiley, New York, 1989.

[Pfe95]   Pfeifer, U. Fuhr, N. Huynh, T. Searching structured documents
            with the enhanced retrieval functionality of freeWAIS–sf and
            SFgate. *Proceedings of the Third International World–Wide Web
            Conference. Computer Networks and ISDN Systems* 27, no. 6,
            1995, 1027–1036.

[Pic88]   Pickles, J. O. *An Introduction to the Physiology of Hearing*.
            Academic Press, London, 1988.

[Pol87]   Polansky, L. Morphological metrics: An introduction to a theory
            of formal distances. *Proceedings of the 1987 International
            Computer Music Conference*, 1987, 197–207.

[Pre93]   *Premiere*. Adobe Systems, Mountain View, CA, 1993.

[Pri57]   Prim, R. C. Shortest connection networks and some generaliza-
            tions. *Tech. Journal, Bell Labs* 36, 1957, 1389–1401.

[Pri93]   Price, B. A. Baecker, R. M., Small, I. S. A principled taxonomy of
            software visualization. *Journal of Visual Languages and
            Computing* 4, no. 3, 1993, 211–266. Also available on–line:
            http://hcrl.open.ac.uk/jvlc/JVLC–Body.html

[Qua85]   Quatieri, T. F. McAulay, R. J. *Speech Analysis/Synthesis Based on
            a Sinusoidal Representation*. Technical Report 693. Lincoln
            Laboratory, MIT, Cambridge, MA, 1985.

[Qui92]   *QuickTime*. Apple Computer, Cupertino, CA, 1992.

[Rad93]   Rada, R. (prod. chair). Proceedings CD–ROM of the First ACM
            International Conference on Multimedia, August 1–6, Anaheim,
            CA, 1993. (CD–ROM)

[Rea95]   RealAudio Technology, http://www.realaudio.com

[Reb95]   Rebelsky, S. Gloor, P. Makedon, F. Metaxas, T. Ford, J. Matthews,
           J. Owen, C. Van Ligten, O. Bright, L. Harker, K. Toth, N. The
           Roles of Video in the Design, Use, and Construction of
           Interactive Electronic Conference Proceedings. Forthcoming,
           1995.

[Rem87]   Remde, J. R. Gomez, L. M. Landauer, T. K. SuperBook: An auto-
           matic tool for information exploration – hypertext? *Proceedings
           Hypertext '87*, Chapel Hill, NC, 1987, 175–188.

[Ria94]   RIAO 94. *Proceedings of the 94 RIAO Conference.*
           Intelligent Multimedia Information Retrieval Systems and
           Management.

[Ric83]   Rich, E. Users are individuals: Individualizing user models.
           International Journal on Man–Machine Studies 18, 1983, 199–214.

[Rob91]   Robertson, G. G. Mackinlay, J. D. Card, S. K. Cone trees:
           Animated 3D visualizations of hierarchical information. *Proc.
           CHI '91.* New Orleans, April 27 – May 2, 1991, 189–194.

[Roe95]   Röscheisen, M. Mogensen, C. Winograd, T. Beyond browsing:
           Shared comments, SOAPs, trails, and on–line communities.
           Computer Networks and ISDN Systems 27, vol. 6, April 1995,
           739–749.

[Sal83]   Salton, G. McGill, M. J. *Introduction to Modern Information
           Retrieval.* McGraw–Hill, New York, 1983.

[Sal88]   Salton, G. Automatic text indexing using complex identifiers.
           ACM Conference on Document Processing Systems, Santa Fe,
           December 5–9, 1988, 135–145.

[Sal89a]   Salton, G. *Automatic Text Processing.* Addison–Wesley, Reading,
           MA, 1989.

[Sal89b]   Salton, G. Buckley, C. *On the Automatic Generation of Content
           Links in Hypertext.* Technical Report TR 89–993. Cornell
           University, Ithaca, NY, April 1989.

[Sal91]   Salton, G. Buckley, C. *Automatic Text Structuring and Retrieval –
           Experiments in Automatic Encyclopedia Searching.* Technical
           Report TR 91–1196. Cornell University, Ithaca, NY, 1991.

[Sal96]   Salton, G. Singhal, A. Buckley, C. Mitra, M. Automatic text decomposition using text segments and text themes. *Proceedings ACM Hypertext '96*, Washington, DC, March 16–20, 1996, 53–65.

[Sar92]   Sarkar, M. Brown, M. Graphical fish–eye views of graphs. *CHI '92 Proceedings*, Monterey, CA, May 3–7, 1992, 83–91.

[Sax90]   Saxer, K. H. Gloor, P. Navigation im Hyperraum: Fish–eye Views in HyperCard. In Gloor, P. Streitz, N. (eds.). *Hypertext und Hypermedia: von theoretischen Konzepten zur praktischen Anwendung.* Proceedings Hypertext/Hypermedia Fachtagung der SI/GI, Basel und Darmstadt, April 1990. Springer Informatikfachberichte 249, Heidelberg, 1990.

[She95]   Sheldon, M. A. Duda, A. Weiss, R. Gifford, D. K. Discover: a resource discovery system based on content routing,*Proceedings of the Third International World–Wide Web Conference. Computer Networks and ISDN Systems* 27, no. 6, 1995, 953–972.

[Sig95]   SIGIR, Proceedings of Annual Conferences of the ACM Special Interest Group on Information Retrieval. Latest proceedings are 1995.

[Sio92]   *SIOD (Scheme–in–one–Defun).* Paradigm Associates, Cambridge, MA, 1992.

[Smo94]   Smoliar, E. Zhang, H. Content–based video indexing and retrieval. , *IEEE Multimedia* 1,no. 2, Summer 1994.

[Sta89]   Stasko, J. T. *Tango: A Framework and System for Algorithm Animation.* Technical Report CS–89–30. Brown University, 1989.

[Sta90]   Stasko, J. T. Tango: A framework and system for algorithm animation. *IEEE Computer,* September 1990, 27–39.

[Sta91]   Stasko, J. T. Using direct manipulation to build algorithm animations by demonstration. *CHI '91 Proceedings,* New Orleans, 1991, 307–314.

[Ste91]   Steinberg, E. R. *Teaching Computers to Teach.* 2d ed. Erlbaum, Hillsdale, NJ, 1991.

[Swa95]   Swart, J. Smith, B. C. A resolution independent video language. *Proceedings ACM Multimedia '95,* San Francisco, November 5–9, 1995.

[Tar83]   Tarjan, R. E. *Data Structures And Network Algorithms*. Society for Industrial and Applied Math, Philadelphia, 1983.

[Ten93]   Tennenhouse, D. Adam, J. Compton, C. Duda, A. Gifford, D. Houh, H. Ismert, M. Lindblad, C. Stasior, W. Weiss, R. Wetherall, D. Bacher, D. Carver, D. Chang, T. *The Viewstation Collected Papers*. MIT Laboratory of Computer Science Technical Report TR–590, Release 1. 1993.

[Tho89]   Thompson, R. H. Croft, W. B. Support for browsing in an intelligent text retrieval system. *International Journal on Man–Machine Studies* 30, no. 6, 1989, 639–668.

[Tho91]   Thomas, Bob. *Disney's Art of Animation*. Hyperion Press. New York, 1991.

[Ton85]   Tong, R. M. Shapiro, D. G. Experimental investigations of uncertainty in a rule–based system for information retrieval. *International Journal on Man–Machine Studies* 22, 1985, 265–282.

[Tra89]   Travers, M. A visual representation for knowledge structures. *Hypertext '89 Proceedings*, Pittsburgh, November 5–8, 1989, 147–158.

[Tri88]   Trigg, R. H. Guided tours and tabletops: Tools for communicating in a hypertext environment. *ACM Transactions on Office Information Systems* 6, no. 4, October 1988.

[Ued91]   Ueda, H., Miyatake, T., Yoshizawa, S. IMPACT: An interactive natural–motion–picture dedicated multimedia authoring system. *CHI '91 Conference Proceedings*, 1991.

[Utt89]   Utting, K. Yankelovich, N. Context and orientation in hypermedia networks. *ACM Transactions on Office Information Systems* 7, no. 1, January 1989, 58–84.

[Van89]   Van Dyke Parunak, H. Hypermedia topologies and user navigation. *Hypertext '89 Proceedings*, Pittsburgh, November 5–8, 1989, 43–50.

[Van96]   Van Hoff, A. Shaio, S. Starbuck, O. *Hooked on Java*. Addison-Wesley, Reading, MA, 1996.

[Vau94]   Vaughan, Tay. *Multimedia: Making It Work*. Osborne McGraw–Hill, Berkeley, CA, 1994.

[Vel92]   Velez–Sosa, A. Gloor, P. Animating hashing algorithms for com-
            puter science education. *Proceedings ACM Computer Science
            Conference 93*, Indianapolis, 1993.

[Wei76]   Weizenbaum, J. *Computer Power and Human Reason: From
            Judgement to Calculation.* W. H. Freeman, San Francisco, 1976.

[Wei96]   Weiss, R. Velez, B. Sheldon, M. Namprempre, C. Szilagyi, P.
            Duda, A. Gifford, D. HyPursuit: A hierarchical network search
            engine that exploits content–link hypertext–clustering.
            Proceedings ACM Hypertext '96, Washington, DC, March 16–20,
            1996, 180–193.

[Wet94]   Wetherall, D. J. *An Interactive Programming System for Media
            Computation.* Technical Report MIT/LCS/TR–640. Laboratory for
            Computer Science, MIT, Cambridge, MA, September 1994.

[Whi86]   White, T. *The Animator's Workbook.* Billboard Publications, New
            York, 1986.

[Win90]   Winkler, D. Kamins, S. *Hypertalk 2.0: The Book.* Bantam Books,
            New York, 1990.

[Wit86]   Wittenburg, K. Natural Language Parsing with Combinatory
            Categorical Grammars in a Graph–Unification–Based Formalism.
            Ph.D dissertation, University of Texas, Austin, 1986.

[Yan88]   Yankelovich, N. Haan, B. Meyrowitz, N. Drucker, S. Intermedia:
            The concept and the construction of a seamless information envi-
            ronment. *IEEE Computer* 21, no. 1, 1988, 81–96.

[Yos94]   Yoshitaka, A. Kishida, S. Hirakawa, M. Ichikawa, T.
            Knowledge–assisted content–based retrieval for multimedia data-
            bases. *IEEE Multimedia* 1, no.4, Winter 1994.

[Zel89]   Zellweger, P. Scripted documents: A hypermedia path mecha-
            nism. *Hypertext '89 Proceedings*, Pittsburgh, November 5–8,
            1989, 1–14.

[Zha93]   Zhang, H. Kankanhalli, A. Smoliar, S. Automatic partitioning of
            full motion video. *Multimedia Systems* 1, no. 1, 1993.

Permissions

Acknowledgments

Permissions for figure and illustration reproduction appear on the appropriate text pages, unlless requested to appear in the permissions Acknowledge.

Figures I.5-7 courtesy of Springer-Verlag, from Chin, D. C. KNOME: Modeling what the user knows in UC. In Kobsa, A. Wahlster, W. (eds.), *User Models in Dialog Systems*. Springer, Berlin, 1989.

Figure I.8 courtesy of International Journal on Man-Machine Studies, Academic Press, Ltd., from Kok, A. J. A Formal approach to user models in data retrieval. *International Journal on Man-Machine Studies* 35, no. 6, 1991.

Text extract, Section 3.1 courtesy of CERN Library, from Berners-Lee, T. Cailliau, R. Groff, J. Pollerman, B. *World-Wide Web: The Information Universe*. CERN, Geneva, Switzerland, 1992.

Figures I.11(a,c), I.12(a), I.13(a,c) courtesy of *Computing Services, Kiewit Computation Center*, Dartmouth College, Hanover, NH. Figure I.13(c) © 1995 Andy J. Williams.

Figures I.11(b), I.12(b), I.13(b), I.14(a), I.34(b), I.35(b), I.64(c), II.10(b), II.16(b), II.25(b), II.26(b), II.28(b), II.41(b), V.14(b),

V.15(b), V.16(b), V.19(b), V.20(b), V.21(b) and Table I.1 Copyright 1994-1995 © Netscape Communications Corporation. All rights reserved.

Figure I.14(b) courtesy of MIT Center for Coordination Science.

Figures I.15-18, I.19(a) courtesy of Dr. Hermann Maurer, Institute for Information Processing and Computer Supported New Media (IICM), Graz University of Technology, Austria; and Institute for HyperMedia Systems (IHM) of Joanneum Research, Graz, Austria.

Figure I.23 courtesy of Prof. Hugh Davis, The Multimedia Research Group, Dept. of Electronics and Computer Science, University of Southampton, U.K.

Figures I.24-27 courtesy of Kevin Hughes.

Figures I.28-30 courtesy of Prof. Jay Bagga, Dept. of Computer Science, Ball State University, Muncie, IN.

Figures I.34(a), I.35(a) courtesy of Prof. Tariq S. Durrani, Dept. Of Electronic and Electrical Engineering, University of Strathclyde, Glasgow, and Project INTERACT.

Figure I.40 © 1994 Association for Computing Imagery, from Furnas, G. W. Zachs, J. Multitrees: Enriching and reusing hierarchical structure. *Human Factors in Computing Systems, CHI 94 Proceedings*, Boston, 1994.

Figure I.41 courtesy of Lawrence Erlbaum Associates, from 1993 Proceedings of World Congress on Neural Networks.

Figure I.49-50 from Goodman, D. *Danny Goodman's Hypercard Handbook*. Copyright © Random House, Inc.

Figure I.51 courtesy of IEEE, from Conklin, J. A Survey of Hypertext. MCC Technical Report No. STP-356-86, Rev. 2. December 3, 1987. © 1987 IEEE.

Figures I.52-54 © 1989 Association for Computing Machinery, from Utting, K. Yankelovich, N. Context and orientation in

Figures I.68-70, III.3 courtesy of Georgia Tech Web Server. I.68-70 reproduced with permission of Sougata Mukherjea, GVU Center, Georgia Institute of Technology. Copyright 1996.

Figure I.71 Copyright © NetCarta Corporation.

Figures I.72-73, I.75-76 and Table 1.3 from Laurel, B. *The Art of Human-Computer Interface Design* (figures 1, 2, 6, and 12 from pages 360, 365, 370, and 376). © 1990 by Apple Computer, Inc. Reprinted by permission of Addison-Wesley Longman Publishing Company, Inc.

Figures I.74, II.17, II.33-37, III.1, IV.1, IV.3(a-e), IV.6(a), IV.6(b-h), V.2, V.8-9 © Apple Computer, Inc. All rights reserved. Apple® and Macintosh® are registered trademarks of Apple Computer, Inc.

Figure I.77 courtesy of Dr. Pattie Maes, MIT Media Lab, Cambridge, MA.

Figures I.78-80 © 1988 Association for Computing Machinery, from Lai, K. Malone, T. W. Yu, K. Object lens: A "spreadsheet" for cooperative work. ACM *Trans. On Office Information Systems*, 6, no. 4, October, 1988.

Figure II.1 courtesy of IEEE Education Society, from Gloor, P. Dynes, S. Animated algorithms: Teaching computer science with hypermedia learning environments. *Proc. IEEE Conference on Frontiers in Education FIE 1993*, Washington, 1993.

Figures II.16(a), V.13, V.14(a), V.15(a), V.20(a), V.21(a) courtesy of Dartmouth Experimental Visualization Laboratory (DEVLAB) and Addison-Wesley Interactive.

Figures II.25(a), II.26(a) from Goodman, D. *Danny Goodman's Applescript Handbook, 2nd Edition*. Copyright © Random House, Inc.

Figures II.38-39 courtesy of Dr. Glorianna Davenport, MIT Media Lab, Cambridge, MA. © 1988 MIT Media Lab.

Figures II.41-43, II.45-47 courtesy of Dr. Chris Langmead, Department of Computer Science, Dartmouth College, Hanover, NH.

Figure III.2 courtesy of Marc H. Brown.

Figure III.4 courtesy of Prof. Gruia-Catalin Roman, Dept. of Computer Science, Washington University, St. Louis, MO.

Figure III.27 courtesy of MIT Press, from Brown, M.H. *Algorithm Animation*. MIT Press, Cambridge, MA. 1988.

Figure IV.1 courtesy of Adobe Systems Incorporated. Adobe® and Adobe Premiere® are trademarks of Adobe Systems Incorporated.

Figure IV.5 courtesy of Elsevier Science-NL, from Nagasaka, A. Tanaka, Y. Automatic video indexing and full-video search for object appearances. IFIP Transactions A (*Computer Science and Technology*) A-7, 1992.

Figures V.2-3, V.4(a,b), V.5(a,b), V.6, V.7(a,b), V.8-10 courtesy of Dartmouth Experimental Visualization Laboratory (DEVLAB), TELOS and Springer-Verlag.

Figures V.11, V.12(a,b) courtesy of Dartmouth Experimental Visualization Laboratory (DEVLAB).

Figures V.16-18 courtesy of Dr. Tim Berners-Lee, Dartmouth Experimental Visualization Laboratory (DEVLAB) and Addison-Wesley Interactive.

Figure V.19(a) courtesy of Dr. Tim Berners-Lee.

Index

3

3D hyperbolic space, 118
3D/Rooms, 114, 115

A

A Web Conference Factory, 348
Abstract Window Toolkit, 45
ACM Multimedia '93, 318
acoustic waveform, 198
action link, 15, 64
AddMotion, 238–239
Adobe Premiere, 283, 287
agent, 125, 130
Agent-Tcl, 47, 131

algorithm definition, 263
algorithm animation
  content, 268
  persistence, 268
  transformation, 268
algorithm animation, 229
  advantages, 229
  automatic, 268
  definition, 229
  educational aspects, 251
  motivation
    enhancement, 251
  proof animation, 257
  pseudocode, 255
  recipe for, 263
  scripting, 271
  skill mastery, 251